FUNDAMENTAL RIGHTS AND BEST INTERESTS OF THE CHILD IN TRANSNATIONAL FAMILIES

With the financial support of: the Jean Monnet Modules on 'European Family Law', Nos. 542609-LLP-1-2013-1-IT-AJM-MO and 553498-EPP-1-2014-1-IT-EPPJMO-MODULE; and of the Research project PRID on 'Continuità transfrontaliera dello status filiationis e tutela dell'interesse superiore del minore', financed by the Department of Legal Sciences of the University of Udine, Italy.

FUNDAMENTAL RIGHTS AND BEST INTERESTS OF THE CHILD IN TRANSNATIONAL FAMILIES

Edited by
Elisabetta BERGAMINI
Chiara RAGNI
in collaboration with
Francesco DEANA

intersentia
Cambridge – Antwerp – Chicago

Intersentia Ltd
8 Wellington Mews
Wellington Street | Cambridge
CB1 1HW | United Kingdom
Tel.: +44 1223 736 170
Email: mail@intersentia.co.uk
www.intersentia.com | www.intersentia.co.uk

Distribution for the UK and Ireland:
NBN International
Airport Business Centre, 10 Thornbury Road
Plymouth, PL6 7PP
United Kingdom
Tel.: +44 1752 202 301 | Fax: +44 1752 202 331
Email: orders@nbninternational.com

Distribution for Europe and all other countries:
Intersentia Publishing nv
Groenstraat 31
2640 Mortsel
Belgium
Tel.: +32 3 680 15 50 | Fax: +32 3 658 71 21
Email: mail@intersentia.be

Distribution for the USA and Canada:
Independent Publishers Group
Order Department
814 North Franklin Street
Chicago, IL 60610
USA
Tel.: +1 800 888 4741 (toll free) | Fax: +1 312 337 5985
Email: orders@ipgbook.com

Fundamental Rights and Best Interests of the Child in Transnational Families

Artwork on cover: New York through the eyes of children (2019)

ISBN 978-1-78068-665-3
D/2019/7849/123
NUR 828

British Library Cataloguing in Publication Data. A catalogue record for this book is available from the British Library.

To Caterina, Costanza, Davide, Luca and Nicola, who not only give colour to our lives but have also given it to the cover of this book

PREFACE

The idea of devoting this book to the relationship between the fundamental rights of the child and European family law stems from the Jean Monnet Modules on European Family Law, funded by the European Commission, in the years 2013/2016 and 2014/2017 at our respective Universities (University of Milano and University of Udine).

During the lectures and seminars that we organised in the framework of these modules, as coordinators, we realised that even though family law is currently considered a hot topic and is subject to intensive research in the academic world, one of the most relevant issues in the European context, that still has not been thoroughly explored, was the one related to the need to protect the rights of children both in the framework of the free movement of citizens and migration law and in the context of international private law. Thirty years have passed since the UN Convention on the Rights of the Child was adopted: the aim of this book is also to assess how and to what extent its provisions have been implemented in family-related matters, with special regard to the European context.

Notwithstanding the lack of any EU competence on family matters that fall into the exclusive jurisdiction of national law, the protection of families and family ties within EU Member States should actually be guaranteed as a means of protecting fundamental rights, and this becomes even more relevant when dealing with minors. The right to family life is indeed included in the Charter of Fundamental Rights of the European Union (the EU Charter) and in the European Convention on Human Rights (ECHR), both of which, according to the EU Treaty, impose legal duties on Member States. Specific norms regarding the rights of children can be found both in the Charter (at Article 24), and in the case law of the ECtHR, which state, in accordance with the 1989 UN Convention on the Rights of the Child, that minors (being EU citizens or third country nationals) have the right to protection and care as is necessary for their well-being. In accordance with both international and European law, minors' views must be taken into account and their best interests must be a primary consideration when taking any action relating to them.

As the analysis of the jurisprudence of both the domestic and the European courts clearly suggests, the protection of minors' rights may prove to be a challenging issue when judges are called to strike a balance between fundamental public values and the individual rights specifically concerned, or between the abstract and the particular dimension of the best interests of the child, in cases where different conclusions may be reached depending on the perspective adopted.

The impact of human rights on EU legislation dealing with matters which are strictly connected with children and family issues (like for example Directives on family reunification, or private international law rules on child abduction and on parental rights) has already been questioned before the Court of Justice of the European Union and the European Court of Human Rights; their case law confirms the need for interpretative tools aimed at coordinating and reconciling European rules with national public concerns and with the need for human rights protection.

Therefore, we decided to involve academics coming from different countries in the making of this book, in order to assess, *de iure condito* and *de iure condendo*, what legal options, among those suggested by both practitioners and scholars, seem to be most effective for the purpose of balancing the different interests that come into play, notably in situations related to migration (within the EU and from outside the EU), and in cross-border circumstances where private international law issues may arise.

The book addresses the matter from two perspectives: on the one hand it examines how the obligations deriving from Article 8 of the ECHR and from Article 7 of the EU Charter can be coordinated with migration policies and rules, especially in the case where these lead to results which are inconsistent with the protection of the children's family ties; on the other hand, it focuses on the impact of human rights values on the recognition of a parent-child relationship formed abroad, on the content of the public policy exception and finally on the implementation of some EU controversial conflict of law rules, such as those regarding child abduction.

Moreover, beyond the sectoral challenges in different areas of European family law, the book aims at offering a contribution to the definition of the content and of the nature of the general principle of the best interests of the child as related not only to the need to have his/her interests prevail over those of the other members of the family and, in some cases, over the public interest in strictly regulating migration flows, but also to the need to strike a balance between the different needs and interests of the single child whose case is being evaluated. These issues are in fact still controversial, as the practice and the existing literature on these matters confirm; this uncertainty has resulted in practical difficulties for those trying to apply it. Therefore, we wanted to offer academics and practitioners not only a solid reconstruction of the existing legal framework and evolution of the supranational and national case law on these issues, but also perspectives on their possible future evolution through a critical analysis of each connected aspect, taking into account all the possible dimensions of the best interests of the child (see General Comment no. 14/2003, where the

Committee on the Rights of the Child underlines that the best interests of the child should be understood as a right, a principle and a rule of procedure).

In the first part of the book, the introductory chapter (Elisabetta Bergamini) analyses the main supranational principles in the field of children's rights and assesses the global impact of such principles on domestic family law in EU Member States, notably on children, in cases related to EU free movement and migration law. The analysis mainly focuses on the CRC (UN Convention on the Rights of the Child of 1989), due to the specificity of its provisions on the best interests of the child, the ECHR and the Charter of Fundamental Rights of the EU, in order to evaluate whether cross-border situations (stemming from free movement of EU citizens and their families or from migration situations) affect the different national legal frameworks leading towards a higher-level of protection of children's rights as well as a more satisfying and comprehensive application of the international instruments meant to protect human (or more specifically children's) rights. The specific issues evaluated (the case of children born out of wedlock, the right of the child to maintain a relationship with an extended family, the right of the child to be heard and the prohibition of inhuman treatment) leads the author to remark that children's rights that are more closely linked to cross-border situations appear to be headed for a higher level of protection based on the international framework, while more general rights that are not strictly linked to free movement, such as the right of the child to be heard, still need to be fully implemented.

The following chapters deal with selective topics concerning the protection of children within EU Member States, mainly chosen due to their particular relevance, sensitiveness and timeliness. Sexual orientation (Alina Tryfonidou), integration of family patterns based on different religions (Alessandra Lang), protection of family identity as a fundamental right (Francesco Deana), derogation from State sovereignty on migration law (Maura Marchegiani and Peter Rodrigues), domestic violence (Sara De Vido), are those that we selected for the above-mentioned reasons.

All the chapters take into consideration EU substantive law and consider situations in which the still existing differences in domestic family law that are felt to be the expression of the States' social, cultural and legal identity, might deprive children from benefiting from their best interests and their family unity protections within the EU. However, the authors had to adopt different kind of approach to each specific topic. Thus, some authors (Tryfonidou and Lang, respectively dealing with rainbow families and *kafala*) consider the analysis of domestic praxis that could breach human rights principles where it rigidly implements EU legislation (thus suggesting a human-rights-oriented interpretation of EU law that advocates the necessity for the EU to clarify that *all* EU Member States are required by EU law to recognise the exact legal ties among the members of a family when EU law on free movement of persons is applied). Consequently, this approach clearly takes into consideration the reforming pressure on Member States to establish new rules in order not to discriminate under national law in purely internal situations (in the case of rainbow families) and examines the difficult balance between the need to protect the child's best interests and to avoid circumvention of national and EU rules on migration (in the case of *kafala*).

Other authors, specifically Deana, Marchegiani and Rodrigues, start from a case law approach on transnational family situations and assess how best interests and human rights are/must be taken into account in order to grant children the highest level of protection through an expanded implementation of the existing EU rules of international protection of child migrants, even though it runs counter to the States' prerogatives in migration policies. In this framework they specifically analyse the centrality of EU citizenship as the key to protect the identity of children (Deana), the need to protect children through a human rights-oriented application of family reunification (Rodrigues) and the impact of the best interests principle in cases of peculiar vulnerability such as in the case of asylum-seeking and refugee children (Marchegiani). Even more detailed is the analysis set in the chapter in which Sara De Vido considers the need to protect children, especially girls, from child marriages and violence, suggesting the need to reform the Directive on family reunification in order to respect the Council of Europe Istanbul Convention on preventing and combating violence against women and domestic violence.

What emerges from all the chapters included in the first part of this book is the clear need to grant a higher level of protection to children in cross-border situations. Furthermore, the development of an EU human rights-oriented approach to these situations – also thanks to the influence of ECtHR case-law – could grant an increased level of protection to children in internal situations too.

The second part of the book is devoted to the analysis of the impact of human rights law on conflict of laws rules. It is introduced by two chapters (Pietro Franzina and Marcella Di Stefano) that address this matter focusing both on the EU and on the domestic perspective. While in fact both national and European private international law rules should be read in the light of a human rights-oriented approach, the means of achieving this result may be different, according to the goals pursued.

In the context of the EU the harmonisation of conflict of law rules is aimed at creating an area of freedom, security and justice in order to promote the free movement of persons, and is also a means of ensuring the cross-border recognition of a person's rights and status. In addition, as far as family and child-related matters are concerned, the protection of the fundamental rights of the persons involved, with specific regard to the child's best interests, are among the considerations underlying how the rules are formulated and how the choice of the appropriate connecting factor is made.

If one considers for example the Brussels II *bis* Regulation, which is the main topic of the last four chapters of Part II, the choice of the habitual residence of the child as a connecting factor was properly guided by the idea that the court, identified on that ground, is presumably the one better placed to conduct a proper and reliable assessment of the child's actual situation and interests. At the same time, the Regulation includes norms on the return procedure in cases of abduction (Ruth Lamont), that are aimed on the one hand at ensuring the right of the child to maintain personal relations with both parents (which is prescribed by both the New York Convention, Article 9 and by the EU Charter, Article 24) and on the other, at granting the possibility of assessing whether the return corresponds to the best interests of the child. To this end the Regulation provides: specific exceptions to the return (in this respect it should be pointed out that one of the most debated issues – as shown in the chapter written by Costanza Honorati – specifically regards the possibility to conceive, also in the light of the 1980 Hague Convention, a general human rights exception to the return); the right of the child to be heard; and the power for the competent judicial authorities to order provisional measures aimed at ensuring protection of the returned child in cases where his/her well-being may be at risk (Lidia Sandrini). Since all these issues were discussed on the occasion of the Recast, chapters dealing with the matter broadly take into account not only the rules included in the Brussels II *bis* Regulation but also the changes introduced with the Recast, the latter mostly being the result of considerations related to the protection of the child's best interests (Laura Carpaneto).

As regards the impact of human rights on the functioning of domestic conflict of law rules in family matters, a question arises as to whether and to what extent the protection of the child's best interests binds states to recognise a parent-child relationship established abroad, notwithstanding that the strict application of private international law rules would lead to the opposite result. The second and third chapters (Marcella Distefano and Roberto Baratta), which adopt a comprehensive and inclusive perspective on the matter, both consider whether private international law could be interpreted and applied consistently with the rights to private and family life, the respect of which may entail the cross-border recognition of personal and family status. They explore different options at stake like the use of interpretative tools that for example allow the inclusion of considerations on human rights among public policy grounds or the adoption of rules that are aimed at achieving specific material results (for example rules that make a choice among different alternative connecting factors contingent upon the establishment of valid a parent-child relationship). The same questions are addressed in the fourth and fifth chapters, with regard to specific topics, namely the cross-border recognition of the status *filii* arising from the recourse to surrogacy agreements

(Katarina Trimmings) and the effects that foreign adoption are likely to produce in countries where, under recurring circumstances, the adoption of minors would not be allowed (Chiara Ragni). In all these situations, as clarified by the ECtHR, States are not under an obligation to automatically recognise the status acquired abroad, but rather to ensure that decisions in this regard are the result of a proper balancing of all the interests involved, with particular regard to those of the child (in this perspective see also the Advisory Opinion which the Court delivered in April 2019 upon the request of the French Court of Cassation). These interests shall prevail over any other consideration and should be taken into account both in the collective and in the individual dimension, especially in the case where these do not coincide.

Elisabetta Bergamini and Chiara Ragni
June 2019

ACKNOWLEDGEMENTS

We wish to thank all the authors for agreeing to be involved in this project, for sharing their passion and knowledge with us and for their patience in the length of the different phases of the project. We are deeply grateful to them, but we are even more greatly indebted to Francesco Deana, who not only wrote a chapter for this book, but also collaborated with us in all the background activities necessary to coordinate and edit the contributions, providing us excellent support in all the different phases of this project. All of his efforts and suggestions were essential in finalising this editorial project and we wish to give him our heartfelt thanks for everything he has done.

We also would like to thank our PhD candidates (Laura Lizzi and Brigida Varesano) for helping us in the final checking phases before publication.

CONTENTS

Preface vii
Acknowledgements xiii
List of Cases xxi
List of Authors xxvii

PART I. THE IMPACT OF HUMAN RIGHTS AND OF THE BEST INTERESTS OF THE CHILD ON EU FREE MOVEMENT AND MIGRATION LAW

Human Rights of Children in the EU Context: Impact on National Family Law
Elisabetta BERGAMINI 3

1. Introduction 3
2. Analyses of Human Rights Rules Relevant in the Field of Interest 5
3. Children's Rights in the Interpretative Activity of the CJEU 10
4. Children's Rights and the Evolution of Domestic Family Law: Specific Issues 12
5. Final Remarks 19

Protecting EU Citizen Minors' Right to Identity in the Transnational Family Context
Francesco DEANA 21

1. Introduction 21
2. Identity as a Fundamental Right under International and EU Law 22
3. The Relevance of Children's Identity-Related Issues to EU Law 24
4. Non-Recognition of a Child's Name as a Hindrance to Free Movement 26
5. Non-Recognition of Other Personal and Family Status Legally Acquired Abroad 28
6. Restrictions on Status Recognition and their Compatibility with EU Law 30
7. Protecting Family Unity and the Enjoyment of Established Family Life 32
8. Final Remarks 35

The Best Interests Principle's Impact on Decisions Concerning Asylum-Seeking and Refugee Children
Maura Marchegiani ... 39

1. Introductory Remarks ... 39
2. A General Instrument of Promotion of the Rights of the Child ... 41
3. The Best Interests Principle in Regional Instruments ... 46
4. Influence of the Best Interests Principle on European Jurisprudence ... 48
5. Implications of the Best Interests Approach for International Protection Procedures ... 52

Human Rights and the Best Interests of the Child in European Family Reunification Law
Peter Rodrigues ... 55

1. Introduction ... 55
2. Best Interests of the Child in European Migration Law ... 56
3. EU Family Reunification Law ... 65
4. *Ruiz Zambrano* Jurisprudence ... 70
5. Conclusions ... 72

Rainbow Families and EU Free Movement Law
Alina Tryfonidou ... 75

1. Introduction ... 75
2. Legal Recognition of Rainbow Families in EU Member States: The Current Situation ... 76
3. Family Reunification Rights under EU Law: The Position of Children ... 78
4. The Current (Uncertain) Position of Rainbow Families under EU Law ... 82
5. Is the Non-Recognition of the Parent-Child Relationship a Breach of EU Law? ... 84
6. Conclusion ... 95

***Kafala* and Family Reunification of Third-Country Nationals**
Alessandra Lang ... 97

1. Introduction ... 97
2. The 1996 Hague Convention and Migration ... 99
3. Entry and Residence of Foreign Nationals within the EU ... 100
4. Family Reunification: EU Legislation ... 101
5. State Practice ... 105
6. Seeking Common Principles ... 110

Against a Girl's Will: Child Marriages, Immigration and the Directive on Family Reunification
Sara De Vido 115

1. Introduction and Scope of Analysis 115
2. Child Marriages 117
3. Family Reunification under EU Law and Child Marriages 125
4. Prohibition of Child Marriages, Family Reunification and the Istanbul Convention 130
5. When Denying Family Reunification Causes Violence against Women 133
6. Conclusions 136

PART II. THE BEST INTERESTS OF THE CHILD AS A CONCERN OF HUMAN RIGHTS AND EUROPEAN PRIVATE INTERNATIONAL LAW

The Place of Human Rights in the Private International Law of the Union in Family Matters
Pietro Franzina 141

1. The Protection of Fundamental Rights in the Union's Legal System 142
2. Harmonisation as a Way to Enhance the Protection of Fundamental Rights 145
3. The Impact of Human Rights on the Design of Private International Law Rules 148
4. A Human Rights-Oriented Interpretation of the Union's Private International Law 152
5. Concluding Remarks 155

The Best Interests of the Child Principle at the Intersection of Private International Law and Human Rights
Marcella Distefano 157

1. The Relationship between Private International Law and Human Rights 157
2. The Best Interests Principle in International Human Rights Law: Three Concepts in One 162
3. Best Interests of the Child and Private International Family Law: Towards a Convergence 165
4. Concluding Remarks 169

Recognition of a Foreign Status *Filii*: Pursuing the Best Interests Principle
Roberto Baratta 171

1. Introduction 171
2. ECtHR Activism as to the *Ordre Public* Exception 174
3. Outlining the Best Interests Test 178
4. Conclusion 184

Surrogacy Arrangements and the Best Interests of the Child: The Case Law of the European Court of Human Rights
Katarina Trimmings 187

1. Introduction 187
2. Case Law Overview 188
3. Recognition of the Legal Parent-Child Relationship 198
4. Conclusion 207

Cross-Border Recognition of Adoption: Rethinking Private International Law from a Human Rights Perspective
Chiara Ragni 209

1. Lack of Harmonisation of Family Law in Europe and its Impact on Recognition of Foreign Adoptions 209
2. The International Legal Framework: The 1993 Hague Convention and its Limits 211
3. The Right to the Continuity of Family Status: Social Reality and Legitimate Expectations v. Legal Relationships 215
4. Reconciling Human Rights and Private International Law 220

Protecting Children's Rights after Child Abduction: The Interaction of the CJEU and ECtHR in Interpreting Brussels II *bis*
Ruth Lamont 225

1. Introduction 225
2. International Child Abduction: The Legal Framework within the EU 226
3. Protecting Children's Rights on Child Abduction in the Supranational Courts 231
4. Conclusions 242

Cross-Border Parental Child Abduction in the EU: Is there Room for a Human Rights Exception?
Costanza Honorati 243

1. Article 20 of the 1980 Hague Convention: Between Public Policy and Fundamental Rights 243

2. The Difficulty of Framing the Scope of Article 20, Particularly with Regard to Article 13(1)(b). 246
3. Application of Article 20 in Purely Conventional Cases 252
4. Is there a Use for Article 20 in EU Abduction Cases? 259

Impact of the Best Interests of the Child on the Brussels II *ter* Regulation
Laura CARPANETO 265

1. The Best Interests of the Child and the 'Brussels II System': Setting Terms of Reference 265
2. Impact of the BIC Principle: The Structure and Scope of Application 270
3. Rules on Jurisdiction 274
4. More Efficient Circulation of Decisions 277
5. The New Proactive Attitude Toward Hearing the Child and Mediation. 279
6. Assessment of the Child's Situation in 'Moving' within the EU Judicial Area 281
7. Is the BIC Better Protected by the New Rules? 284

Provisional Measures and the Best Interests of the Child in the Field of Parental Responsibility
Lidia SANDRINI 287

1. Introduction 287
2. Jurisdiction on the Substance and Jurisdiction to Issue Interim Relief. 289
3. The Presence of the Child or of the Child's Assets as a Ground of 'Interim' Jurisdiction 295
4. Coordination between Measures and Impact on the Notion of 'Provisional and Protective Measures' 302
5. Conclusions 307

Index 311

LIST OF CASES

COURT OF JUSTICE OF THE EUROPEAN UNION

A v. B, case C-184/14, ECLI:EU:C:2015:479 270
A, case C-523/07, ECLI:EU:C:2009:225 . . . . . 272, 290, 296–297, 299, 304–305, 307
A. v. the Netherlands, case C-550/16, ECLI:EU:C:2018:248 66–67
Aguirre-Zarraga v. Simone Pelz, case C-491/10 PPU, ECLI:EU:C:2010:828 . . . 230, 236, 295
Åkerberg Fransson, case C-617/10, ECLI:EU:C:2013:105 . . . . . 25, 65, 86
Anklagemyndigheden v. Peter Michael Poulsen and Diva Navigation Corp., case C-286/90, ECLI:EU:C:1992:453 142
Bogendorff von Wolffersdorff, case C-438/14, ECLI:EU:C:2016:401 . . . . . 27, 86
C, case C-435/06, ECLI:EU:C:2014:2461 272
C. v. M., case C-376/14 PPU, ECLI:EU:C:2014:2268 274
Carpenter, case C-60/00, ECLI:EU:C:2002:434 . . . . . 87, 90
Chakroun v. the Netherlands, case C-578/08, ECLI:EU:C:2010:117 . . . . . 57, 65
Child and Family Agency v. J.D., case C-428/15, ECLI:EU:C:2016:819 . . . 155, 169, 276, 291
Coleman, case C-303/06, ECLI:EU:C:2008:415 93
Coman, case C-673/16, ECLI:EU:C:2018:385 . . . . . 29, 81
Commission v. France, case 167/73, ECLI:EU:C:1974:35 79
De Cavel v. De Cavel, case 143/78, ECLI:EU:C:1979:83 299
Denilauler v. snc Couchet Frères, case 125/79, ECLI:EU:C:1980:130 292
Doris Povse v. Mauro Alpago, case C-211/10, ECLI:EU:C:2010:400 . . . . . 237–238, 240
Dynamic Medien Vertriebs GmbH, case C-244/06, ECLI:EU:C:2008:85 11
Freitag, case C-541/15, ECLI:EU:C:2017:432 27
Garcia Avello, case C-148/02, ECLI:EU:C:2003:539 . . . . . 27, 86
Gerardo Ruiz Zambrano v. Office national de l'emploi (ONEm), case C-34/09, ECLI:EU:C:2011:124 . . . . . 34, 70, 81
Gogova, case C-215/15, ECLI:EU:C:2015:710 291
Grunkin-Paul, case C-353/06, ECLI:EU:C:2008:559 . . . . . 27, 86
H.C. Chavez-Vilchez and Others, case C-133/15 [AG Opinion], ECLI:EU:C:2016:659 11
H.C. Chavez-Vilchez and Others, case C-133/15 [Judgment], ECLI:EU:C:2017:354 . . . . . 34, 71
Health Service Executive v. S.C. and A.C., case C-92/12 PPU, ECLI:EU:C:2012:255 . . . . . 272, 289, 293, 296
HR, case C-512/17, ECLI:EU:C:2018:513 290
Italian Leather spa v. WECO Polstermöbel GmbH & Co., case C-80/00, ECLI:EU:C:2002:342 . . . . . 303, 306
J. McB. v. L.E., case C-400/10 PPU, ECLI:EU:C:2010:582 153
Jasna Deticek v. Maurizio Sgueglia, case C-403/09 PPU, ECLI:EU:C:2009:810 . . . . . 154, 228, 236, 290, 294, 296–298

K. v. Buundesasylamt, case C-245/11, ECLI:EU:C:2012:685 49
K.A. and Others v Belgische Staatcase, case C-82/16, ECLI:EU:C:2018:308............. 34
Konstantinidis, case C-168/91, ECLI:EU:C:1993:115 27
Mario Reichert, Hans-Heinz Reichert and Ingeborg Kockler v. Dresdner Bank AG., case C-261/90, ECLI:EU:C:1992:149.. 305
Mario Vicente Micheletti and others v. Delegación del Gobierno en Cantabria, case C-360/90, ECLI:EU:C:1992:295.. 305
Marjan Noorzia v. Bundesministerin für Inneres, case C-338/13, ECLI:EU:C:2014:2092..127–128
Maruko, case C-267/06, ECLI:EU:C:2008:179... 86
Matouskova, case C-404/14, ECLI:EU:C:2015:653 271
Mercredi, case C-497/10 PPU, ECLI:EU:C:2010:829................................ 290
Mietz v Intership Yachting Sneek BV, case C-99/96, ECLI:EU:C:1999:202 ....303, 306
MRAX, case C-459/99, ECLI:EU:C:2002:461... 86
Murat Dereci and Others v. Bundesministerium für Inneres, case C-256/11, ECLI:EU:C:2011:734 .... 34, 70
Neli Valcheva v Georgios Babanarakis, case C-335/17 [AG Opinion], ECLI:EU:C:2018:242 76
Neli Valcheva v Georgios Babanarakis, case C-335/17 [Judgment], ECLI:EU:C:2018:359 .... 14, 273
Nold, case 4/73, ECLI:EU:C:1974:51 89
O. and S. v Maahanmuuttovirasto and *Maahanmuuttovirasto v. L.*, cases C-356/11 and C-357/11, ECLI:EU:C:2012:776 ....34, 64–65, 81
O. v. Minister voor Immigratie, Integratie en Asiel and Minister voor Immigratie, Integratie en Asiel v. Bcase, case C-456/12, ECLI:EU:C:2014:135 .... 33, 79
OL v PQ, case C-111/17 PPU, ECLI:EU:C:2017:436................................ 290
Opinion of the Court 2/13, 18 December 2014, ECLI:EU:C:2014:2454............ 57, 241
P v. Q, case C-455/15 PPU, ECLI:EU:C:2015:763 304
Parliament v. Council, case C-540/03, ECLI:EU:C:2006:429 .... 10, 57, 103, 111, 228
Parris, case C-443/15, ECLI:EU:C:2016:897... 86
Pfleger, case C-390/12, ECLI:EU:C:2014:281 86
PM v. AH, case C-604/17, ECLI:EU:C:2018:10 292
Pupino, case C-105/03 [AG Opinion], ECLI:EU:C:2004:712.......................... 48
Pupino, case C-105/03 [Judgment], ECLI:EU:C:2005:386 9
Purrucker I, case C-256/09, ECLI:EU:C:2010:437.................... 289–290, 299–300
Purrucker II, case C-296/10, ECLI:EU:C:2010:665 287
Rahman, case C-83/11, ECLI:EU:C:2012/519 ....80, 88, 109
Rendòn Marìn, case C-165/14, ECLI:EU:C:2016:675 .... 34, 70
Rinau, case C-195/08 PPU, ECLI:EU:C:2008:406 ....278, 287
Roux v. Belgium, case C-363/89, ECLI:EU:C:1991:41 79
Runevic-Vardyn and Wardyn, case C-391/09 [AG Opinion], ECLI:EU:C:2010:784...... 23
Runevic-Vardyn and Wardyn, case C-391/09 [Judgment], ECLI:EU:C:2011:291 ..... 27, 32
Sanders, case C-400/13 and C-408/13, ECLI:EU:C:2014:2461 269
Saponaro, case C-565/16, ECLI:EU:C:2018:265..............................271, 291
Sayn-Wittgenstein, case C-208/09, ECLI:EU:C:2010:806 27
Secretary of State for the Home Department v. CS, case C-304/14, ECLI:EU:C:2016:674 .... 11, 34
Secretary of State for the Home Department v. NA, case C-115/15, ECLI:EU:C:2016:487 34

Shirley McCarthy v. Secretary of State for the Home Department, case C-434/09, ECLI:EU:C:2011:277 25
SM, case C-129/18, ECLI:EU:C:2019:248 . . . . . 105, 109
St Paul Dairy Industries NV v. Unibel Exser BVBA, case C-104/03, ECLI:EU:C:2005:255 306
Stauder, case 29/69, ECLI:EU:C:1969:57 89
The Queen, on the application of MA and Others v. Secretary of State for the Home Department, case C-648/11, ECLI:EU:C:2013:367 . . . . . 12, 49, 69, 143
U.D. v. X.B., case C-393/18 PPU, ECLI:EU:C:2018:835 . . . . . 153, 290, 292, 305
Van Uden Maritime BV v. Firma Deco Line, case C-391/95, ECLI:EU:C:1998:543 . . . . . 289, 297, 303
W and V, case C-499/15, ECLI:EU:C:2017:118 . . . . . 290, 292
Wachauf, case 5/88, ECLI:EU:C:1989:321 86
Yoshikazu Iida v. Stadt Ulm, case C-40/11, ECLI:EU:C:2012:691 . . . . . 68, 88, 134
Zhu and Chen, case C-200/02, ECLI:EU:C:2004:639 . . . . . 27, 81

EUROPEAN COURT OF HUMAN RIGHTS

Abdulaziz, Cabales, and Balkandali v. UK, nos. 9214/80, 9473/81 and 9474/81, ECHR 1985 . . . . . 56, 72
Abubakar v. Malta, nos. 25794/13 and 28151/13, 22.02.2017 50
Abubeker v. Austria and Italy, no. 73874/11, 18.06.2013 51
Advisory Opinion [GC], no. P16-2018-001 . . . . . xii, 223
Al Nashif v. Bulgaria, no. 509963/99, ECHR 2002 61
Al-Adsani v. United Kingdom [GC], no. 35763/97, ECHR 2001-XI 48, 176
Anayo v. Germany, no. 20578/07, 21.12.2010 13
Belgian Linguistics Case, nos. 1474/62; 1677/62; 1691/62; 1769/63; 1994/63; 2126/64, ECHR 1968 61
Bosphorous Hava Yollari Turizm ve Ticaret Anonim Sirketi v. Ireland, no. 45036/11, ECHR 2005-VI 48, 238, 240
Brauer v. Germany, no. 3545/04, 28.05.2009 13
Braun v France, no. 1462/18 201
Bronda v. Italy, no. 22430/93, 09.06.1998 14
Chapin and Charpentier v. France, no. 40183/07, 9.6.2016 172
Chbihi Loudoudi and others v. *Belgium*, no. 52265/10, ECHR 2015 112
Ciubotaru v. Moldova, no. 27138/04, 27.04.2010 23
Collins and Akaziebie v. Sweden, no. 23944/05, 08.03.2007 18
Cusan and Fazzo v. Italy, no. 77/07, 07.01.2014 24
D. v Belgium, no. 29176/13, 11.09.2014 192–194
Dudgeon v. the United Kingdom, no. 7525/76, 22.10.1981 23
E.B. c. France [GC], no. 43546/02, 22.01.2008 . . . . . 176, 216
El Ghatet v. Switzerland, no. 56971/10, ... 59, 63
Ferrari v. Romania, no. 1714/10, 28.04.2010 234
Foulon and Bouvet v. France, nos. 9063/14 and 10410/14, 21.07.2016 . . . . . 32, 190–191, 198
Frettè v. France, no. 36515/97, ECHR 2002-I 216
Gas and Dubois v. France, no. 25952/07, ECHR 2012-II 90, 92, 94, 180

Gaskin v. the United Kingdom, no. 10454/83, 07.07.1989 24
Genovese v. Malta, no. 53124/09, 11.10.2011 24
Golder v. United Kingdom, no. 4451/70, 21.02.1975 . . . . 48, 176
Golemanova v. Bulgaria, no. 11369/04, 17.02.2011 26
Goodwin v. United Kingdom [GC], no. 289957/95, ECHR 2002-VI 23
Guillot v. France, no. 22500/93, 24.10.1993. 24
Halimi v. Austria and Italy, no. 53852/11, 18.06.2013. 51
Harroudj v. *France*, no. 43631/09, ECHR 2012. . . . . 111, 221
Hirsi Jamaa and Others v. Italy, no. 27765/09, ECHR 2012-II 51
Hussein Diirshi and others v. Netherland and Italy, no. 2314/10, 10.09.2013 51
Hussin v. Belgium, no. 70807/01, 6.05.2004 . . . . 173, 216
I.A.A. and others v. UK, no. 25960/13 ECHR 2016 72
Iosub Caras v. Romania, no. 7198/04, 27.07.2006 232
Raban v. Romania, no. 25437/08, 26.10.2010 232
Izevbekhai and others v. Ireland, no. 43408/08, 17.05.2011. 18
J.R.M. v. the Netherlands, no. 16944/90, ECHR 1993 90
Jeunesse v. the Netherlands, no. 12738/10, ECHR 2014. . . . . 11, 62
Johansen v. Norway, no. 17383/90, 17.01.1995. 227
Johansson v. Finland, no. 10163/02, 06.09.2007 24
Josef. v. Belgium, no. 70055/10, 27.02.2014 19
K. and T. v. Finland, no. 25702/94, ECHR 2001-VII 90
K.A. and A.D. v. *Belgium*, nos. 42756/98 and 45558/98, 17.02.2005. 23
K.A. v. Finland, no. 27751/95, 14.01.2003. 24
Kanagaratnam v. Belgium, no. 15297/09, 13.12.2011 6
Karner v. Austria, no. 40016/98, ECHR 2003-XI. 172, 180
Keegan v. Ireland, no. 16969/90, 26.05.1994 13
Kozak v. Poland, no. 13102/02, 2.03.2010 180
Kroon and others v. The Netherlands, no. 18535/91, 27.10.1994 177
L. v. The Netherlands, no. 45582/99, ECHR 2004. 61
Laborie v. France, no. 44024/2013, 19.01.2017 . . . . 32, 190–191, 198
Levin v. Sweden, no. 35141/06, 15.03.2012 24
M.S.S. v. Belgium and Greece, no. 30696/09, ECHR 2011 69
MA/Sofia Povse and *Doris Povse v. Austria*, no. 3890/11 . . . . 238, 240
Manuello and Nevi v. Italy, 107/10, 20.01.2015 14
Marckx v. Belgium, no. 6833/74, 13.06.1979 . . . . 13, 30, 61, 90, 92, 177
Mary Green and Ajad Farhat v. Malta, no. 38797/07, 6.07.2010 23
Maslov v. Austria, no. 1638/0323, ECHR 2008. 72
Maumousseau and Washington v. France, no. 39388/05, 06.12.2007. 232
McDonald v. France, no. 18648/04, 29.04.2008 23
Mennesson v. France and *Labassee v. France*, nos. 65192/2011
and 65941/2011,ECHR 2014-III 32, 91, 176, 188, 198
Miruts Hagos v. Netherland and Italy, no. 9053/10, 27.08.2013 51
Mohammed Hassan and others v. The Netherlands and Italy, no. 40524/10,
27.08.2013 51
Mohammed Hussein v. The Netherlands and Italy, no. 27725/10, 02.04.2013 51
Mubilanzila Mayeka et Kaniki Mitunga v. Belgium, no. 13178/03, 12.10.2006 50–51
Muskhadzhiyeva and others v. Belgium, no. 41442/07, 19.01.2010 6
A.M.E. v. The Netherlands, no. 51428/10, 05.02.2015 50
Negrepontis-Giannisis v. Greece, no. 56759/08, 3.05.2011 . . . . 23, 91, 173, 218

Neulinger and Shuruk v. Switzerland [GC], no. 41615/07, 06.07.2010 .... 49, 72, 167, 176, 179, 232–233
Neulinger in *X v. Latvia*, no. 27853/09, 26.11.2011 233–234
Niemietz v. Germany, no. 13710/88, 16.12.1992 23
Nistor v. Romania, no. 14565/05, 02.11.2010 14
Norris v. Ireland, no. 10581/83, 26.10.1988 23
Nunez v. Norway, no. 55597/09, ECHR 2011 62
Nylund v. Finland, no. 27110/95, ECHR 1999-VI 90
Odièvre v. France [GC], no. 42326/98, 13.02.2003 24
Oliari and others v. Italy, nos. 18766/11 and 36030/11, 21.07.2015 .... 172, 180
Olsson v. Sweden, no. 10465/83, 24.03.1988 180
Paradiso and Campanelli v. Italy, no. 25358/12, 27.01.2015 .... 30, 116, 177, 180, 190, 194–197, 217–220
Petrovic v. Austria, no. 20458/92, (156/1996/775/976), 27.03.1998 172
Pini and Others v. Romania, nos. 78028/01 and 78030/01, 22.09.2004 216
Pretty v. United Kingdom, no. 2346/02, ECHR 2002-III 23
R. B. A. B. and others v. The Netherlands, no. 7211/06, 07.06.2016 18
R.M.S. v. Spain, no. 28775/12, 18.06.2013 24
Rahimi v. Greece, no. 8687/08, 05.07.2011 50
Rodrigues da Silva and Hoogkamer v. The Netherlands, no. 50435/99, ECHR 2006 62
S. F. and others v. Bulgaria, no. 8138/16, 07.12.2017 20
Saenz and Saenz Cortes v France, no. 11288/18 201
Sahin v. Germany, no. 30943/96, 08.07.2003 .... 14, 179
Schalk and Kopf v. Austria, no. 30141/04, 22.06.2010 .... 172, 180
Senigo Longue and others v. France, no. 19113/09, ECHR 2014 72
Senigo Longue v. France, no. 19113/09, 10.07.2014 50
Serife Yigit v. Turkey, no. 3976/05, 2.11.2005 129
Severe v. Austria, no. 53661/15, 21.09.2017 .... 234–235, 239
Sharifi and others v. Italy and Greece, no. 16643/09, 21.10.2014 51
Stjerna v. Finland, no. 18131/91, 25.11.1994 23
Streletz, Kessler and Krenz v. Germany [GC], nos. 34044/96, 35532/97 and 44801/98, 22.03.2001 176
Tarakhel v. Switzerland [GC], no. 29217/12, 14.11.2014 .... 50–51, 69
Vallianatos and Others v. Greece [GC], nos. 29381/09 and 32684/09, ECHR 2013-VI 93, 172
Wagner and J.M.W.L. v. Luxembourg, no. 76240/01, ECHR 2007-VII 23, 91, 94, 167, 173, 216–217, 219
X and others v. Austria [GC], no. 19010/07, ECHR 2013-II 72, 180–181
X, Y and Z v. United Kingdom, no. 21830/93, 22.04.1997 228
X. v Latvia [GC], no. 27853/09, ECHR 2013-VI 168, 245
X. v. Germany, no. 6167/73, 18.12.1974 129
Z.H. and R.H. v. Switzerland, no. 60119/12, 08.12.2015 .... 116, 128–130, 132

LIST OF AUTHORS

Roberto Baratta
Professor of International Law and European Union Law at the University of Macerata, Italy

Elisabetta Bergamini
Professor of International Law at the University of Udine, Italy

Laura Carpenato
Associate Professor of European Union Law at the University of Genoa, Italy

Francesco Deana
Lecturer in European Union Law at the University of Udine, Italy

Sara De Vido
Researcher of International Law at the Ca' Foscari University of Venice, Italy

Marcella Distefano
Professor of International Law at the University of Messina, Italy

Pietro Franzina
Professor of International Law at the University of Ferrara, Italy

Costanza Honorati
Professor of European Union Law at the University of Milano-Bicocca, Italy

Ruth Lamont
Senior Lecturer in Family and Child Law at the University of Manchester, United Kingdom

Alessandra Lang
Professor of European Union Law at the University of Milan, Italy

Maura Marchegiani
Professor of International Law at the University of Foreigners of Perugia, Italy

Chiara Ragni
Professor of International Law at the University of Milan, Italy

Peter Rodrigues
Professor of Immigration Law and Chair of the Institute of Immigration Law at Leiden University, The Netherlands

Lidia Sandrini
Professor of International Law at the University of Milan, Italy

Katarina Trimmings
Senior Lecturer in Private International Law at the University of Aberdeen, United Kingdom

Alina Tryfodinou
Professor of Law at the University of Reading, United Kingdom

PART I

THE IMPACT OF HUMAN RIGHTS AND OF THE BEST INTERESTS OF THE CHILD ON EU FREE MOVEMENT AND MIGRATION LAW

HUMAN RIGHTS OF CHILDREN IN THE EU CONTEXT

Impact on National Family Law

Elisabetta BERGAMINI

1. Introduction . . . 3
2. Analyses of Human Rights Rules Relevant in the Field of Interest . . . 5
   2.1. The New York Convention . . . 5
   2.2. The ECHR . . . 8
   2.3. The EU and the Charter of Fundamental Rights . . . 8
3. Children's Rights in the Interpretative Activity of the CJEU . . . 10
4. Children's Rights and the Evolution of Domestic Family Law: Specific Issues . . . 12
   4.1. Children Born Out of Wedlock . . . 12
   4.2. Right of the Child to Maintain a Relationship with Other Family Members . . . 14
   4.3. Right of the Child to be Heard . . . 15
   4.4. Prohibition of Inhuman Treatment and Migrating Children . . . 17
5. Final Remarks . . . 19

1. INTRODUCTION

We had to wait until 1989 for a specific general catalogue of children's rights to be approved at the supranational level (the Convention on the Rights of the Child (CRC)), which was drafted in New York in the framework of the United Nations).[1] However, some general principles applicable to children had already

[1] The Convention on the Rights of the Child was adopted with resolution No. 44/25 of the UN General Assembly on 20.11.1989 and entered into force on 02.09.1990. It is now applied in 193 States (The USA did not ratify it). For more details, see W. VANDENHOLE, 'The Convention on the Rights of the Child' in F. GÓMEZ ISA and K. DE FEYTER (eds.), *International Human Rights Law in a Global Context*, University of Deusto, Bilbao 2009, p. 452; I. BARRIÈRE-BROUSSE, 'L'Enfant et les Conventions Internationales' [1996] *Journal du Droit International* 4, 843.

been included in previously devised instruments concerning human rights. These include the Universal Declaration on Human Rights proclaimed by the UN General Assembly in 1948,[2] the International Covenant on Civil and Political Rights of 1966[3] and the European Convention on Human Rights (ECHR) of 1950, all of which contain references at least to the need to protect family life.

The CRC differs from these previous instruments in that it considers the child as a subject and not only as an object of law.[4] Through this 'Copernican revolution' children have become a focus of legal reasoning and are granted specific and autonomous rights that do not derive from their parents or, more generally, from being part of a 'legitimate' family. Such rights could also diverge from those of other family members. However, as will be illustrated in this chapter, the complex legal framework existing at the international level has yet to be fully implemented at the national level in most cases.

This chapter considers the idea that children's rights need to be protected as human rights, and that such protections are not only reserved for toddlers but are also valid for adolescents and young adults.[5] Accordingly, this work analyses the main supranational instruments concerning children's fundamental rights, and assesses the global impact of the relevant principles on domestic family law in the EU Member States. Such an impact will be considered with particular regard to the role of the Court of Justice of the European Union (CJEU) in tandem with that of the European Court of Human Rights (ECtHR).

This chapter proceeds under the basic assumption that children's rights can be divided into two categories. The first category encompasses the more basic rights that are usually not at risk of violation in EU Member States (e.g. the right to respect for physical integrity and its violation in case of female genital mutilation). Clearly, the risk of violation of such rights increases in cross-border situations, as migrating children could face infringement by their national communities in the host country or, as is more frequently the case, when sent back to their national countries (as we will see is the case for forced marriages, among other situations).[6] The second category refers to rights whose protection

---

On the different approaches in place before and after the approval of the CRC, see N. Cantwell, 'Are Children's Rights Still Human?' in A. Invernizzi and J. Williams (eds.), *The Human Rights of Children: From Visions to Implementation*, Routledge, New York 2016, p. 38.

2 The most relevant provisions of interest for this analysis are Article 16, which considers the family as the natural and fundamental group unit of society, and Article 25, which stresses that childhood is entitled to special care and assistance.

3 Articles 23 and 24 address, respectively, the need to protect the family as the natural and fundamental group unit of society, and the right of children to such measures of protection as are required by their status as minors.

4 Y. Beigbeder, 'Children' in G. T. Weiss and S. Daws (eds.), *The Oxford Handbook on the United Nations*, Oxford University Press, Oxford-New York 2007, p. 513.

5 N. Cantwell, above n. 1, p. 43.

6 See De Vido in this volume.

still needs to be specifically granted to children in their home countries, and where the risk of violation in cross-border situations is even higher. It includes the right of children to be heard in judgments regarding parental responsibility, which is still subject to many violations in domestic proceedings but is at much higher risk in all cross-border situations.

The main research question that this chapter will try to answer is whether cross-border situations (stemming from free movement of EU citizens and their families or from migration situations) affect the different national legal frameworks in a way that leads to higher-level protections of children rights as well as to a more satisfying and comprehensive application of the international instruments meant to protect human (or more specifically children's) rights.

2. ANALYSES OF HUMAN RIGHTS RULES RELEVANT IN THE FIELD OF INTEREST

This analysis of the existing legal framework mainly focuses on three documents among the various sources of international law: the CRC, due to the specificity of its provisions on the best interests of the child, which have been considered a model for the interpretative evolution of children's rights, then the ECHR and the Charter of Fundamental Rights of the EU (because of their relevance at the regional level and the effectiveness of their jurisdictional system). Other existing international instruments will not be considered either because they are too general (e.g. the International Covenant on Civil and Political Rights) or they are too specifically linked to particular situations (e.g. the Convention on Contact Concerning Children of 2003).[7]

2.1. THE NEW YORK CONVENTION

The need to take the child's best interests as the primary consideration is the main pillar of the New York Convention of 1989.[8] No definition of such

7 Council of Europe, CETS No. 192, 15.05.2003. For a more general analysis of the international legal framework on this issue, see E. Canetta, N. Meurens, P. McDonough and R. Ruggiero, *Note on the EU Framework of Law for Children's Rights, European Parliament*, Brussels, [2012] <http://www.europarl.europa.eu/RegData/etudes/note/join/2012/462445/IPOL-LIBE_NT(2012)462445_EN.pdf>.

8 On the limits of the Convention, see M. Freeman, 'The Value and Values of Children's Rights' in A. Invernizzi and J. Williams (eds.), *The Human Rights of Children: From Visions to Implementation*, Ashgate, Surrey 2011, p. 27. For a critical approach to the inadequacies of the CRC and some possible remedies, see U. Kilkelly, 'Using the Convention on the Rights of the Child in Law and Policy: Two Ways to Improve Compliance' in A. Invernizzi and J. Williams (eds.), above n. 1, pp. 179–97.

interests is given in that Convention. However, the relevance of this principle is clearly established by various Articles containing a reference to it. In particular, Article 3, as can be seen in General Comment No. 14, defines the best interests of the child as a threefold concept that is simultaneously a substantive right, a fundamental interpretative principle and a rule of procedure.[9]

If the UN Declaration on Children's Rights (1959) already stated that 'the best interests of the child shall be the paramount consideration',[10] the text of the New York Convention seems to undermine this principle by slightly changing the definition and reducing the best interests of the child to 'a primary consideration', thereby giving space to the urge to balance the different needs that must be considered when taking decisions regarding children.[11]

Notably, some national legal systems, such as the Spanish and the French, refer to the 'best interest of the child' in the singular, thereby implying that there could be only one such best interest. By contrast, the idea as expressed in the English system is that the 'best interests' of children exist and must be considered, thus clarifying that different interests exist for any given child and all should be balanced.

Some children's rights as listed by the CRC are not endangered for EU citizens living inside EU Member States (a clear example is the prohibition of inhuman and degrading treatment found in Article 37; it seems difficult to imagine a violation of this principle perpetrated against national citizens in Europe). However, they could still be at risk when we consider migrant children either lawfully or unlawfully residing in Europe (as was the case for some detention conditions to which migrant children were submitted by European States)[12]

---

9 United Nations (UN), Committee on the Rights of the Child (CRC) (2013), General Comment No. 14 (2013) on the Right of the Child to Have His or Her Best Interests Taken as a Primary Consideration (Art. 3, Para. 1)*, CRC/C/GC/14, 29.5.2013, paras. 6–7. On Article 3 see U. Kilkelly, 'The Best Interests of the Child: A Gateway to Children's Rights?' in E. E. Sutherland and L. A. Barnes Macfarlane (eds.), *Implementing Article 3 of the United Nations Convention on the Rights of the Child – Best Interests, Welfare and Well-being*, Cambridge University Press, Cambridge 2018, p. 64.

10 On the evolution of children protection in international law see G. Van Beuren, *The International Law on the Right of the Child*, Dordrecht, Kluwer 1995, p. 8.

11 For a comparison between the English and the French versions of the Convention see C. Focarelli, 'La convenzione di New York sui diritti del fanciullo e il concetto di "best interests of the child"' [2010] *Rivista di diritto internazionale* 4, 981. On the drafting of Article 3, see E. E. Sutherland, 'Article 3 of the United Nations Convention on the Rights of the Child: The Challenges of Vagueness and Priorities' in E. E. Sutherland and L. A. Barnes Macfarlane (eds.), *Implementing Article 3 of the United Nations Convention on the Rights of the Child – Best Interests, Welfare and Well-being*, Cambridge University Press, Cambridge 2018, p. 22.

12 *Popov v. France*, 19.01.2012. The ECtHR made a specific reference to the CRC encouraging 'States to take the appropriate measures to ensure that a child who is seeking to obtain refugee status enjoys protection and humanitarian assistance, whether the child is alone or accompanied by his or her parents' (§91). See also *Muskhadzhiyeva and Others v. Belgium* No. 41442/07, 19.01.2010, and *Kanagaratnam v. Belgium* No. 15297/09, 13.12.2011, in which

and even more if they are at risk of *refoulement* towards their country of origin (as could be the case for victims of female genital mutilation or forced marriages).

Migrant children clearly need to be considered as particularly vulnerable and must be specifically protected. This was illustrated by the recent Joint General Comments by the Committee on the Protection of the Rights of All Migrant Workers and Members of Their Families and the Committee on the Rights of the Child, on the general principles regarding the human rights of children in the context of international migration as well as State obligations concerning the human rights of children in the context of international migration in countries of origin, transit, destination and return. The two sets of comments were approved on 16 November 2017; although each was issued independently of the other, they should be read and implemented together. These General Comments stress that the best interests of children should be protected

> whether they have migrated with their parents or primary caregivers, are unaccompanied or separated, have returned to their country of origin, were born to migrant parents in countries of transit or destination, or remained in their country of origin while one or both parents migrated to another country, and regardless of their or their parents' migration or residence status (point 9 comment No. 3).[13]

The universal reach of the CRC is granted by its application to any child, irrespective of his or her citizenship. However, with Article 22, a specific protection is extended to refugees and asylum seekers, to whom the State should grant human rights as set forth not only in the CRC but also in all international human rights instruments to which the State is party.

The Committee on the Rights of the Child – a body of independent experts that monitors and reports on the implementation of the CRC – has also clarified the relevance of fundamental rights protections as they apply to the specific situation of migrant children,[14] as the CRC is considered a 'complimentary source of protection' to be combined with the 1951 Refugee Convention, when possible.[15]

---

the ECtHR found a violation of Article 3 (degrading and inhuman treatment) due to the harsh detention conditions in which the migrant children were held by Belgian authorities.

13 Respectively, Comments No. 3 and 4 (2017) of the Committee on the Protection of the Rights of All Migrant Workers and Members of Their Families, and Comment No. 22 and 23 (2017) of the Committee on the Rights of the Child. See Point 9 Comment No. 3.

14 On the main activities of the Committee and its role, see J. Kanics, 'The Best Interests of Unaccompanied and Separated Children: A Normative Framework Based on the Convention on the Rights of the Child' in M. Sedmak, B. Sauer, B. Gornik and D. Senovilla Hernández (eds.), *Unaccompanied Children in European Migration and Asylum Practices: In Whose Best Interests?* [Internet] Routledge, London 2016, p. 41. On its jurisprudence, see C. P. Cohen and S. Kilbourne, 'Jurisprudence of the Committee of the Rights of the Child: A Guide for Research and Analyses', [1998] 19(3) *Michigan Journal of International Law*, 633.

15 J. M. Pobjoy, *The Child in International Refugee Law*, Cambridge University Press, Cambridge 2017, p. 186.

2.2. THE ECHR

The best interests of the child are not expressly mentioned in the ECHR, which mentions the interests of the child (as opposed to other interests) only in Article 5.1.d, which recognises the possibility for the State to take necessary measures in the interests of children upon their lawful detention for educational supervision, and in Article 6, which declares that juveniles have a right to a fair hearing.

Although a specific provision is lacking, the promotion of children's rights has been granted in various cases because most rights listed in the ECHR are not reserved solely for adults, as well as through the application of the right to family life (Article 8 of the ECHR), which is widely used to recognise and preserve family ties. The case law of the Strasbourg court clarifies that the ECHR shall be applied consistently with the CRC and that the best interests of the child shall be thereby preserved (e.g. using Article 3, which prohibits inhuman and degrading treatment) and balanced with the interest of other family members.[16]

Another legal basis frequently used to protect children is Article 14, which prohibits 'discrimination on any ground such as … birth or other status' and – as we will see – is usually applied concurrently with Article 8 to grant protection to children born out of wedlock.

None of these Articles are specifically targeted at protecting the rights of migrant children; however, they are intended to be respected and implemented in both domestic and cross-border situations. Yet, due to unaccompanied minors' general lack of access to the ECtHR, there is still no jurisprudence applying the Convention to asylum (i.e. *non-refoulement*) requests presented by children alone.[17]

2.3. THE EU AND THE CHARTER OF FUNDAMENTAL RIGHTS

The European Economic Community and later European Community Treaties had no specific provisions addressing children's rights, as children were merely indirect beneficiaries of social policy measures.[18] However, human rights, including the right to family life, were already considered part of the general

---

16 J. M. Scott, 'Conflict between Human Rights and Best Interests of Children: Myth or Reality?' in E. E. Sutherland and L. A. Barnes Macfarlane (eds.), *Implementing Article 3*, above n. 9, p. 68.

17 For more remarks on this issue see C. Smyth, 'The Jurisprudence of the European Court of Human Rights Relevant to Child Migrants' in J. Bhabha, J. Kanics and D. Senovilla Hernández (eds.), *Research Handbook on Child Migration*, Edward Elgar Publishing, Cheltenham 2018, p. 141.

18 See E. Caracciolo di Torella and A. Masselot, *Reconciling Work and Family Life in EU Law and Policy*, Palgrave Macmillian, Basingstoke 2010.

principles of EU law thanks to the evolution of the case law of the CJEU. Eventually, the EU Charter included these rights in its provisions and, after the entry into force of the Treaty of Lisbon, they now have the same legal value as the Treaties.[19]

Although most of the provisions of the Charter can be applied equally to children as to any other individual, our primary focus will be Article 24. In accordance with the principles already enshrined in the CRC, Article 24 guarantees the rights of children: 1) to such protection and care as is necessary for their well-being;[20] 2) to be heard and for their opinion to be taken into consideration in accordance with age and maturity; 3) to have their best interests taken as a primary consideration in all actions; and 4) to maintain a personal relationship with both parents. This Article should also be applied concurrently with Article 21 of the Charter, which abjures any kind of discrimination based on birth circumstances (i.e. whether inside or outside wedlock) and on grounds of age. Furthermore, it should be applied with Article 7, which commands respect for private and family life. A specific reference to rights pertaining to children is also contained in Article 14 (the right to receive free compulsory education) and Article 32 (the prohibition of exploitative child labour). Moreover, Articles 3.3 and 3.5 of the Treaty on European Union now specifically address the topic by declaring that the EU shall promote the 'protection of the rights of the child', both in its internal dimensions and in its external relationships.

Recognition of the need to ensure child protection emerged clearly after 2006 with the EU Commission's Communication titled *Towards an EU Strategy on the Rights of the Child*, which granted children their own rights extending beyond those deriving from their parents' status (in particular from their parents' choice to move within or to Europe).[21]

---

19 See H. Stalford and M. Schuurman, 'Are We There Yet? The Impact of the Lisbon Treaty on the EU Children's Rights Agenda' [2011] *International Journal of Children's Rights* 19, 381–403. For an overview, see S. Iglesias Sánchez, 'The Court and the Charter: the Impact of the Entry into Force of the Lisbon Treaty on the ECJ's Approach to Fundamental Rights' [2012] *Common Market Law Review* 49, 1565–1611; K. Lenaerts, 'Exploring the Limits of the EU Charter of Fundamental Rights' [2012] *European Constitutional Law Review*, 375. More specifically, for the provisions of the EU Charter and family matters, see C. Campiglio, 'L'applicazione della Carta dei diritti fondamentali dell'Unione europea in materia familiare' [2015] *Diritti umani e diritto internazionale*, 279. On Article 24 of the EU Charter, see H. Bosse-Platière, 'Le statut de l'enfant et l'européanisation des sources en droit de la famille' in D. Gadbin and F. Kernaleguen (eds), *Le Statut Juridique de l'Enfant dans l'Espace Européen*, Bruylant Bruxelles 2004, pp. 82–88.

20 In her opinion of 11.11.2004 in Case C-105/03, *Pupino*, ECLI:EU:C:2005:386 par. 57, Advocate General Kokott invoked Article 24 of the EU Charter for the first time. For a comment on the case, see J. R. Spencer, 'Child Witnesses and the European Union', [2005] *The Cambridge Law Journal*, 569.

21 See also European Commission, DG Justice, EU Acquis and Policy Documents on the Rights of the Child, December 2015, pp.1–83.

As described by the European Agency on Fundamental Rights, we are currently facing a 'gradual shift from the exclusively economic imperative family entitlement towards a rights-based approach'.[22] However, Article 24 is legally binding only for EU Institutions and Member States when implementing and/or applying EU law. This means that while we clearly apply Article 24 in all situations in which we have a cross-border element (e.g. the free movement of EU citizens or migration law as long as the field is covered by EU law), there still could be situations inside the EU to which Article 24 could not be applied. Fortunately, with the influence of EU law on national legislation as well as the principle of non-discrimination delineated in most national Constitutions, any interpretative evolution that could emerge from the application of Article 24 will also influence internal rules even outside the competence of EU Law.

Article 24 does not provide specific rules for migrant children; however, it clearly sets general rules for any child. Its application to children in transnational situations derives from Directives 2004/38 and 2003/86, both of which contain an express reference to the Charter provisions in their recitals (a reference which is also paired in the 2003/86 Directive with a reference to Article 8 of the ECHR). As described below, the rights of children were extended due to the jurisprudence of the CJEU, specifically by its use of Article 24 and Article 8 of the Charter to grant children the possibility of living with their non-EU parents.

3. CHILDREN'S RIGHTS IN THE INTERPRETATIVE ACTIVITY OF THE CJEU

The CJEU has strongly influenced national legal frameworks by applying the relevant principles of human rights protection to children in cross-border situations, as analysed in the previous sections.

After decades of case law largely focusing on the general right to family reunification (stemming from Article 8 of the ECHR) as a parameter for evaluating compliance with human rights needs in the free movement of persons and migration law, the CJEU openly recognised the relevance of the CRC in 2006 in its judgment on the legality of the Family Reunification Directive (2003/86). Here, the CJEU affirmed the need to consider the CRC when evaluating whether EU measures comply with fundamental rights.[23]

---

22 European Union Agency for Fundamental Rights, Developing Indicators for the Protection, Respect and Promotion of the Rights of the Child in the European Union, Luxembourg, 2010.

23 Case C-540/03, *Parliament v. Council*, ECLI:EU:C:2006:429. See H. Stalford and E. Drwyood, 'Using the CRC to Inform EU law and Policy-making' in A. Invernizzi, and J. Williams (eds.), above n. 1, p. 207.

The best interests of the child – now considered as 'one of the principles permeating the EU legal order'[24]– was defined by the CJEU in the case *Dynamic Medien* as a 'legitimate interest' that 'justifies a restriction on a fundamental freedom guaranteed by the EC Treaty'.[25] Thus, the CJEU recognised the 'constitutional' value of this principle in a case in which legitimacy of restrictions on the free movement of goods were at stake; in balancing different interests, the CJEU determined that the German prohibition on the selling of DVDs not labelled as child-appropriate under domestic law was justified and proportionate as a means to protect children's rights.

The obligation to consider children's best interests has been applied concurrently with the general right to private and family life in recent case law. In the case *Ruiz Zambrano*,[26] for example, the ability of the parents (who were third-country nationals)to benefit from EU Law was affirmed based on the citizenship status of their child, which thereby used the need to protect the child's best interests to extend the EU rules on citizenship and freedom of movement and undermine national competence in the field of migration law. More recently, in case *CS* on the legitimacy of the expulsion of a single parent (third-country national) who was criminally convicted and therefore expelled even though she had a young dependent child,[27] the Court stressed the need to balance the public security requirements of the State with the need to protect the interests of the child. Rejecting any systematic and automatic link between criminal conviction and expulsion, the CJEU recalled the obligation for the national judge to particularly focus on the age of the child, his/her situation in the Member State concerned and the extent to which he/she is dependent on the parent, which was supported by making an express reference to the ECtHR case *Jeunesse* to suggest the parameters to be respected.[28] The ECtHR has frequently stressed the need to evaluate the best interests of the child in all migration cases and to give consideration of Article 8 of the ECHR as implemented in domestic law.[29]

---

24 See Advocate General Szpunar's Opinion, delivered on 8.09.2016 in case C-133/15, *H. C. Chavez-Vilchez and Others*, ECLI:EU:C:2016:659, para. 42.

25 Case C-244/06, *Dynamic Medien Vertriebs GmbH*, ECLI:EU:C:2008:85, paras. 41 and 42. The CJEU states that the 'Member States' right to take the measures necessary for reasons relating to the protection of young persons is recognised by a number of Community-law instruments, such as Directive 2000/31'. A specific reference was made by the CJEU to Article 17 of the CRC. For a comment, see H. Stalford and E. Drywood, 'Using the CRC to Inform EU Law and Policy-making' in A. Invernizzi and J. Williams (eds.), above n. 1, p. 213.

26 See Rodriguez and Deana in this volume.

27 Case C-304/14, *Secretary of State for the Home Department v. CS*, ECLI:EU:C:2016:674.

28 ECtHR, *Jeunesse v. the Netherlands* [GC], No. 12738/10, 3.10.2014.

29 J. M. Pobjoy, *The Child in International Refugee Law*, Blackstone Chambers, London 2017, p. 209. Also see in national case law the UK Supreme Court case *ZH (Tanzania) v SSHD*, [2011] UKSC 4, in which Lord Kerr (para. 46) declared the need to accord a primacy but not a limitless importance to the best interests of a child.

A similar evolution and extensive interpretation of EU law can be found in case *MA and others* on asylum law.[30] The CJEU used Article 24 of the Charter to declare that the child's best interests must be a primary consideration in all decisions adopted by a Member State and therefore also when the State applies the second paragraph of Article 6 of Regulation No 343/2003. The State where the asylum application is lodged is consequently designated as responsible for the application even if the unaccompanied minor now present there had already presented a previous request in a different Member State. The particular situation of minors with no family members legally present in the territory of a Member State requires them to have prompt access to the procedures for determining refugee status and justifies the application of different rules from those applied to adults' asylum requests. However, the general principle of the Dublin Regulation requiring only one State to evaluate the application should always be respected.[31]

The need for a specific approach to children in cross-border situations could therefore lead Member States to adopt a more flexible approach in examining residence permits and asylum requests, thereby strengthening the level of protection of human rights in all cases involving children.

4. CHILDREN'S RIGHTS AND THE EVOLUTION OF DOMESTIC FAMILY LAW: SPECIFIC ISSUES

It is worth exploring in more depth a few particular situations in which children's rights have led to innovative changes in national family law to evaluate the influence of the international framework on the national legal orders.

4.1. CHILDREN BORN OUT OF WEDLOCK

The first example is related to the situation of children born out of wedlock and the need for them to not be discriminated against due to their parents not being married. The European States were largely not bound by the European Convention on the Legal Status of Children Born Out of Wedlock,[32] and many

30 Case C-648/11, *MA and Others*, ECLI:EU:C:2013:367, paras. 59–61.

31 Therefore, the possibility of presenting a new application in another State will be limited to cases in which the minor is present in that State and the first application has not been already rejected. Consequently, the second State shall inform the first one of the change in responsibility.

32 The European Convention on the Legal Status of Children born out of Wedlock, CETS No. 85, 15.10.1975, is in force for 23 States (however, many States did not sign and/or ratify it, including Belgium, France, Germany, Italy and Spain).

maintained for a long time discriminatory rules both on the acquisition of parental rights for the father and regarding inheritance rights.[33]

The ECtHR deeply influenced the evolution of national legislation by declaring the incompatibility of such rules with human rights protection. At the same time, similar discriminatory situations also prohibited by Article 2 (1) of the CRC could hinder the free movement of persons in as much as the rights of a child towards parents and other family members might differ in different European countries due to their diverging national systems.

The *Marckx v. Belgium* decision confirmed that Article 8 applies both to 'illegitimate' and 'legitimate' family members; the protection of family life must be granted to relationships between parents and their children born both in and out of wedlock such that the child should be granted a relationship with other relatives (grandparents in particular) as well as full inheritance rights.[34] In *Keegan v. Ireland*, the Court had to consider the right of the natural father to be appointed as a guardian and informed and asked for consent in case his child born out of wedlock was placed for adoption.[35] Irish law infringed upon the father's right to family life, and therefore, Ireland was led to change its legal framework by introducing a simplified procedure for natural fathers to be appointed as guardians of their children.[36]

The ECtHR pronounced again on the issue in three other cases related to the French and German legal systems. In *Mazurek v. France*, the Court determined that French legislation violated Articles 8 and 14 of the ECHR from the point of view of inheritance rights, as children born outside marriage were recognised as eligible for only half of the inheritance given to legitimate children.[37] In *Brauer v. Germany* in 2009, the still existing discrimination impacting children born out of wedlock before 1949 (a previous reform had already addressed the situation for children born after that date) was also deemed to violate Articles 8 and 14.[38]

---

33 For example, until 2002, a father in the UK could acquire parental rights only through marriage or a court order. It was only with the Children Act 2002 that fathers were allowed parental responsibility when registering the birth of the child, if formally agreed with the mother.

34 *Marckx v. Belgium*, no. 6833/74 13.06.1979. For a comment on this and on the subsequent case law, see C. Draghici, *The Legitimacy of Family Rights in Strasbourg Case Law: 'Living Instrument' or Extinguished Sovereignty?* (Modern Studies in European Law Book 64), Hart Publishing, Oxford 2017.

35 *Keegan v. Ireland*, no. 16969/90, 26.05.1994.

36 The Children's Act 1997 allows unmarried parents to sign a statutory declaration granting guardianship also to the father. For a critical evaluation of the current framework see C. Best, 'The Rights of Unmarried Fathers in Ireland' [2012] *Critical Social Thinking: Policy and Practice* 4, 35.

37 The decision led to the amendment of French legislation with Law no. 1135, approved on 3.12.2001, which established equality between legitimate and natural children. However, a complete equating was introduced only later in 2009. See A. Valongo, 'Children Born Out of Wedlock: The End of an Anachronistic Discrimination' [2015] *Italian Law Journal* 1, 83.

38 ECtHR, *Brauer v. Germany*, No. 3545/04, 28.05.2009; *Anayo v. Germany*, No. 20578/07, 21.12.2010.

In the case of *Sahin*,[39] the Court took the view that the German approach to the position of fathers was a violation of Article 14, as the right to visit a child was dependent on a court ruling finding such contact to be in the child's interests and not only limited, such as for divorced fathers, if it was expressly against the child's interests.

Although the approach of the ECtHR was primarily focussed on general family life rather than the specific position of the child, the results were clearly favourable to his/her best interests. This influenced countries to introduce laws that fully equated marital with non-marital children, as Italy did with *Legge* (Act) no. 219/2012.[40]

4.2. RIGHT OF THE CHILD TO MAINTAIN A RELATIONSHIP WITH OTHER FAMILY MEMBERS

Another relevant problem is the right of the child to maintain a constant relationship with both parents and, more generally, with other family members. Both the CJEU and the ECtHR have recently intervened on this issue, thus influencing national legal frameworks and their interpretation. The situation of parents is well known and generally protected; however, the new frontier seems to be the need to protect the interests of children in having a constant relationship with their grandparents.

The ECtHR applied Article 8 to the child-grandparent relationship for the first time in *Bronda v. Italy* and reaffirmed the principle in *Nistor v. Romania*, and *Manuello and Nevi v. Italy*.[41] In the most recent case, Italy was condemned for a prolonged refusal to grant the right to visit grandparents; however, no reference was made to the best interests of the child in this case, as the evaluation was limited to the right to family life of the grandparents themselves. National judges have usually considered the former as a subordinate to the latter and have linked this right to the best interests of the (grand)children.[42]

The CJEU addressed this issue in relationship with private international law when it interpreted Regulation 2201/2003 in a cross-border situation that was clearly influenced by the free movement of persons. The case of *Babanarakis* stemmed from the request of a Bulgarian grandmother who sought to be granted the right to visit a child who had been taken by the father to live in Greece.[43]

---

39 ECtHR, *Sahin v. Germany*, No. 30943/96, 08.07.2003.

40 Completed with d. lgs. no 154/2013.

41 ECtHR, *Bronda v. Italy*, No. 22430/93, 09.06.1998; *Nistor v. Romania*, No. 14565/05, 02.11.2010; *Manuello and Nevi v. Italy*, 107/10, 20.01.2015.

42 For a comparison between EU and Italian case law, see E. Bergamini, 'La Corte di giustizia e il diritto di visita dei nonni: sentenza Valcheva c. Babanarakis' in *Eurojus.it*, July–September 2018.

43 Case C-335/17, *Neli Valcheva v Georgios Babanarakis*, ECLI:EU:C:2018:359.

Although the focus of this case was not on the child's rights but rather on the grandmother's position (in terms of her relationship with the child), the declaration of the Advocate General was highly relevant to the former in its conclusions that the evolution of society is proceeding at a much faster pace than the process of legislative adaptation and that therefore, some 'grey areas' still exist for which the legislation does not provide an explicit response. In the absence of an existing legal framework, the level of protection to be recognised 'to a child's contact with other persons to whom the child has "family" ties based on law or on fact (such as the former spouse of one of the parents, the child's siblings, grandparents or the partner of a parent who is the holder of parental responsibility)' is one of the grey areas in which the judicial authorities at both the EU and at the national level should intervene to protect the child's best interests.[44]

In fact, as stated by the Advocate General, the relationship between children and grandparents is an 'essential source of stability for children and an important factor in the intergenerational bond which undoubtedly contributes to building their personal identity'.[45]

It will be up to the national legal systems to consider – whether in a general way or, as is more likely, with a case-by-case approach – if this multitude of external relationships contributing to the creation of the child's identity could be considered as essential for his or her best interests. Clearly, transnational situations will force national judges (and consequently national legislators) to face family situations that are distinct from those existing solely at the national level, which will ultimately lead to the integration of new models into the national context and the establishment of higher levels of protection for the interests of the children involved in such cases.

4.3. RIGHT OF THE CHILD TO BE HEARD

The third relevant issue is the right of the child to be consulted and to have access to justice.[46] Children should be permitted to express their opinions before a decision is made regarding their interests, and their views and wishes should

---

44 Para. 31 of the conclusions.

45 Para. 32.

46 Article 12 of the New York Convention shall be read in conjunction with Article 14 of the International Covenant on Civil and Political Rights (ICCPR) on the general right for everybody to have access to the courts for the determination of his or her rights and obligations. On this idea, see G. Lansdown, 'Every Child's Right to be Heard. A Resource Guide on the Committee on the Rights of the Child General Comment no. 12', <https://www.unicef.org/french/adolescence/files/Every_Childs_Right_to_be_Heard.pdf>.

be considered even if they do not enjoy a right of self-determination. This means that they have a right for their opinions to be heard and to be acted upon.[47]

The right of the child to be heard is enshrined in Article 12 of the CRC, Article 24.1 of the EU Charter and the European Convention on the Exercise of Children's Rights (the Strasbourg Convention of 1996). This principle has been given more specific protection than that found in its general framework in all cases involving a cross-border situation (migrating children as well as simple relocation cases in which one parent wants to take the child to live in a different country against the other parent's will) on the premise that children in such a situation are at greater risk of not having their opinions heard and duly considered.

The EU legal framework attempted to implement the principle in Directives 2003/9 and 2004/83 regarding asylum seekers and refugees, respectively, which establish the need to grant appropriate assistance and legal representation to children. However, the failure to consult the child has never been found to be in breach of the ECHR in the Strasbourg case law, and national legislations have yet to reach a full compliance with this principle, particularly in cross-border situations.[48] For instance, in the UK, a draft order intended to limit access to legal aid to persons (children included) who were lawfully resident in the UK (or had been for at least 12 continuous months) was deemed not to respect children's right to be heard.[49]

Italy introduced legal changes only in 2006 to comply with this principle;[50] however, even earlier, the Italian Constitutional Court found that the international conventions on the need to hear the child had to be applied to make up for the shortcomings in the country's national legal framework.[51] The Court sought to extend the principle by ruling that the child must be heard as part of relevant proceedings, and as such, the child may also be subjected

47 On this view, see G. Van Bueren, *The International Law on the Rights of the Child*, The Hague/Boston/London, Martinus Nijhoff Publishers 1998, p. 138. More generally on this principle see A. Parkes, *Children and International Human Rights Law/The Right of the Child to be Heard*, Taylor & Francis Ltd, London 2013.

48 U. Kilkelly, *The Child and the European Convention on Human Rights*, Routledge, New York 2016, p. 118.

49 For this opinion, see the Equality and Human Rights Commission, Updated submission to the UN Committee on the Rights of the Child in advance of the public examination of the UK's implementation of the Convention on the Rights of the Child, April 2016, <https://www.equalityhumanrights.com/en/file/18726/download?token=mXNH6S2D>. The Supreme Court allowed the appeal (not discussing the discrimination issue) in *R (Public Law Project) v Lord Chancellor* [2016] UKSC 39.

50 Article 1 of Law No. 54 of 8.2.2006, which came into force on 16.03.2006.

51 See the decision of the Italian Constitutional Court 30.01.2002 no. 1. The same principle was expressed again in 2009 (Constitutional Court 12 June 2009 no. 179). For a comment, see also J. Long, 'L'impatto della Convenzione delle Nazioni Unite sui diritti del minore sull'ordinamento giuridico italiano' [2008] *Famiglia* 4, 24–43.

to cross-examination. The more recent domestic case law therefore focuses on the need to combine the application of Italian law and international law such as Article 12 of the CRC, Article 6 of the Strasbourg Convention of 1996 and Article 24 of the EU Charter.[52]

Clearly, most national legal systems still lack a coherent and full application of this principle, as can be seen in the Reports of the CRC Committee;[53] therefore, it will be relevant to check whether the future evolution of laws linked to cross-border situations could lead to a higher level of protection.

4.4. PROHIBITION OF INHUMAN TREATMENT AND MIGRATING CHILDREN

Another situation in which a new approach to children rights protection is emerging is linked to the *non-refoulment* principle.

In a recent case, the Committee on the Rights of the Child attempted to link the positive recognition of asylum demands and the national principles regulating it with the need to protect the best interests of the child in a more extensive manner.[54] The individual case was started by a Somali mother on behalf of her child born in Denmark. The mother and daughter had been subject to a deportation order; however, the mother claimed that such a deportation would have endangered her daughter, who would be subjected to female genital mutilation if returned to Somalia.[55] As established in the Committee's General

52 Supreme Court of Cassation, judgment rendered on 15.05.2013 (Case 11687/13).

53 All States have to submit a first report to the Committee on how the CRC is being implemented after two years as well as periodic reports (every five years). The Committee responds to such reports with 'concluding observations' in which concerns and recommendations to the State party are addressed. In the Observations regarding France (2016), for instance, the Committee stressed 'the little progress made to systematically ensure and implement respect for the views of the child in all relevant contexts of life'. In the Observations regarding Spain (2018), the situation was considered critical, as the Committee 'reiterates its previous concluding observations (see CRC/C/ESP/CO/3-4, para. 30) and recommends that the State party increase its efforts to promote due respect for the children's view'.

54 State parties to the Protocol on a communication procedure (which came into force in April 2014) allow individuals to submit complaints regarding specific violations of the CRC and its first two optional protocols.

55 Views adopted by the Committee on the Rights of the Child under the Optional Protocol to the Convention on the Rights of the Child on a communications procedure in respect of communication No. 3/2016*, 25.1.2018, CRC/C/77/D/3/2016. As clearly stated in General Comment No. 18, female genital mutilation can have various immediate and/or long-term health consequences, and therefore, immigration and asylum policies at the national level should consider such risk as a ground for granting asylum and also protect the accompanying relative. Therefore, States assessing refugee claims shall 'take into account the development of, and formative relationship between, international human rights and refugee law, including positions developed by UNHCR in exercising its supervisory functions under the 1951 Refugee Convention' (for this wording, also see General Comment No. 6 para. 74).

Comments No. 13 and No. 18, States shall not only prohibit but also prevent and respond to all forms of physical violence against children. This means that national immigration and asylum policies must consider harmful practices, such as female genital mutilation, as grounds for granting asylum.

The mother asked for the *non-refoulement* principle to be applied, thus giving extraterritorial effect to the Convention to protect the best interests of the child. As a single mother, she claimed she would not be able to avoid genital mutilation for her daughter even though Somali law currently prohibits it,[56] as the law is not enforced in practice.

Similar cases are frequently subject to national and supranational judgments;[57] however, the outcome of this specific one was striking. The Committee decided to apply a precautionary principle and strongly protect the child by declaring that 'the State party failed to consider the best interests of the child when assessing the *alleged* risk of the author's daughter to be subjected to female genital mutilation … and to take proper safeguards to ensure the child's wellbeing upon return in violation of Articles 3 and 19 of the Convention'.[58]

This interpretation of the CRC – considering the best interests of the child as decisive, since they are per se a reason for *non-refoulement*, rather than requiring the obstacle/exceptional circumstances test (as in *Jeunesse*) – could therefore be a relevant instrument for national authorities to enhance best interests assessments, as it reminds them to balance different needs without requiring full proof of the risk of violation (which is frequently impossible to obtain).[59]

Although it is well known that the CRC has been strongly criticised for being more focused on the parent-children relationship and not sufficiently concerned with the problems of migrant children,[60] this new interpretative deal could lead

---

56 Reference is made to the thematic paper used by Danish authorities to underpin the refusal for asylum: Southcentral Somalia: Female Genital Mutilation/Cutting, Country of Origin Information for Use in the Asylum Determination Process, January 2016, <https://www.nyidanmark.dk/NR/rdonlyres/D011EB99-7FB6-4693-921A-8F912F4079CB/0/female genital mutilationnotat2016.pdf>.

57 Although it is not in dispute that subjecting a child or adult to female genital mutilation amounts to treatment proscribed by Article 3 of the ECHR, in this context, see ECtHR, *Collins and Akaziebie v. Sweden*, no. 23944/05, 08.03.2007; *Izevbekhai and others v. Ireland*, no. 43408/08, 17.05.2011. The ECtHR usually bases its decisions on similar cases focussing on the necessity for the asylum request to be accepted in order to prove a real risk of being subjected to FGM upon the child return to the country of origin. See recently *R. B. A. B. and others v. The Netherlands*, no. 7211/06, 07.06. 2016.

58 Emphasis added.

59 See General Comment No. 14 (2013) para. 46; N. Cantwell, 'Are Children's Rights Still Human?', above n. 1, p. 50. U. Kilkelly, above n. 9, pp. 51–66.

60 At the crossroads of power relations: B. Gornik, 'The Convention of the Rights of the Child and Unaccompanied Minor Migrants' in M. Sedmak, B. Sauer, B. Gornik and D. Senovilla Hernández (eds.), *Unaccompanied Children*, above n. 14, p. 18.

to a new approach in the Convention's application at the national level. However, the ECtHR follows a different approach, as exemplified in *Josef v. Belgium*.[61] In this case, three children were sent back to Nigeria with their HIV positive mother and the Court considered Article 8 of the ECHR to have been respected despite the risk of leaving the children alone in a State where they had no family links in case the mother died.[62]

5. FINAL REMARKS

As we have seen, notwithstanding the international framework legally binding all European States, the protection extended to the rights of the child is not uniform at the national level. The free movement of persons and the protection of migrants have become key elements to assure better protection of human rights, particularly children's rights, by heightening the level of protection that would otherwise be granted by national legislators. These fields include the right of the child to maintain a relationship with his/her family members and the right not to be subject to inhuman or degrading treatment.

In fact any attempt to discriminate against children whose parental link is created in non-traditional circumstances (meaning not only outside wedlock but also through medically assisted reproduction methods, surrogacy agreements or adoption) and to prohibit their relationship with family members violates the fundamental rights of the child and hinders the free movement of persons outside the State in which the family link was created.[63] The new trend to protect similar situations in cross-border cases will consequently also influence the evolution of national legal systems in domestic situations.

The same protection extends to the prohibition of inhuman or degrading treatment. However, we need to distinguish between: 1) *non-refoulement* cases in which the fundamental rights of migrant children could be subject to a higher level of protection due to the new approach of a supranational authority such as the Committee on the Right of the Child, in the hope that that this new approach will influence national legislators even if the ECtHR still remains anchored to its

61 ECtHR, *Josef. v. Belgium*, 70055/10, 27.02.2014.

62 C. Smyth, 'The Jurisprudence of the European Court of Human Rights Relevant to Child Migrants' in J. Bhabha, J. Kanics and D. Senovilla Hernández (eds.), *Research Handbook on Child Migration*, Edward Elgar Publishing, Cheltenham 2018, p. 151.

63 The free movement of persons and protection of migrants have become the key elements to assure a better protection of human rights, particularly children rights, by heightening the levels of protection that would otherwise be granted by national legislators.

previous restrictive interpretation; and 2) detention cases in which the ECtHR approach already grants extensive interpretative scope to protect migrating children's rights in host countries.[64]

Although children's rights more closely linked to cross-border situations appear to be headed for a higher level of protection based on the international framework, more general rights that are not strictly linked to free movement, such as the right of the child to be heard, still need to be fully implemented. Even if the impact on children is perhaps less directly relevant in such cases, international instruments make it compulsory for European States to respect them. Therefore, it is highly desirable that national legal systems focus on respecting these rights in both domestic and international situations in the future.

[64] See *S. F. and Others v. Bulgaria*, no. 8138/16, 07.12.2017, in which the Court held that there had been a violation of Article 3 despite the fact that the period of detention was for just a couple of days due to the awful conditions in which the children were kept (i.e. delayed access to food and drink and even to the toddler's baby bottle and milk, limited access to toilet facilities).

PROTECTING EU CITIZEN MINORS' RIGHT TO IDENTITY IN THE TRANSNATIONAL FAMILY CONTEXT

Francesco DEANA

1. Introduction 21
2. Identity as a Fundamental Right under International and EU Law. 22
3. The Relevance of Children's Identity-Related Issues to EU Law 24
4. Non-Recognition of a Child's Name as a Hindrance to Free Movement . . . 26
5. Non-Recognition of Other Personal and Family Status Legally Acquired Abroad. 28
6. Restrictions on Status Recognition and their Compatibility with EU Law 30
7. Protecting Family Unity and the Enjoyment of Established Family Life . . . 32
   7.1. The Right to Family Reunification. 32
   7.2. Removal of a Child's Family Member 33
8. Final Remarks 35

1. INTRODUCTION

This chapter considers how living in a transnational context might affect the identity of children who are EU citizens and how EU law protects their identity against Member State (MS) measures that could threaten its integrity and cross-border continuity just because of the children's transnational situation. The key question is whether, despite the lack of a specific competence, the EU legal framework provides effective protection for constitutive elements of children's identity in transnational situations and, then, under which circumstances this legal framework applies to prevent national measures from jeopardising that identity.

In answering this question, this chapter goes beyond the traditional approach that circumscribes research to the question as to how the denial of recognition of personal and family status in cross-border situations could jeopardise people's identities within the EU. First, the traditional approach considers just cross-border situations, i.e. in which the exercise of free movement rights within EU territory give rise to issues affecting identity, whereas this chapter also considers situations in which a static EU citizen minor invokes the right to reside in and to not leave a MS territory. Moreover, the approach here adopted demonstrates that, even when dealing with cross-border situations, children's identity can be affected in various ways beyond the non-recognition of family status and, notably, the denial of the right to family reunification (with a certain family member).

Ultimately, this chapter traces the evolution of the CJEU's approach to the issue; it began as an 'all about internal market or migration' approach and then became an approach also significantly based on fundamental rights.

2. IDENTITY AS A FUNDAMENTAL RIGHT UNDER INTERNATIONAL AND EU LAW

Issues of 'identity' can arise on numerous grounds – nationality, gender, sexuality, ethnicity, family relationships and so on – relating to the concrete, unequivocal circumstances of someone's personality and social life as cultural, professional, religious, political and social experiences. Starting from birth, an individual's identity is formed and preserved by registration as somebody's son or daughter, the bestowal of a name and the acquisition of State citizenship. Then, as an individual develops a personality, enters social groups and gains various social experiences, identity becomes more complex, needing broader legal protection from public or private interference.

Growing interest in legal protection for various aspects of the human personality, which progressively emerged from Western legal systems in the late 20th century, can be considered the origin of many 'new' personal rights, such as the right to identity itself.[1] Nowadays, therefore, international and domestic legislation universally recognises the fundamental right to (personal and social) identity,[2] which can be described as the right everybody has to be, and to be represented in social life, in a way that expresses or fits his or her personality and personal history as an individual and a member of a social group.

The most relevant supranational provisions in the European area concerning identity as a fundamental right are those protecting the right to private and family life, namely Article 7 of the EU Charter and Article 8 of the ECHR. Although such provisions do not mention the concept of identity, the CJEU

1 The first reference to a right to personal identity under civil law is commonly attributed to A. De Cupis, *Il diritto all'identità personale*, Giuffré, Milan 1949. However, his approach was still restricted to a static view of identity, limited to classic categories of personality rights, such as the right to a name.

2 J. Marshall, *Human Rights Law and Personal Identity*, Routledge, Oxon 2014.

and the ECtHR broadly interpret the right to private and family life,[3] now considered to include many aspects of a person's identity, such as name,[4] gender identification,[5] sexual orientation,[6] ethnic identity,[7] personal autonomy and development,[8] the right to establish and develop relationships with other human beings and the outside world,[9] and the right to cross-border continuity of family status and relationships.[10] Although the ECtHR has played the greater role in developing such case law, since rights guaranteed by Article 7 of the EU Charter[11] correspond to those guaranteed by Article 8 ECHR, Article 52 of the EU Charter establishes that the former should be interpreted in line with the latter, giving both provisions the same meaning and scope. The same goes for the kinds of limitations that national legislation can legitimately impose.[12]

Legal protection of identity gives rise to some peculiar issues when dealing with children, considered as vulnerable individuals, and thus special care is due when granting them an appropriate level of protection.[13] First of all, the 'best interests of the child' principle[14] binds any authority with which a child must deal to pursue his/her best interests under a really broad range of factors capable of affecting the child's welfare. Moreover, many other specific facets of children's identity are protected as part of their fundamental rights. Article 8 CRC expressly mentions nationality, name and family relations as part of such identity, while other fundamental rights linked to the preservation of children's identity are covered by the right to private and family life under

---

3 Private life is a broad concept incapable of exhaustive definition, and may 'embrace multiple aspects of the person's physical and social identity'. See the ECtHR judgment in cases *Niemietz v. Germany*, no. 13710/88, 16.12.1992, §29; *Pretty v. the United Kingdom*, no. 2346/02, 29.04.2002, §61; *Peck v. the United Kingdom*, no. 44647/98, 28.01.2003, §57.

4 ECtHR, *Stjerna v. Finland*, no. 18131/91, 25.11.1994.

5 ECtHR, *Goodwin v. United Kingdom*, no. 289957/95, 11.04.2001.

6 ECtHR, *Dudgeon v. the United Kingdom*, no. 7525/76, 22.10.1981, para. 52, and *Norris v. Ireland*, no. 10581/83, 26.10.1988, para. 46.

7 ECtHR, *Ciubotaru v. Moldova*, no. 27138/04, 27.04.2010.

8 ECtHR, *K.A. and A.D.* v. *Belgium*, no. 42756/98 and 45558/98, 17.02.2005

9 ECtHR, *Niemietz v. Germany*, cit., para. 29; *Pretty v. the United Kingdom*, cit., paras. 61 and 67.

10 ECtHR, *Wagner and J.M.W.L. v. Luxembourg*, no. 76240/01, 28.06.2007; *McDonald v. France*, no. 18648/04, 29.04.2008, *Mary Green and Ajad Farhat v. Malta*, no. 38797/07, 6.07.2010; *Negrepontis-Giannisis v. Greece*, no. 56759/08, 3.05.2011.

11 Under which the protection of private and family life is considered a fundamental right of EU citizens.

12 See the explanations prepared under the authority of the Praesidium of the Convention that drafted the Charter of Fundamental Rights of the European Union (Official Journal of the European Union C-303/17, 14.12.2007). See also the Opinion of 16.12.2010 of Advocate General Jääskinen in case *Runevic-Vardyn*, ECLI:EU:C:2010:784, para. 77.

13 See Y. Ronen, *Re-understanding the Child's Right to Identity: On Belonging, Responsiveness and Hope*, Brill-Nijhoff, Leiden 2016.

14 J. Zermatten, 'The Best Interests of the Child Principle: Literal Analysis and Function', (2010) *International Journal of Children's Rights*, 483. J. M. Pobjoy, 'The Best Interests of the Child Principle as an Independent Source of International Protection', (2015) *International and Comparative Law Quarterly* Part 2, 327.

Article 8 ECHR and Article 7 of the EU Charter. Worth mentioning are rights to identity and personal development,[15] to know and be cared for by parents,[16] to be registered after birth,[17] *not* to be separated from parents,[18] *not* to be deprived of a family environment,[19] and, to some extent, to citizenship.[20]

Thus, the best interests of the child principle does not exclude children from the protection granted by other fundamental rights; on the contrary, as we will see, the best interests principle strengthens all rights granted to children, shaping their interpretation, broadening their scope and narrowing the margin of appreciation in imposing restrictions on such rights. Moreover, the best interests principle fills normative lacunas because there is still the possibility of applying the general principle wherever specific provisions do not cover every issue concerning children's identity.

3. THE RELEVANCE OF CHILDREN'S IDENTITY-RELATED ISSUES TO EU LAW

The EU legal system grants the highest level of protection to the right to identity and the best interests of the child. Nonetheless, EU law does not expressly rule on identity's constituent elements because they fall outside EU competence. Therefore, Member States regulate those elements, potentially affecting the identity of EU citizens (adults or children) who move to or reside in a MS other than that of their nationality. Thus, the key question is when and how EU law protects EU children's identity in transnational contexts.

The first preliminary issue is whether an individual's identity, where it is alleged to be affected by a domestic measure, comes within the scope of EU law, given that no national rule can infringe EU law in its application, even in an area regulated exclusively by a MS. The second preliminary issue is whether an

---

15 I.e. information concerning highly personal aspects of someone's childhood, development and history. See ECtHR, *Odièvre v. France* [GC], no. 42326/98, 13.02.2003, para. 29; ECtHR, *Gaskin v. the United Kingdom*, no. 10454/83, 07.07.1989, para. 36. In the field of family relationship, this right particularly includes the child's right to know his or her origins in the context of adoption.

16 ECtHR, *R.M.S. v. Spain*, no. 28775/12, 18.06.2013.

17 ECtHR, *Guillot v. France*, no. 22500/93, 24.10.1993, paras. 21-22; *Johansson v. Finland*, no. 10163/02, 06.09.2007, para. 28; *Cusan and Fazzo v. Italy*, no. 77/07, 07.01.2014, para. 56.

18 ECtHR, *Levin v. Sweden*, no. 35141/06, 15.03.2012.

19 Placing a child in an alternative care setting should be just a temporary measure: in respect of the right to private and family life the final goal has to be eventually to reunite the child with his/her family. See ECtHR, *K.A. v. Finland*, no. 27751/95, 14.01.2003.

20 Even though the ECHR does not guarantee a right to citizenship, an arbitrary refusal of citizenship could fall anyway within the scope of the right to private life in the light of its particular consequences for the social identity of the child. See ECtHR, *Genovese v. Malta*, no. 53124/09, 11.10.2011, para. 33.

existing link between such a situation and EU law is sufficient enough to satisfy the requirement established by Article 51 of the EU Charter, which affirms that the Charter applies only when EU legislation has to apply or to be implemented by a MS.[21] Finally, under which circumstances can a MS infringe EU law by adopting a national measure that affects an EU citizen minor's identity?

As to the first issue, the CJEU traditionally affirms that a link with EU law does exist for any individual who is a national of one MS and is lawfully resident in another MS's territory. It is irrelevant whether the individual has freely relocated to another MS or whether (s)he has always resided in a MS other than that of his/her citizenship. More recently,[22] however, the Court affirmed that also situations in which the EU citizen has not moved from the State of his/her only nationality cannot, for that reason alone, be assimilated into a purely internal situation; thus the citizen could be linked with EU law as well. This link is EU citizenship and the possibility of exercising rights enshrined in it.

As to the second issue, the CJEU broadly interpreted Article 51 of the EU Charter; therefore, fundamental rights guaranteed by the Charter must be complied with wherever national legislation falls within the scope of EU law.[23]

As to the third and final question, issues of personal identity were generally not addressed at the EU level until the CJEU incidentally ruled on them from the perspectives of Articles 18, 20 and 21 TFEU.

Thus, from CJEU case law emerge three peculiar situations – strictly linked to families' transnational circumstances – in which a MS could harm an EU citizen minor's identity. The first is to deny recognition/transcription of a status legally acquired by the child in another MS or under another MS's legislation where that denial infringes the principle of non-discrimination and/or the right to move freely and reside within the EU. This is a typical cross-border issue involving either individuals who have exercised their freedom to move to another MS or nationals of a MS other than that in which they reside. The second peculiar situation concerns the denial of family reunification when a child is the sponsor[24] requesting reunification. This is another cross-border issue because the right to family reunification arises when an EU citizen moves to another MS and wants his/her family member to join him/her in the host State. Although the matter is strictly governed by Directive 2004/38/EC, the CJEU has recognised a similar right on the grounds of EU primary law, even in cases falling outside

---

21 If the Charter does not apply to a specific situation, the latter shall be assessed in the light of the ECHR, which is binding for every EU MS.

22 Case C-434/09, *Shirley McCarthy v. Secretary of State for the Home Department*, ECLI:EU:C:2011:277.

23 Case C-617/10, *Åkerberg Fransson*, ECLI:EU:C:2013:105, paras. 19–22. This interpretation has been considered compatible with Article 6(1) TEU, according to which the provisions of the Charter are not to extend in any way the competences of the European Union as defined in the Treaties.

24 The person who wants to be joined by his/her family members in the host MS.

the Directive's scope, when protecting EU citizens' family life is necessary. The third situation is where the MS where the child resides removes a close family member who is a third country national (TCN). This situation involves static EU citizens; therefore, it should fall outside the scope of EU law. Nonetheless, the CJEU found a link with the EU legal system, namely the necessity to prevent Member States from adopting measures which infringe the genuine enjoyment of rights conferred on individuals by virtue of their status as EU citizens.

4. NON-RECOGNITION OF A CHILD'S NAME AS A HINDRANCE TO FREE MOVEMENT

First, this section will address the attribution or recognition of a surname given to an EU citizen under legislation of a State other than that of his/her residence. The name (combination of first name and surname) is part of one's personal identity and thus an expression of a fundamental right of personality.[25] It fulfils various relevant functions. A name is a means by which the State identifies citizens, but it also denotes a person's belonging to a family and kinship with other people. More generally, a name expresses an individual's identity towards public authority and towards other associates.[26] It distinguishes (from others) and identifies (oneself towards others).[27]

Therefore, if a name is the symbol of one's personal identity and of a fundamental human right, we should argue,

> every subject should have the right to bear the name he or she identifies with, irrespective of the integration of that individual into a specific family, or of the will of the State to give that individual a different name.[28]

However, each State regulates the attribution, modification, conservation and transcription of a person's name in civil status records. The existence of international measures aimed at harmonising rules of private international law,[29] at the most, attenuates the effects of existing normative heterogeneity, and

---

25 ECtHR judgments in case *Stjerna v Finland*, cit, para. 42, and *Golemanova v. Bulgaria*, no. 11369/04, 17.02.2011.

26 D. Gutmann, *Le sentiment d'identité, étude de droit des personnes et de la famille*, LGDJ, Paris 2000.

27 V. Zeno Zencovich, *Onore e reputazione nel sistema del diritto civile*, Jovene, Naples 1985.

28 G. Rossolillo, 'Personal Identity at a Crossroad Between Private International Law, International Protection of Human Rights and EU law', (2009) *Yearbook of Private International Law*, Volume 11, 143.

29 E.g. the Convention on changes of names and surnames, signed at Istanbul on 04.09.1958, and the Convention on the law applicable to surnames and forenames, signed at Munich on 05.09.1980.

the negative consequences possibly arising from it, for citizens connected to a legal system other than that in which they live. Two, in particular, are the most common consequences:

a) The law of the forum does not allow recognition of the validity and/or the effectiveness of the 'foreign' name, making it therefore irrelevant for that legal order, and replaces it with a name determined on the basis of the *lex fori*;
b) The law of the forum precludes application of the foreign law invoked for determination of the name by the interested party who has a particular connection with a foreign legal order.

In both cases, the result is the attribution to the same person of different names in different States. This can hinder the exercise of free movement by EU citizens.[30] This is exactly the moment in which domestic rules on names become relevant to the EU legal order, despite the lack of any competence in this field: by invoking EU citizens' right to free movement (Article 21 TFEU) and, under some circumstances, the principle of non-discrimination (Article 18 TFEU). This is what actually happened in some relevant CJEU cases,[31] in which the Court broadly interpreted the principle of non-discrimination and the right to free movement,[32] thus allowing linkage of their compliance to the previous mutual recognition of personal status, as long as the denial of recognition would have consisted in denying the relevance of citizenship in another MS (and thus discrimination on the grounds of nationality)[33] or a restriction on the exercise of free movement.

30 This can essentially happen in two cases: 1) a MS refuses to recognise the name of one of its nationals who has acquired that name following the exercise of the right to move and reside freely in the territory of another MS, as there determined under national legislation; 2) a MS refuses to recognise the name already given to a national of another State who has subsequently moved to the first MS and then has requested the transcription of the name.

31 See the judgments in Cases C-168/91, *Konstantinidis*, ECLI:EU:C:1993:115; C-148/02, *Garcia Avello*, ECLI:EU:C:2003:539; C-353/06, *Grunkin-Paul*, ECLI:EU:C:2008:559; C-208/09, *Sayn-Wittgenstein*, ECLI:EU:C:2010:806; C-391/09, *Runevic-Vardyn and Wardyn*, ECLI:EU:C:2011:291; C-438/14, *Bogendorff von Wolffersdorff*, ECLI:EU:C:2016:401; C-541/15, *Freitag*, ECLI:EU:C:2017:432.

32 That is consistent with previous judgments of the Court on free movement of people, where it stated that EU rules granting such right must be interpreted in a broad way. See the judgment in Case C-200/02, *Zhu and Chen*, EU:C:2004:639, notably at para. 31.

33 In case *Garcia Avello* it appeared that the nationals of a MS residing in that State and who were also endowed with the citizenship of another State were treated, in the attribution of the surname, in the same way as those who had only the citizenship of the State of the forum. Indeed, in both cases only the national law of the State of the forum was applied. This situation was therefore considered to integrate discrimination on the ground of nationality towards those who had dual citizenship because they were prevented without any justification from the possibility of carrying the surname they would have been entitled to by virtue of the law and tradition of the other MS of nationality. See J. Meeusen, 'Le droit international privé et le principe de non-discrimination', (2011) *Recueil des cours*, vol. 353, 9, 127.

Refusal to recognise a name acquired in another MS or to allow acquisition of a name under another MS's law amounts to discrimination on grounds of nationality or a restriction of free movement only where it generates for the citizen – even only potentially – a 'serious inconvenience' at administrative, professional and private levels.[34] Thus, we can conclude that EU law eventually interferes with domestic legislation to protect the right to identity in its peculiar form of EU citizens' right to a name's cross-border continuity. At the same time, however, we must stress that EU law guarantees this right only in situations linked with its legal order, and only insofar as this functions to guarantee the effective exercise of free movement rights or to prevent discrimination on grounds of nationality. Indeed, the CJEU has never applied Article 7 of the EU Charter as the main or only reference to preclude the refusal to recognise a surname determined in another MS or under another MS's law.

5. NON-RECOGNITION OF OTHER PERSONAL AND FAMILY STATUS LEGALLY ACQUIRED ABROAD

The continuity of personal and social identities in space and time is probably the most relevant issue in the matter of identity. While both name and nationality deal mostly with the child's personal, individual sphere within society, family relations are the grounds on which an individual identifies himself or herself in a more intimate and limited context. Family is ideally the group in which a child receives the protection and support necessary to develop his or her personality and family and personal identity. Just as a name's non-recognition could prevent the exercise by EU citizens of rights to move freely and reside in another MS, non-recognition of other personal and family status can lead to the very same outcome, eventually affecting someone's identity. First, non-recognition of personal and family status might initiate 'serious inconveniences', such as the impossibility of establishing inheritance rights between the individuals concerned, or of ensuring that pensions, social security benefits and hospital visiting rights are granted. Moreover, non-recognition can preclude a

---

34 The CJEU has considered as a serious inconvenience the risk of being obliged to dispel doubts as to one's identity because of the discrepancy in names used in different countries (*Grunkin-Paul*, para. 26, and *Sayn*, para. 70); the risk of encountering difficulties in proving family links with your own family members (*Runevic-Vardyn*, para. 77, *Bogendorff von Wolffersdorff*, para. 46); the risk of being obliged to dispel doubts as to the authenticity of personal documents or the truthfulness of the information contained in those documents (*Runevic-Vardyn*, para. 77); the risk that potential clients might confuse a professional with others due to a surname spelling modification (*Kostandinidis*); the risk of difficulties in benefiting from the legal effects of diplomas or certificates drawn up in the name recognised in another MS (*Garcia Avello*, para. 36).

status required by EU law for the exercise of the right to free movement[35] or necessary for gaining citizenship of a MS and thus EU citizenship itself.[36] The recognition of personal or family status referred to in EU law must therefore be considered a 'preliminary issue', the solution of which is a logical precondition for the application of EU law.[37]

Children are affected by such a phenomenon mainly when their status *filii* is involved.[38] Non-recognition of parental links usually happens when parents ask for recognition of the parental relationship in States that prevent access to parenthood in the very same way as in the child's country of birth. However, this might also happen when the *child* asks for recognition. In practice, most cases of non-recognition involve children born through artificial reproductive technologies strictly prohibited in the State where recognition is sought or in parental relationships between a child and same-sex parents.[39] With respect to this status, legislation (in the term's broadest sense) is uncertain or, at least, not synchronised with society's evolution. This encourages discriminatory treatment compared to the treatment of daughters and sons of opposite-sex parents, whose status might instead be recognised. Thus, to grant a child's identity broader protection and keeping in mind the best interests of the child principle, applying the *Grunkin Paul* principle to every EU citizen minor's status would be particularly relevant.

The CJEU provided no explicit suggestion on whether this reasoning should also be applicable to any EU citizens' personal and family status other than their name. Following the argument developed in *Grunkin Paul*, however, the right to mutual recognition of every EU citizen's personal and family status could be envisaged insofar as that status contributes to building someone's identity as a

---

35 Not being recognised as someone's spouse means not having the right to family reunification under Directive 2004/38. See the recent judgment of the CJEU in case C-673/16, *Coman*, ECLI:EU:C:2018:385, and its annotation by A. Tryfonidou, 'Free Movement of Same-Sex Spouses within the EU: The ECJ's Coman judgment', (2018) *European Law Blog* (19.06.2018).

36 Usually, a key concern on the right to acquire citizenship is the avoidance of statelessness. In the EU context, the concern is to avoid the situation whereby a child who would be entitled to be an EU citizen cannot gain EU citizenship. If I'm not recognised as the son of an EU citizen and I was born in the territory of a MS that applies a *iure sanguinis* criteria for the attribution of citizenship, I won't been given EU citizenship.

37 As highlighted by M. Fallon, 'Constraints of Internal Market law on Family Law' in J. Meeusen et al. (eds.), *International Family Law for the European Union*, Intersentia, Antwerp 2007, p. 164, the regulation of family status referred to by EU secondary law act as a preliminary question to the application of the EU law itself. On the protection of family status within the free movement of people and the EU policy on migration, see L. Tomasi, *La tutela degli status familiari nel diritto dell'Unione europea*, CEDAM, Padua 2010.

38 A. Tryfonidou, 'Rainbow Families and EU Free Movement Law', in this book, mentions some examples of serious inconveniences that may affect children when their status *filii* is not recognised by the requested State.

39 See the contributions of R. Baratta and A. Tryfonidou in this book.

means of personal identification and as a link to family, and since the denial of recognition causes inconveniences of the utmost relevance in moving freely across EU territory. The recent judgment in *Coman* confirms that free movement of family status other than name may be based on the same reasoning and arguments. Moreover, recognition is encouraged where MS legislations share relevant guiding principles on personal and family statuses – which is considered to strengthen the mutual trust upon which the principle of mutual recognition is inevitably grounded.[40] In particular, such sharing exists (to some extent) in the recognition of parent-child relationships since any treatment differing between legitimate and illegitimate children has been progressively eliminated.[41]

When the prerequisites mentioned above are met and account is taken of the child's best interests, EU citizen minors should legitimately be able to expect their family status to be recognised by the host State's authorities.[42]

CJEU case law has not yet intervened in recognition of the child's status *tout court*. However, the need to protect the child's interests and not to deprive him/her of an effective family life forces even EU law to enlarge the elements necessary to resolving the recognition issue, including children's protection as vulnerable individuals in family relationships; thus these pressures lead to an almost absolute compression of the margin of discretion afforded to Member States in such matters. Indeed, no doubt the host State's failure to recognise the parent-child relationship would deprive the child of almost any legal protection and could ultimately lead to the child's separation from the intended parents.[43]

6. RESTRICTIONS ON STATUS RECOGNITION AND THEIR COMPATIBILITY WITH EU LAW

EU law protects the right to cross-border continuity of personal and family status as a means of granting EU citizens free movement rights; therefore, this right is protected as long as a restriction on people's free movement would be unacceptable. EU law might tolerate a hindrance to free movement or a

---

40 C. Honorati, 'Free Circulation Of Names For EU Citizens?', (2009) *Diritto dell'Unione Europea*, p. 379.

41 In *Marckx v. Belgium* (application no. 6833/74) the ECtHR declared that Belgian law on inheritance breached Article 14 ECHR because it discriminated between illegitimate children and legitimate ones. In this case, the Court acknowledges that a common *consensus* about the legal recognition of equality between legitimate and illegitimate children exists among the Council of Europe's Member States.

42 See R. Baratta, 'Recognition of a Foreign Status Filii – Pursuing the Best Interests Principle', in this book.

43 As in the case of *Paradiso and Campanelli v. Italy* before the ECtHR. See K. Trimmings, in this book.

discriminatory measure grounded on nationality if objectively justified by the necessity of protecting an opposing general interest by domestic measures that pursue that goal and are proportionate to it. At the same time, however, the fundamental right to private and family life and the best interests of the child principle protect children's personal and family statuses under EU law. Therefore, non-recognition respectively requires justification also under Articles 7 and 24(2) of the EU Charter. Thus, free movement cases must be assessed in light of fundamental rights, insofar as these rights are considered a parameter for assessing whether justifications invoked by Member States amount to a legitimate interference with free movement.[44]

The CJEU devolves the proportionality test to the national judge's discretion; however, the Court provides that the test must balance inconveniences deriving from restrictive measures and the relevance of conflicting interests.[45] Based on the corresponding jurisprudence on Article 8 ECHR,[46] a State's interference is allowed under Article 7 of the EU Charter when, in accordance with national law,[47] it pursues one (or more) legitimate aims mentioned in Article 8(2) and is considered 'necessary in a democratic society' (meaning it is based on a 'pressing social need' and is proportionate to its pursued aim). Thus, Member States have a margin of appreciation in determining what is deemed necessary to protect a collective interest such as to justify the restriction of an individual citizen's fundamental rights. The proportionality assessment is based on specific standards by which to assess the degree of protection that the interests at stake specifically deserve. Some standards strictly concern subjective criteria expressing

> the link between the relationship and the state of its creation that will be considered as giving rise to a legitimate expectation as to its stability.[48]

---

44 See the judgment in *Coman*, para. 47.

45 The interest of the child – in terms of his/her personal and social identity – and the interest pursued by the State that interferes with the child's identity

46 See above n. 10.

47 The Strasbourg Court has established a threefold test to determine whether an interference is in accordance with the law. The scheme leads the Court to evaluate: 1) the presence of a national law; 2) the clearness and precision of its wording; and 3) the aim it pursues. See I. Roagna, *Protecting the Right to Respect for Private and Family Life under the European Convention on Human Rights*, 2012, p. 37, online on www.echr.coe.int/LibraryDocs/Roagna2012_EN.pdf.

48 P. Kinsh, 'Recognition in the Forum of a Status Acquired Abroad – Private International Law and European Human Rights Law', in K. Boele-Woelki, T. Einhorn, D. Girsberger, S. Symeonides (eds.), *Convergence and Divergence in Private International Law – Liber Amicorum Kurt Siehr*, Schulthess, Zurich 2010, p. 266. However, the Author cannot tell whether 'stability' means 'a real and substantial link, a preponderant link, or even an exclusive link', and refers the issue to the ECtHR.

At first, this concept is linked to 'social reality'[49] (i.e. a relationship deeply rooted in the social fabric and in the families of the individuals involved)[50] and the 'intensity' of the family ties affected by non-recognition.[51] Moreover, the proportionality test must consider the gravity of the inconvenience caused to citizens seeking recognition.[52] Finally, the balancing stage must address the nature of the interests at stake, including the child's best interests – which are considered as primary whenever recognition is sought for a status involving a minor because a status's cross-border continuity is fundamental to the child's identity.[53] Therefore, whenever recognition realises the child's best interests, it is likely to prevail over the opposing interest invoked by the authorities of the State where recognition is sought: very few interests indeed have greater relevance than a child's protection.

7. PROTECTING FAMILY UNITY AND THE ENJOYMENT OF ESTABLISHED FAMILY LIFE

7.1. THE RIGHT TO FAMILY REUNIFICATION

One facet of a child's right to identity is the right *not* to be separated from parents and to grow up in the family environment. Therefore, moving freely from one MS to another might affect children's identity every time family members cannot legally join the child in the State of destination. Notably, this can occur when the host State does not grant family reunification with a TCN. When the sponsor is

---

49 L. R. Kiestra, *The Impact of the European Convention on Human Rights on Private International Law*, Springer, Berlin 2014, p. 225.

50 Social reality depends, for example, on the duration of the undisturbed enjoyment of the status in question, as held by the ECtHR in *Negrepontis-Giannisis*, para. 75.

51 The intensity is higher when the status at issue has been established by the firm will of two adults, who were conscious of the legal implications of their act, such as in a marriage or a registered partnership or an adoption of a grown-up (see again *Negrepontis-Giannisis*).

52 There must be a certain degree of seriousness or significance in order for a failure to respect the right to private life to be established. See the ECtHR judgment in *Stjerna v Finland*, at para. 42. The second one is the possibility that an EU citizen's identity has no protection even in case of really serious inconveniences. The European Court of justice, in *Runevic-Vardyn* at para. 91, stated that a serious inconvenience to EU citizens does not necessarily imply that the State's interest must be disregarded, as a fair balance between the interests in issue may nonetheless be sought and may eventually lean on the State's interest.

53 See ECtHR, *Mennesson v. France* and *Labassee v. France*, no. 65192/2011 and no. 65941/2011, 26.06.2014. These were the first cases in which the Court of Strasbourg examined the refusal to recognise the parent-child relationship between children born from a surrogate mother abroad and the couples who had resorted to surrogacy. Other similar cases were then brought before the Court: *Laborie v. France*, no. 44024/2013, 19.01.2017; *Foulon v. France* and *Bouvet v. France*, no. 9063/2014 and no. 10410/2014, 21.07.2016.

an EU citizen, family reunification is governed by Directive 2004/38/EC, whose Article 7 grants family reunification only in a State other than that of the sponsor's citizenship. Therefore, if the child's family resides in a MS other than that of the child's citizenship, and then the child moves back to the State of which (s)he is a national and asks for family reunification, the TCN should not be eligible for a derived right of residence in that MS. Indeed, in such a case, domestic legislation could deny reunification without apparently infringing EU law while evidently affecting the child's family unity and eventually his/her family identity. This is true particularly when the TCN is the child's parent, since a separation – even a temporary one – from parents is likely to be detrimental to the child's interest in ensuring his/her personal development in a continuing family relationship.

Within the EU legal order, such a situation might constitute an obstacle to EU citizens' free movement rights and therefore must be scrutinised in the light of Article 21 TFEU. Indeed, citizens could be discouraged from leaving a MS of which they are nationals to exercise rights of movement and residence because the question of whether they can continue, in the original MS, a family life created in the host MS remains uncertain. Therefore, although Directive 2004/38 does not apply to cases of inbound free-movers, in *O. and B.*,[54] the CJEU did not neglect EU citizens' need for protection; instead, it developed a derivative right of residence for TCNs based on Article 21 TFEU in order to preserve EU citizens' family life when they return to the MS of which they are nationals. However, the Court set specific limits to such a right, which is granted only if family life has been established or strengthened during a Union citizen's 'genuine residence' in the host MS in conformity with conditions set forth in Directive 2004/38.

7.2. REMOVAL OF A CHILD'S FAMILY MEMBER

EU law protects the enjoyment of established family life for static EU citizens too. This applies where an EU citizen minor lives in his/her State of citizenship and is dependent upon a TCN family member who has to leave or cannot enter EU territory due to a decision of the local authorities. While EU citizens are entitled to the autonomous right to move and reside in a MS other than that of their nationality, there is no right to reside in one's MS of citizenship that stems expressly from EU primary or secondary law. This also means that TCN family members cannot claim a derived right of residence under either Article 21 TFEU or Directive 2004/38/EC in order to maintain family unity.

---

[54] Case C-456/12, ECLI:EU:C:2014:135, para. 54

The CJEU overturned this scenario by its well-known judgments in the cases of *Ruiz Zambrano*[55] and *Dereci*,[56] in which the Court noted that the expulsion of an EU citizen minor's family member could force the child to leave the Union too. If this happened, the child would be unable to benefit in the future from his rights as an EU citizen. Therefore, based upon the principle that EU citizenship is the fundamental status of the nationals of a MS, the CJEU concluded that Article 20 TFEU precludes national measures from depriving EU citizens of genuine enjoyment of core rights conferred by virtue of their status as citizens of the Union.[57]

In *Ruiz Zambrano* and in other subsequent judgments,[58] EU citizenship became the means through which family unity and all elements of a child's identity as part of a family were protected. The CJEU affirmed that a MS cannot jeopardise the effectiveness of EU citizenship by refusing to grant a right of residence to the parents[59] of an EU child[60] citizen and then obliging them to leave the EU territory as a whole. Previously, this could have happened where: (a) a relationship of dependency existed between the child and the TCN; (b) the TCN was intended to be the child's primary caregiver; (c) a refusal could have led the child to leave EU territory to accompany the concerned TCN, thus undermining the possibility of making future use of any of the core rights derived from being an EU citizen, and eventually breaching the right to family life.

Therefore, the key point is to define 'dependency'. In its most recent judgment in *K.A. and others*,[61] the Court stressed that the mere existence of a family link, whether natural or legal, cannot be sufficient grounds to justify

---

55 Case C-34/09, *Gerardo Ruiz Zambrano v. Office national de l'emploi (ONEm)*, ECLI:EU:C:2011:124. See P. Corneloup, 'Citoyenneté européenne: la Cour de justice apporte une nouvelle pierre à son édifice', (2011) *Recueil Le Dalloz*, 1325; R. Grand, 'Consécration d'un droit de séjour européen independent de la libre circulation', (2011) *L'actualité juridique droit administratif*, 38; K. Hailbronner and D. Thym, (2011) *Common Market Law Review*, 1253; A. Hinarejos, 'Extending Citizenship and the Scope of EU law', (2011) *Cambridge Law Journal*, 309.

56 Case C-256/11, *Murat Dereci and Others v. Bundesministerium für Inneres*, ECLI:EU:C:2011:734, commented on by N. Nic Shuibhne, (2012) *Common Market Law Review*, 349.

57 See *Ruiz Zambrano*, paras. 42–43; *Dereci*, para. 66.

58 Joint cases C-356/11 and C-357/11, *O. and S. v Maahanmuuttovirasto* and *Maahanmuuttovirasto v. L.*, ECLI:EU:C:2012:776; C-115/15, *Secretary of State for the Home Department v. NA*, ECLI:EU:C:2016:487; C-165/14, *Rendòn Marìn*, ECLI:EU:C:2016:675; C-304/14, *Secretary of State for the Home Department v. C.S.*, ECLI:EU:C:2016:674; C-133/15, *H.C. Chavez-Vilchez and Others*, ECLI:EU:C:2017:354.

59 In joint Cases C-356/11 and C-357/11, *O., S. & L.*, ECLI:EU:C:2012:776, the Court affirmed that the principle established in *Ruiz Zambrano* can also be applied to situations in which there is not a blood relationship between the TCN and the minor EU citizen (para. 55).

60 However, in *Dereci*, the Court suggests that, even if it is unlikely, it cannot be excluded *a priori* that the 'Ruiz Zambrano' principle applies to relationships involving adults.

61 Case C-82/16, ECLI:EU:C:2018:308.

granting a derived right of residence. Thus account must be taken of all relevant circumstances, including the child's age and physical and emotional development, the extent of emotional ties to the EU citizen parent and to the TCN parent, the co-habitation situation and the risk to the child's equilibrium resulting from eventual separation. That the child has an EU citizen parent who is 'able and willing to assume sole responsibility for the primary day-to-day care of the child' is relevant, but does not automatically lead to the conclusion that no relationship of dependency exists between the TCN parent and the child.[62] In the light of this criterion, dependency occurs not 'only in exceptional circumstances' in which separation of the EU citizen from the TCN family member is not possible, but also in circumstances in which separation is 'just' undesirable because it runs counter the child's best interests.

We cannot conclude, however, that only the existence of dependency can automatically prevent a MS from exercising immigration control. The Court simply suggests that the MS must seek the right balance between the interests at stake, including the child's interest in not being separated from the parents and not being deprived of the family environment. Therefore, the MS can still apply proportionate restrictive measures when keeping the family together is not in the child's best interests.[63]

8. FINAL REMARKS

The CJEU's case law considered in this chapter shows the increasing inclination to protect children's identity by EU law. It develops protection aimed at preserving EU citizens' identity through the determination of principles the necessary compliance with which requires the displacement of national rules which are not justifiable under Articles 18, 20 and 21 TFEU and 7 and 24(2) of the EU Charter. This chapter highlights the eventual centrality of the individual – that is, the citizen of the European Union – in the process of European integration,[64] even in matters beyond those directly harmonised by the EU, and even in contexts that only a few years ago we would have defined as extraneous to the scope of EU law. Legal protection of the citizen's personal sphere, particularly of its cross-border dimension, is now an absolute priority that requires Member States to cooperate as effectively as possible, including by lowering their respective legal systems' cultural barriers and legal borders. Free movement, EU citizenship's

62 *Chavez-Vilchez*, cit., para. 72.

63 *Rendon-Marin*, cit., para. 81.

64 See B. Nascimbene, 'La centralità della persona e la tutela dei suoi diritti', (2013) *Studi sull'integrazione europea*, 9.

true core, can never become in this context an occasion for denying a right considered fundamental to the Union's order, that is the right to the continuity and stability of the identity of the EU citizen minor in transnational families. Only general interests expressing inalienable needs – not for States themselves, but for their citizens (e.g. human dignity, life, equality) – can justify restriction of that right, unless children's interests – by definition, superior to others' – should nonetheless prevail over these general interests. If this were not so, the ensuing illogicality would jeopardise the process of integration undertaken in the European Union.

Therefore, we can only welcome the direction towards the protection of situations initially unknown to EU law or regarded as extraneous and external to it. At the same time, the effective weight of the right to identity in CJEU case law remains unclear. Do the EU single market and EU citizenship strengthen protection of human rights, or is it the opposite? Even though all these situations ultimately affect the child's fundamental right to identity, as interpreted through the right to private and family life and the best interests principle, only recently has the CJEU expressly stated that the situations as explored above have a fundamental rights dimension. Moreover, when the Court dealt with cases of non-discrimination and/or freedom to move and reside in EU territory, the issue of fundamental rights arose only when the Court had to explore a possible justification for a restriction on the right stemming from the TFEU. However, the fact that the Court attributes to Article 7 of the EU Charter a limited role, circumscribed within the test of proportionality of the restrictive measure (as a means of reviewing a MS's justifications) should not lead us to conclude that the right to identity is marginal and instrumental with respect to the right to move and reside freely, so widely referred to by the Court. Article 7 of the EU Charter expresses a fundamental human right, which by its very definition cannot be an instrument for furthering other interests, but is itself the ultimate goal. On closer inspection, then, the fundamental right to move and reside and the fundamental right to identity operate synergistically, without establishing any instrumental relationship.

The Court's approach, heavily tilted towards the protection of rights enshrined in Articles 20 and 21 TFEU, is necessary, on the one hand, and reasonable, on the other. Establishing its reasoning on the concept of EU citizenship – and the consequent right to free movement – was necessary to bring additional situations within the scope of EU law and has thus permitted a broader interpretation of pre-existing rights – in turn triggering the obligation of Member States to recognise the rights and statuses established under EU law or MS legislation. This is reasonable because citizenship still necessarily covers citizens' fundamental rights under the EU Charter and because the Court itself has long recognised the fundamental nature of free movement rights in the process of European integration. Therefore, cases such as *Sayn-Wittgenstein*, *O. B. & S.* and *Ruiz Zambrano* are not merely about the internal market or migration but have become cases about the fundamental right to identity, though not in a traditional way (that is, in the way a human rights court would have treated and solved these cases).

Moreover, one can reasonably argue – without exaggeration – that through its case law, the CJEU has highlighted EU citizenship and the right to reside and move freely in the EU, with the intention of underlining the distinction between citizens of the Union and TCNs. Indeed, while fundamental rights can be universally claimed by any individual against MS and EU institutions under the condition of Article 51 of the EU Charter, Union citizenship stresses that some individuals belong – while others do not – to a certain political community (the EU) that recognises privileges (specific rights) that cannot be exercised by individuals not belonging to that political community. As a matter of fact, we could not have had the *Ruiz Zambrano* judgment or the 'Grunkin Paul' principle if Mr Ruiz Zambrano's children and Leonard Mathias Grunkin Paul had not been Union citizens.

THE BEST INTERESTS PRINCIPLE'S IMPACT ON DECISIONS CONCERNING ASYLUM-SEEKING AND REFUGEE CHILDREN

Maura MARCHEGIANI*

1. Introductory Remarks 39
2. A General Instrument of Promotion of the Rights of the Child 41
3. The Best Interests Principle in Regional Instruments 46
4. Influence of the Best Interests Principle on European Jurisprudence 48
5. Implications of the Best Interests Approach for International Protection Procedures 52

1. INTRODUCTORY REMARKS

Children's migration in the European Union represents a broad, difficult challenge for both European and international systems. Migrant children are a heterogeneous category, including unaccompanied children outside their country of origin, children accompanied by their families, other relatives or previous legal or customary primary caregivers and children seeking asylum or other forms of international protection.[1]

---

* This contribution was funded by the MIUR under SIR 2014 Action. This chapter reflects only the author's view.

[1] It is difficult to assess the number of refugee, asylum-seeking and migrant children in Europe. In 2017, European countries recorded 209,756 asylum claims by children, including 50,325 newly registered asylum claims during the last quarter of 2017. This represents a 47% drop from 2016, when 396,740 children claimed asylum in Europe. Children make up more than 30% of all asylum seekers across Europe (UNICEF, 'Refugee and Migrant Crisis in Europe Humanitarian Situation, Report no. 28', January-June 2018, <https://www.unicef.org/eca/sites/unicef.org.eca/files/sitreprandm.pdf>). On the one hand, the number of unaccompanied minors seeking asylum in the EU increased dramatically in 2015, reaching a total of 99,995 minors (an increase of 315% in comparison to the previous year), before returning to 31,975 in 2017. On the other hand, the number of unaccompanied minors who arrived in the EU and did not seek asylum is unknown. There is a general lack of comprehensive and comparable data on the numbers of and outcomes both for non-asylum-seeking unaccompanied minors,

Despite the extent and complexity of children's migration in Europe, their common feature is extreme vulnerability. According to the United Nations High Commissioner for Refugees (UNHCR), child asylum seekers and refugees are among the world's most vulnerable groups, needing appropriate protection and humanitarian assistance.[2] Recognition of this special vulnerability determines States' obligation to take appropriate measures to ensure that every child seeking refugee status or considered a refugee according to applicable international or domestic law and procedures, whether unaccompanied or accompanied, receives appropriate protection and humanitarian assistance in the enjoyment of the applicable rights set forth in international and European human rights or humanitarian instruments relevant to the States.

Because of such children's vulnerability, States are obliged in particular to ensure an especially broad, complete protection at every stage of the migration process, from their access to the territory to the identification procedure, from interim care and protection measures to determination of refugee or protection status: child asylum seekers and refugees should not be refused access to the territory; their identification should be prioritised and prompt, they should be registered through age-appropriate interviews to collect bio data and social history information immediately after arrival, and every child's views and wishes should be elicited and considered. Children's applications to refugee status should be prioritised and every effort made to reach a decision promptly and fairly.[3] Considering their vulnerability and special needs, asylum-seeking children, particularly the unaccompanied, are actually entitled to special care and protection, to avoid a condition of legal uncertainty that risks undermining the full enjoyment of their rights and proper development.[4]

The challenge of guaranteeing these children special protection is, however, very difficult due to the level of fragmentation that generally characterises the

---

and those minors seeking asylum in the EU (EMN, 'Unaccompanied Minors Following Status Determination in the EU plus Norway', July 2018, <https://ec.europa.eu/home-affairs/sites/homeaffairs/files/00_eu_synthesis_report_unaccompanied_minors_2017_en.pdf>).

2 UNHCR, 'Refugee Children, Guidelines on Protection and Care', Geneva 1994, <http://www.unhcr.org/protect/PROTECTION/3b84c6c67.pdf>. See also: UNHCR, Executive Committee Conclusions, no. 47 (1987) on Refugee Children; no. 59 (1989) on Refugee Children; no. 84 (1997) on Refugee Children and Adolescents; no. 88 (1999) on Protection of the Refugee's Family; UNHCR, 'Summary Note on UNHCR's Strategy and Activities concerning Refugee Children', Geneva 2002, <http://www.unhcr.org/3ee8af944.pdf>.

3 UNHCR, 'Guidelines on Policies and Procedures in dealing with Unaccompanied Children Seeking Asylum', Geneva 1997, <http://www.unhcr.org/3d4f91cf4.pdf>.

4 See J. M. Pobjoy, *The Child in International Refugee Law*, Cambridge University Press, Cambridge 2017, p. 22; F. Ippolito, '(De)Constructing Children's Vulnerability in European Law', in F. Ippolito and S. Iglesias Sanchez (eds.), *Protection of Vulnerable Groups. The European Human Rights Framework*, Hart Publishing, Oxford 2015, p. 23; A. Annoni, 'The Protection of Child Victims of Trafficking in Europe', in F. Ippolito and G. Biagioni (eds.), *Migrant Children: Challenges for Public and Private International Law*, Editoriale Scientifica, Napoli 2016, p. 31.

legal framework of migrant children's protection, but in particular children seeking asylum.

Despite the regional or universal absence of a general instrument specifically dedicated to children involved in migration, multiple levels of protection can be identified. These multilevel protections are based on various, differing systems (e.g. the international legal order, European Union (EU), domestic systems) and case law (e.g. domestic jurisprudence, the European Court of Justice, the European Court of Human Rights). This situation determines a perspective of 'transversal' protection, the coordination of which is not easy and in which guaranteed fundamental rights should go beyond and cross every territorial border, to adequately protect the children's extremely situation.[5]

Indeed, recourse to the best interests of the child principle, representing this chapter's *leitmotif*, can be identified as a connecting element that not only allows for the realisation of children's general and entire protection, but which also has specific relevance in the migratory context, especially because of the migration phenomenon's *heterogeneity* and the various categories of children involved in migration procedures, as well as the applicable laws' *fragmentation*. Application of children's best interests in migration procedures should allow decisions on their admission to a host country or their return to a home country as the first priority.[6]

This coordination criterion can actually guarantee adequate protection to migrant children as an entire category and to each child, considered in her or his individual specificity. From this perspective, this chapter analyses the condition and treatment of child refugees and asylum seekers through the principle of the best interests of the child, as provided by conventional norms and as applied by relevant jurisprudence, to trace problems and the evolution of protection for this particularly vulnerable category of migrants.

2. A GENERAL INSTRUMENT OF PROMOTION OF THE RIGHTS OF THE CHILD

The 1989 United Nations Convention on the Rights of the Child stated in general terms the principle of the best interests of the child, thus introducing, as

5 In this light, see G. Van Bueren, *The International Law on the Rights of the Child*, Martinus Nijhoff, The Hague 1998, p. 46; B. Gornik, 'At the Crossroads of Power Relations: the Convention of the Rights of the Child and Unaccompanied Migrant Minors', in M. Sedmak, B. Sauer and B. Gornik (eds.), *Unaccompanied Children in European Migration and Asylum Practices: In Whose Best Interests?*, Routledge, Abingdon/New York 2017, p. 10.

6 In this sense, see M. Kalverboer, D. Beltman, C. Van Os and E. Zijlstra, 'The Best Interests of the Child in Cases of Migration: Assessing and Determining the Best Interests of the Child in Migration Procedures', (2017) *International Journal of Children's Rights*, 114.

is well known, a change of perspective in international protection of children's rights.[7] In fact, this principle corresponds to the Convention's spirit as a whole, with particular regard to the consideration of children as individuals, with their own opinions, needs and feelings, as subjects of civil and political rights and, at the same time, in need of special protection.[8] The Convention's purpose is essentially to safeguard children's well-being by providing them with independent, autonomous rights. States that have signed and ratified this treaty are responsible for applying its content fully: *de facto*, this means States must refrain from infringing the Convention's obligations and must attempt to implement its requirements in domestic legal orders.[9] Thus, this universal treaty is an important instrument for promoting children's rights by offering general protection; in this sense, it is relevant to migrant children, particularly refugees and asylum seekers.[10]

7 Article 3 of the CRC stated that 'In all actions concerning children, whether undertaken by public or private social welfare *institutions, courts of law, administrative authorities or legislative bodies, the best interests of the child shall be a primary consideration*'. Several other articles of the Convention make explicit reference to this principle, in relation to family ties (Article 9) and parental responsibility (Article 18), the right to have a family (Arts 20–21), and the deprivation of liberty (Article 37(c)). Every other provision of the CRC must be interpreted in the light of the principle. For a detailed analysis of this provision, M. Freeman, 'Article 3. The Best Interests of the Child', in A. Alen, J. Vande Lanotte, E. Verhellen, F. Ang, E. Berghmans and M. Verheyde (eds.), *A Commentary on the United Nations Convention on the Rights of the Child*, Martinus Nijhoff Publishers, Leiden 2007.

8 In this sense, R. Hodgkin and P. Newell, *Implementation Handbook for the Convention on the Rights of the Child*, UNICEF, Geneva 2007, p. 37.

9 For a more detailed analysis, see L. Lundy, U. Kilkelly and B. Byrne, 'Incorporation of the United Nations Convention on the Rights of the Child in Law: A Comparative Review' (2013) *International Journal of Children's Rights*, 442; U. Kilkelly 'Using the Convention on the Rights of the Child in Law and Policy: Two Ways to Improve Compliance' in A. Invernizzi and J. Williams (eds.), *The Human Rights of Children: From Visions to Implementation*, Ashgate, Aldershot 2011.

10 See the New York Declaration for Refugees and Migrants, 2016 (A/RES/71/1); the Statement by the Committee on Economic, Social and Cultural Rights on the Duties of States towards Refugees and Migrants under the International Covenant on Economic, Social and Cultural Rights, 2017 (E/C.12/2017/1); CRC, General Comment no. 6 (2005) on Treatment of Unaccompanied and Separated Children outside their Country of Origin, 2005; CRC, Report of the 2012 Day of General Discussion on the Rights of all Children in the context of International Migration <www.ohchr.org/EN/HRBodies/CRC/Pages/Discussion2012.aspx>, accessed 30.09.2018; the endorsement in 2016 by the Committee on the Protection of the Rights of All Migrant Workers and Members of Their Families of the recommended principles to guide actions concerning children on the move and other children affected by migration, <www.ohchr.org/Documents/HRBodies/CMW/Recommended-principle_EN.pdf>. For a doctrinal reconstruction, see J. Bhabha, 'Arendt's Children: Do Today's Migrant Children Have a Right to Have Rights?', in M. Sedmak, B. Sauer and B. Gornik, above n. 5, p. 203; J. Kanics, 'The Best Interests of Unaccompanied and Separated Children: A Normative Framework Based on the Convention on the Rights of the Child', in M. Sedmak, B. Sauer and B. Gornik, above n. 5, p. 98; M. Kalverboer, D. Beltman, C. Van Os and E. Zijlstra, above n. 6, p. 114.

This Convention provides a general legal framework for children's rights based on the best interests principle, which considers children's involvement in forced migration or the requirements for international protection, giving special attention to their vulnerabilities.[11] While in general children are considered a vulnerable group of people,[12] so children involved in migration procedures or asylum may be considered even more vulnerable because migration itself can negatively impact their health, development and well-being.[13]

The Convention contains four interrelated guiding principles that also connect with the Convention's other provisions. These principles are obviously relevant to all children, and consequently, they also apply to migrant children, for whom they acquire particular meaning. These four principles are the non-discrimination clause,[14] the right to life and development,[15] the right to be heard,[16] and the best interests of the child,[17] which is considered an umbrella provision safeguarding the involved child's interests in all kinds of decision-making procedures.[18]

For migrant children, Article 2 is highly important because it protects them from discrimination in exercising their rights as described by the Convention's other provisions on their legal status. In fact, this provision imposes the obligation to apply the Convention to Member States' entire territories and to all minors under their jurisdiction, and thus also to migrant children, even if only temporarily present and regardless of irregular or regular conditions. According to the Committee on the Rights of the Child, Article 2 stipulates that State parties must apply their obligations under the Convention

> to each child within their jurisdictions, including the jurisdiction arising from a State exercising effective control outside its borders. Those obligations cannot be arbitrarily and unilaterally curtailed either by excluding zones or areas from the

---

11 J. M. Pobjoy, 'A Child Rights Framework for Assessing the Status of Refugee Children', in S. Juss and C. Harvey (eds.), *Contemporary Issues in Refugee* Law, Edward Elgar Publishing, Cheltenham/Northampton 2013.

12 H. Biggs and C. Jones, 'Legally Vulnerable: What is Vulnerability and Who is Vulnerable?' in M. Freeman, S. Hawkes and B. Bennett (eds.), *Law and Global Health: Current Legal Issues*, Oxford University Press, Oxford 2014; J. Herring, 'Vulnerability, Children, and the Law' in M. Freeman (ed.), *Law and Childhood Studies: Current Legal Issues*, Oxford University Press, Oxford 2012.

13 In this sense, see M. Kalverboer, D. Beltman, C. Van Os and E. Zijlstra, above n. 6, p. 117.

14 Article 2.

15 Article 6.

16 Article 12.

17 Article 3.

18 J. Zermatten, 'The Best Interests of the Child Principle: Literal Analysis and Function', (2010) *International Journal of Children's Rights*, 483; M. Freeman, 'Article 3: The Best Interests of the Child', above n. 7.

> territory of a State or by defining particular zones or areas as not or only partly under the jurisdiction of the State, including in international waters or other transit zones where States put in place migration control mechanisms. The obligations apply within the borders of the State, including with respect to those children who come under its jurisdiction while attempting to enter its territory.[19]

In this sense, States should ensure that children in the context of international migration are treated first and foremost as children. State parties to the Convention have a duty to comply with obligations established therein to respect, protect and fulfil children's rights in the context of international migration, regardless of their, their parents or legal guardians' migration status. This statement implies States' specific obligation to ensure adequate guarantees in respect of migrant children, with particular reference to the rights to receive health care and education.[20] As the Committee insisted, the principle of non-discrimination must be fully applied by State parties. who are required to take all necessary measures to ensure

> the rights of illegal immigrant children and unaccompanied foreign minors are fully guaranteed.[21]

The Committee has repeatedly found that migrant workers' children – even if present irregularly – belonging to minorities or indigenous communities, must benefit without discrimination from rights guaranteed by the Convention, regardless of citizenship.[22] In other words, the non-discrimination principle of the Convention obliges State parties to respect and safeguard the rights set forth in the Convention for all children, whether they are considered, inter alia, migrants in regular or irregular situations, asylum seekers, refugees, stateless persons or victims of trafficking, including in situations of return or deportation to the country of origin, irrespective of the child's, parents or legal guardians' nationality, migration status or statelessness.[23]

The Convention on the Rights of the Child contains several provisions that establish specific obligations in the context of international migration in

---

19 Joint General Comment no. 3 (2017) of the Committee on the Protection of the Rights of All Migrant Workers and Members of Their Families, and no. 22 (2017) of the Committee on the Rights of the Child on the general principles regarding the human rights of children in the context of international migration, 16.11.2017, CMW/C/GC/3-CRC/C/GC/22, §12.

20 CRC, Norway, Initial Report Final Observations (IRFO), Add. 23, §12; Denmark, IRFO, Add. 33, §30; Belgium, IRFO, Add. 38, §9.

21 CRC, Portugal, IRFO, Add. 45, §21.

22 CRC, Indonesia, Prel. Obs., Add. 7, §8, Mexico, IRFO, Add. 13, §9, Portugal, IRFO, Add. 45, §13.

23 See also CRC, General Comment no. 6 (2005), above n. 10, §12.

countries of origin, transit, destination and return.[24] Specifically with reference to entry of a migrant child, the Convention imposes on the territorial State the obligation to examine any application for family reunification in a positive and humane way, to recognise the need for protection and special aid[25] considering the child's particular vulnerability,[26] to collaborate with other States, to assist the child in tracing any family and, if family members are untraceable, to provide special assistance on a par with that granted to every other citizen minor in a similar situation. Article 22 also provides for the child's right to humanitarian protection, which should be extended, according to the Committee, to the phase of waiting for recognition of refugee status.[27]

Furthermore, under Article 37, every child, at all times, has a fundamental right to liberty and freedom from immigration detention.[28] Detention of children because of their or their parents' migration status violates their rights and contravenes the principle of children's best interests.[29] The Committee has clarified that 'immigration detention' must be understood 'as any setting in which a child is deprived of his/her liberty for reasons related to his/her or his/her parents' migration status, regardless of the name and reason given to the action of depriving a child of his or her liberty, or the name of the facility or location where the child is deprived of liberty'.[30]

Finally, implementation of the Convention's obligations and principles in the context of migration is supported by an underlying principle: standards established by the Convention should have primacy over any other aspect or policy involved. One implication is that children's rights should never be subject

24 In this sense, see in particular CRC, General Comment no. 19 (2016) on Public Budgeting for the realization of children's rights, §§28–34, concerning the interpretation of Articles 2 and 4 of the CRC.

25 Article 10 §1.

26 Article 20.

27 J. Bhabha, 'Lone Travellers: Rights Criminalization and Transnational Migration of Unaccompanied Children', (2000) *Journal of Interdisciplinary Legal Studies*, 269; ibid., 'Minors or Aliens? Inconsistent State Intervention and Separated Child Asylum-Seekers', (2001) *European Journal of Migration Law*, 288.

28 See also the International Convention on the Protection of the Rights of All Migrant Workers and Members of Their Families, Articles 16 and 17; the Universal Declaration of Human Rights, Articles 3 and 9; and the International Covenant on Civil and Political Rights, Article 9.

29 CRC, Report of the 2012 Day of General Discussion, §78. See also the United Nations Basic Principles and Guidelines on Remedies and Procedures on the Right of Anyone Deprived of Their Liberty to Bring Proceedings Before a Court (A/HRC/30/37, annex), in particular principle 21, §46, and guideline 21.

30 Joint General Comment no. 4 (2017) of the Committee on the Protection of the Rights of All Migrant Workers and Members of Their Families, and no. 23 (2017) of the Committee on the Rights of the Child on State obligations regarding the human rights of children in the context of international migration in countries of origin, transit, destination and return, 16.11.2017, CMW/C/GC/4-CRC/C/GC/23, §5.

to migration goals defined by any State.[31] From this perspective, children's rights should be explicitly included in any migration policy, legislation and/or decision that might impact them.[32]

3. THE BEST INTERESTS PRINCIPLE IN REGIONAL INSTRUMENTS

Since the inception of the Convention on the Rights of the Child,[33] the principle of the best interests of the child, universally established first by this international multilateral treaty,[34] has also been repeated, in slightly different formulations, in relevant legal instruments on the rights of the child; it is widely invoked by international, European and national jurisprudence and in widely differing legal and cultural contexts.

This principle's universal relevance in the migration context is particularly evident from the Draft Articles' reference to it in relation to the expulsion of aliens, adopted by the International Law Commission in 2014: Article 15, concerning vulnerable persons, explicitly refers to the principle of the best interests of the child.[35] The relevance of the best interests principle is particularly evident in the EU legal order. In elaborating legal and political solutions to cope with EU migratory flows, the best interests approach was progressively applied, initially with specific reference to unaccompanied minors, and then gradually to all minors involved in migration, with significant implications for their families.[36] Indeed, several EU legal instruments, specifically focusing on

---

31 M. Kalverboer, D. Beltman, C. Van Os and E. Zijlstra, above n. 6, p. 117.

32 P. Ceriani Cernadas, 'The Human Rights of Children in the Context of International Migration' in W. Vandenhole, E. Desmet, D. Reynaert and S. Lembrechts (eds.), *Routledge International Handbook of Children's Rights Studies*, Routledge, London/New York 2015.

33 This universal treaty has been signed and ratified by almost all the countries in the world: <http://indicators.ohchr.org> accessed 30.09.2018.

34 Some general references to the best interests of the child can also be found in previous legal documents and the concept was in fact invoked by other international human rights instruments: in the context of the 1959 Declaration on the Rights of the Child (Principle 2) and in some articles of the 1979 Convention on the Elimination of All Forms of Discrimination against Women (Articles 5(b) on family education and 16(1)(d) on marriage and family relations). The principle does not appear in either of the International Covenants, but the Human Rights Committee, in two of its General Comments on interpretation of the International Covenant on Civil and Political Rights, has referred to the interests of the child as 'paramount' in cases of parental separation or divorce (Human Rights Committee, General Comment 17 and 19, HRI/GEN/1/Rev.5, pp. 133, 138).

35 Draft articles on the Expulsion of Aliens, adopted by the International Law Commission in 2014 and submitted to the General Assembly as a part of the Commission's Report (A/69/10), Article 15, §2.

36 In this light, see Regulation (EU) 2016/1624 of the European Parliament and of the Council of 14.09.2016 on the European Border and Coast Guard and amending Regulation (EU) 2016/399

asylum and international protection, such as the EU Regulations and Directives constituting the Common European Asylum and Immigration Policy, include increasing references to the Convention and to the best interests principle.[37]

The introduction of Article 3's provision into the consolidated version of the Treaty on European Union,[38] which elevates 'protection of the rights of the child' to a general EU objective, has profoundly impacted EU political institutions' actions, which are increasingly oriented towards the child's best interests in exercising legislative power concerning migration, asylum and international protection. This principle has finally been enshrined in the EU Charter of Fundamental Rights,[39] which mainly covers the EU human rights framework, specifically in Article 24.[40] This provision

> guarantees the right of children to such protection and care as is necessary for their well-being. In all actions relating to children taken by public authorities the child's best interests must be a primary consideration. Since according to the foregoing,

---

of the European Parliament and of the Council and repealing Regulation (EC) 863/2007 of the European Parliament and of the Council, Council Regulation (EC) 2007/2004 and Council Decision 2005/267/EC [2016] (OJ L251/1), especially considering Articles 38 and 34.3, under whose terms 'the European Border and Coast Guard shall in all its activities pay particular attention to children's rights and ensure that the best interests of the child are respected'.

37 The best interests of the child principle can be found in many Regulations and Directives concerning asylum and migration. From the most recent, see particularly Regulation (EU) No 604/2013 of the European Parliament and of the Council of 26.06.2013 establishing the criteria and mechanisms for determining the Member State responsible for examining an application for international protection lodged in one of the Member States by a third-country national or a stateless person, [2013] OJ L 180/31 (Article 6); Directive 2013/33/EU of the European Parliament and of the Council of 26.06.2013 laying down standards for the reception of applicants for international protection, [2013] OJ L 180/96 (Article 23). In this light, see also the European Parliament's Draft Report on the Proposal for a Regulation of the European Parliament and of the Council Establishing the Criteria and Mechanisms for Determining the Member States responsible for Examining an Application for International Protection Lodged in One of the Member States by a Third-country National or a Stateless Person (Recast), Rapporteur C. Wikström, 24.02.2017, 2016/0133(COD). On the doctrine, see K. Hailbronner (ed.), *EU Immigration and Asylum Law: Commentary on EU Regulations and Directives*, Hart Publishing, Oxford/Portland 2013; H. Stalford and E. Drywood, 'Using the CRC to Inform EU Law and Policy-making' in A. Invernizzi and J. Williams, above n. 9.

38 For a general overview of the amendments on fundamental rights following the Lisbon Treaty, see, *ex multis*, S. De Vries, U. Bernitz and S. Weatherill, *The Protection of Fundamental Rights in the EU After Lisbon*, Hart Publishing, Oxford/Portland 2013.

39 For a detailed analysis of the Charter and of its impact on the EU legal order, see S. Peers, T. K. Hervey, J. Kenner and A. Ward (eds.), *The EU Charter of Fundamental Rights: A Commentary*, Hart Publishing, Oxford 2014.

40 According to the Explanations relating to the Charter of Fundamental Rights (2007/C 303/02), this provision is directly based on Article 3 of the Convention: consequently, the meaning of the principle of the best interests of the child should be determined in accordance with the interpretation provided by the Committee in its general comments. From this perspective, see M. Kalverboer, D. Beltman, C. Van Os and E. Zijlstra, above n. 6, p. 118.

> children are, in principle, particularly in need of protection, they must in general also be regarded as particularly vulnerable.[41]

Therefore, the EU legal framework concerning children involved in migration and asylum procedures tends to converge on the 1989 Convention's object and scope: children, including those involved in migratory procedures, are individually considered an independent subject of rights, whose pre-eminent interest is not limited to guaranteeing protection, but has a broader perspective, including development and participation.[42]

4. INFLUENCE OF THE BEST INTERESTS PRINCIPLE ON EUROPEAN JURISPRUDENCE

The absence of a general legal instrument specifically devoted to the promotion and protection of children's rights in Europe has also profoundly impacted developments in European courts, which are committed to compliance with international standards and with the best interests of the child principle in resolving cases concerning migration, asylum and international protection.[43] In this process, the European Court of Human Rights (ECtHR) and the European Court of Justice have played fundamental roles.[44] The ECtHR has applied the principle of the best interests of the child essentially as an interpretative tool: to guarantee effective protection of fundamental rights, the ECtHR initially assumed this principle as a constant reference in interpretation and application of Article 8.[45] From the perspective of international rules on treaties' interpretation, the Court justified this orientation, traditionally referring to Article 31(3)(c) of the 1969 Vienna Convention on the Law of Treaties. Application of this coordination mechanism is quite frequent in the ECtHR's jurisprudence.[46]

---

41 Opinion of Advocate General Kokott delivered on 11.11.2004, in Case C-105/03, *Pupino*, ECLI:EU:C:2004:712, §§57–58.

42 In these terms, see C. Danisi, 'Il principio del preminente interesse del minore in ambito migratorio: verso una convergenza?' in G. Nesi (ed.), *Migrazioni e diritto internazionale: verso il superamento dell'emergenza?*, Editoriale scientifica, Napoli 2018, p. 507, 511.

43 See E. Brems, E. Desmet and W. Wandenhole (eds.), *Children Rights Law in the Global Human Rights Landscape*, Routledge, Oxford 2017.

44 The jurisprudence concerning refugee and migrant children is broad and heterogeneous and cannot obviously be examined systematically in this context. Therefore, some emblematic cases, particularly relevant for the purposes of this analysis, have been selected.

45 Article 8 provides for the right to respect for private and family life. It states that 'everyone has the right to respect for his private and family life, his home and his correspondence' (§1).

46 On the general rules of interpretation, see ECtHR, *Golder v. United Kingdom*, No. 4451/70, 21.02.1975, §29. On Article 31(3)(c), see *Al-Adsani v. United Kingdom*, No. 35763/97, 21.11.2001, §55; *Bosphorus v. Ireland*, No. 45036/98, 30.06.2005, §150.

Concerning the best interests of the child, the Court does not find any particular obstacle to use of the mechanism of interpretation provided in Article 31(3)(c), because all State parties to the ECHR are equally subject to obligations deriving from the United Nations Convention on the Rights of the Child 1989, which all European States have ratified.[47]

Moreover, the Court has managed a gradual transition from an approach based on 'general and abstract prevention', founded on the general consideration of the interests of the child, to an enhancement of the principle, considered in individual cases' particular dimension.[48]

If, initially, recourse to the principle was strictly connected to the right covered by Article 8 ECHR, the realisation of the best interests of the child has gradually affected the whole Convention's comprehension and interpretation, in order to guarantee all rights and liberties to all children, without distinctions.[49] The European Court of Justice, for its part, bases its decisions on a specific, internal source, directly relevant for the EU legal order, represented by Article 24 of the Charter of Fundamental Rights, which, in any case, has to be interpreted by considering relevant international norms. Concerning migration, asylum and international protection, solutions adopted in jurisprudence are also affected by the specific situation in which the best interests principle has been concretely interpreted and applied by the two European Courts. From this perspective, cases of expulsion, detention, international protection or reception can show flexible convergence on international standards and principles.

In any case, it should be stressed that European jurisprudence has exercised a significant influence on the evolution of the Common European Asylum System, as demonstrated by the European Court of Justice's famous ruling in the case of *M.A. v. Secretary of State of the Home Department*, thanks to which some important modifications were made to the Dublin II Regulation, precisely to consider the best interests of the child: this amendment was then codified in the text of Article 8 of the Dublin III Regulation.[50] In the *M.A.* case, the

---

47 On Article 31(3)(c) of the VCLT, see, generally, *Fragmentation of International Law: Difficulties Arising from the Diversification and Expansion of International Law*, Report of the Study Group of the International Law Commission, finalised by Martti Koskenniemi, UN doc. A/CN.4/L.682, 13.04.2006, §410. See also the WTO Panel in *EC-Measures Affecting the Approval and Marketing of Biotech Products*, 07.02.2006, WT/DS291-293/INTERIM, especially §§7.70–7.72.

48 This passage starts particularly from the case of *Neulinger and Shuruk v. Switzerland*, No. 41615/07, 06.07.2010 (GC), concerning a case of international abduction of children.

49 On the use of the principle in a migration context, see C. Smyth, 'The Best Interests of the Child in the Expulsion and First-entry Jurisprudence of the European Court of Human Rights: How Principled is the Court's Use of the Principle?', (2015) *European Journal of Migration and Law*, 70.

50 Case C-648/11, *M.A. v. Secretary of State of the Home Department*, ECLI:EU:C:2013:367, §§55–60; see also case C-245/11, K. *V. Buundesasylamt*, ECLI:EU:C:2012:685, §52.

Court established the child's condition of extreme vulnerability and therefore affirmed that, if he has applied for international protection in more than one Member State, the State responsible for examining his application may also be considered that in which the child is located, to avoid further and unnecessary movements. The Dublin system's purpose is, in fact, to guarantee rapid access to asylum procedures and to prevent unnecessary procedural delays that could be detrimental to the child. In this case, the Court gave fundamental weight to the best interests of the child. Taking into account the observations of the UN Committee on the Rights of the Child, the Court found that only rapid access to asylum procedures could comply with the best interests of that unaccompanied minor, especially since any further transfer would aggravate the condition of vulnerability, rather than remedy it.

The direction followed by the European Court of Human Rights is considered more incisive: despite absence in the European Convention of Human Rights of any provision concerning protection of migrants and of children, the Court developed its jurisprudence based on an evolving interpretation, in conjunction with the best interests of the child,[51] giving rise to changes of great impact.[52]

From this perspective, the *Tarakhel* case is particularly emblematic. The underlying facts concerned the transfer of an Afghan family, two parents and six minor children, in application of the Dublin Regulation. According to the ECtHR, compliance with the execution of a removal measure with the best interests of the child is conditional on the securing of specific guarantees, especially concerning the children's location in the destination State and the family unit's maintenance. In other words, the best interests approach excludes basing the transfer on the mere general presumption that the destination State respects fundamental rights, but entails specific socio-economic obligations, *vis-à-vis* the reception State and the destination State, to meet special needs

> related in particular to their age and lack of independence, but also to their asylum-seeker status.[53]

The Court also clarified that pursuing the best interests of a child under a State party's jurisdiction implies the duty 'to bear in mind that the child's extreme

---

51 From this perspective, see K. A. McSweeney, 'The Potential for Enforcement of the United Nations Convention on the Rights of the Child: The Need to Improve the Information Base' (1993) *Boston College of International and Comparative Law Review*, 467.

52 See in this context, ECtHR, *Mubilanzila Mayeka et Kaniki Mitunga v. Belgium*, No. 13178/03, 12.10.2006, §55; *Rahimi v. Greece*, No. 8687/08, 05.07.2011; *Popov v. France*, Nos. 39472/07 and 39474/07, 19.01.2012, §91; *Senigo Longue v. France*, No. 19113/09, 10.07.2014, §67; *Abubakar v. Malta*, No. 25794/13, 22.11.2016; C. Smyth, above, n. 49.

53 See ECtHR, *Tarakhel v. Switzerland*, No. 29217/12, 14.11.2014 (GC), §99. See also, *mutatis mutandis*, *A.M.E. v. the Netherlands*, No. 51428/10, 05.02.2015.

vulnerability is the decisive factor and takes precedence over considerations relating to the status of illegal immigrant'.[54] According to the Court, the condition of vulnerability is inherent to childhood and is exacerbated because of migration.[55]

Before the ECtHR, the best interests approach may have significant implications at both substantial and procedural levels. First, application of the best interests of the child principle might impact the admissibility of individual applications, resulting in a broadening of the Court's jurisdiction to embrace consideration of the notion of best interests.

In this sense, the solution adopted in *Tarakhel* is emblematic, especially when compared with other decisions on inadmissibility given in a series of cases also concerning transfers to Italy, according to the Dublin system, but in the absence of children seeking asylum.[56] Furthermore, the best interests approach can also affect the required standard of proof, and it might impact the adoption of interim measures pursuant to Article 39 of the Rules of the Court. As stated by former President Costa of the European Court of Human Rights,

> application of Rule 39 has preserved the physical integrity, the liberty and even the lives of many people who by definition are vulnerable.[57]

Finally, the concept of the child's best interests impacts the extension of the margin of appreciation afforded to the State: application of the best interests of the child principle raises the relevant standard, requiring States to consider children's special vulnerability, thus considerably limiting States' sphere of discretion. This situation implies that consideration of the child's special needs, to be removed or transferred, acquires a significantly greater weight than that attributed to other interests, including security and border control.[58]

---

54 ECtHR, *Mubilanzila Mayeka and Kaniki Mitunga v. Belgium*, above n. 52, §55; Popov v. France, above n. 52, §91.

55 ECtHR, *Tarakhel v. Switzerland*, above n. 53, §119.

56 ECtHR, *Mohammed Hussein v. Netherland and Italy*, No. 27725/10, 02.04.2013, §78; *Halimi v. Austria and Italy*, No. 53852/11, 18.06.2013, §58; *Abubeker v. Austria and Italy*, No. 73874/11, 18.06.2013, §69; *Mohammed Hassan and others v. Netherland and Italy*, No. 40524/10, 27.08.2013, §176; *Miruts Hagos v. Netherland and Italy*, No. 9053/10, 27.08.2013, §38; *Hussein Diirshi and others v. Netherland and Italy*, No. 2314/10, 10.09.2013, §138.

57 Speech given by Mr Jean-Paul Costa, Former President of the European Court of Human Rights, 28.012011, ECtHR, Annual Report 2011, Registry of the European Court of Human Rights, Strasbourg 2012, pp. 35, 40.

58 ECtHR, *Hirsi Jamaa and Others v. Italy*, No. 27765/09, 23.02.2012; *Sharifi and Others v. Italy and Greece*, No. 16643/09, 21.10.2014.

5. IMPLICATIONS OF THE BEST INTERESTS APPROACH FOR INTERNATIONAL PROTECTION PROCEDURES

During the last three decades, the principle of the best interests of the child has gained ground, especially in the context of human rights instruments and international courts. The frequency with which legal analysis invokes this principle forms the most evident proof of its universal acceptance internationally.[59]

However, despite frequent, broad references to the best interests principle in such legal instruments as conventions, resolutions, recommendations, declarations and reports, this notion remains partially unclear and transient at both European and international levels: some difficulties arise in relation to its specific content's definition and to its scope's exactness in international law.[60] Actually, in its General Comment No. 14, the UN Committee on the Rights of the Child has clarified functions and the scope of best interests without providing a definition.[61] However, the absence of a complete definition can have positive effects, as the notion of the 'best interests of the child' is not static, but can evolve over time and may vary depending on context, namely when the best interests approach has to be applied in migration and asylum procedures. A rigorous definition would therefore risk reducing or limiting the notion's application.

The best interests of the child principle could be considered to have basically two dimensions: individual and collective, as it can refer to a single child or to children as a group. In its collective dimension, the principle imposes on States the obligation to consider children's special needs that can be associated through common conditions, such as involvement in migration or asylum; in this dimension, the principle represents a useful tool and an important criterion for identifying some collective solutions, capable of guaranteeing children involved in the migratory process, by a holistic approach, all their rights. These include even those rights more likely to be compromised in migration or asylum, such as rights to non-discrimination, to life, to survival and development, to participation and being heard, regardless of their conditions' regularity or irregularity.[62]

---

59 In this sense, see P. Alston, *The Best Interests of the Child: Reconciling Culture and Human Rights*, Clarendon Press, Oxford 1994. More recently, see G. Aguillar Cavallo, 'El principio del interés superiore del niño y la Corte interamericana de derechos humanos' (2008) *Estudios Costitucionales*, 223, 226.

60 According to a part of the doctrine, Art. 3 of the Convention does not impose specific obligations on States, but rather establishes a general principle which should inform 'every action concerning children' (see, inter alia, P. Alston, above n. 59, p. 15; G. Van Bueren, above n. 5, p. 47).

61 The Committee identifies a threefold concept about the child's best interests: a substantive right; a fundamental, interpretative legal principle; and a rule of procedure (General Comment no. 14 (2013) on the Right of the Child to have his or her best interests taken as a primary consideration (Art. 3 §1), 29 May 2013, CRC/C/GC/14).

62 UNHCR, 'Guidelines on Determining the Best Interests of the Child', Geneva 2008 <http://www.unhcr.org/4566b16b2.pdf>; in the context of the Council of Europe, see Parliamentarian

In its individual dimension, the notion of best interests stipulates a specific link between each child, on the one hand, and an obligation of the State, on the other hand, so as to afford special or additional protection in specific situations, such as migration, while considering the child's specific characteristics to ensure some degree of priority of consideration. The best interests of the child, from a personal development perspective, depend in fact on a variety of individual circumstances, particularly age and level of maturity, presence or absence of parents and environment and individual experiences. For that reason, those best interests must be assessed individually.[63]

The relevance of the best interests principle might prove particularly problematic when the child's condition is particularly vulnerable, as occurs in the migration, asylum and international protection context. In its *Guidelines on Determining the Best Interests of the Child*, the UNHCR provides, inter alia, that

> the term "best interests" broadly describes the well-being of a child. Such well-being is determined by a variety of individual circumstances, such as the age, the level of maturity of the child, the presence or absence of parents, the child's environment and experiences.[64]

Clearly, when the best interests principle is applied to children involved in migration, asylum and international protection procedures, a cumulative effect is produced, entailing a higher degree of vulnerability and therefore of protection.[65] In these situations, clarifying the relations between the notion of vulnerability and the best interests principle would be useful. Jurisprudence has offered opportunities to adopt a comprehensive, consistent approach to vulnerability and best interests by considering both notions. Actually, the starting point would be the consideration of children involved in migration and asylum as vulnerable *per se*, and the best interests approach allows the enhancement to another level of protection through analysis of individual and situational conditions. Such an approach allows the flexibility essential to a case-by-case determination of these complex notions.

Assembly, Protection and Assistance for Separated Children Seeking Asylum, 18 April 2005, and Undocumented Migrant Children in an Irregular Situation, 7 October 2011; Committee of the Ministers, Strategy for the Rights of the Child, 3 March 2016, especially §§22 and 32; Special Representative of the Council of Europe, Migrant and Refugee Children, 10 March 2017. In the EU context, see European Commission, Communication from the Commission to the European Parliament and the Council, The Protection of Children in Migration, 12 April 2017, COM(2017)211 Final.

63 In these terms, ex multis, ECtHR, *Neulinger and Shuruk v. Switzerland*, cit., para. 138. See also Quadri, 1999; Alston and Gilmour Walsh, 1996, p. 10.

64 UNHCR, 'Guidelines on Determining the Best Interests of the Child', above n.62.

65 ECtHR, *Rahimi v. Greece*, above n. 52; *Popov v. France*, above n. 52; *Elmi and Aweys Abubakar v. Malta*, nos. 25794/13 and 28151/13, 22 November 2016, and *S.F. and Others v. Bulgaria*, no. 8138/16, 7 December 2017; IACtHR, *Yean and Bosico Children v. The Dominican Republic*, 8 September 2005, and *Pacheco Tineo Family v. Bolivia*, 25 November 2013.

HUMAN RIGHTS AND THE BEST INTERESTS OF THE CHILD IN EUROPEAN FAMILY REUNIFICATION LAW

Peter RODRIGUES

1. Introduction 55
2. Best Interests of the Child in European Migration Law 56
   2.1. Convention on the Rights of the Child 58
   2.2. Article 8 of the European Convention on Human Rights 61
   2.3. Charter of Fundamental Rights 64
3. EU Family Reunification Law 65
   3.1. Family Reunification Directive 65
   3.2. Free Movement Directive 67
   3.3. Dublin III 68
4. *Ruiz Zambrano* Jurisprudence 70
5. Conclusions 72

1. INTRODUCTION

Family unity is a strong natural concept protected in European human rights law through the right to family life under Article 8 of the European Convention of Human Rights (ECHR) and Article 7 of the EU Charter on Fundamental Rights (the Charter). Furthermore, Article 10 of the UN Convention on the Rights of the Child (CRC) provides that States must handle applications for family reunion involving children in a positive, humane, and expeditious manner. Article 9(1) further specifies that children shall not be separated from their parents against their will if separation is not in the best interests of the child. The principle of the best interests of the child is codified in Article 3(1) CRC and in Article 24(2) of the Charter. It is a guiding concept in migration cases involving children. Nevertheless, we have to face the difficulties that exist in making this concept operational in legal reasoning.[1]

---

1 M. E. KALVERBOER, D. BELTMAN, E. C. C. VAN OS and A. E. ZIJLSTRA, 'The Best Interests of the Child in Cases of Migration', *International Journal of Children's Rights* 25 (2017), 114–139.

Due to migration, family members are sometimes separated from each other by borders. The European Court of Human Rights (ECtHR) jurisprudence holds that, as a matter of well-established international law and subject to its treaty obligations, a State has the right to control the entry of non-nationals into its territory.[2] Furthermore, a conditional right to family reunification follows from EU migration law.[3] Where minors are involved, this right is even stronger because of their vulnerability and the special protection afforded to them by international and European law. The key question is as follows: in EU law, how should the interests of the State be balanced against that of family unity and the best interests of the child?

This chapter analyses various legal situations in which the host country interferes in the relationship of the minor with his or her parent(s) by denying access. The right to family reunification in these situations is then examined, and the balance between the right of States to secure their borders and the right of migrant minors to be reunited with their parents, or vice versa, are discussed. Decisions concerning non-admission of a parent or child may lead to the separation of parents and children, leading to the family's ability to exercise the right of unity of the family and the right to family reunification. Consequently, the position of unaccompanied or separated migrant minors is considered only if family reunification is an option.

Section 2 first examines the role of the best interests of the child in European migration law and analyses the relevant provisions in international (CRC) and regional human rights law (ECHR and the Charter) related to family life and children's rights. Section 3 examines EU family reunification law in relation to migrant minors and their parents. It discusses the different EU migration law regimes of the Family Reunification Directive, Free Movement Directive, and the Dublin Regulation. Section 4 examines recent developments in the so-called *Ruiz Zambrano* case law. The chapter concludes with some final observations.

2. BEST INTERESTS OF THE CHILD IN EUROPEAN MIGRATION LAW

Article 6 of the Treaty on European Union (TEU) states that the ECHR and the constitutional traditions of Member States are sources of the general principles of EU law. If necessary, the Court of Justice of the European Union (CJEU) may refer to these principles to supplement the fundamental rights protected

2 *Abdulaziz, Cabales, and Balkandali v. UK*, Nos. 9214/80; 9473/81; 9474/81, ECHR 1985, para. 67.

3 P. Boeles, M. den Heijer, G. Lodder and K. Wouters, *European Migration Law*, Intersentia, Antwerp 2014, p. 130.

in the Charter. Article 6(2) TEU states that the EU shall accede to the ECHR, and a draft EU Accession Agreement to the ECHR between Member States of the Council of Europe and the EU was finalised on April 5, 2013.[4] Asked by the Commission to deliver an opinion pursuant to Article 218(11) of the Treaty on the Functioning of the European Union (TFEU), on the draft agreement's compatibility with EU law, the CJEU identified problems and gave negative advice in its opinion of December 18, 2014.[5] Consequently, the EU is not a party to the ECHR; unlike its Member States, it is not a party to other human rights treaties such as the CRC. EU courts have generally not directly applied these treaties, but they do so indirectly using them as a source of inspiration for EU fundamental rights and general principles of EU law. International human rights law is often a source of inspiration for the CJEU in developing its case law. Fundamental rights form an integral part of the general principles of law, and the CJEU ensures its observance.[6]

The right to family life can be found in many international human rights treaties.[7] Family life may be severely affected by migration, particularly in the family reunification context. Therefore, the right to family reunification can be identified as a key element of integration policies[8] and a right that should be promoted and fulfilled within migration policies.[9] Considering the research question – concerning balancing State interests against those of family unity and the best interests of the child in EU law – analyses of relevant provisions in international and regional human rights treaties should be restricted to the CRC, ECHR, and the Charter. Before discussing these treaties, first, some remarks must be made on UNHCR guidelines (1983) on refugee families' reunification.[10] Guidelines state that circumstances in which refugees leave their country of origin frequently involve the separation of families. Such separation invariably leads to hardship and, sometimes, tragic consequences. It may also create serious obstacles to a refugee's integration into a new homeland. The principle of the unity of the family takes precedence, and the importance of integration comes second.

---

4 Fifth Negotiation Meeting Between the CDDH ad hoc Negotiation Group and the European Commission on the Accession of the European Union to the European Convention on Human Rights, Council of Europe, Strasbourg, April 5, 2013.

5 Opinion of the Court 2/13, 18 December 2014, ECLI:EU:C:2014:2454.

6 Case C-540/03, *Parliament v. Council*, ECLI:EU:C:2006:429.

7 For instance, Article 17(1) and 23(1) of the International Covenant on Civil and Political Rights (ICCPR), Article 10(1) of the International Covenant on Economic, Social and Cultural Rights (ICESCR), Article 16 of the Convention for the Elimination of All Forms of Discrimination against Women (CEDAW) and Articles 14 and 44 of the International Convention on the Protection of the Rights of All Migrant Workers and Members of their Families.

8 V. Abramovich, P. Ceriani Cernadas and A. Morlachetti, *The Rights of Children, Youth and Women in the Context of Migration*, UNICEF, Geneva, April 2011, p. 39.

9 Case C-578/08, *Chakroun v. the Netherlands*, ECLI:EU:C:2010:117, 47.

10 *UNHCR Guidelines on Reunification of Refugee Families*, July 1983.

Besides unaccompanied minors, the guidelines have no specific rules for the protection of minors.

2.1. CONVENTION ON THE RIGHTS OF THE CHILD

The CRC was adopted by the General Assembly of the UN in 1989.[11] With more than 190 signatory states, it is the world's most multilateral human rights treaty.[12] All EU Member States are party to the CRC. The Committee on the Rights of the Child monitors the implementation of the Convention and issues General Comments on the interpretation of the Convention's content. Committee documents are considered to be of high authority but are not legally binding.

The definition of the child under the CRC provides rights and protection until the age of 18 years (Article 1 CRC). This age limitation will be followed in this chapter. In its preamble, the CRC points to the position of children within the family unit and states that the family unit is the natural environment for the growth and well-being of all its members, particularly children. According to the preamble, children should grow up in a family environment for the full and harmonious development of their personalities. The general human right to respect for family life is laid down in Article 16 CRC, but the Convention provides more specific rights relating to family unity. Under Article 7(1), children have the right to know and be cared for by their parents, while Article 8(1) states that children have the right to preserve their family relations as recognised by law, without unlawful interference. Under Article 9(1), meanwhile, children have the right not to be separated from their parents against their will, except when such separation is necessary and in their best interests. Regarding best interests, Article 3(1) CRC is the Convention's leading principle and reads as follows:

> In all actions concerning children, whether undertaken by public or private social welfare institutions, courts of law, administrative authorities or legislative bodies, the best interests of the child shall be a primary consideration.

The main questions concerning the best interests of the child in family reunification law have regard to determining what is in the best interests of the child and the importance to be given to this concept. In General Recommendation 14 of the Committee on the Rights of the Child, the Committee promulgates a rights-based approach; the best interests concept should be understood as an umbrella provision for the rights of the child laid down in the Convention.[13] According to this General Comment, the best

[11] Adopted on November 20, 1989, and entered into force on September 2, 1990.

[12] To date only the USA has not ratified the CRC.

[13] General Comment No. 14 (2013) on the right of the child to have his or her best interests taken as a primary consideration (art. 3, para 1), 2013, UN Doc. CRC/C/GC/14.

interests concept can have three distinct functions: (1) to be an interpretative device for other substantive rights; (2) to serve as a bridge between two rights; and (3) to serve as a mediator when there is a conflict of rights.[14] Traditionally, States hold the sovereign right to control the entry and residence of foreign nationals in their territory. In recent decades, this State competence has somewhat declined with the proliferation of human rights and the increasing implications of EU law for domestic immigration law.[15] However, according to the ECtHR, the best interests of the child cannot be a 'trump card' that requires the admission of all children who would be better off living in a contracting State.[16]

Article 10 exclusively deals with family reunification. Article 10(1) provides that States shall handle applications for family unification by a child or parents in a positive, humane, and expeditious manner. Article 10(2) provides that a child whose parents reside in different States has the right to maintain personal relations and direct contact with both parents on a regular basis. Notably, the wording of Article 10 is weaker than that of Article 9, as the latter prescribes that children shall not be separated from their parents. Klaassen concludes that the CRC does not propose an explicit right to family reunification.[17] It merely states that applications to that end should be handled in a positive, humane, and expeditious manner. In the Concluding Observations concerning country reports, the Committee has made some critical remarks on Article 10's implementation. The age limit of 18 years for minors to be eligible for family reunification of minors was deemed incompatible with the Convention,[18] and lengthy procedures for family reunification were deemed incompatible with Article 10.[19] In the General Comment on unaccompanied children, the Committee underlines the importance of the right to family reunification by considering the following:[20]

> Whenever family reunification in the country of origin is not possible, irrespective of whether this is due to legal obstacles to return or whether the best-interests-based

14 General Comment No. 14, above n. 13, para 6.

15 M. A. K. Klaassen and P. R. Rodrigues, 'The Best Interests of the Child in EU Family Reunification Law: A Plea for More Guidance on the Role of Article 24(2) Charter', *European Journal of Migration and Law* 19 (2017), 198 (191–218).

16 *El Ghatet v. Switzerland*, No. 56971/10, ECHR 2-16, para. 46.

17 M. A. K. Klaassen, *The Right to Family Unification: Between Migration Control and Human Rights*, Leiden Law School, Leiden 2015, p. 33.

18 UN Committee on the Rights of the Child, Concluding Observations, Denmark (23 November 2005) (UN Doc CRC/C/DNK/CO/3 2005), paras. 30–31.

19 UN Committee on the Rights of the Child, Concluding Observations, Austria (March 31, 2005) (UN Doc CRC/C/15/Add251 2005), paras. 35–36. See also: Protection of children in migration, European Council 3 May 2018, no. 13.

20 General Comment No. 6 (2005), Treatment of Unaccompanied and Separated Children Outside their Country of Origin, 2005, UN Doc. CRC/GC/2005/6, para. 83.

balancing test has decided against return, the obligations under Article 9 and 10 of the Convention come into effect and should govern the host country's decisions on family reunification therein.

Furthermore, the International Convention on the Protection of the Rights of All Migrant Workers and Members of Their Families and the CRC contain legally binding obligations that relate both in general and specifically to the protection of human rights of children and migrants. Both Conventions contain several provisions that establish specific obligations related to the rights of children in the context of international migration in the countries of origin, transit, destination, and return. The Committees of the Conventions published a joint General Comment No. 4 (2017) on the human rights of children in the context of international migration in countries of origin, transit, destination, and return.[21] In this joint General Comment, the aforementioned consideration of General Comment No. 6 is repeated, and it adds that countries should facilitate family reunification procedures to reunify children with their parents and/or regularise their status.[22]

According to General Comment No. 4, children who remain in their countries of origin receive special attention because they may migrate irregularly and unsafely, seeking to be reunited with their parents and siblings in destination countries. States should develop effective and accessible family reunification procedures that allow children to migrate in a regular manner, including children remaining in countries of origin who may migrate irregularly. Family reunification in the country of origin should not be pursued where there is a 'reasonable risk' that return would lead to the violation of the human rights of the child, also known as the principle of *non-refoulement*.[23] The standard of Article 3 ECHR requires a 'real risk' of inhuman treatment upon return, and both Committees advise lowering this requirement for minor migrants. As mentioned previously, General Comments are of high authority but not binding on the contracting states.

---

21 Joint General Comment No. 4 (2017) of the Committee on the Protection of the Rights of All Migrant Workers and Members of Their Families, and No. 23 (2017) of the Committee on the Rights of the Child on State obligations regarding the human rights of children in the context of international migration in countries of origin, transit, destination and return, 2017, CMW/C/GC/4-CRC/C/GC/23. At the same time another joint general recommendation was published, No. 22 (2017 of the CRC Committee.

22 Joint General Comment No. 4 (2017), above n. 21, para. 35.

23 K. Wouters, *International Legal Standards for the Protection from Refoulement*, Intersentia Publishers, Antwerp 2009.

2.2. ARTICLE 8 OF THE EUROPEAN CONVENTION ON HUMAN RIGHTS

Article 8 ECHR is the European cornerstone of family rights. It grants everyone the right to respect for private and family life. The essential objective of Article 8 is to protect the individual against arbitrary interference by public authorities.[24] The text of Article 8 reads as follows:

> 1. Everyone has the right to respect for his private and family life, his home and his correspondence.
> 2. There shall be no interference by a public authority with the exercise of this right except such as is in accordance with the law and is necessary in a democratic society in the interests of national security, public safety or the economic well-being of the country, for the prevention of disorder or crime, for the protection of health or morals, or for the protection of the rights and freedoms of others.

The ECtHR interpretation of the concept of family life is broad, and numerous factors may be relevant, including whether a couple lives together, the length of their relationship, and whether they have demonstrated their commitment to each other by having children together or by any other means.[25]

Without analysing this interpretation further, Strasbourg jurisprudence leads to the conclusion that determining whether family life exists requires considering biological, legal, and social facts.

Regarding the parent-child relationship, standing jurisprudence holds that irrespective of whether the child is born in or outside marriage, family life exists between a mother and her child from the moment of the child's birth.[26] The situation for the father is more complicated since mere biological paternity is not in itself sufficient to constitute the existence of family life.[27] Further legal or factual elements must demonstrate whether the relationship between the biological father and the child has sufficient constancy and substance to create family ties.[28]

---

24 *Belgian Linguistics Case*, Nos. 1474/62; 1677/62; 1691/62; 1769/63; 1994/63; 2126/64, ECHR 1968, para. 7.

25 *Al Nashif v. Bulgaria*, No. 509963/99, ECHR 2002, para. 112.

26 *Marckx v. Belgium*, No. 6833/74, ECHR 1979, para. 31.

27 N. Ismaili, *Who Cares for the Child? Regulating Custody and Access in Family and Migration Law in the Netherlands, the European Union and the Council of Europe*, forthcoming, VU Migration Law Series 18, Amsterdam, para. 2.1.2.

28 *L. v. the Netherlands*, No. 45582/99, ECHR 2004, para. 37.

In the event of expulsion, the question is whether State interference in family life, which is a negative obligation, is legitimate and in accordance with Article 8(2) ECHR. States must consider admission cases as part of their positive obligation and should judge them by the fair balance test. A balance needs to be struck between the competing interests of the individual and the community as a whole. It took a long time before the ECtHR recognised the best interests of the child as a major consideration in an entry case. In the case *Rodrigues da Silva*, the ECtHR stated that the mother should have the right to entry because of the best interests of her young daughter and the emotional damage that the mother's departure would cause her child.[29] In the case's particular circumstances, the country's economic well-being does not outweigh the applicants' rights under Article 8. However, the Court made no explicit reference to Article 3(1) CRC. In the *Nunez* case, the ECtHR referred to this for the first time in relation to an Article 8 ECHR expulsion procedure.[30] According to the Court, the deportation of the applicant was legitimate because of her identity fraud and criminal convictions. Nevertheless, the Court found that the rights of the child under Article 8 ECHR must be read in conjunction with Article 3 CRC and concluded that it was not in the interest of the young children to be separated from their mother:[31]

> (...) the Court is not convinced in the concrete and exceptional circumstances of the case that sufficient weight was attached to the best interests of the children for the purposes of Article 8 of the Convention. Reference is made in this context also to Article 3 of the UN CRC, according to which the best interests of the child shall be a primary consideration in all actions taken by public authorities concerning children.[32]

Since *Nunez*, the ECtHR has dealt with the best interests of the child in numerous cases but has never concluded that Article 8 ECHR had been violated.[33] The Grand Chamber case *Jeunesse* changed that.[34] The Court examined whether any exceptional circumstances warranted finding that the Netherlands authorities had failed to strike a fair balance in denying the applicant residence in the Netherlands. The ECtHR considered four factors: one of these was the best interests concept:[35]

> The Court observes that the best interests of the applicant's children must be taken into account in this balancing exercise (see above §109). On this particular point,

---

29 *Rodrigues da Silva and Hoogkamer v. the Netherlands*, No. 50435/99, ECHR 2006, para. 44.
30 *Nunez v. Norway*, No. 55597/09, ECHR 2011.
31 Ibid., para 84.
32 Ibid.
33 M. A. K. Klaassen, above n. 17, para. 3.3.7.
34 *Jeunesse v. the Netherlands*, No. 12738/10, ECHR 2014.
35 Ibid., para. 118.

> the Court reiterates that there is a broad consensus, including in international law, in support of the idea that in all decisions concerning children, their best interests are of paramount importance (see Neulinger and Shuruk v. Switzerland, cited above, §135, and X v. Latvia, cited above, §96). Whilst alone they cannot be decisive, such interests certainly must be afforded significant weight. For that purpose, in cases concerning family reunification, the Court pays particular attention to the circumstances of the minor children concerned, especially their age, their situation in the country or countries concerned and the extent to which they are dependent on their parents (see Tuquabo-Tekle and Others v. the Netherlands, cited above, §44).

The way the Court fills in the best interests concept in family reunification cases is important. Children's best interests are of paramount importance, and although alone they cannot be decisive, such interests certainly must be afforded significant weight. The Court particularly focuses on the circumstances of the children concerned, especially their ages, their situation in the country or countries concerned, and the extent to which they depend on their parents. In the cases discussed in this paragraph, there were always two parents, and denying entry or deportation would separate the mother from her child. In the *El Ghatet* case, family reunification with a son was refused by the Swiss immigration service because, after acquiring a legal residency in Switzerland, the son had voluntarily returned to Egypt and lived there for years:[36]

> For that purpose, in cases regarding family reunification the Court pays particular attention to the circumstances of the minor children concerned, especially their age, their situation in their country of origin and the extent to which they are dependent on their parents (see Tuquabo-Tekle and Others, cited above, §44). While the best interests of the child cannot be a "trump card" which requires the admission of all children who would be better off living in a Contracting State (I.A.A. and Others v. the United Kingdom, cited above, §46; see also Berisha, cited above, §§60–61), the domestic courts must place the best interests of the child at the heart of their considerations and attach crucial weight to it (see, mutatis mutandis, Mandet v. France, no. 30955/12, §§56–57, 14 January 2016).

The ECtHR repeated the relevant circumstances that should be considered and that the principle of best interests is not a 'carte blanche' for a residence permit. The reference to the child's best interests not being a trump card is relatively new and underlines the need to balance the State's interests in immigration control and the individual interests of the child concerned. The instruction to domestic courts that they must place the best interests of the child at the heart of their considerations and attach crucial weight to it is important. Bhabha notes that the ECtHR has difficulty in maintaining a consistent approach regarding the

---

[36] *El Ghatet v. Switzerland*, above n. 16, para. 46.

prerogative of sovereign States to exercise border control and a human being's right to respect for family life.[37]

2.3. CHARTER OF FUNDAMENTAL RIGHTS

In Article 3 TEU, the protection of the rights of the child is formulated as a task for the EU and Member States. This becomes more concrete in Article 24(2) of the Charter:

> In all actions relating to children, whether taken by public authorities or private institutions, the child's best interests must be a primary consideration.

This Article is based on Article 3 CRC, but its text is more succinct. The Explanation to the Charter states that Article 24 is based on the CRC, particularly Articles 3 (best interests), 9 (unity of the family), 12 (own view), and 13 (freedom of expression).[38] Similar to Article 3 CRC, Article 24 of the Charter should be read in conjunction with other Charter rights. The codification of the best interests concept in the Charter marks a shift from seeing children as objects of EU law to seeing them as independent rights holders within the EU.[39] This change is also reflected in European migration law and most recent Directives; the Preamble or specific Articles refer to the best interests of the child.[40]

Article 24 of the Charter highlights two additional children's rights. Paragraph 1 states that children have the right to the protection and care necessary for their well-being and the right to have their views considered. Article 24(3) establishes that every child has the right to maintain a personal relationship and direct contact with his/her parents on a regular basis. Usually, bodies that handle human rights treaties consider that Member States should have a certain margin of appreciation on how to implement these rights in their local situation and domestic law. The same applies to Article 24. In the joined family reunification cases of third-country nationals *O., S., and L.*, the CJEU stated that neither Article 7 (private life) nor Article 24 deprives the Member State of their margin of appreciation in applying the law.[41] The CJEU also cited

---

37 J. Bhabha, *Child Migration & Human Rights in a Global Age*, Princeton University Press, Princeton and Oxford 2014, pp. 48–49.

38 Explanations relating to the Charter of Fundamental Rights, *OJ* 2007/C 303/25.

39 S. Peers, T. Hervey, J. Kenner and A. Ward (eds.) *The EU Charter of Fundamental Rights: A Commentary*, Hart, Oxford and Portland 2014, p. 687.

40 See among others: Preamble 18 of the Qualification Directive 2011/95, Preamble 33 of the Procedures Directive 2013/32, Article 23 of the Reception Directive 2013/33, Preamble 16 of Dublin III 604/2013, Preamble 22 of the Return Directive 2008/115 and Article 5(5) of the Family Reunification Directive 2003/86.

41 S. Peers et al., above n. 39, p. 680; case C-356/11, *O and S*, ECLI:EU:C:2012:776 and case C-357/11, *Maahanmuuttovirasto*, ECLI:EU:C:2012:776.

Article 24 of the Charter in several other family reunification cases, some of which are discussed below.

With the commencement of the Lisbon Treaty on December 1, 2009, the Charter of Fundamental Rights of the EU acquired the status of primary EU law. However, the scope of the Charter is limited. Article 51(1) of the Charter states that the Charter's provisions are addressed to institutions, bodies, offices, and agencies of the EU and to Member States when they are implementing the EU law. In *Åkerberg Fransson*, the CJEU clarified that Article 51(1) of the Charter is applicable in all situations in which national legislation falls within the scope of EU law.[42] To determine whether a national measure falls within the scope of EU law, what must be assessed is whether a direct link exists between the impugned national measure and an EU obligation.[43] Article 51(2) of the Charter states that none of its provisions extend the application of EU law or has the ability to establish new powers or tasks for it. Most Charter provisions correspond to provisions in the ECHR, and insofar as this is the case, must be interpreted in line with the corresponding provision and ECtHR case law.[44] Nevertheless, Article 52(3) shall not prevent Union law providing more extensive protection.

3. EU FAMILY REUNIFICATION LAW

The child's position in EU family reunification law is now discussed by analysing the following legal instruments: the Family Reunification Directive, the Free Movement Directive, and the Dublin III Regulation.

3.1. FAMILY REUNIFICATION DIRECTIVE

Directive 2003/86/EC on the right to family reunification grants a clearly defined subjective right to family reunification to third-country applicants who comply with the conditions defined in the Directive.[45] In *Chakroun*, the CJEU found that authorisation of the Directive is the general rule and that Member States have a certain margin of appreciation as long as they do not undermine the Directive's objective to promote family reunification and the effectiveness thereof.[46]

The Directive's objective is to promote family reunification because the integration of families will contribute to their economic activities. According to

42 Case C-617/10, *Åkerberg Fransson*, ECLI:EU:C:2013:105, 18.

43 Ibid., paras. 28–29.

44 Article 52(3) of the Charter.

45 Council Directive 2003/86/EC of September 22, 2003 on the right to family reunification, *OJ* L 251, 3.10.2003, p. 12.

46 Case C-578/08 *Chakroun*, above n. 9, 43.

the Court, States must adopt family reunification measures in conformity with the obligation to protect the family and respect family life. More specifically, the Directive contains a provision to protect minors. Article 5(5) prescribes that when examining an application, Member States shall have due regard to the best interests of minor children. Nevertheless, Court decisions that refer to best interests are rare. The case of *O., S., & L.* concerns the family reunification of the partner of a third-country national lawfully residing in Finland; however, the sponsor did not comply with the income requirement.[47] Although Article 7(1)(c) of the Family Reunification Directive allows these requirements, the Court emphasises that Member States may not apply the implementation of an EU law instrument in such a way that it disregards fundamental rights such as the right to respect for family life (Article 7 of the Charter) and the best interests of the child (Article 24(2) of the Charter). In general, the CJEU approach is that even when the Directive allows requirements, the administration or domestic courts should always consider the case's particular circumstances and must be aware of the child's best interests. The guidelines of the European Commission (EC) take a similar approach. In 2014, the EC published a communication containing guidance on the interpretation of the Family Reunification Directive.[48]

With regard to the family reunification of parents of an unaccompanied minor who has received international protection, the CJEU recently addressed the question of the relevant moment at which the unaccompanied minor must be deemed a minor to be eligible for family reunion. The Dutch Council of State held that unaccompanied children left behind in the country of origin are eligible for family reunification with their parents if they were minors when the application for family reunification was lodged. According to the Council of State, events occurring after the applicant applied for asylum must be considered in establishing whether a right to family reunification exists. A district court disagreed and referred preliminary questions to the CJEU. The CJEU decided that the date on which it must be determined whether a right of family reunification exists is purely a matter of EU law and not at the discretion of the Member States:[49]

> In those circumstances, while Directive 2003/86 does not explicitly determine the moment until which a refugee must be a minor in order to be able to benefit from the right to family reunification referred to in Article 10(3)(a), it follows however from the objective of that provision, the fact that it confers no discretion on

[47] Cases C-356/11 and C-357/11, *O., S. & L*, ECLI:EU:C:2012:776.

[48] COM(2014)210 final communication from the Commission to the European Parliament and the Council on guidance for application of Directive 2003/86/EC on the right to family reunification.

[49] Case C-550/16, *A. v. the Netherlands*, ECLI:EU:C:2018:248.

Member States and the lack of a reference to the national law in that regard, that the determination of that moment cannot be left to each Member State to assess.[50]

The Court establishes that the right to family reunification of unaccompanied children does not depend on the moment at which Member States decide to recognise the applicant as a refugee.[51] According to the Court, doing so would question the relevant provision's effectiveness. It would go against that Directive's aim – to promote family reunification and grant in that regard a specific protection to refugees, particularly unaccompanied minors – and the principles of equal treatment and legal certainty. Reference is made to Article 24(2) of the Charter and Article 5(5) of the Family Reunification Directive, prescribing that the principle of the best interests of the child is a primary consideration for Member States in the Directive's application. The Court establishes that the relevant moment to decide whether an unaccompanied asylum-seeking child is eligible for family reunification is the moment at which the child applies for international protection. The Family Reunification Directive not only promotes family reunification but also protects the rights of the child. Long-term separation from families has an immensely negative impact on refugees and on minors. However, the CJEU is more an economic rights court than a human rights court, and a consistent child right-based approach is still missing.[52]

3.2. FREE MOVEMENT DIRECTIVE

The free movement of persons is one of the four fundamental freedoms under EU law, and its legal basis is the Treaty. Article 21 TFEU outlines that every EU citizen has the right to move freely and reside within EU territory. The Free Movement Directive 2004/38/EC defines the right of free movement for citizens of the European Economic Area (EEA), which includes Member States of the EU and the three European Free Trade Association (EFTA) members, Iceland, Norway and Liechtenstein.[53] Third-country national family members are also covered by the right to free movement, but only as dependants of EEA citizens. Family reunification is possible without further requirements based on this

---

50 Ibid., 45.

51 See also M. A. K. Klaassen, 'Unaccompanied Children Becoming Young Adults and the Right to Family Reunion', *Leiden Law Blog*, April 23, 2018.

52 See also H. Stalford, *Children and the European Union*, Hart Publishing, Oxford and Portland, Oregon 2012, p. 72.

53 Council Directive 2004/38/EC of April 29, 2004 on the right of citizens of the Union and their family members to move and reside freely within the territory of the Member States amending Regulation (EEC) No 1612/68 and repealing Directives 64/221/EEC, 68/360/EEC, 72/194/EEC, 73/148/EEC, 75/34/EEC, 75/35/EEC, 90/364/EEC, 90/365/EEC and 93/96/EEC, *OJ* L 158 30.4.2004, p. 77.

Directive when an EU citizen has excercised his or her free movement rights if the EU citizen qualifies for residence longer than three months. Several cases concern the free movement of persons in which children were involved; in most of these cases, the Citizenship Directive was not applicable.[54] The CJEU directly based the right of residence of the parents of the children on a Treaty provision.

One notable case is that of *Yoshikazu Iida v. Stadt Ulm* (Germany).[55] Mr. Iida is a Japanese national married to a German national. Their daughter was born in America and has German, Japanese and American nationalities. The family moved to Germany from the USA, whereupon Mr. Iida obtained a residence permit as the spouse of a Union citizen. Unfortunately, the relationship soured and his wife moved to Austria with their daughter. Both spouses jointly hold and exercise parental responsibility for their daughter, even though the mother and daughter have been habitually resident in Vienna since March 2008, where the daughter attends school. After their separation, Germany revoked Mr. Iida's spousal residence permit, and he applied for a residence card as a family member of a Union citizen. The CJEU states that outside situations governed by Directive 2004/38/EC, in which no other connection exists to EU law's provisions on citizenship, a third-country national cannot claim a right of residence derived from a Union citizen.[56] With regard to fundamental rights, particularly the right to respect for private and family life and the rights of the child (Articles 7 and 24(2) of the Charter), according to the Court, it must be borne in mind that according to Article 51(1) of the Charter, its provisions are addressed to Member States only when they are implementing EU law. Accordingly, the Court is called on to interpret, in light of the Charter, EU law within the limits of the powers conferred on it. It would be in the best interests of his daughter that Mr. Iida has a residence card as a family member of a Union citizen; however, in the CJEU's reasoning, there was no connection with EU law. Hence, Article 24(2) of the Charter is not at stake.[57]

3.3. DUBLIN III

One of the most debated EU legal instruments is the Dublin Regulation.[58] The Dublin III Regulation prescribes that the Member State in which family

---

54 An analysis of this jurisprudence can be found in M. A. K. Klaassen & P. R. Rodrigues, above n. 15, pp. 204–206.

55 Case C-40/11, *Yoshikazu Iida v. Stadt Ulm*, ECLI:EU:C:2012:691.

56 Ibid.

57 See also paragraph 4 on the *Ruiz Zambrano* jurisprudence.

58 J. Mitchell, 'The Dublin Regulation and Systemic Flaws', (2017) *San Diego International Law Journal*, Vol. 18 Issue 2; M. Mouzorakis, 'We Need to Talk about Dublin: Responsibility under the Dublin System as a Blockage to Asylum Burden-Sharing in the European Union', *Refugee Studies Centre*, Oxford 2014.

members have obtained or applied for international protection is responsible for handling asylum procedures of other family members.[59] During times of high migrant influx into the EU, Member States at EU borders, for instance, Greece, Malta, Italy and Spain, have had to handle (too) many asylum applications. The EC published the evaluation of Dublin III on March 18, 2016.[60] Of the 84,000 requests for transfers in 2014, only 4,500 actually occurred. This amounts to little more than 5 per cent of all requests. Consequently, there are serious doubts whether border Member States still register all migrants who have entered the EU. The presence of family members is the highest in the hierarchy of criteria for determining which Member State is responsible for examining an application for international protection. Member States have the obligation to examine each application for international protection.[61] According to Recital 15,

> The processing together of the applications for international protection of the members of one family by a single Member State makes it possible to ensure that the applications are examined thoroughly, the decisions taken in respect of them are consistent and the members of one family are not separated.

Areas of concern include enforcing transfers of asylum seekers,[62] separation of families[63] and protection of children,[64] the lack of available effective remedies to appeal against transfers,[65] and limited use of discretionary provisions within Dublin III to prevent these problems.[66] Nevertheless, Article 6(1) of Dublin III states that the best interests of the child shall be a primary consideration for Member States with respect to *all* procedures provided for in this Regulation. This concern is demonstrated by the case of *M.A. and others v. UK*.[67] This case's preliminary question concerned an unaccompanied minor with no member of his family legally present in a Member State's territory, who has lodged asylum applications in more than one Member State. Which State is responsible for his asylum application? Is it the State where the minor lodged his first application

---

59 Regulation (EU) No 604/2013 of the European Parliament and of the Council of 26 June 2013 establishing the criteria and mechanisms for determining the Member State responsible for examining an application for international protection lodged in one of the Member States by a third-country national or a stateless person (recast), *OJ* L 180/31.

60 Evaluation of the Implementation of Dublin III Regulation, March 18, 2016.

61 Article 3(1) Dublin III Regulation.

62 T. Poli, 'Immigration Detention and the Rule of Law: The ECJ's First Ruling on Detaining Asylum-Seekers in the Dublin System', *EU Law Analysis*, 5 May 2017.

63 *Tarakhel v. Switzerland*, No. 29217/12, ECHR 2014.

64 S. Peers, 'The Dublin Regulation: Is the End Nigh? Where Should Unaccompanied Children Apply for Asylum?', *EU Law Analysis*, 21 January 2016.

65 See *M.S.S. v. Belgium and Greece*, No. 30696/09, ECHR 2011.

66 *Realising the Right to Family Reunification of Refugees in Europe*, Council of Europe, Strasbourg 2017.

67 Case C-648/11, *M.A. & Others v. UK*, ECLI:EU:C:2013:367.

or that in which the minor is present after having lodged his most recent asylum application? According to the CJEU, unaccompanied minors form a category of particularly vulnerable persons; therefore, it is important not to prolong the procedure for determining the Member State responsible more than is strictly necessary. This entails that unaccompanied minors should not be transferred to another Member State. The Court based its judgment on Article 24(2) of the Charter. The family reunification criteria in Dublin III can be applied only when a Member State makes a 'take charge request' to another Member State. Without such a request, an individual asylum applicant does not have the right to initiate proceedings under Dublin III. This creates a void in protection since an individual minor may be eligible for transfer under the Dublin III Regulation but does not have the ability to enforce it.[68]

4. *RUIZ ZAMBRANO* JURISPRUDENCE

Since the *Ruiz Zambrano* case in 2011, EU citizenship has also effectively been a source of family reunification law. Based on Article 20 TFEU, the CJEU states in this landmark case that an EU citizen may not be forced to leave EU territory.[69] The case concerns the right of residence in Belgium of a Colombian family, the parents having unsuccessfully applied for asylum. One child was born in Columbia and two others in Belgium. At that time, Belgian law provided Belgian nationality to children who would become stateless if they were not granted Belgian nationality; thus, the two younger children obtained Belgian nationality. The CJEU decided that the refusal of the right to reside in Belgium for EU citizen minors' parents would deprive the children of the enjoyment of rights attached to their EU citizenship. Interestingly, no reference was made to children's rights. In subsequent case law, the Court specifies its judgment's meaning. Regarding the right to respect for private and family life, the CJEU notes that the meaning and scope of Article 7 of the Charter are the same as those laid down in Article 8 ECHR; however, the Charter addresses Member States only when they are implementing EU law.[70] The CJEU leaves to the referring court's determination the questions of whether the situation falls within the scope of EU law and whether the applicants' family members were deprived of genuine enjoyment of the rights' substance. In the case of *Rendón Marín*, the Court explicitly refers to Article 24(2) of the Charter.[71] The case concerns a Colombian father who lives in Spain, where he has been granted sole care and custody of his two minor

[68] For a UK case, see M. A. K. Klaassen and P. R. Rodrigues, above n. 15, p. 215.

[69] Case C-34/09, *Ruiz Zambrano*, ECLI:EU:C:2011:124.

[70] Case C-256/11, *Dereci*, ECLI:EU:C:2011:734.

[71] Case C-165/14, *Rendón Marín*, ECLI:EU:C:2016:675, para. 66.

children with Union citizenship. Mr. Rendón Marín applies for a residence permit based on family circumstances, but this request is refused because of his criminal record. According to the CJEU, national legislation which, on the sole ground that the third-country national has a criminal record, automatically refuses a residence permit to a third-country national who is the parent and sole carer of one or more minor Union citizens, violates Article 21 TFEU and the Free Movement Directive.

In 2017, the CJEU delivered its much-anticipated ruling in *Chavez-Vilchez*,[72] which is a follow-up to the *Ruiz Zambrano* case. The *Chavez-Vilchez* case considers eight different families, and the preliminary question is whether the third-country national mother of a minor child with EU citizenship must be allowed to remain in the EU if denial of the parent's residence would force the child to leave the EU territory with this parent. Leaving the EU territory would prevent the child from exercising rights as an EU citizen. All eight families comprised one or more children with EU citizenship, one third-country national mother and an EU citizen father who did not take real parental responsibility for his child. Because applications for the mothers' residence permits were rejected, Dutch authorities refused to grant social assistance and child benefit to the mothers. The mothers claim that their EU citizen children would be forced to leave the EU territory even though they have a father who is a Dutch citizen.

According to the Court, when considering whether a child would be forced to leave the EU territory if a derived right of residence were denied to a third-country national parent, it should be determined whether that parent is the child's actual caregiver and to what extent the child depends on that parent. The Court finds it important to determine which parent is the child's primary caretaker and whether the child factually depends on the third-country national parent.[73] According to the Court, Member State authorities must consider the right to respect for family life (Article 7 of the Charter) in conjunction with the best interests of the child (Article 24(2) of the Charter).[74]

> In this case, in order to assess the risk that a particular child, who is a Union citizen, might be compelled to leave the territory of the European Union and thereby be deprived of the genuine enjoyment of the substance of the rights conferred on him by Article 20 TFEU if the child's third-country national parent were to be refused a right of residence in the Member State concerned, it is important to determine, in each case at issue in the main proceedings, which parent is the primary carer of the child and whether there is in fact a relationship of dependency between the child and the third-country national parent. As part of that assessment, the competent authorities must take account of the right to respect for family life, as stated in Article 7 of the

72 Case C-133/15, Chavez Vilchez, ECLI:EU:C:2017:354.
73 Ibid., para. 70.
74 Ibid.

> Charter of Fundamental Rights of the European Union, that article requiring to be read in conjunction with the obligation to take into consideration the best interests of the child, recognised in Article 24(2) of that charter.

Consequently, establishing that the child could live with the EU citizen parent is not sufficient. It is indeed a relevant factor but should be considered in combination with other individual factors. Other factors the Court mentions are the child's age, his/her physical and emotional development, the strength of the affective bond between the child and both parents and the risks to the child's development and well-being if separated from the third-country national parent. The CJEU also states that national authorities must discover where the Union citizen parent lives and whether that parent is actually able and willing to assume sole responsibility for the child's daily care. These determination criteria and investigation conditions are new and make *Chaves-Vilchez* a landmark case because the Court has included fundamental rights and children's rights in determining whether a right of residence for a third-country national parent can be derived from a child's EU citizenship.[75]

5. CONCLUSIONS

In *El Ghatet v. Switzerland*,[76] the ECtHR held that 'there is a broad consensus, including in international law, in support of the idea that in all decisions concerning children, their best interests must be paramount' and referred to the landmark case of *Neulinger and Shuruk v. Switzerland*.[77] In other cases, the ECtHR even directly referred to the best interests principle of Article 3 CRC.[78] It can be concluded that interaction exists between legal systems and that the ECtHR has referred to both the CRC and to European family reunification law.[79] Furthermore, standing ECtHR case law holds that the right to family life does not entail a right to family reunification: States are still entitled to control aliens' entry into their territory.[80] However, the importance of children's rights has been emphasised, and the Court states that these interests cannot act as a 'trump card' allowing the admission of all children who would be better off living in a Member State.[81] Even the ECtHR admits that in cases concerning

75 M. A. K. Klaassen, *The Right of Residence for Non-EU Parents of EU Citizen Children: The Chavez-Vilchez Case*, Leiden Law Blog, May 12, 2017.

76 *El Ghatet*, above n. 16, para. 46.

77 *Neulinger and Shuruk v. Switzerland* No. 41615/07, ECHR 2010, para. 135.

78 *Maslov v. Austria*, No. 1638/0323, ECHR 2008, para. 82; *X and others v. Austria*, No. 19010/07, ECHR 2013, para. 49.

79 *Senigo Longue and others v. France*, No. 19113/09, ECHR 2014, para. 69.

80 *Abdulaziz, Cabales & Balkandali*, above n. 2, para. 67.

81 *I.A.A. and others v. UK*, No. 25960/13 ECHR 2016, para. 46.

children, strong immigration policy considerations could, in principle, militate in favour of associating children with their parents' conduct. Failing that, there would be a great risk that parents would exploit their children's situation to secure a residence permit for themselves and for the children.[82] Whether parents actually exploit their children's situation and can thus be blamed for abusing rights is a question that remains unanswered. One of the objections against this reasoning is Article 2(2) CRC that prohibits unfavourable treatment of children because of their parents' behaviour or acts.[83]

Examination of EU family reunification law demonstrates that in CJEU jurisprudence, the best interests of the child is a concept rarely used. To date, the Court's case law contains few examples, but the fact that best interests are determinative in cases involving minors is not a standing practice. The best interests of the child should be a primary consideration in all family reunification decisions, and requests for family reunification must be dealt with in a positive, humane and expeditious manner. Nonetheless, over the last decade, Article 3 CRC and Article 24(2) of the Charter have increasingly influenced policy papers, legal instruments and case law. The EU citizenship jurisprudence of *Ruiz Zambrano* demonstrates an implicit assessment of best interests, made explicit in *Chavez-Vilchez*. Considering Member States' fear that parents will abuse the law, new preventive legal measures are likely to be introduced. The only way to tackle these back and forth movements is to develop a substantive best interests test and weigh its outcome against the interests of the host state's migration control. The right to family reunification of minors is certainly a human right but is not unconditional.

---

82 *Butt*, No. 47017/09,ECHR 2012, para. 79.

83 P. R. Rodrigues, 'Misbruik van migratierecht', *Graag nog even bespreken*, Liber amicorum Henk Lubberdink, Drukkerij Van der Linden, Leiden 2016, pp. 273–280.

RAINBOW FAMILIES AND EU FREE MOVEMENT LAW

Alina Tryfonidou

1. Introduction 75
2. Legal Recognition of Rainbow Families in EU Member States: The Current Situation 76
3. Family Reunification Rights under EU Law: The Position of Children 78
4. The Current (Uncertain) Position of Rainbow Families under EU Law 82
5. Is the Non-Recognition of the Parent-Child Relationship a Breach of EU Law? 84
   5.1. Does the EU have the Competence to Act? 86
   5.2. Is there a Breach of the EU Free Movement Provisions? 87
   5.3. Is there a Breach of EU Fundamental Human Rights Protection? . . . 89
      5.3.1. Breach of the Right to Private and Family Life 90
      5.3.2. Breach of the Prohibition of Discrimination on the Ground of Sexual Orientation 93
6. Conclusion 95

1. INTRODUCTION

This chapter examines the position of the children of rainbow families (i.e. families comprising a same-sex couple and their children) in cases where such families move between European Union (EU) Member States and include at least one EU citizen. Currently, a division exists in the EU between Member States that provide legal recognition to same-sex couples and to the parental linkage between such couples and their children and Member States that provide only limited or no legal recognition. When same-sex couples move with their children from a Member State where they are fully legally recognised as a family to a Member State that refuses to afford full (or any) recognition, this is problematic from several perspectives. The free movement and fundamental (human) rights that both children and their parents enjoy under EU law are clearly affected when recognition is refused. This chapter explores whether

EU law can assist the children of rainbow families when they seek legal recognition in a host Member State as children of both their parents under EU law.[1]

2. LEGAL RECOGNITION OF RAINBOW FAMILIES IN EU MEMBER STATES: THE CURRENT SITUATION

The 'nuclear family', comprising different-sex married spouses and their legitimate and biologically linked children, was never the only form of family that existed. However, until recently it has been the main form of family recognised under the law. Nonetheless, 'the family' is a flexible and adaptable unit. Recent years have seen an increase in 'alternative families', with many families now comprising (unmarried) cohabitants, children and their step-parents, children and their single parents, and children and their same-sex parents. Therefore, the law must not only recognise such alternative families, but also provide a system that is sensitive and responsive to their specific needs.[2]

Same-sex couples are incapable of having children who will be biologically related to both members. Such couples can, however, become *de facto* parents in several ways, such as through donor insemination (known or anonymous), assisted conception, surrogacy, a prior opposite-sex relationship, or adoption. This means that in some situations, one of the members of the couple will be biologically connected to the child (e.g. when one of the female partners in a same-sex couple undergoes medically assisted insemination using her own egg or when the sperm of one of the male partners in a same-sex couple is used in a surrogacy arrangement). In other situations (mainly adoption), the child will be biologically connected to neither of the couple's members.

In terms of same-sex parenthood, the important questions that arise are whether, under a specific legal system, same-sex couples are allowed *de facto* to become parents of a child *as a couple*; and, if they act as parents of a child, whether they can both be recognised under the law as the child's parents (either automatically or after taking specific steps, e.g. adoption).

This short section summarises the current legal landscape in EU Member States regarding parenting by same-sex couples.[3]

---

1 For a more detailed exploration of this question see A. Tryfonidou, 'EU Free Movement Law and the Children of Rainbow Families: Children of a Lesser God?' (2019) 38 *Yearbook of European Law* (forthcoming).

2 Opinion of AG Szpunar in Case C-335/17, *Babanarakis*, ECLI:EU:C:2018:242, para. 29. For an analysis of this argument see, inter alia, A. Bainham, 'Family Law in a Pluralistic Society', (1995) 22 *Journal of Law and Society*, 234.

3 For a comparison between Europe and the US in relation to the legal recognition of same-sex relationships and the parental ties between same-sex couples and their children, see S. Titshaw, 'A Transatlantic Rainbow Comparison: "Federalism" and Family-Based Immigration for Rainbow Families in the US and the EU' in C. Casonato and A. Schuster (eds.),

Lack of EU competence on this matter and lack of guidance at the European level means that the family rights that same-sex couples enjoy at the national level with regard to parenting vary considerably throughout the EU. The most recent edition of ILGA Europe's Rainbow Map[4] demonstrates that only a minority of EU Member States provides full parental rights to same-sex couples. As Nikolina has noted, '[t]he idea that in order to thrive a child needs two parents of different sex who are in a committed relationship, translates in many jurisdictions into laws precluding different-sex cohabitants from adopting children and same-sex partners from both being acknowledged as legal parents of their children'.[5]

At the moment of writing, joint adoption by same-sex couples is allowed in only 14 EU Member States,[6] as is the case for second-parent adoption for same-sex couples.[7] Surrogacy is largely prohibited across EU Member States, which in effect limits parenting options for male same-sex couples to adoption. The law allows medically assisted insemination by same-sex couples (*as a couple*) in only 12 EU Member States,[8] while same-sex couples enjoy automatic recognition as co-parents only in 9 EU Member States.[9] In countries where medically assisted insemination is not open to same-sex couples (i.e. they cannot go through the process *as a couple*), one of the members can go through it if it is open to single persons. In the current EU context, 18 Member States allow medically assisted insemination for single persons.[10] However, EU Member States that do not allow medically assisted insemination for same-sex couples but allow it for single women[11] do not recognise the child produced through

---

Rights on the Move: Rainbow Families in Europe, Conference Proceedings, Trento 16–17 October 2014 <http://eprints.biblio.unitn.it/4448/1/Casonato-Schuster-ROTM_Proceedings-2014.pdf> accessed 27.06.2018. For an analysis of social attitudes toward adoption by same-sex couples in Europe, see J. Takács, I. Szalma and T. Bartus, 'Social Attitudes Toward Adoption by Same-Sex Couples in Europe', (2016) 45 *Arch Sex Behav* 1787.

4 See ILGA Europe Rainbow Europe Package: Annual Review and Rainbow Europe Map <https://www.ilga-europe.org/rainboweurope/2019> accessed 08.07.2019.

5 N. Nikolina, 'Evolution of Parenting Rights in Europe – a Comparative Case Study about Questions in Section 3 of the LawsAndFamilies Database' in K. Waaldijk, *More and More Together: Legal Family Formats for Same-Sex and Different-Sex Couples in European Countries: Comparative Analysis of Data in the LawsAndFamilies Database*, Working Paper 75 (2017) in the Families and Societies Working Paper Series, 102 <https://openaccess.leidenuniv.nl/bitstream/handle/1887/54628/Waaldijk%20-%20More%20and%20more%20together%20-%20FamiliesAndSocietiesWorkingPaper%2075%282017%29.pdf?sequence=3> accessed 22.06.2018.

6 Austria, Belgium, Denmark, Finland, France, Germany, Ireland, Luxembourg, Malta, the Netherlands, Portugal, Spain, Sweden, and the UK.

7 Austria, Belgium, Denmark, Finland, France, Germany, Luxembourg, Malta, the Netherlands, Portugal, Slovenia, Spain, Sweden, and the UK.

8 Austria, Belgium, Denmark, Finland, Ireland, Luxembourg, Malta, the Netherlands, Portugal, Spain, Sweden, and the UK.

9 Austria, Belgium, Denmark, Ireland, Malta, the Netherlands, Portugal, Spain and the UK.

10 Belgium, Bulgaria, Croatia, Cyprus, Denmark, Estonia, Finland, Greece, Hungary, Ireland, Latvia, Luxembourg, Malta, the Netherlands, Portugal, Spain, Sweden, and the UK.

11 This is the case in Bulgaria, Croatia, Cyprus, Estonia, Greece, Hungary, and Latvia.

insemination as the couple's child. Instead, the child will be legally recognised only as the child of the woman who gave birth to him/her. Since EU Member States that do not allow medically assisted insemination for same-sex couples do not allow second-parent adoptions for such couples, the woman who did not give birth to the child will not be legally recognised as the second parent.

Accordingly, it can be seen that currently, in EU Member States, a legal patchwork exists regarding the recognition of same-sex couples' parental status, reflecting how the matter of same-sex couples' parental rights remains controversial.[12] Only a rather slim minority of EU Member States (8) grants full parental rights to same-sex couples. It allows them to adopt a child jointly, undergo artificial insemination as a couple and be automatically recognised as a child's legal parents.[13] At the same time, almost half of EU Member States (13) do not provide any rights whatsoever to same-sex couples to act (legally) as co-parents.[14] Between these two extremes, some EU Member States allow only limited ways through which same-sex couples can become co-parents and be legally recognised as such. For instance, France allows joint adoption by same-sex couples but does not allow women to undergo medically assisted insemination if they are in a relationship with another woman or if they are single.[15]

3. FAMILY REUNIFICATION RIGHTS UNDER EU LAW: THE POSITION OF CHILDREN

EU law grants to all EU citizens (i.e. all persons possessing the nationality of an EU Member State)[16] the right to move and reside freely in the territory of another Member State. This right is derived from the free movement of persons provisions of the Treaty on the Functioning of the European Union (TFEU),[17]

---

12 See P. Dunne, 'Who is a Parent and Who is a Child in a Same-Sex Family? – Legislative and Judicial Issues for LGBT Families Post-Separation, Part I: The European Perspective', (2017) 30 *Journal of the American Academy of Matrimonial Lawyers* 27, 31 (and the references in footnote 13 of that article).

13 The EU Member States which offer such *full* recognition of the parental status of same-sex couples are Austria, Belgium, Denmark, Malta, the Netherlands, Portugal, Spain and the UK.

14 These are Bulgaria, Croatia, Cyprus, Czech Republic, Estonia, Greece, Hungary, Italy, Latvia, Lithuania, Poland, Romania, Slovakia.

15 The nuances and specificities of the exact entitlements granted to same-sex couples in different EU Member States will not concern us here since our focus is simply on *cross-border* recognition of the parental link between a child and *both* of his/her same-sex parents. For a rather recent analysis of the laws and trends regarding same-sex parenting in different EU Member States see N. Nikolina (above n. 5). See, also, E. Falletti, 'LGBTI Discrimination and Parent-Child Relationships: Cross-Border Mobility of Rainbow Families in the European Union', (2014) 52 *Family Court Review*, 28.

16 Article 20 TFEU.

17 The right is now laid down in Article 21 TFEU and – the *leges speciales* to it – Articles 45, 49, and 56 TFEU.

which have always prohibited obstacles to the free movement of persons between Member States. These provisions have also granted numerous additional rights to Member State nationals, most notably the right to be treated equally with the nationals of the host State and the right to reside in the territory of the Member State to which they have moved.[18] These provisions have, nonetheless, never referred to the family of the migrant Union citizen. However, being aware of the importance of family life and – more pragmatically – that Union citizens would be discouraged from moving if the host State refused to admit their close family members into its territory, the EU legislature has included family reunification rights in secondary legislation complementing the free movement of persons provisions.[19]

Currently, the main source of family reunification rights for Union citizens is Directive 2004/38.[20] This Directive applies only to 'Union citizens who move to or reside in a Member State other than that of which they are a national';[21] however, the European Court of Justice (ECJ) has extended its application 'by analogy' to Union citizens who return to their Member State of nationality after spending a period residing in the territory of another Member State ('returnees').[22]

Directive 2004/38 grants to Union citizens the *automatic* right to be joined or accompanied by their 'family members' in the territory of the Member State to which they move, i.e. the host State is *required* by EU law to admit family members into its territory without applying its own immigration requirements, irrespective of whether or not the family member is a Union citizen.[23]

For the Directive, 'family members' are defined in Article 2(2) as follows:

(a) the spouse;
(b) the partner with whom the Union citizen has contracted a registered partnership on the basis of the legislation of a Member State if the legislation of the host Member State treats registered partnerships as equivalent to marriage and in accordance with conditions laid down in the relevant legislation of the host Member State;
(c) the direct descendants who are under the age of 21 or are dependants and those of the spouse or partner as defined in point (b); and
(d) the dependent direct relatives in the ascending line and those of the spouse or partner as defined in point (b).

---

18 See, e.g. Case 167/73, *Commission v. France*, ECLI:EU:C:1974:35 (non-discrimination on the ground of nationality); Case C-363/89, *Roux v. Belgium*, ECLI:EU:C:1991:41 (right of residence).

19 G. Barrett, 'Family Matters: European Community Law and Third-Country Family Members', (2003) 40 *CMLRev*, 369.

20 Council and Parliament Directive 2004/38 on the right of citizens of the Union and their family members to move and reside freely within the territory of the Member States [2004] OJ L 158/77.

21 Ibid., Article 3.

22 Case C-456/12, *O. and B.*, ECLI:EU:C:2014:135.

23 Recital 5 of Directive 2004/38 (above n. 20).

For family members who do not fall into the list above, Article 3(2) of the Directive mentions that

> Without prejudice to any rights to free movement and residence the persons concerned may have in their own right, the host Member State shall, in accordance with its national legislation, facilitate entry and residence for the following persons:
>
> (a) any other family members, irrespective of their nationality, not falling under the definition in point 2 of Article 2 who, in the country from which they have come, are dependants or members of the household of the Union citizen having the primary right of residence or where serious health grounds strictly require the personal care of the family member by the Union citizen;
>
> (b) the partner with whom the Union citizen has a durable relationship duly attested.

Family members who fall within the categories of Article 3(2) cannot *automatically* require the host State to accept them into its territory but can require it to justify its decision not to admit them by demonstrating that it has undertaken an extensive examination of their personal circumstances.[24]

A quick glance at the provisions above demonstrates that the EU legislature has employed gender-neutral and sexual-orientation neutral terms when listing family members who must be allowed to join or accompany a Union citizen in the host Member State. In relation to parents and their children, in particular, the 2004 Directive speaks simply about 'descendants' and 'relatives in the ascending line' without interpreting these terms in more detail. This lack of clarity has encouraged Member States that do not provide for rainbow families within their national legal systems to believe that they are free to refuse to recognise such families when they move into their territory in exercise of EU free movement rights.

Given that this chapter focuses on the position of the children of rainbow families, it will be useful to summarise the four ways in which such children can benefit from family reunification rights under EU free movement law and the difficulties they may encounter in Member States that refuse to recognise one or both of their parents as their legal parent(s).

First, a child can fall under Article 2(2)(c) of Directive 2004/38 when (s)he is the direct descendant of a Union citizen who moves, or of the spouse or registered partner of the Union citizen. The child can fall within this category irrespective of whether (s)he is a Union citizen, but (s)he can only be covered if under the age of 21, or a dependant of his/her parents. The child of a rainbow family can, clearly, be covered by this category, if the parent recognised by the host State as his/her legal parent (usually the birth mother or the biological parent)

[24] Case C-83/11, *Rahman*, ECLI:EU:C:2012/519.

is the Union citizen. In addition, the child can be covered by this category even if the Union citizen is the other parent and the host State refuses to legally recognise him/her as the child's parent, provided that the parent who is recognised as the legal parent is considered by the host State to be the spouse or registered partner of the Union citizen. Following the ECJ's judgment in *Coman*,[25] if the child's parents are married (and the marriage was concluded in an EU Member State), the host State is obliged to recognise them as married for the purposes of Directive 2004/38; thus, the child has to be recognised in the host State at least as the child of the spouse of the parent who is not recognised as the legal parent.

Second, under Article 2(2)(d) of the 2004 Directive, if the child is a Union citizen and is not dependent on his/her parents, then (s)he may wish to act as the 'sponsor' of family reunification rights for his/her parents who are not EU citizens and thus do not have free movement rights. However, a rainbow family moving to a Member State that refuses to recognise the parental linkage between the child and one or both parents will be confronted with a refusal to admit the parent(s) into its territory, unless the parent(s) can claim the right to move there on another basis.

Third, in *Zhu and Chen*,[26] the ECJ held that minors who are Union citizens and wish to exercise their right to move and reside in the territory of another Member State can claim the right to be joined or accompanied by their primary carer in the host State, provided that the family is economically self-sufficient.[27] This principle can be useful for a child in a rainbow family who is a Union citizen but whose parents are third-country nationals and cannot move to that Member State on another basis. If the aim is to claim a right of residence for the parent who is legally recognised by the host State as the parent of the child, the claim is unlikely to present any difficulties. The situation may be more complicated if the primary carer is the parent that the host State refuses to recognise as the legal parent. This is usually the case when the primary carer is not biologically connected to the child. However, in the *O, S and L* case – a case that did not involve a rainbow family – the ECJ noted that a child who is a Union citizen can sponsor a right of residence for his(her) primary carer irrespective of a blood relationship between the two.[28]

Fourth, if a child does not fall within any of the categories above, (s)he can try to rely on Article 3(2)(a) of Directive 2004/38 as a dependant or a member of

---

25 Case C-673/16, *Coman*, ECLI:EU:C:2018:385.

26 Case C-200/02, *Zhu and Chen*, ECLI:EU:C:2004:639, paras. 26–34.

27 Given that this chapter is about the *free movement* rights of rainbow families, it should be noted that the possibility of employing the principle established in Case C-34/09, *Ruiz Zambrano* ECLI:EU:C:2011:124, which enables children who are Union citizens to reside in the territory *of the Member State of their nationality* with their primary carer, will not be considered here.

28 Joined Cases C-356-357/11, *O, S and L*, ECLI:EU:C:2012:776, para. 55.

the Union citizen's household. Alternatively, if the child is a Union citizen, (s)he can be the sponsor if the person or persons who wish to join the child can prove that they are members of the child's household in the home Member State or are dependent on the child. The Article 3(2)(a) category may, in fact, be the only acceptable solution for Member States as it grants family reunification rights to a rainbow family without this presupposing or leading to a recognition of the familial links between the child and his/her parents. At the same time, the actual familial links between child and parents are not recognised, which is exactly what the host Member State usually wishes to avoid.

4. THE CURRENT (UNCERTAIN) POSITION OF RAINBOW FAMILIES UNDER EU LAW

As noted in the Introduction, this chapter focuses on the rights *of the children* of rainbow families; hence, the right of Union citizens to be joined in another Member State by their same-sex spouse, registered partner, or partner will not be discussed here.[29] The question in this chapter, therefore, is whether same-sex couples' children can rely on EU law to require the Member State to which the family moves to legally recognise the legal links between them and their parents, as these have been lawfully established in the family's Member State of origin.

The problematic position in which rainbow families currently find themselves is clearly demonstrated by a petition made recently to the Committee of Petitions (PETI) of the European Parliament by Eleni Maravelia, a Greek national married to a British woman.[30] Ms. Maravelia gave birth to a daughter in Spain in 2014. The Spanish birth certificate of the couple's daughter indicates both Ms. Maravelia and her spouse as the child's mothers. Yet, in Greece – which does not legally

---

29 The ECJ has very recently held that the term 'spouse' in Article 2(2) of Directive 2004/38 must be interpreted as including the same-sex spouse of a Union citizen – see *Coman* (above n. 25). For a discussion of the judgment, see A. Tryfonidou, 'The ECJ recognises the right of same-sex spouses to move freely between EU Member States: the *Coman* ruling', (2019) 44 *European Law Review* (forthcoming). The terms 'registered partner' in the same provision and 'partner' in Article 3(2) of the Directive have not been interpreted yet by the Court, although it has been argued elsewhere that these should also be clearly interpreted to include same-sex registered partners and partners – see A. Tryfonidou, 'EU Free Movement Law and the Legal Recognition of Same-Sex Relationships: The Case for Mutual Recognition' (2015) 21 *Columbia Journal of European Law*, 195. On the same issue, see U. Belavusau and D. Kochenov, 'Federalizing Legal Opportunities for LGBT Movements in the Growing EU' in K. Slootmaeckers, H. Touquet and P. Vermeersch (eds.), *The EU Enlargement and Gay Politics: The Impact of Eastern Enlargement on Rights, Activism and Prejudice* (Palgrave 2016).

30 Petition No 0513/2016 by Eleni Maravelia (Greek) on the non-recognition of LGBT families in the European Union <https://petiport.secure.europarl.europa.eu/petitions/en/petition/content/0513%252F2016/html/Petition-No-0513%252F2016-by-Eleni-Maravelia-%2528Greek%2529-on-the-non-recognition-of-LGBT-families-in-the-European-Union> accessed 22.06.2018.

recognise same-sex couples as co-parents – they were told that only the birth mother is recognised as the child's parent, thus making Ms. Maravelia the child's sole parent under Greek law. The petition noted that 'The petitioner believes that families like hers are being refused their right to free movement and that their children are vulnerable, since their parents are not equally recognized across the EU. The petitioner urges that the EP and the Commission work toward making official civil status documents, such as birth certificates, to be accepted *de facto* across Member States. She believes that children of parents in similar situations deserve the same rights as all children, with both their parents recognized'.

This petition makes it obvious that, as with cross-border legal recognition of same-sex marriages, in relation to which the EU had – until recently – washed its hands, with regards to the *cross-border* recognition of the legal ties between children and their parents who happen to be of the same sex, the EU has, so far, chosen to remain silent.

This gives leeway to Member States that do not recognise that members of a same-sex couple can be the joint parents of a child to extend the application of their restrictive laws to situations in which rainbow families legally recognised in other Member States come to their territory to exercise their free movement rights. Consequently, if the only sponsor of family reunification rights in the family is the child, either or both parents will be unable to join the child in the host State. Similarly, if the only sponsor of family reunification rights in the family is the non-biological parent, then the family may simply not be able to move together to the host State unless the latter admits the other parent as the same-sex spouse or registered partner of a Union citizen. In this case, the child will be able to join the couple as 'the child of the spouse or partner' of the Union citizen.

In any event, research has shown that host States facilitate the entry and residence of the children of a rainbow family even if their laws do not recognise them as children of one or either parent.[31] Hence, in practice, the main issue appears to be not so much whether rainbow families can move and reside in the territory of another Member State. Rather, the issue is *how* they will be able to move, i.e. whether they will be recognised as a family in the host State, with the legal ties established in the State of origin remaining intact.

This is critical since, in addition to the negative symbolic value that results from non-recognition under the law of the links between a child and one or both of his/her parents, such non-recognition will also have a host of adverse practical consequences. The child will not be recognised as the child of the parent (or parents) for any legal purposes. Thus, the parent or parents will not be able, for instance, to give consent for the child's medical treatment, open a

31 'Handbook on the Rights of Rainbow Families: Rights on the move', Cara-Friend, Northern Ireland 2014, p. 28 <https://www.ilga-europe.org/sites/default/files/rights_on_the_move_-_handbook_on_the_rights_of_rainbow_families_2015.pdf> accessed 10.05.2018.

bank account for the child, travel (alone) with the child, or place the child in school. In addition, the child will not have any inheritance rights on intestacy in case the parent who is not legally recognised as a parent dies, and will not be able to take the nationality of that parent. In case the parent who is legally recognised dies, the child becomes an orphan and can be placed in the care of a guardian or a foster family, whilst if the biological parent's family takes care of the child, they can decide whether they will allow the other parent (who is not legally recognised as a parent) to continue to play a part – and, if so, what part – in the child's life.

Research on the cross-border legal recognition of rainbow families and the legal status of their members has 'revealed a chaotic mosaic of full, partial, unclear, and denied recognitions'.[32] The non-recognition of legal ties between a child and one or both of his/her parents demonstrates that some EU Member States insist on refusing to recognise the realities of the familial relationships of children of rainbow families, jeopardising their legal security in addition to breaching several rights that children (and their parents) enjoy under EU law. The next section, therefore, analyses how the failure of the host Member State to recognise legal ties (as these are recognised in another EU Member State) between a child and his/her parent can breach several rights that the child enjoys under EU law.

5. IS THE NON-RECOGNITION OF THE PARENT-CHILD RELATIONSHIP A BREACH OF EU LAW?

Traditionally, and until relatively recently, different-sex married spouses and their legitimate (biological) children have constituted the only recognised form of 'family' for legal purposes. This has underpinned the approach not merely of EU Member States but also of the EU.[33] Such an approach ignores the existence of rainbow families despite evidence which suggests that the number of such families is increasing.[34]

The European Parliament – the most pro-LGBTI among the EU institutions – has called on the other EU institutions to create a legal framework at EU level

---

32 K. Waaldijk, 'The Right to Relate: A Lecture on the Importance of Orientation in Comparative Sexual Orientation Law' (2013) 24 *Duke Journal of Comparative and International Law*, 161, 198.

33 H. Stalford, 'Concepts of Family under EU Law – Lessons from the ECHR' (2002) 16 *International Journal of Law, Policy and the Family*, 410; C. McGlynn, *Families and the European Union: Law, Politics and Pluralism*, Cambridge University Press, Cambridge 2006.

34 L. Hodson, 'The Rights of Children raised in lesbian, gay, bisexual or transgender families: A European perspective', ILGA-Europe 2008, p. 8 <https://www.ilga-europe.org/resources/ilga-europe-reports-and-other-materials/rights-children-raised-lesbian-gay-bisexual-or> accessed 25.06.2018.

which will ensure that the rights of rainbow families which move between Member States are respected, whilst the Member States' competence in the family law field is respected. In particular, in its recent resolution on protection and non-discrimination with regard to minorities in the EU Member States,[35] it recommended, inter alia, the provision of clear and accessible information on the recognition of cross-border rights for LGBTI persons and their families in the EU.[36] It urged the Commission to ensure that Member States correctly implement Directive 2004/38, and consistently respect, inter alia, the provisions related to family members and prohibiting discrimination on any grounds.[37] In the same resolution, the Parliament called on the Commission to take action to ensure that LGBTI individuals and their families can exercise their right to free movement in accordance with both Article 21 TFEU and Article 21 EUCFR.[38]

Importantly, however, this is not the first time that the European Parliament has made such suggestions. In 1994 – when only one Member State (Denmark) had offered some form of legal recognition to same-sex relationships – the Parliament issued a resolution noting, inter alia, that the Commission should draft a recommendation on equal rights for lesbians and homosexuals, which would, as a minimum, seek to end 'the barring of lesbians and homosexual couples from marriage or from an equivalent legal framework, and should guarantee the full rights and benefits of marriage, allowing the registration of partnerships' as well as 'any restrictions on the rights of lesbians and homosexuals to be parents or to adopt or foster children'.[39]

Yet, despite the Parliament's repeated calls for a legal framework that caters to the needs of rainbow families and that grants them the same protection and rights as those enjoyed by the traditional nuclear family, the EU has, to date, buried its head in the sand on this matter. Other EU institutions have chosen to ignore social reality, and as a result rainbow families continue to live in a state of legal uncertainty: a mere attempt to exercise the core – free movement – rights they enjoy under EU law often brings them face to face with the harsh reality that their family is not recognised in many EU Member States.

---

35 2017/2937(RSP), available at <http://www.europarl.europa.eu/sides/getDoc.do?pubRef=-%2f%2fEP%2f%2fTEXT%2bMOTION%2bB8-2018-0064%2b0%2bDOC%2bXML%2bV0%2f%2fEN&language=EN> accessed 25.06.2018. This motion was, in fact, the European Parliament's response to the PETI public hearing organised by the Committee on Petitions (PETI) titled 'Fighting against discrimination of EU citizens in the EU Member States and the protection of minorities' that took place on 4 May 2017, where the Petition submitted by Eleni Maravelia (above n. 30) was heard.

36 Ibid., para. 19.

37 Ibid., para. 20.

38 Ibid., para. 21.

39 European Parliament Resolution on equal rights for homosexuals and lesbians in EC A3-0028/94 (1994) OJ C 61/40.

Accordingly, the next sub-section examines whether the EU has the competence and tools to require its Member States to recognise familial links between the members of rainbow families, as these are recognised in the family's Member State of origin.

5.1. DOES THE EU HAVE THE COMPETENCE TO ACT?

As is well known – and as has been repeatedly confirmed by the ECJ[40] – family law and the regulation of civil status still fall broadly within Member State competence. The EU does not have competence, except when measures concerning family law 'having cross-border implications' are concerned.[41] Therefore, Member States have largely been left to decide what legal recognition, if any, will be given to same-sex couples. Similarly, EU Member States are left to decide whether they will allow same-sex couples to become *de facto* parents and whether a same-sex couple can be legally recognised as the joint legal parents of a child.

Yet, as stressed in numerous different contexts,[42] Member States must act in a way that respects their obligations under EU law even in areas that fall within their competence. Among these is the obligation to respect the free movement rights of Union citizens. In particular, in situations that fall within the scope of EU law by virtue of an actual or potential exercise of free movement rights by a Union citizen, Member States must comply with their obligations under the EU free movement provisions and the secondary legislation complementing them. In addition, the EUCFR (and fundamental human rights that are part of the general principles of EU law) binds EU institutions in all instances and Member States 'when they are implementing EU law',[43] which has been interpreted, in some cases, to mean situations that fall within the scope of EU law.[44] Hence, in situations that fall within the scope of EU law, by virtue of the fact that a Union citizen has exercised free movement rights, the EU institutions and Member States must act in a way that complies with the free movement provisions and fundamental human rights protected under EU law.

Accordingly, the remainder of this section examines whether the host State's refusal to recognise the legal links between children and their same-sex parents

---

40 Case C-267/06, *Maruko*, EU:C:2008:179, para. 59; Case C-443/15, *Parris*, EU:C:2016:897, para. 59; *Coman* (above n. 25), para. 37.

41 Article 81(3) TFEU.

42 Case C-148/02, *Garcia Avello*, EU:C:2003:539, para. 25; Case C-353/06, *Grunkin and Paul*, EU:C:2008:559, para. 16; Case C-438/14, *Bogendorff von Wolffersdorff*, EU:C:2016:401, para. 32; *Coman* (above n. 25) para. 38.

43 Article 51 EUCFR (for the Charter); Case 5/88, *Wachauf*, ECLI:EU:C:1989:321 (for the general principles of EU law).

44 See, inter alia, Case C-459/99, *MRAX*, ECLI:EU:C:2002:461; Case C-617/10, *Åkerberg*, ECLI:EU:C:2013:105; Case C-390/12, *Pfleger*, ECLI:EU:C:2014:281.

when the family moves to its territory (and the resultant refusal of several rights which would have been enjoyed, had there been such recognition) breaches the free movement provisions of the Treaty and fundamental (human) rights as these are protected *under EU law*.[45]

5.2. IS THERE A BREACH OF THE EU FREE MOVEMENT PROVISIONS?

As noted earlier, the free movement of persons provisions in the TFEU prohibit national measures that obstruct the free movement of Union citizens between Member States. Union citizens have been given the right to be accompanied or joined by their close family members in the host State because the refusal to allow them to do so would deter them from exercising their free movement rights, thus creating an obstacle to free movement. To paraphrase the ECJ in its judgment in *Carpenter*,[46] the separation of the members of a rainbow family would be detrimental to their family life and, therefore, to the conditions under which the member(s) of the family who hold(s) Union citizenship exercise(s) free movement rights.

Clearly, when a child is a Union citizen and (s)he is not allowed to be accompanied or joined by both of his/her parents in the host State – because the legal links between members of the family are not recognised in the host State – the child's right to move and reside in the territory of another Member State will be infringed. Similarly, when, for the same reason, a Union citizen cannot be accompanied or joined by his/her spouse or partner *and/or any children of the couple*, (s)he will be deterred from exercising free movement rights.

Assuming that a rainbow family is actually admitted to the host State, this is not the end of the story. If the host Member State does not legally recognise the family ties between family members for other legal purposes (e.g. taxation, nationality, pensions, intestacy and so on), this will cause great inconvenience to those family members, thereby impeding the exercise of their free movement rights. In *Garcia Avello*[47] and *Grunkin Paul*,[48] the ECJ noted that the host State's denial of surname recognition to Union citizens registered in another Member State, and the resultant discrepancy in surnames in different Member States, led

45 The words 'EU law' have been italicised to emphasise that this chapter is concerned with the rights of the children of rainbow families only *under EU law* – the rights enjoyed under the ECHR or under other international instruments for the protection of children's rights will not be considered, unless and to the extent that this is necessary when examining the position under EU law.

46 Case C-60/00, *Carpenter*, ECLI:EU:C:2002:434.

47 Above n. 42.

48 Ibid.

to serious inconvenience for the persons concerned which, in turn, was likely to deter them from exercising their free movement rights.[49] If we transpose this reasoning to the context of rainbow families, the refusal of the host State to legally recognise family ties between family members once the family is within its territory can constitute an obstacle to free movement. In recent cases, the ECJ has highlighted the need to ensure that Union citizens can *continue* a way of family life that may have come into being in the Member State from which they come, if they are not to be deterred from exercising their free movement rights.[50]

As is well known, obstacles to free movement can be justified on numerous grounds. In cases involving rainbow families and the refusal to recognise them, Member States would probably try to rely on the ground of public policy and particularly their interest in preserving their national identity, as was done in the recent case of *Coman*, which concerned the cross-border legal recognition of marriages. However, as the ECJ pointed out, an obligation to recognise the status attached to a same-sex relationship in another EU Member State and – importantly – to recognise the parental linkage (as established in another Member State) between one or both of the parents in a same-sex relationship and their child, for the sole purpose of granting family reunification rights under EU law, 'does not undermine the national identity or pose a threat to the public policy of the Member State concerned'.[51]

Moreover, as laid down in Article 27(2) of Directive 2004/38, measures taken by the host State relying on public policy 'shall be based exclusively on the personal conduct of the individual concerned'. This will not be satisfied when Member States engage in a blanket refusal to admit within their territory, and/or to recognise, the exact family ties of all members of a rainbow family. This is because, by doing so, they exclude a whole category of persons (LGB individuals who are in a same-sex relationship and their children) simply because they fall within that category; hence, their exclusion is not based on their personal conduct.

Finally, (again) according to the ECJ's judgment in *Coman*, 'a national measure that is liable to obstruct the exercise of freedom of movement for persons may be justified only where such a measure is consistent with the fundamental rights guaranteed by the Charter, it being the task of the Court to ensure that those rights are respected'.[52] As will be seen in the next sub-section, the refusal of the

---

49 For a similar argument with regard to the legal status attached to same-sex relationships, see G. Biagioni, 'On Recognition of Foreign Same-Sex Marriages and Partnerships' in D. Gallo, L. Paladini and P. Pustorino (eds.), *Same-Sex Couples Before National, Supranational and International Jurisdictions*, Springer Publishing, New York 2014, pp. 376–377.

50 *O. and B.* (above n. 22), para. 50; Case C-291/05, *Eind*, ECLI:EU:C:2007:771, para. 36; Case C-40/11, *Iida*, ECLI:EU:C:2012:691, para. 70.

51 *Coman* (above n. 25), para. 46.

52 Ibid., para. 47.

host State to recognise the legal links between a child and his/her parent in a rainbow family is capable of breaching several fundamental human rights that the child and parents derive from the EUCFR and which are also protected as general principles of EU law.

Therefore, the obstacle to free movement that emerges from the non-recognition of rainbow families by the host State cannot be justified and thus such non-recognition can clearly be found to amount to a breach of the EU free movement of persons provisions.

5.3. IS THERE A BREACH OF EU FUNDAMENTAL HUMAN RIGHTS PROTECTION?

Under EU law, fundamental human rights have been protected as part of the general principles of EU law since the late 1960s.[53] Following the changes made to the Treaty on European Union (TEU) by the Treaty of Lisbon in 2009, Article 6 TEU provides that the EUCFR has the same legal value as the Treaties. Hence, in the EU, we have two parallel sources of fundamental human rights protection which significantly overlap: the EUCFR and the general principles of EU law.

Although the European Convention on Human Rights (ECHR) is *not* an EU instrument, it has nonetheless always had an important impact on the development of fundamental human rights protection in the EU, being recognised as a source of 'guidelines' for the ECJ when determining which fundamental human rights form part of the general principles of EU law and how these should be interpreted.[54] In addition, it plays an equally important role in the interpretation of the EUCFR, as Article 52(3) of the latter instrument provides that 'In so far as this Charter contains rights which correspond to rights guaranteed by the Convention for the Protection of Human Rights and Fundamental Freedoms, the meaning and scope of those rights shall be the same as those laid down by the said Convention. This provision shall not prevent Union law providing more extensive protection'.

Accordingly, given that no *ECJ* case law deals with rainbow families and parenting by same-sex couples in particular, a large part of the analysis that follows examines the Strasbourg court's jurisprudence, as the latter can clearly inform the ECJ's reasoning in situations falling within the scope of EU law. So far, all cases of the European Court of Human Rights (ECtHR) involving rainbow families have been approached from the parental point of view – in other words, the question has been whether the rights enjoyed by parents have

53 Case 29/69, *Stauder*, ECLI:EU:C:1969:57.
54 Case 4/73, *Nold*, ECLI:EU:C:1974:51.

been breached as a result of the contested measure of a State.[55] In this chapter, however, a different perspective is taken – that of the child – and thus the question is whether the contested non-recognition of familial ties in rainbow families in situations where the families move between Member States can breach the fundamental human rights of the children of rainbow families.

5.3.1. Breach of the Right to Private and Family Life

The right to private and family life is protected as a general principle of EU law[56] as well as under Article 7 EUCFR.

The ECtHR held in *Gas and Dubois v. France* that a same-sex couple and their child can together enjoy 'family life' within the meaning of Article 8 ECHR, irrespective of whether one or both parents are not biologically connected to the child.[57] This follows the general approach of the ECtHR, according to which biological ties are not an overriding factor in establishing family life and some evidence of real and constant relationship is normally needed before such relationships are afforded the protection of Article 8 ECHR.[58]

However, can the refusal of a host Member State to recognise legal links established between a child and both of her/his parents in their Member State of origin amount to a breach of the child's right to family life, provided that the family does enjoy family life within the meaning of Article 8 ECHR?

In *Marckx v. Belgium*,[59] the ECtHR held that Article 8 ECHR 'does not merely compel the State to abstain from' arbitrary interference with the exercise of the right to family life. It also imposes positive obligations on it, such as 'when the State determines in its domestic legal system the regime applicable to certain family ties such as those between an unmarried mother and her child, it must act in a manner calculated to allow those concerned to lead a normal family life. As envisaged by Article 8, respect for family life implies in particular, in the Court's view, the existence in domestic law of legal safeguards that render possible as from the moment of birth the child's integration in his family'.[60] The case, of course, involved facts confined within one and the same State; however, it is important for our purposes, since it underlined the significance of ensuring that

---

55 For a criticism of this approach that seems to be leaving the question of the child's best interests outside the equation, see the dissenting opinion of Judge Villiger in *Gas and Dubois v. France*, no. 25952/07, ECHR 2012-II.

56 See, e.g. *Carpenter* (above n. 46), para. 41.

57 *Gas and Dubois v. France* (above n. 55), para. 37.

58 *J.R.M. v. the Netherlands*, no. 16944/90, ECHR 1993; *Nylund v. Finland*, no. 27110/95, ECHR 1999-VI; *K. and T. v. Finland*, no. 25702/94, ECHR 2001-VII.

59 *Marckx v. Belgium*, no. 6833/74, ECHR 1979.

60 Ibid., para. 31.

in situations in which two or more persons enjoy family life together (as can be the case in the context of a rainbow family), States have the positive obligation to see that their legal system allows for the child's integration into his/her family by being legally recognised as a part of it.

In a subsequent case, *Wagner v. Luxembourg*,[61] the ECtHR was confronted with an alleged breach of Article 8 ECHR in a case that involved the *cross-border* recognition of an adoption, albeit not involving a rainbow family. At issue was the refusal of the Luxembourg authorities to recognise the Peruvian court's decision pronouncing the full adoption by Ms. Wagner – a Luxembourg national – of her child, JMWL, of Peruvian nationality. The refusal resulted from the absence in Luxembourg legislation of provisions allowing an unmarried person to obtain full adoption of a child. The Court held that this refusal amounted to an unjustified interference with the right to respect for Ms. Wagner and her child's family life and, thus, amounted to an infringement of Article 8 ECHR. The Court, in particular, noted that '[b]earing in mind that the best interests of the child are paramount in such a case … the Court considers that the Luxembourg courts could not reasonably disregard the legal status validly created abroad and corresponding to a family life within the meaning of Article 8 of the Convention'.[62]

More recently, the Court was confronted with the same issue in two cases that involved the cross-border recognition of a legal parent-child relationship lawfully established abroad as the result of a surrogacy agreement (*Mennesson v. France* and *Labassee v. France*).[63] The Court, following the principles established in *Wagner v. Luxembourg*, found that the contested refusals amounted to a breach of Article 8 ECHR, albeit not of the 'family life' aspect (in relation to which it found that the infringement was justified) but of the 'private life' aspect. This was in view of the fact that 'respect for private life requires that everyone should be able to establish details of their identity as individual human beings, which includes the legal parent-child relationship';[64] 'legal uncertainty' caused as a result of non-recognition in the host State is liable to have negative repercussions on the children's definition of their personal identity.

Hence, the ECtHR has clarified in numerous judgments that Article 8 ECHR is breached where there is *de facto* family life and the host State refuses to recognise the legal status of those family ties as formally recognised in the country of origin. Although the cases in which this was held did not involve rainbow families, similar cases and legal argumentation in situations involving

---

61 *Wagner v. Luxembourg*, no. 76240/01, ECHR 2007-VII.
62 Ibid., para. 133. See, also, *Negrepontis-Giannisis v. Greece*, no. 56759/09, ECHR 2011.
63 *Mennesson v. France*, no. 65192/11, ECHR 2014. See, also, *Labassee v. France*, no. 65941/11, ECHR 2014.
64 *Mennesson v. France* (above n. 63), para. 96.

the cross-border legal recognition of the legal status of members of a rainbow family are likely to arise in national and international courts.[65] Hence, transposing this interpretation of Article 8 ECHR into the EU context, the failure of a host Member State to legally recognise the family ties between a child of a rainbow family and one or both of his/her parents places that child in a legal vacuum; this can breach his/her right to private and family life, which is protected as a general principle of EU law as well as under Article 7 EUCFR.

Like Article 8 ECHR, Article 7 EUCFR and the right to private and family life as a general principle of EU law, do not impose an absolute prohibition but allow Member States to justify measures which constitute an interference with the exercise of this right. The most likely ground of justification in cases in which the children of rainbow families are ignored by the law of the host Member State would be the aim of supporting and encouraging the traditional family. However such a justification would fail. This is because 'in the achievement of this end recourse must not be had to measures whose object or result is … to prejudice the rainbow family', given that members of the rainbow family can – as noted in *Gas and Dubois v. France* – 'enjoy the guarantees of Article 8 on an equal footing with the members of the traditional family'.[66] Moreover, as Dunne has rightly argued,

> 'The standard "traditional family" defense would suggest that by reducing non-heterosexual family rights to the greatest extent possible, national laws disincentivise non-traditional family structures, prioritise heterosexual marriage relationships and encourage individuals into a socially optimal family model. However … such an argument would be intellectually weak (not to mention wholly removed from social reality). Severing the legal connection between gay, lesbian and bisexual parents and their non-biological children does not persuade such individuals to enter an opposite-gender heterosexual marriage … instead of reinforcing the *de facto* social superiority of traditional families, the absence of LGB family rights has no appreciable impact on heterosexual marriage, but significantly impedes lesbian, gay and bisexual family life'.[67]

This argument can, obviously, be extended to situations where there is no *cross-border* legal recognition of the familial ties among members of rainbow families.

Accordingly, the failure of a host Member State to recognise the legal links between a child in a rainbow family and both parents – as these are recognised in the home State from which the family is moving – can clearly amount to an unjustified breach of the child's right to private and family life under Article 7 EUCFR and as a general principle of EU law.[68]

---

65 K. Waaldijk (above n. 32), 197.
66 *Marckx v. Belgium* (above n. 59), para. 40.
67 P. Dunne (above n. 12), 48–49.
68 For a similar argument see P. Dunne (ibid.), 43–44.

5.3.2. *Breach of the Prohibition of Discrimination on the Ground of Sexual Orientation*

In situations in which a host Member State refuses to recognise the parental ties between a child of a same-sex couple and both parents, as these are recognised in the Member State of origin, this is based on the child's parents being of the same sex. Accordingly, the children of same-sex couples face discrimination because of their parents' sexual orientation; hence they face discrimination *by association with their LGB parents*.

As established by the ECJ in the *Coleman* case,[69] the prohibition of discrimination under Directive 2000/78[70] – the instrument that prohibits discrimination on, inter alia, grounds of sexual orientation in the context of employment – includes discrimination by association. There is no reason why this would not be recognised as the case also for Article 21 EUCFR, which generally prohibits discrimination on, inter alia, the ground of sexual orientation.[71]

The question is whether a host Member State may nonetheless be justified in drawing a distinction between the children of rainbow families and children of opposite-sex couples – as regards the legal recognition of their ties with their parents – in situations in which EU free movement rights have been exercised. After all, it is very rarely – if ever – that the legal links between children and their opposite-sex parents are severed when the family moves between Member States, and, if they ever are, this is certainly *not* based on the (heterosexual) sexual orientation of the parents.

As the ECtHR has repeatedly noted, discrimination on the ground of sexual orientation requires 'particularly convincing and weighty reasons' to be justified, and differences solely based on considerations of sexual orientation are unacceptable under the ECHR.[72] In line with Article 52(3) EUCFR, the same approach should be adopted in the EU context when considering justifications in situations in which discrimination occurs on the ground of sexual orientation, as this is prohibited under the Charter.

The usual argument for justifying discrimination in cases of non-recognition in the context of rainbow families is the need to protect the child's best interests. However, same-sex couples should continue to be legally recognised as the joint parents of their children in the host State, not despite the children's best

---

69 Case C-303/06, *Coleman*, ECLI:EU:C:2008:415.

70 Council Directive 2000/78 establishing a general framework for equal treatment in employment and occupation (2000) OJ L 303/16.

71 There has not been a case to date that precedes recognition of the EUCFR as a legally binding document and which involved the need to establish whether the prohibition of discrimination on the ground of sexual orientation is a fundamental human right protected as a general principle of EU law.

72 *Vallianatos v. Greece*, no. 29381/09 and 32684/09, ECHR 2013, para. 77.

interests but precisely because this is required if the children's best interests are considered, as is, after all, required by Article 24 EUCFR.

Considerable social, scientific and psychological research argues that successfully raising a child does not depend on his or her parents' sexual orientation.[73] Moreover, increasing numbers of children in Europe are being raised in families comprising a same-sex couple. Failing to provide legal recognition to such families will not reduce the numbers of such families but will complicate their lives and – as already seen in this chapter – result in a breach of several rights enjoyed under EU law both by the parents and by the children themselves. As Judge Villiger rightly noted in his dissenting opinion in the *Gas and Dubois v. France* case,

> 'joint parental custody is in the best interests of the child. I fail to see a justification for this difference in treatment [between the children of a same-sex and an opposite-sex couple]. In my view, all children should be afforded the same treatment. I cannot see why some children, but not others, should be deprived of their best interests, namely of joint parental custody. Indeed, how can children help it that they were born of a parent of a same-sex couple rather than of a parent of a heterosexual couple? Why should the child have to suffer for the parents' situation?'[74]

Or, as asked by another commentator, 'Why prejudice children living in a certain kind of relationship?'[75] After all, as laid down in Article 2(2) of the UN Convention on the Rights of the Child – to which all EU Member States are parties – 'States Parties shall take all appropriate measures to ensure that the child is protected against all forms of discrimination or punishment on the basis of the status, activities, expressed opinions, or beliefs of the child's parents, legal guardians, or family members'.

Accordingly, the children of rainbow families should not be 'penalised in [their] daily existence'[76] simply because of their association with parents who are of homosexual sexual orientation. Children of opposite-sex couples who move to a host Member State in exercise of their free movement rights have the right to benefit from family reunification rights granted by EU law and, once admitted, to be recognised as the children of both of their parents. In the same

---

73 See the sources referred to in this website <https://whatweknow.inequality.cornell.edu/topics/lgbt-equality/what-does-the-scholarly-research-say-about-the-wellbeing-of-children-with-gay-or-lesbian-parents/> accessed 25.06.2018. See, also, the American Psychological Association Policy Statement on Sexual Orientation, Parents, and Children (2004) <http://www.apa.org/about/policy/parenting.aspx> accessed 25.06.2018.

74 Dissenting opinion of Judge Villiger in *Gas and Dubois v. France* (above n. 55).

75 K. Lundström, 'Family Life and the Freedom of Movement of Workers in the European Union' (1996) 10 *International Journal of Law, Policy and the Family*, 250, 262.

76 *Wagner v. Luxembourg* (above n. 61), para. 158.

way, children of same-sex couples who move to another Member State should be able to maintain the legal ties lawfully established between them and their parents in the Member State of origin.

6. CONCLUSION

This chapter examined the position of children of rainbow families (comprising at least one EU citizen) who move between EU Member States in exercise of EU free movement rights.

Since family law and issues regarding family and civil status are still areas that fall within Member State competence, there is currently a legal patchwork regarding the recognition of same-sex couples' parental status. The sad reality is that in many EU Member States, same-sex parents lack not only automatic recognition of their parental status but also the means to become *de facto* parents.

This, in itself, is not problematic from the point of view of EU law. What *is* problematic, however, is that because of the lack of clarity in EU legislation governing the family reunification rights of EU citizens who move between Member States, the Member States that do not allow same-sex couples to be registered as joint parents of their child *in their territory* refuse to recognise them as such even in situations in which they were lawfully registered as joint parents of their child in another Member State.

There are different legal and cultural conceptions of what constellations may form a family. However, in addition to the traditional nuclear family, the ECtHR has recognised that alternative families, including rainbow families, can enjoy 'family life' and merit equal protection with families whose basis is an opposite-sex couple. Moreover, *all* children enjoy human rights equally, and their best interests must be protected, irrespective of who their parents are.

As explained in this chapter, the host State's refusal to legally recognise the parental ties between the child of a rainbow family and both parents breaches the right to free movement that rainbow families comprising at least one Union citizen enjoy under EU law; breaches the right to private and family life that the child and his/her parents enjoy under Article 7 EUCFR and as a general principle of EU law; and breaches the right that children of rainbow families enjoy under Article 21 EUCFR, not to be discriminated against on the ground of their parents' sexual orientation (discrimination by association).

Accordingly, the EU should clarify that *all* EU Member States are required by EU law to recognise the exact legal ties among the members of a rainbow family *as these are recognised under the law of another Member State*. It should, nonetheless, be emphasised that this chapter does not advocate that EU Member States are now obliged under EU law to allow same-sex couples to become *de facto* parents of a child and to be legally recognised as the child's parents in situations in which the couple is nowhere recognised as such and where there has been no exercise of EU free movement rights. Rather, this chapter argues that in situations in which (legal) links among the members of a rainbow family have been lawfully established in another Member State, the host Member State is obliged under EU law to mutually recognise those links. The (implicit) reforming pressure that will emerge following the recognition of rainbow families from other Member States should not be ignored, however. While space does not allow an analysis of this point, it is submitted that if the host Member State has to recognise – for the purposes of EU law – a same-sex couple as a child's joint parents, it will certainly feel the pressure to do so for same-sex couples whose situation is confined within its territory and is not governed by EU law.

KAFALA AND FAMILY REUNIFICATION OF THIRD-COUNTRY NATIONALS

Alessandra LANG

1. Introduction 97
2. The 1996 Hague Convention and Migration 99
3. Entry and Residence of Foreign Nationals within the EU 100
4. Family Reunification: EU Legislation 101
   4.1. Directive 2003/86 102
   4.2. Directive 2004/38 104
5. State Practice 105
6. Seeking Common Principles 110

1. INTRODUCTION

Kafala[1] is an institution for children's protection. It is mentioned in the 1996 Hague Convention on Jurisdiction, Applicable Law, Recognition, Enforcement and Cooperation in Respect of Parental Responsibility and Measures for the Protection of Children (1996 Hague Convention), drawn up within the Hague Conference on Private International Law. All European Union (EU) Member States are bound by the Convention, which they have also ratified in the interest of the EU.

The Convention concerns a matter that falls within the EU's competence, which the EU has exercised through the adoption of regulations on jurisdiction and the recognition and enforcement of judgements in matters of parental responsibility,[2] including measures for children's protection, although *kafala* is

[1] In this chapter, the spelling '*kafala*' will be used since this is the spelling used in the 1996 Hague Convention, as opposed to other alternative and equally common spellings such as *kafalah*, *kafāla*, or *kefalah*.

[2] Council Regulation 2201/2003 of 27.11.2003, concerning jurisdiction and the recognition and enforcement of judgments in matrimonial matters and the matters of parental responsibility, repealing Regulation (EC) No 1347/2000 ([2003] OJ L338/1), hereinafter the Brussels IIa Regulation.

not mentioned.[3] Clearly, the Union can conclude international agreements on matters for which the Treaties have conferred internal competence.[4] But it could not conclude the 1996 Hague Convention because only States could become parties to it.[5] Nonetheless, the Convention's ratification was desirable, and States were authorised to ratify it and make a declaration to coordinate the Convention's respective scope and regulation.[6] The Union cannot, therefore, be considered to be formally bound by the Convention, but States are obliged to respect it on the basis of international law and EU law (in this case, only between Member States themselves and between Member States and the Union).[7] For States to fulfil their obligations, including those that do not fall within its competence, is in the Union's interest.

The 1996 Hague Convention requires contracting parties to recognise the effects of child protection measures adopted by another contracting party. However, nothing is mentioned about granting an entry and residence permit to a child, respecting the traditional margin of appreciation afforded to States in admitting foreign nationals. However, for recognition to take effect, it is often necessary for the child to move from his or her State of origin where the *kafala* was established, to another State where the adult or adults with whom the child is placed live or intend to live. In the EU, admission of foreign nationals is a matter over which institutions have shared competence.

This chapter tries to find out which rules regulate the entry and residence in an EU Member State of a child placed in *kafala* care. Two situations can be identified: 1) the child and the adult (or adults) with whom the child is placed live together in the State in which the *kafala* was ordered, and wish to move to a

---

3 L. Carpaneto, 'Recognition of Protection measures affecting Migrant Children' in F. Ippolito and G. Biagioni (eds.), *Migrant Children: Challenges for Public and Private International Law*, Editoriale scientifica, 2016, p. 444, emphasises that the material scopes of the Convention and of the regulation are broadly similar, with the exception of *kafala* and related measures.

4 In general, P. Eeckhout, *EU External Relations Law*, Oxford University Press, Oxford 2011.

5 It is worth recalling that the EU has been party to the HCCH since 03.04.2007: see Council Decision 2006/719 on the accession of the Community to the Hague Conference on Private International Law. The EU can therefore be a contracting party to conventions negotiated after its accession but not those concluded previously.

6 Decision 2008/431 authorising certain Member States to ratify, or accede to, in the interest of the European Community, the 1996 Hague Convention on Jurisdiction, Applicable Law, Recognition, Enforcement and Cooperation in respect of Parental Responsibility and Measures for the Protection of Children and authorising certain Member States to make a declaration on the application of the relevant internal rules of Community law [2008] OJ L151/36. See E. Pataut, 'The External Dimension of Private International Family Law' in M. Cremona and H.-W. Micklitz (eds.), *Private Law in the External Relations of the EU*, Oxford University Press, Oxford 2016, p. 109, who entitles the paragraph with the significant words 'Forcing Ratification' of the 1996 Hague Convention.

7 The obligation arises from the principle of fair cooperation. See M. Cremona, 'Member States as Trustees of the Community Interest: Participating in International Agreements on Behalf of the European Community', EUI Working papers. Law, 2009/17, p. 10.

Member State of the European Union; and 2) the adult (or adults) already resides in the European Union and the child was entrusted to his or her *kafala* care by the competent authority in the child's State of habitual residence. The answer is not straightforward because the entry and residence of foreigners is a matter that can be regulated by both the EU and its Member States. Therefore, it is necessary to test whether EU legislation applies: for this purpose, Directive 2003/86 on family reunification of third-country nationals and Directive 2004/38 on the free movement of Union citizens will be scrutinised. If the two directives turned out not to be applicable, the relevant rules are those laid down by the Member States. The Member States approach the entry and residence of children placed in *kafala* in different ways. Among them, Italy stands out for its 'creative' interpretation of the law and for this reason deserves a closer analysis. The chapter concludes by examining whether common principles can be identified to guide decision-making in this area.

2. THE 1996 HAGUE CONVENTION AND MIGRATION

The 1996 Hague Convention mentions *kafala* – or, more precisely, 'the provision of care by kafala' – as an institution for the protection of children, in addition to 'the placement of the child in a foster family or in institutional care' (Article 3, sub-paragraph e), and includes *kafala* in its scope.[8] *Kafala* is not defined in the Convention itself. However, the Explanatory Report by Paul Lagarde specifies that the Morocco delegation supplied a description according to its internal law, which can be summarised as follows: 'a child in need of protection may be entrusted either by a decision of the guardianship judge or by an administrative commission to a public or social institution or to a Muslim family which care for the child's person (shelter, maintenance, education) and, if needed, for the property of the child and who, if necessary, would receive delegation of guardianship over the child. The *kafala* is not an adoption, which would be forbidden by Islamic law, and it produces no effect on the parent-child relationship. The child who benefits from it does not become a member of the family of the *kafil*'.[9] Similar institutions are also established in other countries,[10]

8 Article 3 of the Convention lists a series of 'measures directed to the protection of the person or property of the child' that are included in its scope. On the Convention see M.C. Baruffi, 'Sulla tutela internazionalprivatistica dei diritti dei minori stranieri nella Convenzione dell'Aja del 1996', in C. Fratea and I. Quadranti (a cura di), *Minori e immigrazione: quali diritti?*, [2015] Edizioni Scientifiche italiane, pp. 151–182.

9 Lagarde Report, para. 23. *Kafil* refers to the adult with which the child is placed.

10 In Algeria and Tunisia according to N. Yassari, 'Adding by Choice: Adoption and Functional Equivalents in Islamic and Middle Eastern Law', (2015) *The American Journal of Comparative Law*, 927; in Muslim States, with the exception of Indonesia, Tunisia and Turkey, according to the Strasbourg Court, in *Harroudj*, para. 16.

but only Morocco is a contracting party to the Convention. The institution's key feature is that the child is placed within the *kafil*'s family but does not have a legal child status.

The Convention requires contracting States to recognise child protection measures, including *kafala*, adopted by the competent authority, i.e. the State authority of the child's habitual residence. However, it does not deal with matters relating to residence permits, as is clear from Article 4(j), which excludes 'decisions … on immigration'.[11] On the other hand, it does establish a procedure to be followed if the child is placed abroad. Failure to follow the procedure constitutes grounds for refusal of recognition.[12] According to Article 33, a competent authority contemplating a child's placement in *kafala* with a *kafil* based abroad must contact the competent authority in the State where the decision will take effect to explain the reasons for the child's proposed placement with a family abroad. If the requested State's authority consents to the placement after considering the child's best interests, the requesting authority may pronounce the decision establishing the *kafala*. In the absence of consent, the decision cannot be made, or, if already made, recognition of that decision can be refused. As the Lagarde Report clarifies, the procedure serves 'to determine in advance the conditions under which the child will stay in the receiving State, in particular in respect to the immigration laws in force in that State'.[13] Article 33 is a provision that the States must implement; therefore, defining the procedure to be followed is necessary.

The Convention does not specify any procedural obligation in situations where the child has been placed in *kafala* with an adult residing in the State that ordered the placement and the family subsequently wishes to move abroad – perhaps years later.

3. ENTRY AND RESIDENCE OF FOREIGN NATIONALS WITHIN THE EU

The Treaties conferred competence on the Union to define the conditions governing foreign nationals' entry and residence. However, the legal basis differs according to the foreign national's status or nationality. A distinction is made, including from a terminology perspective, between free movement of persons and immigration policy. Free movement of persons concerns the right of Union

11 The Lagarde report justifies the exclusion, which concerns only 'the granting … of a residence permit,' by stating that these are 'decisions which derive from the sovereign power of the States' (para. 36).

12 Article 23 of the Convention lists reasons for refusal of recognition, including, under letter f), where the procedure provided in Article 33 has not been complied with.

13 Lagarde Report, paragraph 143.

citizens and their family members (whatever their nationality) to enter and reside in a Union State of which they are not nationals. Its legal basis lies in Article 21 of the Treaty on the Functioning of the EU (TFEU), which also gives the Union the power to establish conditions and limits on that right's exercise. In contrast, conditions governing entry and residence of third-country nationals (who are not family members of Union citizens) form part of immigration policy and can be defined by the Union under Article 79 TFEU.[14] That provision does not confer any right on third-country nationals but simply confers competence on the Union. With regard to immigration, the Union has not yet drawn up a common policy but has adopted a series of acts that establish conditions of entry and residence for particular categories of third-country nationals or of the treatment to be afforded to certain categories of foreign nationals legally residing in the Union territory.

Free movement and immigration are matters of shared competence in the sense that both the Union and Member States can legislate in those areas. The Union can issue binding acts only if the measure being contemplated passes the subsidiarity test. If a Union act is in force, the principle of the primacy of Union law means that States cannot adopt acts that conflict with those of the Union. If, however, the Union has not exercised its competence, States may legislate, while respecting the Union's objectives. Any matter not governed by Union law will continue to be a matter for the national law.

4. FAMILY REUNIFICATION: EU LEGISLATION

The law applicable to family reunification in the EU is not unitary but reflects the difference in legal basis – as described in the previous paragraph – which in turn depends on the sponsor's nationality, i.e. the person applying for reunification. Specifically, if the sponsor is a Union citizen residing in a different Member State from the State of nationality, family reunification is governed by Directive 2004/38. If the sponsor is a third-country national residing in a Member State, family reunification comes under Directive 2003/86. If the sponsor is a Union citizen residing in his or her own State of nationality, this is not a case governed by EU law but is a matter for national law.[15]

---

14 If third-country nationals are seeking protection in the European Union, relevant provisions are contained in Article 78 TFEU (which we do not analyse here).

15 Article 3(3) of Directive 2003/86/EC expressly states that it does not apply to reunification of family members of the citizen of the State concerned. The Commission's initial proposal was to extend rules laid down for Union workers (which, at the time, were contained in Regulation 1612/68/EEC) to the situation in question (COM/1999/638). However, the proposal was subsequently dropped. The Commission justifies this by reference to the contemporaneous start on work to recast the law on free movement of Union citizens and to the need to wait

Directive 2003/86 and Directive 2004/38 outline different rules. Both confer a right of family reunification on members of a nuclear family (who are also defined somewhat differently, as will shortly be seen in relation to children); however, they give States a margin of appreciation with respect to reunification of other categories of family members. Conditions governing reunification also differ. They are more favourable if the sponsor is a Union citizen (and more favourable still if the Union citizen is self-employed or a worker)[16] and less favourable if the sponsor is a third-country national.[17] First, it is important to remember that Union acts intend to establish uniform rules applicable in all Member States while recognising national legal systems' distinctive characteristics. Legal notions must therefore be considered autonomous; in other words, they must be construed according to the letter and purpose of the act and not by reference to national law unless an express reference is made to the national law.

4.1. DIRECTIVE 2003/86

Directive 2003/86 applies to the family reunification of a foreign national who holds a residence permit that lasts for at least one year and who has reasonable prospects of obtaining the right of permanent residence. The aim is to maintain the nuclear family's unity regardless of when the family relationship arose.[18] The State may impose a waiting period before a foreign national can apply for reunification.

---

until that recasting is complete before reviewing how to ensure 'the alignment of the rights of all Union citizens to family reunification' (COM/2002/225). However, the fact remains that Directive 2004/38/EC applies only to Union citizens residing in a State other than the State of origin. For the sake of completeness, it should be added that European Union law governs a number of very specific situations relating to family reunification of a Union citizen in his or her State of nationality. Due to the ancillary nature of these situations, together with reasons of limited space, we cannot discuss them in this article.

16 No conditions are laid down for reunification of workers. If the Union citizen is a student or is economically self-sufficient, s/he must have, both personally and for their family members, sickness insurance and sufficient resources not to become a burden on the host State (Article 7 of Directive 2004/38).

17 Under Article 7 of Directive 2003/86, applicants must provide evidence that they have accommodation regarded as normal for a comparable family, sickness insurance, and stable and regular resources without the need to have recourse to State assistance. In addition, States may impose further integration measures that the family member must satisfy before achieving reunification.

18 S. Peers, E. Guild, D. Acosta Arcarazo, K. Groenendijk and V. Moreno-Lax (eds.), *EU immigration and Asylum Law (Text and Commentary), Second revisited edition. Volume 2: EU immigration Law*, Nijhoff, Leiden 2012, p. 247–272; K. Hailbronner, C. Arévalo and T. Klarmann, 'Directive 2003/86' in K. Hailbronner and D. Thym (eds.), *Immigration and Asylum Law: A Commentary*, C.H. Beck, München 2016, pp. 300–426.

According to the European Court of Justice's interpretation, the Directive confers a right to reunification on family members listed in Article 4(1).[19] Article 4 applies to minor children and unmarried children according to the requested State's law. If the sponsor is married, the child may be a common child, the sponsor's child alone, or the spouse's child alone. An adopted child is included within the notion of child. The adoption may, however, be ordered by the competent authority in the host State; if ordered by the authority of another State, the decision must be automatically enforceable due to international obligations of the host Member State or must be recognised in accordance with its international obligations. It is not sufficient for the adoption decision to be recognisable in the State on the basis of private international law rules. It must be a decision whose recognition is governed by international agreements. The reference here is obviously to the 1993 Hague Adoption Convention[20] and to bilateral treaties that States have concluded on the subject of adoption. The 1993 Convention 'covers only adoptions which create a permanent parent-child relationship' (Article 2(2)).

The report accompanying the proposed Directive provides that 'the entry of children 'entrusted' in accordance with certain local customs is not possible, unless the relevant authority of the Member State recognizes that such customs have the same effect as adoption'.[21]

Clearly, from Article 4's wording, given the Directive's objective, a 'child' means a person who has that status on account of biological ties or legal ties (adoption) that confer child status by operation of law. Therefore, the family unit exists if this status is present regardless of whether the parties actually live together.[22] A family relationship with a child other than the relationship arising with a person having legal child status is not included within the Directive's scope; the Directive does not include relationships between family members mentioned in Article 4(2) and (3) to whom States have the right to grant reunification.[23]

---

19 Case C-540/03 *Parliament v. Council*, ECLI:EU:C:2006:429, para. 60.

20 Convention of 29.05.1993 on Protection of Children and Co-operation in Respect of Intercountry Adoption.

21 COM/99/638.

22 During preparatory works, the Netherlands sought an addition to the effect that children must have a 'genuine relationship' with their parents. This position was not shared by the Commission (Working Party on Migration and Expulsion, Outcome of the Proceedings, 19-20.02.2001, 6450/01). Nonetheless, the Directive allows States to take account of effective ties between children and parents if the children have resided for a long period of time in the country of origin without the parents.

23 Paragraph 2 concerns adult children and first-degree relatives in the direct ascending line, and paragraph 3, the partner and the partner's children.

In light of its wording and preparatory works, analysis of Directive 2003/86 demonstrates that entry and residence of children placed in *kafala* care do not come within its scope.

4.2. DIRECTIVE 2004/38

Directive 2004/38 concerns family reunification of Union citizens residing in the host State as workers or self-employed workers, students, or financially self-sufficient individuals. Family members entitled to reunification include the Union citizen's descendants or those of the spouse. There is no mention of minor children because the age of the person being reunited is of limited importance. Indeed, all descendants under 21 years enjoy an unconditional right of residence. Above that age, they must be 'dependents' of the Union citizen or of the spouse. The use of the term 'descendant' as opposed to that of 'child' is intentional. The aim is to cover not only situations in which a parent is reunited with a child but also those in which a grandparent is reunited with a grandchild.[24] During preparatory works within the Council, several interesting questions were raised but were not ultimately included in the final adopted text. In particular, as far as the definition of children is concerned, Belgium, Denmark and Austria asked for the same wording as the Directive on family reunification of third-country nationals, which was being developed at the same time. The Presidency, Italy and the Commission responded 'that the two proposals referred to different situations and that it would be misguided to attempt a uniform definition to apply to all situations'.[25]

In the Communication to the European Parliament and to the Council on guidance for better transposition and application of Directive 2004/38/EC on the right of citizens of the Union and their family members to move and reside freely within the territory of the Member States,[26] the Commission writes that the notion of 'descendant' includes adopted children[27] as well as 'minors in custody of a permanent legal guardian' without further elaboration. It adds that

---

24 '[T]he persons within the scope of Article 2(2)(c) *obviously* include the children, grandchildren et al of the EU citizen': E. Guild, S. Peers and J. Tomkin, *The EU Citizenship Directive. A Commentary*, Oxford University Press, Oxford 2014, p. 44 (emphasis added). Preparatory works back this interpretation. In response to a specific question, the Commission stated that provisions on descendants and ascendants 'referred to the whole line of parentage (children/grandchildren/parents/grandparents)': Working Party on Free Movement of Persons, outcome of the proceedings of 14 and 28.11 and 11.12.2001, 15380/01, p. 8.

25 Working Party on Free Movement of Persons, outcome of the proceedings of 08.02, 11.03, 15.04 and 14.06.2002, 10572/02, p. 12.

26 COM/2009/313, Brussels, 02.07.2009.

27 During preparatory works, the Commission had already specified that the notion of descendant includes 'legitimate, adopted, and natural children' (15380/01 cit. p. 8).

'foster children and foster parents who have temporary custody may have rights under the Directive, depending upon the strength of the ties in the particular case'. As far as adopted children are concerned, unlike Directive 2003/86, no conditions are established limiting the group of beneficiaries.

When a child is placed in *kafala* care with grandparents, he or she is a descendant benefitting from reunification rights. If the child is placed with other relatives, e.g. uncles and aunts, or with persons who have no family ties with that child, Article 3 of the Directive could apply, requiring States to 'facilitate' reunification of other family members beyond the nuclear family (for which see below). The European Court of Justice rejected the alternative interpretation of considering the child placed in *kafala* care as a 'descendant'. It said that when there is no child-parent relationship between the child and the adult, Article 2 of the Directive is not applicable.[28] The protection of family life provided for in Article 8 ECHR, which underlies Directive 2004/38, could have justified a different reading of the provision. As is discussed below, the Strasbourg Court has defined family life so as to include the relationship between child and *kafil*, at least in cases referred to it. One could have therefore relied on the need to protect family life to extend the notion of 'descendant' as to include cases in which, despite the absence of a legal parent-child relationship, the child is placed in the protection of a Union citizen (or of the spouse).

5. STATE PRACTICE

Given that *kafala* is not included within the scope of Directive 2003/86 and Directive 2004/38 (although the latter lends itself to an interpretation whereby it could be included), this raises the question as to how Member States deal with the issue. Moreover, if the *kafil* is a citizen of the State in which reunification is applied for, Union law is not applicable.

However, investigating national laws and practices is extremely difficult. To this author's knowledge, no comprehensive, systematic and up-to-date study is available.[29] Nonetheless, certain indications can be gathered from various sources that have studied the subject or from which indicative information can be gleaned.[30] More detailed comments will be given about how Italy deals with

---

28 Case C-129/18, *SM*, ECLI:EU:C:2019:248, para. 52.

29 A certain number of studies have examined the problem of recognising a *kafala* measure from the perspective of private international law and how *kafala* compares with institutions for protection of children under national law. For instance, see C. Tuo, 'Riconoscimento degli effetti delle adozioni straniere e rispetto delle diversità culturali', (2014) *Rivista di diritto internazionale privato e processuale*, 43–79.

30 The following sources have been taken into consideration: two reports by the European Migration Network (an EU network of migration and asylum experts who work together

the issue because it is more straightforward to gather and interpret sources there and because Italian case law on this subject matter is unquestionably interesting.

In general, no express rules govern children placed in *kafala* care. Nonetheless, at least in certain States, the child may be granted a residence permit to live with the *kafil*. With the exception of Italy, the entry of a child placed in *kafala* does not fall within the scope of family reunification in a strict sense. This is because a *kafala* child is not considered equivalent to a child for the purposes of immigration law but is considered to fall within the margin of appreciation afforded to national authorities. This can point to the existence of family ties leading to the conclusion of there being life in common and the best interests of the child as being served by living with the *kafil*.[31]

The situation in Italy is somewhat unusual. In the absence of any legislative provisions, the Italian Court of Cassation has reconstructed, through interpretation, a right of entry for a child placed in *kafala*.[32] This case law developed before Italy ratified the 1996 Hague Convention.[33]

The approach followed depends on the *kafil*'s nationality. If the sponsor is a third-country national, the relevant legislation is the Consolidated Immigration Act (*Testo Unico sull'Immigrazione*).[34] This Act provides that family reunification rights also apply to children placed in foster care, not just children in the legal sense. If the sponsor is an Italian citizen, the applicable legislation is Legislative Decree No. 30/2007, which is the transposition of Directive 2004/38 and extends application of that Directive to family members of Italian citizens.[35] The Court

---

to provide objective, comparable policy-relevant information: <https://ec.europa.eu/home-affairs/content/about-emn-0_en>) entitled 'Misuse of the right to family reunification: marriage of convenience and false declaration of parenthood' (2012) and 'Family Reunification of third country nationals in the EU plus Norway: national practices' (2016); two studies by the Directorate General for Internal Policies, Policy Department for Citizens' Rights and Constitutional Affairs, Legal Affairs, of the European Parliament, 'Private International Law in a Context of Increasing International Mobility: Challenges and Potential' (2017) and 'Children on the Move: A Private International Law Perspective' (2017); and two articles by R. Duca, 'Family Reunification: The Case of the Muslim Migrant Children in Europe', (2014) *Athens Journal of Social Sciences*, 111–120 (which examines practice in Italy, France and United Kingdom), and 'Diffusion of Islamic Law in the UK: the Case of the 'Special Guardianship' in S. Farran, J. Gallen, J. Hendry and C. Rautenbach (eds.), *The Diffusion of Law: the Movement of Laws and Norms*, Routledge, Abingdon 2015, pp. 47–58.

31 According to documents mentioned in the previous footnote, this is the case in France, Belgium, Germany, and the United Kingdom.

32 For a summary of relevant Italian case law, see A. Marotta, 'Italy and Kafalah: Reinventing Traditional Perspectives to Accommodate Diversity?', (2016) 2 *The Italian Law Journal* No. 1, 191–211.

33 Italy ratified the 1996 Hague Convention on 30.09.2015. See C. Peraro, 'Il riconoscimento degli effetti della kafalah: una questione non ancora risolta', (2015) *Rivista di diritto internazionale privato e processuale*, 541.

34 Legislative Decree 25.07.1998, No. 286.

35 Article 23 of Legislative Decree 2007/30 reads: 'The provisions of this legislative decree, if more favourable, shall apply to the family members of Italian citizens who do not have Italian

of Cassation has held that a child placed in *kafala* cannot be considered the same as a legal child but treats a *kafala* child as being among other family members under Article 3. No cases have yet arisen in which the applicant is a Union citizen, but presumably the interpretation followed would be the same as that for an Italian citizen. The case law is not entirely satisfactory and deserves a more detailed analysis.

With regard to the interpretation of the Consolidated Immigration Act, Article 29 implements Directive 2003/86. In fact, Italy has amended the Consolidated Immigration Act to incorporate relevant Directives adopted over time by the Union but has retained the original terminology. Thus, Article 29(1) reproduces the list of family members entitled to reunification using language similar to that of the Directive ('minor children, including those of the spouse or those born outside of marriage, unmarried children, provided the other parent, where existing, has given his or her agreement').[36] Article 29(2) specifies that 'Children who are adopted or fostered or under guardianship are considered as children in the legal sense',[37] a provision that has not been amended and which appeared in the provision's original version. According to the Court of Cassation, *kafala* is analogous to the institution of fostering under Italian law, and this justifies treating a *kafala* child in the same way as a legal child under Article 29 of the Consolidated Immigration Act.[38]

With regard to the interpretation of Legislative Decree No. 30/2007 (Article 2 and Article 3 of which merely reproduce the same Articles in Directive 2004/38), the Court of Cassation[39] does not ascribe proper importance to the fact that

nationality.' ('Le disposizioni del presente decreto legislativo, se più favorevoli, si applicano ai familiari di cittadini italiani non aventi la cittadinanza italiana.') This is a choice that Italy has made without any obligation arising from Union law, but which has the advantage of avoiding reverse discrimination through which Italian citizens are treated less favorably than Union citizens.

36 'Figli minori, anche del coniuge o nati fuori del matrimonio, non coniugati, a condizione che l'altro genitore, qualora esistente, abbia dato il suo consenso'.

37 'I minori adottati o affidati o sottoposti a tutela sono equiparati ai figli.'

38 Judgment no. 7472 of 20.03.2008.

39 Initially, in its judgment no. 4868 of 01.03.2010, the Court of Cassation had stated that Legislative Decree No. 30/2007 could not be construed as justifying a right of entry and residence for a child placed in *kafala* with an Italian citizen because the notion of 'descendant' requires a biological tie between parent and child. Despite noting the difference in treatment where the applicant is an Italian citizen and where the applicant is a third-country national, the Court of Cassation deemed that this was not discriminatory, stating that an Italian citizen could have pursued the route of adoption to establish the legal parent-child relationship required for reunification. To resolve the clear discrepancy between the two approaches identified, Section VI of the Court of Cassation, Civil Division, asked the Combined Sections, in Order no. 996 of 24.01.2012, to assess whether family reunification of a child placed in *kafala* with an Italian citizen could also be governed by Article 29 of the Consolidated Immigration Act, given that Article 23 of Legislative Decree No. 30/2007 provides that more favorable provisions can be applied. The Combined Sections gave their ruling in judgment no. 21108 of 16.09.2013, which is the approach now followed and which will be considered below.

this decree is the transposition of Directive 2004/38. According to the Court, the family reunification of an Italian citizen is governed by Legislative Decree No. 30/2007 alone but as interpreted in light of two guiding principles: the best interests of the child and conformity with the Constitution. The need to ensure the best interests of the child derives from international law and from the Italian Constitution. With regard to conformity with the Constitution, the Court of Cassation emphasises that an interpretation of Legislative Decree No. 30/2007 that completely prohibits any reunification of a child of an Italian citizen would violate the principle of equality enshrined in Article 2 of the Constitution insofar as it would bring about unequal treatment between foster families based on nationality. Specifically, the best interests of the child and conformity with the Constitution justified the interpretation of Article 29 of the Consolidated Immigration Act whereby *kafala* was recognised as a suitable basis for reunification rights of a foreign national, as mentioned above.

Having clarified the appropriate method to be followed, the Court of Cassation turns to Article 2 and Article 3 of Legislative Decree No. 30/2007 to interpret them so that they can be consistently applied with the Constitution and in accordance with international law. It specifies that a child placed in *kafala* cannot be considered a 'descendant' within the meaning of Article 2 because the notion, broadly interpreted, 'implies a parental relationship, founded on the biological reality or also on the legal reality of the legitimising adoption'.[40] In contrast, a *kafala* child may fall within the scope of Article 3 under 'other family members'. Article 3 is interpreted along the lines that if established conditions are met (namely if, in the country of origin, the child is a dependent or a member of the applicant's household or where serious health grounds require the applicant to take care of the child), a right of entry and residence for the child arises. Therefore, the right to reunification arises not only if the child placed in *kafala* and Italian citizens have lived together in the country in which the arrangement was ordered but also where they have not lived together but the child is the Italian citizen's dependent or where serious health grounds strictly require the personal care of the Italian citizen with whom the child is placed.

In the system established under Directive 2004/38, Article 3 concerns family members other than those who are part of the restricted family defined in Article 2. If family members under Article 2 enjoy a right of entry and residence, other family members under Article 3 are left only with the expectation that the State will favourably assess their application for entry and residence.[41] In contrast, the

[40] 'Implica un rapporto parentale, fondato sulla realtà biologica o anche solo giuridica dell'adozione legittimante.'

[41] The State has the obligation to 'facilitate' the entry and residence of 'other family members', but is not obliged to accord such right: according to the Court of Justice, 'that provision imposes an obligation on the Member States to confer a certain advantage, compared with

Court of Cassation states that if conditions established in Article 3 of Legislative Decree No. 30/2007 are met, family reunification cannot be refused. The Italian Court therefore anticipates the legal reasoning that the European Court of Justice will adopt a few years later.

The Court of Cassation initially held that the interests of the child meant that the requirements for reunification could be met only if *kafala* was ordered by a judge but not in the case of consensual *kafala*. The Court seems to consider judicial *kafala* an abstract institution established in the interests of the child, with an assessment conducted by the authority that ordered it as sufficient for ensuring that the placement is in the interests of that particular child. In contrast, in consensual *kafala*, placement results from an agreement between private individuals, which does not require the authority's prior assessment as to the interests of the child. Subsequently, however, the Court changed its stance and confirmed that consensual *kafala* can also constitute the basis for family reunification rights under Article 3 of Legislative Decree No. 30/2007.[42]

In interpreting the applicable Italian law, the Court of Cassation does not consider that these acts implement Union law. The Consolidated Immigration Act is interpreted more broadly than the Directive, but always consistently with the latter, because States are free to specify what happens in situations without rules. By contrast, Legislative Decree No. 30/2007 is interpreted in a manner inconsistent with its nature. Indeed, the Italian Supreme Court uses specific categories of Italian law and employs other national legislative acts to clarify terms in the Decree. In particular, it states that a child placed in *kafala* cannot be considered a 'descendant' because, in the Court's view, the term presupposes a parent-child relationship and specifies that the child instead falls under the category of 'other family members' because the concept of family, as is well known in Italian law, 'does not necessarily require the existence of parental ties'.[43] The Court overlooks the fact that the Legislative Decree is the transposition of Directive 2004/38/EC. Therefore, notions of 'descendant' and 'other family members', which the Legislative Decree takes directly from the Directive, should

---

applications for entry and residence of other nationals of third States, on applications submitted by persons who have a relationship of particular dependence with a Union citizen' (Case C-83/11, *Rahman*, ECLI:EU:C:2012:519, para. 21). However, with regard to a child under *kafala* care, the same Court said that the fundamental right to enjoy a genuine family life and the best interest of the child demand that a right to entry and residence is granted (Case C-129/18, *SM*, ECLI:EU:C:2019:248, para. 71).

42 Court of Cassation, Civil Division, Section I, judgments no. 6204 of 18.03.2014 and no. 1843 of 02.02.2015. In the second of the two cases mentioned, it is clear from the judgment that the child was placed with his uncle and aunt, within the same family according to its extended meaning. It remains to be seen whether this detail is relevant for the Court of Cassation, in other words, whether it is willing to follow the same reasoning in cases in which the child placed in consensual *kafala* is outside the foster parent's family.

43 'Non richiede necessariamente l'esistenza di legami di tipo parentale.'

not be interpreted in relation to Italian law (or that of any other Member State); however, the objective and system from which they derive must be considered.

The Court of Cassation seems rather casual in its interpretation of the legal notions of a Decree implementing a Directive. The Court finds itself ruling on cases that do not fall within the Directive's scope. However, Legislative Decree No. 30/2007 specified that family reunification for an Italian citizen is subject to the same rules as those governing family reunification for a Union citizen. Although not imposed by the Directive, the solution is compatible with Union law and has a bearing on the requirement that legal notions must be interpreted in a manner consistent with Community law.

6. SEEKING COMMON PRINCIPLES

Bringing children placed in *kafala* within the scope of Directive 2003/86 is not straightforward, given the Directive's wording and the provision's origin that associates the notion of child with a legal parent-child relationship. In contrast, it is more straightforward, again based on wording and origin, to include *kafala* children within the notion of 'family member' under Directive 2004/38. If the child does not fall within the scope of Union law, rules governing the child's entry and residence will continue to be determined by national law. However, for Member States to follow uniform criteria in examining visa and residence permit applications would not be inappropriate. They share obligations and values and have common concerns in tackling the question; these circumstances could justify a certain convergence in approaching and resolving questions associated with the entry of a child placed in *kafala*.

First, as already mentioned, Member States acceded to the 1996 Hague Convention in the interest of the Union. On the basis of that Convention, States are obliged to recognise a foreign child protection measure. Failing to establish a specific procedure for examining an application for entry and residence or systematically refusing entry and residence would compromise the Convention's effectiveness and render the commitment made by contracting parties in ratifying the Convention devoid of meaning. This would breach the general principle of good faith. Member States have the specific obligation to adopt measures to enforce Article 33 of the Convention.[44]

Second, States share common values based on human rights, codified in sources that are formally outside the EU but part of the European legal system.

---

44 In 2014, the Hague Conference published a *Practical Handbook* to guide States in the process of ratification and enforcement of the Convention. Specifically, the *Handbook* lists provisions of the Convention that may require enforcement measures to be applicable and, among these, it refers to Article 33, on cross-border provision of care by *kafala*.

The 1989 New York Convention on the Rights of the Child establishes the fundamental principle of the best interests of the child as a guiding principle in all decisions concerning children and mentions *kafala* as a form of child protection (Article 20). Member States are bound by this, and the European Court of Justice includes this among the international instruments for the protection of human rights which it considers in reconstructing the fundamental rights applicable to Community law.[45] The *General Comment on the right of the child to have his or her best interest taken as a primary consideration* provides that 'The term 'family' must be interpreted in a broad sense to include biological, adoptive or foster parents or, where applicable, the members of the extended family or community as provided for by local custom'.[46] If the child's biological parents are known, the best interests of the child could be served by refusing entry if those interests are identified as being served by living with the biological family.

Furthermore, Member States are all bound by the ECHR, which forms part of the Union's general principles. The Strasbourg Court has recognised that family life, protected under Article 8 ECHR, can exist between a *kafil* and a child placed in *kafala*. This interpretation is particularly helpful if the family moves together but is less so if the child is placed abroad.

The Strasbourg Court has examined the issue of *kafala* in two judgments. In both cases, the *kafil* was a citizen of the State of residence (France, Belgium) with whom the authorities (of Algeria and Morocco, respectively) had placed a child. The child lived with the *kafil* in the host State, highlighting that family reunification is possible in certain cases at least. In both cases, the applicants complained that the national authorities rejected their application to adopt the child and to establish the legal parent-child relationship. The Court dismissed the appeals because the ECHR does not guarantee the right to adopt. These cases are of interest here because the Court agreed to examine the question within the framework of Article 8 ECHR, recognising that the relationship between child and *kafil* can constitute 'family life'.

In *Harroudj*,[47] the applicant complained of a violation of Article 8 ECHR because France had not allowed her to adopt a child (of unknown parents and abandoned at birth) placed in her *kafala* care, as the child's national law prohibited adoption, and, in so doing, did not allow a legal parent-child relationship to be established with the child, whom she regarded as her daughter. The Court examined the French authorities' decision from the perspective of its possible interference with the applicant's family life, thus taking it as given (which, moreover, France did not dispute) that family life existed between the applicant and the child. The application was dismissed because, even without

45 Case C-540/03, *Parliament v. Council*, ECLI:EU:C:2006:429, para. 37.

46 Committee on the Rights of the Child. General Comment No. 14 (2013), CRC/C/GC/14.

47 *Harroudi* v. *France*, no. 43631/09, ECHR 2012.

adoption and formal recognition of the legal parent-child relationship, family life between applicant and child could exist without impediment.

In *Chbihi Loudoudi*,[48] a child had been placed in *kafala* care with her uncle and aunt residing in Belgium. Both father and mother were known but were not looking after the child and had consented to the placement. The child was allowed to reunite with the uncle and aunt due to a short-term visa pending her adoption and to live with them. She had been granted a temporary residence permit, which was renewed several times. In the meantime, adoption proceedings commenced and, following rejection, an application was submitted for a permit of unlimited duration. Indefinite leave to remain was finally granted right before the Court's judgment.

In this case, the Court is more explicit in stating that the relationship between *kafil* and child is considered as family life. It states that even *de facto* family ties can be protected by Article 8 if the relationship between the parties concerned is genuine. The Court must assess the genuine nature of the relationship, considering time spent together, the relationship's quality and the role played by adults *vis-à-vis* the child.[49] In this case, the *kafil* and the child had lived together since the time of placement in a manner no different from that of a 'traditional family'. The Court then states that when ties are maintained with the biological family (in this case, only very occasional contacts, with the mother only), this is not sufficient to exclude the existence of family ties between the parties.[50]

The second complaint brought by the child in this case was that her precarious situation, brought about by the issue of a residence permit of limited duration and of uncertain renewal, constituted interference with her private life. The Court indicates that Article 8 does not confer the right to receive a particular type of residence permit. Any permit that enables the party concerned to reside in the host State and to freely exercise his or her right to respect for private and family life is, in principle, a sufficient measure (paragraph 135). Although special attention is paid on the best interests of the child, this is not sufficient cause to impose on the State an obligation to grant a residence permit of unlimited duration to protect family life.[51]

---

48 *Chbihi Loudoudi and Others* v. *Belgium*, no. 52265/10, ECHR 2015.

49 'Ce qui importe dans ce type de situations, c'est la réalité concrète de la relation entre les intéressés. La Cour se penchera donc sur l'effectivité de la relation entre les requérants en tenant compte du temps vécu ensemble, de la qualité des relations ainsi que du rôle assumé par les adultes envers l'enfant' (para. 78).

50 '[La Cour] accepte, avec les requérants, que la persistance des liens entre l'enfant et sa famille d'origine n'exclut pas l'existence d'une vie familiale avec d'autres personnes' (para. 79).

51 'La Cour est d'avis que même en accordant, comme le veut la jurisprudence rappelée ci-dessus (voir paragraphe 131), un poids important à l'intérêt de l'enfant, il serait déraisonnable de considérer, sur la base de cette seule conséquence, que l'État belge était tenu, dans l'exercice de ses compétences en la matière, d'accorder un titre de séjour à durée illimité pour protéger la vie privée de la troisième requérante' (para. 137).

In the two cases above, the family life protected by Article 8 ECHR had arisen in the *kafil*'s State of nationality. However, nothing should prevent the States from protecting family life where this situation has arisen abroad.

Although the international texts mentioned above favour a residence permit being granted to enable the *kafala* measure to take effect in the Union, protecting family life and the best interests of the child, there is no denying that the institution's peculiarities could justify a certain degree of caution by States. The problem is not so much that *kafala* is not provided for in Member States' law. Clearly, its inclusion in international conventions as a child protection measure prevents it from being automatically rejected. The problem has more to do with the risk of rules on adoption or immigration being circumvented. These fears are particularly justified if the *kafil* is already a resident in the Union or is a citizen of the State in which recognition of the placement measure is sought.

In the presence of conflicting interests, it seems right to conduct an individual examination of each case to weigh the interest of family life against other public interests deserving protection. National authorities should, however, consider international obligations that Member States have assumed in their own and in the EU's interests.

AGAINST A GIRL'S WILL

Child Marriages, Immigration and the Directive on Family Reunification

Sara De Vido

1. Introduction and Scope of Analysis 115
2. Child Marriages 117
   2.1. Prohibition of Child Marriages in International Law 118
   2.2. Child Marriages as a Violation of Human Rights 121
3. Family Reunification under EU Law and Child Marriages 125
   3.1. The Age for Family Reunification in ECJ Jurisprudence 127
   3.2. Family Reunification in the ECtHR Jurisprudence 128
4. Prohibition of Child Marriages, Family Reunification and the Istanbul Convention 130
5. When Denying Family Reunification Causes Violence against Women 133
   5.1. Autonomous Residence Permits 134
6. Conclusions 136

1. INTRODUCTION AND SCOPE OF ANALYSIS

Family reunification constitutes one of the main reasons for immigration into the European Union (EU). This chapter reflects on a specific aspect of migration issues, i.e. the manner and extent to which the prohibition of child marriages as affirmed at the international level can limit family reunification in the EU. Directive 2003/86/EC on the right to family reunification is the key legal instrument in this respect; it leaves States discretion in requiring the sponsor and his/her spouse to be of a minimum age 'before the spouse is able to join him/her' (Article 4(5)).[1] The provision was interpreted by the European Court

[1] Council Directive 2003/86/EC of 22 September 2003, on the right to family reunification [2003] OJ L 251/12.

of Justice, which considered the decision of a State to assess the age limit *at the time of the application* for family reunification to be legitimate.[2]

This chapter argues that the prohibition of forced child marriages *always* constitutes a limit to family reunification, even when the spouse, sponsor, or both, has reached the minimum age for reunification. Moreover, it is contended that child marriages are forced – hence not a ground for family reunification – in *all* cases in which they constitute gender-based violence against women and girls, as defined at the international level: this is the case of a marriage between a girl and a male adult. To support the main argument, this chapter relies on the recent Council of Europe Convention on preventing and combating violence against women and domestic violence (Istanbul Convention) of 2011,[3] which the EU has signed but not yet ratified. The Convention enshrines pivotal provisions prohibiting forced marriages, and these can be applied in cases of child marriages.

This analysis is guided by the best interest of the child, a principle clearly recognised at the international level[4] and codified in Article 24(2) of the EU Charter of Fundamental Rights.[5] Despite being aware of the existence of child marriages that involve boys, the focus here will be on female brides because girls are disproportionately affected by the practice.

The analysis begins with a definition of and some data on child and forced marriages before investigating the main legal instruments that contain the prohibition of the practice and outline the child's basic human rights that are thus violated. Thereafter, it considers Directive 2003/86/EC, which ensures the right to family reunification for applicants who fulfil the requirements defined in the legal instrument and the jurisprudence related to Article 4(5). The research scope then expands to analyse the European Court of Human Rights (ECtHR) judgment in *Z.H. and R.H. v. Switzerland*.

Eventually, the chapter revisits the main argument by posing a key question: does combating a form of violence against children, such as forced marriages,

---

2 See below, section. 2.

3 CETS No. 210.

4 See, among others, UNHCR, *Guidelines on Determining the Best Interests of the Child*, Geneva 2008; M. Distefano, *Interesse superiore del minore e sottrazione internazionale di minore*, Cedam, Padova 2012; H. Keller and C. Heri, 'Protecting the Best Interests of the Child: International Child Abduction and the European Court of Human Rights' (2015) 84 *Nordic Journal of International Law*, 270; J. M. Pobjoy, 'The Best Interest of the Child Principle as an Independent Source of International Protection' (2015) 64 *ICLQ*, 327. The best interest of the child might even overcome the limit of *ordre public* as it is defined in Italian rules prohibiting surrogacy in order to respect the right to personal identity of minors born through surrogacy. See *Paradiso and Campanelli v. Italy*, No. 25358/12, ECtHR 27 January 2015; S. Tonolo, 'L'evoluzione dei rapporti di filiazione e la riconoscibilità dello status da essi derivante tra ordine pubblico e superiore interesse del minore' (2017) 4 *Rivista di diritto internazionale* 1069, 1079.

5 See M. Klaassen and P. Rodrigues, 'The Best Interests of the Child in EU Family Reunification Law: A Plea for More Guidance on the Role of Article 24(2) Charter', (2017) 19 *European Journal of Migration and Law*, 191.

lead to other forms of violence? If so, do legal instruments exist that can prevent this? In light of the Istanbul Convention, this chapter reflects on the possibility of granting permanent and autonomous residence permits and refugee status to the victims of child marriages.

2. CHILD MARRIAGES

Child or early marriage is any marriage 'where at least one of the parties is under 18 years of age'.[6] As reported by the United Nations Children's Fund in 2014, girls are disproportionately affected by child marriages, even though boys are married as children.[7] In the joint General Recommendation No. 31 elaborated by the CEDAW and CRC Committees, a child marriage can also be considered a form of forced marriage because at least one of the two parties has not expressed full, free and informed consent.[8]

The data on child marriages is extremely concerning. More than 700 million women alive today get married before the age of 18 years, and more than one in three get married before the age of 15 years. Child marriages are most common in South Asian and Sub-Saharan African countries, but they are not unknown in Europe. Europe has recently registered hundreds of cases of child marriages. For example, research conducted by an NGO among slum-dwellers in Rome, Italy, indicated that of 71 marriages from 2014 to 2016, almost 50 per cent of spouses got married before the age of 18 years.[9] In the Netherlands, the Dutch Immigration and Naturalisation Service registered 210 cases of Syrian 'child brides' from 2014 to 2016.[10] The British newspaper *The Guardian* has recently revealed that more than 3,500 reports of forced marriages have been made to the police over three years (2014–2016). In 2014, the European Agency for Fundamental Rights published data related to five EU countries. It indicated a lack of available data for France and the Netherlands, and incomplete data that show only the 'tip of the iceberg' for the UK, Germany and Sweden.[11] Many cases of early/forced marriages go unreported.

---

6 Joint general recommendation No. 31 of the Committee on the Elimination of Discrimination against Women/general comment No. 18 of the Committee on the Rights of the Child on harmful practices, 14 November 2014, CEDAW/C/GC/31-CRC/C/GC/18, para. 20.

7 UNICEF, *Ending Child Marriages*, 2014 <https://www.unicef.org/media/files/Child_Marriage_Report_7_17_LR.pdf>.

8 Joint general recommendation No. 31, above n. 6, para. 20.

9 Associazione 21 luglio onlus, *Non ho l'età*, November 2017, <http://www.21luglio.org/21luglio/wpcontent/uploads/2017/11/report_21_novembre_web_ita.pdf>.

10 See the report in Dutch quoted in A. Wijffelman, 'Child Marriage and Family Reunification: An Analysis under the European Convention on Human Rights and Dutch Forced Marriage Prevention Act', (2017) 35 *Netherlands Quarterly of Human Rights*, 104, 105.

11 FRA, *Addressing Forced Marriage in the EU: Legal Provisions and Promising Practices*, 2014.

This chapter does not thoroughly investigate the reasons for the existence of child marriages around the world. Early marriage is caused by a combination of economic and social elements. A child marriage might be imposed by culture and tradition, might constitute a 'strategy for economic survival',[12] or it might even represent a form of protection for many girls who escape their country of origin during their long journey to Europe. As demonstrated in the report *Protecting refugee women and girls from gender-based violence*, Syrian girls got married in refugee camps or in transit when their parents decided to marry their daughters to an older man who could protect them from violence.[13]

I do not discuss child marriages from a cultural/religious perspective because, as Alston has interestingly argued, 'just as culture is not a factor which should be excluded from the human rights equation, so too must it not be accorded the status of a metanorm which trumps rights'.[14] Even though child marriages are admitted – or were admitted in the past – either by law or by religion, they inevitably conflict with children's human rights, which are protected at both international and national levels and cannot be either admitted or justified.[15] Furthermore, with regard to women's and girls' rights, Nussbaum has interestingly contended that 'brutal and oppressive discrimination on grounds of race is taken to be unacceptable in the global community; but brutal and oppressive discrimination on grounds of sex is often taken to be a legitimate expression of cultural differences'.[16]

2.1. PROHIBITION OF CHILD MARRIAGES IN INTERNATIONAL LAW

The elimination of child marriages is one of the targets of the Agenda 2030 elaborated by the United Nations.[17] With regard to international legal

---

12 R. Gaffney-Rhys, 'International Law as an Instrument to Combat Child Marriage', (2011) 15 *The International Journal of Human Rights*, 359, 360.

13 Committee on Equality and Non-Discrimination. Rapporteur: Gisela Wurm, Doc. 13890, Reference 4161 of 27 November 2015. 2017 – second part-session, para. 28.

14 P. Alston, 'The Best Interests Principle: Towards a Reconciliation of Culture and Human Rights', (1994) 8 *International Journal of Law, Policy and the Family*, 1.

15 See, with regard to Islam, M. Badran, *Feminists, Islam and Nation: Gender and the Making in Modern Egypt*, Princeton University Press, Princeton, NJ, 1995; A. Anjum Ashraf, *Child Marriage in Islamic Law*, Master's Thesis, McGill University, Canada 2000, <http://digitool.Library.McGill.CA:80/R/-?func=dbin-jump-full&object_id=31082&silo_library=GEN01>, who stressed the existence of feminist movements against this practice (see also related references both in Arabic and in English); and J. Bradley, *Behind the Veil of Vice: The Business and Culture of Sex in the Middle East*, Palgrave MacMillan, Basingstoke 2010, p. 113; I. Ibrahim and others, 'The Child Bride: Rights under the Civil and Shariah Law', (2012) 38 *Social and Behavioural Science*, 51, 58.

16 M. C. Nussbaum, *Frontiers of Justice*, Belknap Press, Cambridge 2006, p. 260.

17 Target 5.3.

instruments, child marriages are prohibited under the 1979 UN Convention on the elimination of all forms of discrimination against women. The Convention states in Article 16(2) that 'the betrothal and the marriage of a child shall have no legal effect, and all necessary measures, including legislation, shall be taken to specify a minimum age for marriage and to make the registration of marriages in an official registry compulsory'. This provision mirrors Article 2 of the UN Convention on Consent to Marriage, Minimum Age for Marriage and Registration of Marriages, adopted in 1962. It obliges States to define a minimum marriageable age below which marriage cannot be celebrated.[18] In addition, it mirrors Article 2 of the UN Supplementary Convention on the abolition of slavery, slave trade and institutions and practices similar to slavery of 1956, which requires States parties to define a 'suitable minimum age of marriage'.[19] The UN Convention on the Rights of the Child, adopted in 1989, which defines a child as 'every human being below the age of eighteen years unless, under the law applicable to the child, majority is attained earlier', does not explicitly refer to marriage.

Despite the margin left to States in defining the minimum age for marriage, the CEDAW Committee established by the 1979 Convention determined the minimum age for marriage at 18 years for both boys and girls in its General Recommendation No. 21.[20] The Committee stressed that some countries provide a lower age for marriage for women, relying on the incorrect assumption that they develop at a different rate than men.[21] Considering the severe consequences of marriage for a child, including violation of his/her right to health and reproductive rights, as shown in the next paragraph, and considering that girls are often forced to marry, the Committee concluded that national provisions that allow different ages for marriage for men and women violate women's right to choose a partner freely. This argument was reinforced in the already mentioned CEDAW and CRC General Recommendation No. 31. According to the two Committees, marriages at an earlier age can be allowed but only in exceptional circumstances and never below 16 years, provided that grounds for obtaining permission are legitimate and strictly defined by law and that the marriage is permitted by a court of law 'upon the full, free and informed consent of the child or both children, who must appear in person before the court'.[22]

---

18 Convention on Consent to Marriage, Minimum Age for Marriage and Registration of Marriages, opened for signature and ratification by General Assembly resolution 1763 A (XVII) of 7 November 1962.

19 Supplementary Convention on the Abolition of Slavery, the Slave Trade, and Institutions and Practices Similar to Slavery, adopted by a Conference of Plenipotentiaries convened by Economic and Social Council resolution 608(XXI) of 30 April 1956 and done at Geneva on 7 September 1956.

20 General Recommendation No. 21 on equality in marriage and family relations (1994), para. 36.

21 General Recommendation, above n. 20, para. 38.

22 General Recommendation, above n. 20, para. 55(f). See in Italy, for example (Article 84 of the civil code). In Latin American countries, see the recent example of Guatemala, which adopted

Regional legal instruments contain some provisions on the minimum age for marriage. For example, the Maputo Protocol to the African Charter on the rights of women in Africa of 2003 provides that the minimum age of marriage for women shall be 18 years.[23] The American Convention on human rights of 1969 only focuses on the consent of spouses, providing in Article 17 that 'no marriage shall be entered into without the free and full consent of the intending spouses'. The Council of Europe Istanbul Convention, which is a criminal law and a human rights law treaty, is far more extensive in its scope.[24] The Convention requires States to criminalise the intentional conduct of forcing an adult or a child to enter into a marriage and of luring an adult or a child to the territory of another State to get married (Article 37). Moreover, State parties are obliged to ensure that marriages concluded under force are voidable, annulled, or dissolved (Article 32).

In the resolution adopted on 28 June 2018 by the Parliamentary assembly of the Council of Europe, whose draft was prepared by the Committee on equality and non-discrimination, Member States of the Council of Europe were encouraged to 'criminalise, as a specific offence, intentional conduct forcing an adult or a child to enter into a marriage, as well as luring an adult or a child abroad for the purpose of forcing him or her to enter into a marriage, and provide for effective sanctions against the perpetrators and those who aid, abet, or attempt to commit such offences'; to prohibit 'without exceptions' child marriages; to abolish differences between girls and boys in terms of the minimum age for marriage; to establish mechanisms to verify true consent by both spouses; to adopt civil law measures, such as protection orders against forced marriages, 'together where appropriate with a ban on leaving the country', 'in order to prevent forced marriages when cases involving persons at risk are reported'.[25] Similarly to the Istanbul Convention, the resolution recommends Member States take measures to ensure that forced marriages may be 'voidable, annulled or dissolved without undue financial or administrative burden placed on the victim'.[26] The resolution also recommends that forced marriages are

---

a law in 2015 raising the marriageable age to 18 for both men and women. Marriage at the age of 16 is allowed upon authorisation by a judge: J. A. Behravesh, 'Guatemala's Ban on Child Marriage: A Step Toward Compliance with CEDAW', (2017) 41 *Fordham International Law Journal*, 53, 55.

23 Girls can marry at a lower age than boys in some countries.

24 C. Chinkin, 'International Human Rights, Criminal Law and the Women, Peace and Security Agenda', (2018) *LSE Centre for women, peace and security* paper no. 12, <http://blogs.lse.ac.uk/wps/2018/01/11/international-human-rights-criminal-law-and-the-women-peace-and-security-agenda-christine-chinkin-122018/>.

25 Resolution of the Parliamentary Assembly of the Council of Europe No. 2233 (2018), 28 June 2018, para. 7.5.

26 Resolution above n. 25, para. 7.5.6. The resolution also recommends States ratify the Istanbul Convention.

recognised as a ground for international protection and that States collect accurate and comparable data on forced marriages.[27]

At the EU level, the Committee on women's rights and gender equality for the Committee on Foreign Affairs took steps towards an EU external strategy against early and forced marriages when it condemned child, early and forced marriages and other harmful coercive practices imposed on women and girls, recognising that child and forced marriages are a 'real problem' within the EU.[28] On 4 July 2018, the European Parliament adopted a resolution which acknowledged that child, early and forced marriages constitute a 'serious violation of human rights and, in particular, women's rights',[29] then it called on Member States and third countries to 'set the minimum uniform age for marriage at 18 years', and 'to adopt necessary administrative, legal and financial measures to ensure effective implementation of this requirement'.[30] It encouraged the ratification of the Istanbul Convention and asked Member States to include a complete ban on child, early and forced marriages.[31] The resolution also encouraged Member States 'to guarantee migrant women and girls an autonomous residence permit which is not dependent on the status of their spouse or partner, in particular for victims of physical and psychological violence'.[32]

2.2. CHILD MARRIAGES AS A VIOLATION OF HUMAN RIGHTS

In this section, it is contended that forced child marriages – we assume here that they are forced in all cases that involve a girl and a male adult – constitute a violation of human rights and a form of gender-based violence against women.[33]

Child marriages violate several children's rights enshrined in the Convention on the Rights of the Child, as analysed in two pivotal resolutions adopted by

---

27 Resolution above n. 25, paras. 7.8, 7.10. See also the Declaration of the Committee of ministers of the Council of Europe on the need to intensify efforts to prevent and combat female genital mutilation and forced marriage in Europe, 13 September 2017, Decl (13/09/2017).

28 Opinion of the Committee on Women's Rights and Gender Equality for the Committee on Foreign Affairs Towards an EU external strategy against early and forced marriages – next steps 2017/2275(INI) Rapporteur Daniela Aiuto, 18 April 2018, paras. 1–3.

29 European Parliament Resolution of 4 July 2018, Towards an EU external strategy against early and forced marriages – next steps (2017/2275(INI)), letter A.

30 Resolution above n. 29, para. 1.

31 Resolution above n. 29, para. 6.

32 Resolution above n. 29, para. 12.

33 In that sense see also General Recommendation No. 35 (CEDAW) 2017, para. 31: 'Provisions that allow, tolerate or condone forms of gender-based violence against women, including child or forced marriage and other harmful practices, provisions allowing medical procedures on women with disabilities without their informed consent, as well as legislation that criminalises abortion, being lesbian, bisexual, or transgender, women in prostitution, adultery or any other criminal provisions that affects women disproportionally including those resulting in the discriminatory application of the death penalty to women.'

the Human Rights Council in 2015 and 2017. The first resolution stressed that child, early and forced marriages constitute a violation of children's rights and are a 'harmful practice that prevents individuals from living their lives free from all forms of violence.'[34] The second resolution builds on this precedent and mentions the impact of marriages on children, particularly on girls, stressing as follows:

> Early and forced marriage constitutes a violation, abuse or impairment of human rights and a harmful practice that prevents individuals from living their lives free from all forms of violence, and that ... has wide-ranging and adverse consequences for the enjoyment of human rights, such as the right to education and the right to the highest attainable standard of physical and mental health, including sexual and reproductive health, and ... every girl and woman at risk of or affected by these practices must have equal access to quality education, counselling, shelter and other social services, psychological, sexual and reproductive health-care services and medical care.[35]

Child marriages have serious health consequences for both boys and girls, especially when we consider the psychological impact of a marriage with a person of a different age. Children, especially girls, who are most affected by the practice, experience isolation and depression.[36] Early marriages are also a risk factor for HIV infections and human papilloma virus transmission with the possible consequence of cervical cancer. Girls are commonly considered to be reproductive objects; therefore, they become pregnant quite early without receiving proper medical care during pregnancy.[37] As reported by the WHO, in low- and middle-income countries, complications during pregnancy and childbirth are the leading cause of death in women aged 15–19 years.[38] One dangerous effect of childbirth is obstetric fistula, which is a hole between the birth canal and the bladder or rectum caused by obstructed labour without treatment. An estimated 2 million women in Sub-Saharan Africa, Asia, the Arab Region, Latin America and the Caribbean live with this injury. In a resolution adopted in 2012, the UN General Assembly identified the causes of the injury as 'poverty, lack of or inadequate access to health-care services, early childbearing and child marriage'.[39]

---

34 Strengthening efforts to prevent and eliminate child, early, and forced marriage, Resolution A/HRC/29/L.15, 1 July 2015, para. 1.

35 Child, early, and forced marriage in humanitarian settings, Resolution A/HRC/RES/35/16, 12 July 2017.

36 N. M. Nour 'Child Marriage: A Silent Health and Human Rights Issue', (2009) 2 *Rev Obstet Gynecol*, 51, 53.

37 UNICEF, *Ending Child Marriages*, p. 4 <https://www.unicef.org/media/files/Child_Marriage_Report_7_17_LR.pdf>.

38 Early marriages, adolescent and young pregnancies, WHO, Report by the Secretariat, A65/13, 16 March 2012, <http://apps.who.int/gb/ebwha/pdf_files/WHA65/A65_13-en.pdf>.

39 67/147. Supporting efforts to end obstetric fistula, 5 March 2013, para. 1.

Child brides often drop out of school after marriage; therefore, their right to education is adversely affected.[40]

Girls who marry before 18 years are vulnerable and might experience domestic violence by their husbands or his relatives. In a recent analysis related to 34 countries, domestic violence was 'substantially higher' among women who married as children compared with those married as adults.[41] Arguably, child marriages pave the way to children's abuse within households, including domestic violence and non-consensual sexual intercourse. In this respect, the Supreme Court of India ruled on October 11, 2017, that 'sexual intercourse with a girl below 18 years of age is rape regardless whether she is married or not'.[42] Despite the exception to Section No. 375 of the Indian Penal Code stating that sexual intercourse with a wife who is not under 15 years is not rape, the Court argued that allowing such an exception is 'not only contrary to the philosophy and ethos of Article 15(3) of the Constitution but also to Article 21 of the Constitution' and – which is particularly relevant – to 'our commitments in international conventions'.[43]

Nonetheless, another perspective is as follows: child marriages might not only lead to forms of violence against girls within households but also constitute *per se* a form of violence because they deprive children of their liberty and constitute a violation of their right to health and reproductive rights. The definition of violence against women (VAW) and girls is well consolidated at the international level. According to the Council of Europe Istanbul Convention,

> 'Violence against women' is understood as a violation of human rights and a form of discrimination against women and shall mean all acts of gender-based violence that result in, or are likely to result in, physical, sexual, psychological or economic harm or suffering to women, including threats of such acts, coercion or arbitrary deprivation of liberty, whether occurring in public or in private life (Article 3).
>
> Gender-based violence against women 'shall mean violence that is directed against a woman because she is a woman or that affects women disproportionately' (Article 3).

Forced child marriages, i.e. if they involve a girl under 18 years and a male adult, violate girls' human rights, are a form of discrimination against women and

---

40 See also the report *A Statistical Analysis of Child Marriage in India based on Census 2011*, prepared by the organisation called Young Lives and the National Commission for the Protection of Child Rights, June 2017, quoted in the judgment by the Supreme Court of India (see below n. 42).

41 R. Kidman, 'Child Marriage and Intimate Partner Violence: A Comparative Study of 34 Countries', (2017) 46 *International Journal of Epidemiology*, 662, 665.

42 *Independent Thought v. Union of India* on 11 October 2017, Justice Madan B. Lokur and Justice Deepak Gupta.

43 *Independent Thought v Union of India*, para. 1. Article 15(3) concerns special provisions for women and girls and Article 21 the right to life and personal liberty.

constitute a case of gender-based violence against women. They affect women due to their being women, and they affect them disproportionately. As this analysis anticipated, although boys are affected by the practice, girls are the main victims according to the data provided by major international bodies. Child marriages might result in physical, sexual, psychological or economic harm, and they might also cause arbitrary deprivation of life. In 2006, the Secretary General of the United Nations wrote about the gender-based aspect of child marriages in his report, stating that early marriage is one of the most commonly identified forms of VAW within the family.[44] More recently, the Deputy UN High Commissioner for Human Rights stressed that 'Child marriage is rooted in unequal gender status and power relations that can result in the perpetual subjugation of girls and women. In the absence of viable legal remedies, discriminatory cultural practices based on stereotypical views of women's roles and sexuality are among the structural causes of child and forced marriage'.[45] Forced marriages, irrespective of the spouse's age, are considered to be a form of gender-based VAW in the EU Victims' Directive[46] and in the Council of Europe Istanbul Convention.

The Special Court for Sierra Leone affirmed in several judgments, starting from the landmark Appeals Chamber decision in *Brima, Kamara and Kanu*, that forced marriages may amount to crimes against humanity under customary international law, in the sub-category of 'other inhumane acts'.[47]

The 'public/private' divide, well-known in feminist legal scholarship,[48] still seems to play a role in child marriages. Although they are illegal in most European States and in many countries in the world, child marriages can be celebrated with religious or traditional ceremonies without the need to record

---

44 UN SG, *In-depth Study on all forms of violence against women*, paras. 111, 118–121.

45 Flavia Pansieri's statements are available at <https://www.ohchr.org/EN/NewsEvents/Pages/Childandforcedmarriagemanifestationofgenderdiscrimination.aspx>. See also the association Girls not Brides factsheet available at <https://www.girlsnotbrides.org/why-does-it-happen/>.

46 2012/29/EU.

47 *Prosecutor v. Brima, Kamara, and Kanu* (SCSL-04-16-T), AFRC case, Appeals Chamber, 22 February 2008. See also *Prosecutor v. Sesay, Kallon & Gbao* (SCSL-04-15-T), Trial Chamber I, 2 March 2009. In legal scholarship, among others, see M. Frulli, 'Advancing International Criminal Law The Special Court for Sierra Leone Recognizes Forced Marriage as a "New" Crime against Humanity', (2008) 6 *Journal of International Criminal Justice*, 1033; S. Thompson, 'Forced Marriage at the Special Court for Sierra Leone: Questions of Jurisdiction, Legality, Specificity, and Consistency' in C. Jalloh (ed.), *The Sierra Leone Special Court and its Legacy: The Impact for Africa and International Criminal Law*, Cambridge University Press, Cambridge 2013, p. 215; V. Oosterveld, 'The Gender Jurisprudence of the Special Court for Sierra Leone: Progress in the Revolutionary United Front Judgments', (2011) 44 *Cornell International Law Journal*, 49.

48 See, for example, C. Chinkin, 'A Critique of the Public/Private Dimension', (1999) 10 *EJIL*, 387.

them in the civil register.[49] Victims need their situation to be recognised as child marriage to obtain support from authorities. Despite the phenomenon of child marriages being widespread, it rarely goes to court: indeed, girls are not capable of reporting the case to authorities, marriages are not registered because they are celebrated within a community, marriages occur abroad, and the couple is reunified once the girl is 18 years. It is therefore worth reflecting further on this latter aspect in light of EU law.

3. FAMILY REUNIFICATION UNDER EU LAW AND CHILD MARRIAGES

Family reunification is regulated by Directive 2003/86/EC. Scholars have extensively discussed the Directive's legal basis, its main provisions and its implications for EU migration policy.[50] However, the issue of child marriages and family reunification has not received much attention. This section, therefore, will focus on the Directive's elements relevant to the main argument. Directive 2003/86 is a unique legal instrument that, according to some authors, provides a 'clearly defined subjective right to family reunification to applicants who comply with the conditions defined in the Directive' and includes a minimum set of guarantees that prevents States from deciding further restrictions in their family reunification laws and policies.[51] Another scholar has stressed that despite initial expectations, the Directive's outcome has been quite modest because the legal instrument did not introduce a true right to family reunification but merely a set of minimum requirements.[52] If we consider the right to redress envisaged by the Directive, it can be reasonably argued that the right to family reunification is a justiciable right (Article 18); on the other hand, however, the margin of *manoeuvre* States have is significant, and restrictive

49 Report submitted by the Committee on equality and non-discrimination on 5 June 2018, para. 34.

50 On the evolution of the Directive and the negotiations that led to its adoption, see extensively R. Palladino, *Il ricongiungimento familiare nell'ordinamento europeo*, Cacucci, Bari 2012, p. 143 and related references; E. Bergamini, *La famiglia nel diritto dell'Unione europea*, Giuffrè, Milano 2012. See also, *inter alia*, E. Bribosia, 'La directive 2003/86 relative au regroupement familial dans l'Union européenne', (2003) 125 *Revue des étrangers*, 539; S. Peers, 'Family Reunion and Community Law' in N. Walker (ed.), *Europe's Area of Freedom, Security and Justice*, OUP, Oxford 2005, p. 143; S. Van den Broucke, L. Vanduynslager and P. De Cuyper, *The EU Family Reunification Directive Revisited: An Analysis of Admission Policies for Family Reunification of Third Country Nationals in EU Member States*, factsheet 2016, <https://lirias2repo.kuleuven.be/bitstream/handle/123456789/547583/Fact+sheet+family+reunification.pdf;jsessionid=54FC7F564D099D8C00AB66959F84C4C1?sequence=1>.

51 M. Klaassen and P. Rodrigues, above n. 5, p. 199.

52 E. Bergamini, above n. 50, p.118.

national laws can jeopardise the Directive's main scope, which aims at protecting the family and establishing or preserving family life.[53]

Reunification is requested by a 'sponsor', which, according to the Directive, means a third-country national residing lawfully in a Member State who applies or whose family members apply for family reunification to be joined with him/her (Article 2(c)). The provision on the age of the sponsor's spouse seems – at first sight – quite clear. Article 4(5) reads as follows: 'In order to ensure better integration and to prevent forced marriages Member States may require the sponsor and his/her spouse to be of a minimum age, and at maximum 21 years, before the spouse is able to join him/her'. In the Communication containing the amended draft Council Directive, the European Commission explained that a new provision was added 'to impose a minimum age on the applicant and his or her spouse – which may not exceed the age of legal majority – to combat the practice of forced marriages, at least where minors are concerned'.[54]

Nonetheless, the Directive does not seem enough to ensure the protection of children, particularly girls, from forced marriages for two main reasons. On the one hand, the provision does not prohibit child marriages *per se* since the spouse could join his/her partner when reaching the minimum age provided by law. In other words, 21 years is not the age at which a girl marries but the age at which the request is lodged, as will be discussed further,[55] or even the age at which reunification occurs. On the other hand, it only concerns 'sponsors' of the reunification who are non-EU nationals and does not affect marriages concluded abroad between an (adult) EU national with a minor.

Rules prohibit family reunification where the indications of child and/or forced marriages already exist, for example, in Germany, Italy, UK and the Netherlands. In Germany, Article 27 of the General Administrative Regulation prohibits family reunification if there are concrete indications that one of the spouses has been forced into marriage and that one spouse is under 18 years.[56] The Netherlands,[57] UK and Italy have introduced rules for raising the age limit for family reunification: the Netherlands to 21 years, the UK[58] and Italy to 18 years.[59] If age is assessed at the moment of application or at the moment

---

53 Preamble, recital No. 6.

54 COM (2002) 225 Def., p. 7.

55 See also below, *Noorzia;* I. Queirolo, *EU Law and Family Relationships*, Aracne, Roma 2015, p. 145.

56 FRA, Forced marriages, above n. 11, p. 25.

57 Aliens Decree 2000, Section 3.14 and 3.15.

58 In 2008 the UK raised the age limit to 21, but, following a decision of the Supreme Court, the limit was returned to 18 years of age. FRA, Forced marriages, above n. 11, p. 25.

59 Decreto legislativo 3 ottobre 2008, n. 160, Modifiche ed integrazioni al decreto legislativo 8 gennaio 2007, n. 5, recante attuazione della direttiva 2003/86/CE relativa al diritto di ricongiungimento familiare (GU Serie Generale n. 247 del 21-10-2008).

of reunification, how can provisions of law that determine the age limit be successful in effectively protecting children from child marriages?

European Court of Justice jurisprudence will be discussed in relation to the interpretation of Article 4(5) of Directive 2003/86. Thereafter, the discussion will move to European Court of Human Rights jurisprudence concerning reunification as related to the right to private and family life before discussing the main argument of this chapter by relying on the Council of Europe Istanbul Convention, which, once ratified by the EU, can be used to interpret Article 4(5) of the Directive.

3.1. THE AGE FOR FAMILY REUNIFICATION IN ECJ JURISPRUDENCE

The European Court of Justice analysed the scope of Article 4(5) of the Directive in the *Marjan Noorzia v. Bundesministerin für Inneres* judgment, in which the Court was referred the following question by the *Verwaltungsgerichtshof* (Austrian Administrative Court):[60]

> Is Article 4(5) of Directive [2003/86] to be interpreted as precluding a provision [of national law] under which spouses and registered partners must have reached the age of 21 by the date when the application seeking to be considered family members entitled to family reunification is lodged?

The case originated in the application of an Afghan national, who, at the age of 21 years, applied for a residence permit for family reunification with her spouse, aged 20 years, of Afghan origin and residing in Austria. The *Bundesministerin für Inneres* (Interior Minister) refused the application because the spouse had not reached the minimum age of 21 years, as required by Austrian law, at the time of the application, but at the time of the reunification. The Austrian authorities argued that the national provision was adopted to guarantee that all applicants in the same chronological situation were treated identically.[61] The Court explained that the minimum age corresponds to the age at which a person is presumed to have sufficient maturity to voluntarily choose whether to move to a different country to join his/her spouse.[62] The national measure, which fixed the age at which the application was lodged at 21 years, was not considered to be a way to prevent the exercise of the right to family reunification or to render family reunification more difficult.[63] The Court, therefore, concluded that Article 4(5)

---

60 Case C-338/13, *Marjan Noorzia v. Bundesministerin für Inneres*, ECLI:EU:C:2014:2092.

61 Case C-338/13, above n. 60, para. 18.

62 Case C-338/13, above n. 60, para. 15.

63 Case C-338/13, above n. 60, para. 16.

must be interpreted to mean that the provision does not preclude a rule of national law that requires that spouses and partners must have reached the age of 21 years at the time of application, not at the time of actual reunification.[64] In this case, the spouse and the sponsor were not children according to the definition of the UN Convention of the Rights of the Child. Nonetheless, they were minors for the purpose of the application of Austrian law related to family reunification.

The European Court of Justice's main argument in the *Noorzia* case departed from the legal reasoning of Advocate General (AG) Mengozzi, who contended that the spouse's age must be considered when the spouse is able to join the sponsor, not at the time of application, according to a literal and schematic interpretation of the Directive.[65] The AG also considered it necessary to analyse reunification on a case-by-case basis: on the one hand, establishing a minimum age is not sufficient for avoiding child marriages; on the other hand, the effect of the provision's formalistic interpretation might lead to infringement of the right to family reunification of those who 'have married sincerely and genuinely'.[66] Similarly, a few days before the release of AG Mengozzi's opinion, the European Commission in its Communication on the implementation of Directive 2003/86 argued that Member States 'should consider making an exception thus allowing for family reunification in cases in which the minimum age requirement is not fulfilled. For instance, when it is clear from the individual assessment that there is no abuse, e.g. in the case of a common child'.[67]

On the one hand, we might agree in principle with the position of the European Commission and the AG that a case-by-case analysis might be useful to prevent the non-recognition of marriages where no abuse was committed. On the other hand, from an international feminist law perspective, it is dangerous to consider the birth of a child as proof of non-abuse. Having in mind this chapter's previous affirmation – all child marriages are forced if a girl marries a male adult, and it is a form of VAW – considering the birth of a child as proof of non-abuse leads to the primacy of the rights of the couples' children over a woman's rights, a fact that reinforces gender-based discrimination.

3.2. FAMILY REUNIFICATION IN THE ECtHR JURISPRUDENCE

One year after the European Court of Justice's *Noorzia* judgment, the European Court of Human Rights dealt with *Z.H. and R.H. v. Switzerland*, a case of family

64 Case C-338/13, above n. 60, para. 19.

65 Advocate General Opinion, ECLI:EU:C:2014:288, para. 63.

66 Ibid., para. 42.

67 Brussels, 3.4.2014 COM (2014) 210 final Communication from the Commission to the European Parliament and the Council on guidance for application of Directive 2003/86/EC on the right to family reunification, para. 2.3.

reunification involving a boy and a girl who married in a religious community in Iran when the girl was aged 14 years.[68] The judgment is relevant in this part because it acknowledges a margin of appreciation for the State in deciding whether to recognise a marriage of a child and will be useful in identifying a form of *de facto* family life. Under the European Convention on Human Rights, which refers to 'marriageable age' in Article 12, a State is under no obligation to recognise a marriage 'exclusively' celebrated in accordance with a religious rite chosen by the parties and without respecting the requirements provided by the law.[69] The European Commission of Human Rights, as early as 1986, further argued that the imposition of a minimum marriageable age is compatible with Article 12 of the ECHR and that marriage cannot fall under the right to religious freedom.[70]

In the case under scrutiny, Z.H. and R.H., of Afghani origin, married in Iran during a religious ceremony that was not formally registered. Ms Z.H. was a child at that time. When the applicants entered Switzerland in 2011, the girl being a minor, and asked for asylum, their application was separately examined because the couple was not considered to be legally married under Swiss law. R.H. was expelled to Italy, which, according to the EU asylum system, was the country of the applicants' first entry. Swiss courts rejected the application by affirming that the law in Afghanistan prohibited marriages of girls under the age of 15 years, and that in Switzerland sexual intercourse with a child under the age of 16 years was a crime. R.H. illegally returned to Switzerland a few days later. Once back to Switzerland, R.H. requested the reexamination of his asylum request, which was again rejected because he did not pay the required advance judicial fee. On 18 September 2012, the applicants lodged an application before the ECtHR. In 2013, the applicants requested the recognition of the religious marriage in Switzerland, when the girl was aged 16 years and 11 months. The subsequent application for asylum submitted by the couple to the Swiss government was granted. The applicants decided to maintain their application in front of the ECtHR, complaining that their right to respect for private and family life (Article 8 of the ECHR) was violated at the time the second applicant

---

68 *Z.H. and R.H. v. Switzerland*, No. 60119/12, ECtHR 8 December 2015.

69 *X. v. Germany*, No. 6167/73, ECtHR 18 December 1974; and more recently *Serife Yigit v. Turkey*, No. 3976/05, ECtHR 2 November 2005; C. Draghici, *The Legitimacy of Family Rights in Strasbourg Case Law*, Bloomsbury, Portland 2017, p. 43.

70 *Janis Khan v. UK*, No. 11579/85, Commission decision of 7 July 1986. A Muslim 21-year-old UK national had undergone an Islamic wedding with a girl aged 14 and a half. Under Islamic law, a girl aged 12 or above can marry without her parents' consent. The father forcibly removed her from the household, and the husband was charged with abduction and sexual intercourse with a girl under the age of 16 and sentenced to 9 months in prison. Dispelling myths on the minimum age for marriage in Islam, see Islamic Relief, *An Islamic Human Rights Perspective on Early and Forced Marriages*, 2018, <https://www.girlsnotbrides.org/wp-content/uploads/2018/05/IRW-Islamic-persepctive-on-CM.pdf>.

was expelled to Italy. On the merits, the Court reiterated that the notion of 'family' under the Convention also encompasses *de facto* relationships and that 'family life' can be assessed according to numerous factors, including 'whether the couple lived together, the length of their relationship and whether they have demonstrated their commitment to each other by having children together or by any other means'.[71] The Court then affirmed the margin of appreciation States have when it comes to recognising child marriages: 'Article 8 of the Convention cannot be interpreted as imposing on any State party to the Convention an obligation to recognise a marriage, religious or otherwise, contracted by a 14 year old child'.[72] The Court added that it 'must not rush to substitute its own judgment in place of the authorities who are best placed to assess and respond to the needs of society'.[73] National provisions on marriageable age are part of the *ordre public* of a State, which can legitimately refuse the recognition of such marriages. The moment in which non-recognition happened is relevant. According to the Court, at the time of the removal of the second applicant to Italy, the national authorities were justified in 'considering that the applicants were not married, all the more so, given the fact that the applicants had not yet taken any steps to seek recognition of their religious marriage in Switzerland'.[74] Without clearly stating whether their life could qualify as 'family life' under Article 8 of the Convention, the fact that the second applicant returned to Switzerland after three days and, even though he entered illegally, that he was allowed to stay and to lodge another application for asylum protection had to be considered. Reaffirming the margin of appreciation States have in that respect, the Court found that the Swiss authorities struck a fair balance between the competing interests at stake: on the one hand, the 'personal interests of the applicants in remaining together in Switzerland while waiting for the outcome of the asylum application'; on the other hand, 'the public order interest of the respondent Government in controlling immigration'.[75] No violation of Article 8 of the European Convention on Human Rights was found.

4. PROHIBITION OF CHILD MARRIAGES, FAMILY REUNIFICATION AND THE ISTANBUL CONVENTION

To support the main argument, this section will now read Article 4(5) of the Directive in light of the Charter of Fundamental Rights of the EU and the Council of Europe Istanbul Convention. The EU has already begun the process

71 *Z.H. and R.H. v. Switzerland*, above n. 68, para. 42.
72 Ibid., para. 44.
73 Ibid.
74 Ibid.
75 Ibid., para. 46.

of joining the Convention. In 2017, the Council of the EU adopted two Decisions on the signature, on behalf of the EU, of the Council of Europe Convention on preventing and combating VAW and domestic violence: one regarding matters related to judicial cooperation in criminal matters and the other on asylum and *non-refoulement*.[76] The EU signed the Convention on June 13, 2017 but has not yet ratified it. Once in force for the EU, the Convention will become EU law (Article 216 TFEU). It is argued that the entry into force of the Convention for the EU could impact the interpretation of EU secondary legislation in light of provisions of the Istanbul Convention.[77] The Convention contains several provisions that might be useful for this chapter's main argument, even though it does not encompass provisions on early marriages or marriageable age. It defines, as anticipated above, VAW, and Article 37 criminalises forced marriages, including the act of luring a person abroad with the purpose of forcing that person to enter into marriage. This provision might be relevant for this discussion. Let us imagine that a child arrives in one of the countries of the EU with her family, and she is forced to go back to her country of origin to marry an older man, who, in turn, would be able to enter Europe for family reunification. The criminalisation of the behaviour of the girl's relatives who force a child to marry abroad seems an effective preventive measure, although quite limited if we see it in light of Directive 2003/86. The man, who can even be a member of the family,[78] can wait for his spouse to reach marriageable

76 Council Decision (EU) 2017/865 of 11 May 2017 on the signing, on behalf of the European Union, of the Council of Europe Convention on preventing and combating violence against women and domestic violence with regard to matters related to judicial cooperation in criminal matters [2017] OJ L 131/11; Council Decision (EU) 2017/866 of 11 May 2017 on the signing, on behalf of the European Union, of the Council of Europe Convention on preventing and combating violence against women and domestic violence with regard to asylum and *non-refoulement* [2017] OJ L 131/13.

77 See, in that respect, S. De Vido, 'La violenza di genere contro le donne nel contesto della famiglia: sviluppi nell'Unione Europea alla luce della Convenzione di Istanbul', (2017) 3 *Federalismi*, 1; and forthcoming, *The Istanbul Convention as a Tool for Interpretation*, in J. Niemi, L. Peroni and V. Stoyanova (eds.), *Violence Against Women: Transformations and Challenges After the Istanbul Convention*, Abingdon, Routledge 2020.

78 See, in that respect, the case of transnational cousin marriages. In the Netherlands, a law prohibiting cousin marriages as opposed to forced marriages was discussed for many years. Reunification constitutes 'an important motive for families to engage in cousin marriages between a family member already living in the Netherlands and one living in Turkey or Morocco.' See M. de Koning, O. Storms and E. Bartels, 'Legal Ban on Transnational Cousin Marriages: Citizen Debate in the Netherlands', (2014) 4 *Transnational Social Review*, 226, 229. The authors, however, warn against what they call 'culturalization of citizenship': 'Culture, ethnicity, and tradition, in the views held on citizenship, belong to non-native ethnic minorities, while the moral community of the "native" Dutch is seen as being characterized by freedom, autonomy, and equality between the sexes. The attribution of culture to non-native immigrant groups occurs in ways that identifies this culture as one which is disadvantageous to women and dominated by men and, furthermore, as one which denies all autonomy and agency for women and men.' (p. 237).

age in the destination country before the latter begins to sponsor the family reunification procedure.

In light of the Istanbul Convention and due to the consolidation of the prohibition of child marriages in international law, it is argued that the expression 'before the spouse is able to join him/her'[79] in Article 4(5) must be interpreted as considering the minimum age, fixed at a maximum of 21 years, at the time of *the celebration of the marriage*. The conclusion is supported by the affirmation that child marriages, when they are forced, constitute a form of gender-based VAW prohibited by the Istanbul Convention. In this manner, States maintain a margin of *manoeuvre* in deciding any exception to this rule when child marriage is not a form of VAW. It is argued that it is not a form of VAW, when, for example, two minors freely decide to marry and their free consent and their *de facto* family – as in the case *Z.H and R.H. v. Switzerland* – is assessed by a judge. Provisions that recognise marriages between minors are already included in national legal systems, even though there is a trend to prohibit all child marriages without exceptions.[80] One might argue that it is difficult to assess the age at which spouses marry, whether registers in the country of origin actually exist or are difficult to access, or whether spouses lied about their age. It is possible to counter-argue that given the jurisprudence of the European Court of Human Rights, States are not obliged to recognise marriages concluded with exclusively religious or other private ceremonies. Hence, no marriage or other relationship can be said to exist for the purpose of family reunification if it is not proved by a document, or, as in the aforementioned case, investigated by the ECtHR unless a form of *de facto* family life is confirmed.

Let us now see whether the interpretation proposed here conforms to Directive 2003/86. According to the Directive's literal interpretation and using AG Mengozzi's legal reasoning, the answer should be no. The sponsor and his/her spouse must *be* of a minimum age 'before the spouse is able to join him/her', reads Article 4(5) of the Directive. Hence, according to this line of reasoning, marriageable age must be achieved before reunification, not necessarily at the time of marriage. Nonetheless, this reasoning does not align with the scope of Directive 2003/86, which, in its preamble, states that its purpose is to *prevent* child and forced marriages, not to *postpone* reunification until the

---

79 'Avant que le conjoint ne puisse rejoindre le regroupant' in the French version.

80 See, for example, the recent case of Norway: <http://news.trust.org/item/20180522152944-2cnil/news.trust.org/item/20180522152944-2cnil/>. Even though it is not the purpose of this chapter to analyse this aspect, this author agrees with an author that contended that all child marriages are not legitimate because this practice constitutes a violation of the rights of the children, and, in many cases, the consent of the parents and the judge is not enough to prevent child abuse. With regard to the practice in the US, see T. Dobbins Baxter, 'Child Marriage as Child Abuse and Constitutional Violation', draft, forthcoming, *Legal Studies Research* paper no. 340, available on ssrn.com (last accessed on 29.12.2018).

girl reaches marriageable age. It also contradicts the purpose of some activities undertaken pursuant to EU foreign and security policies, such as the three-year project funded and launched in Tanzania in 2017 to counter child marriages and female genital mutilation in cooperation with local NGOs.[81]

As emphasised by AG Mengozzi in his opinion on the *Noorzia* case, it is true that defining an age limit does not automatically prevent child marriages. It is argued, however, that when it comes to child marriages as forced marriages – in all of which a girl marries a male adult – they are prohibited by the Istanbul Convention because they are a form of gender-based VAW. Waiting for the girl to reach the minimum age does not guarantee that the girl is not coerced into staying in a relationship to which she has not consented. The paradox is that in the hypothetical situation of the girl being the sponsor of the relationship, she might be coerced by the family and the community to lodge an application for family reunification to let her husband, probably married in the country of origin, enter the EU, subjecting her to the risk of violence and other violations of her rights.

5. WHEN DENYING FAMILY REUNIFICATION CAUSES VIOLENCE AGAINST WOMEN

The main argument proposed in the preceding paragraphs might lead to further violations of human rights and a form of VAW. If the girl, for example, is a spouse coming from a country where child marriages are allowed, refusing reunification means that she will have to stay in the community of origin, where she can face discrimination, social exclusion and marginalisation. If she wanted to escape from war or a situation of persecution, denying family reunification would lead to a form of VAW.[82] The dilemma is, from an ethical point of view, almost unbearable: both recognition and non-recognition of child marriages as a ground for family reunification can lead to a form of gender-based VAW.

Let us now see whether, following the reasoning of the European Court of Justice and allowing reunification when the spouse and/or the sponsor are of minimum age at the time of the application – or, as argued by AG Mengozzi – at the time of reunification, provisions on autonomous residence permits included in Directive 2003/86 and in the Council of Europe Istanbul Convention once in force for the EU would protect girls from forced child marriages.

---

81 See <https://eeas.europa.eu/delegations/tanzania_en/30605/EU%20ijects%20TZS.%201.4%20billion%20to%20counter%20child%20marriage%20and%20FGM>.

82 See above the case of girls who marry on their way from Syria to Europe. Article 12 of Directive 2003/86 protects the right to family reunification for refugees.

5.1. AUTONOMOUS RESIDENCE PERMITS

A form of protection for girls who are victims of forced child marriages can come from autonomous residence permits in all cases in which the girl is not the sponsor for family reunification but rather the spouse is. If the girl enters the EU after reaching the minimum age at the time of application or at the time of reunification, she might receive protection from the Directive's other provisions. Article 15 of Directive 2003/15 provides that the spouse can be granted a residence permit, independent of that of the sponsor, 'not later than after five years of residence'. Paragraph 3 of the same article reads as follows:

> In the event of widowhood, divorce, separation, or death of first-degree relatives in the direct ascending or descending line, an autonomous residence permit may be issued, upon application, if required, to persons who have entered by virtue of family reunification. Member States shall lay down provisions ensuring the granting of an autonomous residence permit in the event of particularly difficult circumstances.

The European Commission explained in its Communication of 2014 that 'particularly difficult circumstances' can include child marriages.[83] This might be the correct interpretation also in light of the Council of Europe Istanbul Convention. The wording 'particularly difficult circumstances' is indeed also present in Article 13(2) of Directive 2004/38 on the rights of citizens of the EU and their families[84] and in Article 59 of the Council of Europe Istanbul Convention. Article 59 (1) of the latter reads as follows:

> Parties shall take the necessary legislative or other measures to ensure that victims whose residence status depends on that of the spouse or partner as recognised by internal law, in the event of the dissolution of the marriage or the relationship, are granted in the event of particularly difficult circumstances, upon application, an autonomous residence permit irrespective of the duration of the marriage or the relationship. The conditions relating to the granting and duration of the autonomous residence permit are established by internal law.

---

83 COM (2014) 2010 final, 3 April 2014 at point 5.3.

84 Directive 2004/38/EC of the European Parliament and of the Council of 29 April 2004 on the right of citizens of the Union and their family members to move and reside freely within the territory of the Member States amending Regulation (EEC) No 1612/68 and repealing Directives 64/221/EEC, 68/360/EEC, 72/194/EEC, 73/148/EEC, 75/34/EEC, 75/35/EEC, 90/364/EEC, 90/365/EEC and 93/96/EEC, [2004] OJ L 158/77. It provides, indeed, that 'divorce, annulment of marriage or termination of the registered partnership [...] shall not entail loss of the right of residence of a Union citizen's family members who are not nationals of a Member State' where 'this is warranted by particularly difficult circumstances, such as having been a victim of domestic violence while the marriage or registered partnership was subsisting' under Article 13(2)(c).

According to paragraph 3, States shall issue a renewable residence permit to victims in one of the two envisaged cases or both, particularly 'where the competent authority considers that their stay is necessary owing to their personal situation'. As has been correctly argued, this provision of the Istanbul Convention is not devoid of criticism and surely does not expressly cover all cases;[85] clearly, however, these provisions, if correctly transposed by Member States, might lead to the granting of autonomous residence permits to girls who are victims of child marriages.

There are two issues to discuss. The first concerns the fact that girls must enter the EU *before* asking protection. This means, in other words, that they enter the EU at the age considered to be acceptable by the destination country, notwithstanding that they might have been coerced as children to marry. Could the woman invoke the child (and forced, as explained above) marriage to ask for an autonomous residence permit even though she has reached the age for family reunification? If so, is she no longer a child? Or should the woman demonstrate other forms of violence, such as domestic violence, in order to ask for a residence permit? The Directive does not provide any answer to that, and the European Court of Justice has never dealt with a case having this factual background. It can be reasonably argued, however, that, in light of the Council of Europe Istanbul Convention, an autonomous residence permit should be granted when there is proof that the marriage was celebrated at a lower age than the one accepted for marriages by the destination country. In this case, the reasoning leads us back to the main argument, namely, the recognition of all forms of child *and* forced marriages – all cases in which a girl marries a male adult – as gender-based VAW.

The second issue regards the expression 'upon application' included in both the Directive 2003/86 and the Council of Europe Istanbul Convention: would a woman, probably a young woman who has just achieved minimum marriageable age, be able to report to authorities? Coercion by the community and the family, and other forms of violence such as domestic violence, coupled with the lack of education these girls commonly suffer, might dramatically reduce the number of opportunities for girls to report to the authorities.

The Council of Europe Istanbul Convention contains a specific provision that can be used to interpret Directive 2003/86. Article 59(4) provides as follows:

> Parties shall take the necessary legislative or other measures to ensure that victims of forced marriage brought into another country for the purpose of the marriage and who, as a result, have lost their residence status in the country where they habitually reside, may regain this status.

---

85 V. Stoyanova, 'A Stark Choice: Domestic Violence or Deportation?', (2018) 20 *European Journal of Migration and Law*, 53.

In the explanatory report, the *ratio* of the norm is well clarified. In most Council of Europe Member States, a person loses his/her residence permit whether he/she leaves the country for more than a given number of consecutive months. However, 'this condition only bears in mind persons that leave the country voluntarily'; for this reason, Article 59(4) obliges parties to the Convention 'to provide for the possibility for such victims to regain their residence status on account of them being forced to leave the country where they habitually reside, in particular in the event of the dissolution or annulment of the marriage'.[86] Despite constituting an important step forward, this provision encounters practical obstacles, as acknowledged in the 2014 of the FRA report, because to re-enter 'appears to be subject to a varying degree of pre-conditions, which, depending on the individual case, may be difficult to fulfil'.[87]

In principle, if the European Court of Justice confirms its jurisprudence on Article 4(5) of Directive 2003/86, or in the case in which it opens to the proposal of the European Commission – namely, that the minimum age for reunification must be met at the time of reunification – girls subject to child marriages in their country of origin might receive a form of protection by means of Directive 2003/86 as strengthened by the Council of Europe Istanbul Convention. However, there are two major obstacles: the level of implementation of the Directive and of the Council of Europe Istanbul Convention by States[88] and practical difficulties in fulfilling all the requirements to obtain the residence permit.

6. CONCLUSIONS

Through the argument elaborated in these pages, a two-fold objective can be achieved by means of interpretation: to have a case-by-case analysis where marriages are among minors and they are assessed by a judge in line with existing provisions in EU countries[89] and to prevent the practice of child marriages and contribute to its eradication worldwide.

Interpretation of Directive 2003/86, whether or not it occurs in light of the Council of Europe Istanbul Convention, could reinforce the prohibition of *all* child forced marriages, as defined in this article, as an obstacle to family reunification. In principle, all marriages between a girl and a male adult can be considered a form of gender-based VAW. As argued, the prohibition of child marriages always constitutes a limit to family reunification, even if the spouse, sponsor, or both, has achieved the minimum age for reunification. The Istanbul

86 Explanatory Report to the Istanbul Convention, para. 308.

87 FRA Report, above n. 11, p. 28.

88 Several States, for example, appended reservations to Article 59 of the Istanbul Convention.

89 Although, as noted above, the prohibition of *all* child marriages seems compatible with national constitutions and will allow effective protection of children's human rights.

Convention's main provisions, which the EU has already signed, support this argument when used as means of interpretation of EU law.

Furthermore, if the girl is the sponsor of family reunification, she can have her marriage be voidable, annulled, or dissolved in the country where she resides. States that ratified the Council of Europe Istanbul Convention – all EU States have at least signed it – have an obligation in that respect (Article 32). This provision would be extremely relevant to addressing cases of child marriages in the EU and marriages in which an EU citizen is involved.

By contrast, if the girl is the spouse who joins her sponsor in the EU and reunification is rejected, with the consequence of the girl being discriminated against and marginalised in her country of origin, she can apply for refugee status, more likely in a country that ratified the Istanbul Convention.[90] Indeed, Article 60(1) of the Istanbul Convention reads as follows:

> Parties shall take the necessary legislative or other measures to ensure that gender-based VAW may be recognised as a form of persecution within the meaning of Article 1, A (2), of the 1951 Convention relating to the Status of Refugees and as a form of serious harm giving rise to complementary/subsidiary protection.

In cases of forced marriages as set out in this chapter, girls are entitled to international protection in the destination country. It may be difficult to prove the existence of a marriage, especially if exclusively celebrated with a religious ceremony, and the girl might need to demonstrate having suffered other forms of VAW, such as domestic violence, to obtain refugee status.

Protection of children, especially girls, from child marriages and violence requires coordinated action at international, regional and national levels. Provisions that prohibit child marriages in domestic criminal codes are surely important, but they do not prevent private parties circumventing prohibition through family reunification when the girl reaches a minimum age. Thus, interpretation of the Directive on family reunification in the way here discussed seems a desired outcome, although it does not replace a consideration of possible amendments to the Directive itself, which will transform the latter into a legal instrument more in conformity with the Istanbul Convention.

---

90 One of the Council decisions, no. 866/2017, above n. 76, on the ratification of the Istanbul Convention precisely referred to migration issues.

PART II

THE BEST INTERESTS OF THE CHILD AS A CONCERN OF HUMAN RIGHTS AND EUROPEAN PRIVATE INTERNATIONAL LAW

THE PLACE OF HUMAN RIGHTS IN THE PRIVATE INTERNATIONAL LAW OF THE UNION IN FAMILY MATTERS

Pietro FRANZINA

1. The Protection of Fundamental Rights in the Union's Legal System...... 142
 1.1. Article 6 of the Treaty on European Union and Other Sources..... 142
 1.2. Fundamental Rights Concerning Family and Child-Related Matters.......... 143
 1.3. The Functions Performed by Private International Law Rules 143
2. Harmonisation as a Way to Enhance the Protection of Fundamental Rights 145
3. The Impact of Human Rights on the Design of Private International Law Rules.......... 148
 3.1. Fundamental Rights as a Factor of Openness Towards Foreign Judgments and Foreign Law.......... 148
 3.2. The Relevance of Human Rights to the Choice of Connecting Factors 150
  3.2.1. Rules Primarily Reflecting a Concern for Fundamental Rights 150
  3.2.2. 'Corrections' Aimed at Ensuring the Protection of Human Rights in Particular Circumstances............ 151
4. A Human Rights-Oriented Interpretation of the Union's Private International Law 152
 4.1. Human Rights as a Key to the Interpretation of the Union's Autonomous Notions.......... 153
 4.2. Human Rights as a Guideline in the Exercise of Judicial Discretion 154
5. Concluding Remarks 155

1. THE PROTECTION OF FUNDAMENTAL RIGHTS IN THE UNION'S LEGAL SYSTEM

1.1. ARTICLE 6 OF THE TREATY ON EUROPEAN UNION AND OTHER SOURCES

Article 6(1) of the Treaty on European Union states that the Union recognises the rights set out in the Charter of Fundamental Rights of the European Union (CFREU), the legal value of which is the same as that of the Treaties. Article 6(3) further provides that fundamental rights, as guaranteed by the ECHR and as they result from constitutional traditions common to Member States, constitute general principles of the Union's law. The Union is thus committed to promoting the realisation of fundamental rights in any field where its action unfolds. This means that measures adopted by institutions are only consistent with primary law if they comply with the applicable human rights standards.[1]

References to human rights can be found in other provisions of the TEU, as well. Article 2 lists the respect for fundamental rights among the founding values of the Union. According to Article 3(3), the Union's aims include the promotion of 'equality between women and men' and the 'protection of the rights of the child'. Article 21(1) makes clear that the Union's action on the international scene is guided by, among others, the principles of 'universality and indivisibility of human rights and fundamental freedoms' and 'respect for human dignity'.

The Union's duty to protect fundamental human rights also rests on international conventions to which the Union itself is a party, like the United Nations Convention of 13 December 2006 on the rights of persons with disabilities.[2] Based on Article 216(2) of the TFEU, international conventions that bind the Union on the international plane further serve as a yardstick for assessing the validity of secondary legislation.

Other international conventions, although not binding as such on the Union, play a role in the protection of fundamental rights within the Union's legal system. This holds true, inter alia, for the United Nations Convention on the Rights of the Child of 20 November 1989 (UNCRC), which is in force for all Member States. Some of its rules are believed to reflect international customary law,[3] which the Union is under an obligation to respect.[4] More generally, the

---

1 On the whole topic, see the essays collected in S. Douglas-Scott and N. Hatzis (eds.), *Research Handbook on EU Law and Human Rights*, Edward Elgar Publishing, Cheltenham/Northampton 2017.

2 [2010] OJ L 23/35.

3 See, for further references, L. D. Elrod, 'Please Let Me Stay: Hearing the Voice of the Child in Hague Abduction Cases', 63 *Oklahoma Law Review* (2011), 663, 672.

4 See, in this regard, in the case law of the European Court of Justice, among other judgments, case C-286/90, *Anklagemyndigheden v. Peter Michael Poulsen and Diva Navigation Corp.*, ECLI:EU:C:1992:453, para. 9.

UNCRC was a source of direct inspiration for the CFREU, as acknowledged in the relative Explanations,[5] and has a bearing, as such, on the interpretation of its provisions.[6]

1.2. FUNDAMENTAL RIGHTS CONCERNING FAMILY AND CHILD-RELATED MATTERS

The fundamental rights that the Union is called upon to safeguard and realise include those connected to family relations and the rights of the child. These encompass civil rights, such as the right of a child to be heard in any judicial or administrative proceedings in connection with his or her rights and interests, and cultural, economic and social rights, like the right to education.

Some of these rights have a broad scope. This is the case, for example, for the right to personal identity, the implications of which range from the legal determination of a person's name to the establishment of his or her origins in the case of adoption. Other rights, instead, refer to specific situations (for instance, migration and asylum), or address particular concerns (such as the protection of children against violence and exploitation).

This chapter focuses on civil rights. They typically call for consideration in judicial proceedings relating to divorce or legal separation, or in situations in which custody of a child is at issue. For instance, one such right is the right of parents and their children to the mutual enjoyment of each other's company. This right is enshrined, in particular, in Articles 7 and 24 of the CFREU, taken in conjunction with Article 8 of the ECHR. These result in a positive obligation for the Union and its Member States to take measures aimed, inter alia, at facilitating contacts between family members living apart and combating unlawful abduction.[7]

1.3. THE FUNCTIONS PERFORMED BY PRIVATE INTERNATIONAL LAW RULES

The law of the Union regards the protection of the fundamental rights of children and other family members as a *general* concern, that is, one arising in

---

5 [2007] OJ C 303/17, 25.

6 See, for an application, case C-648/11, *The Queen, on the application of MA and Others v. Secretary of State for the Home Department*, ECLI:EU:C:2013:367.

7 On rights enshrined in Article 7 of the CFREU, see generally M. González Pascual and A. Torres Pérez (eds.), *The Right to Family Life in the European Union*, Routledge, London/New York 2017.

any situation in which the interests of a child and those of his or her parents or relatives are at issue.

Specifically, fundamental rights call for consideration regardless of whether the case has ties with only one country, or rather comes with a foreign element. The latter scenario occurs, for example, when an order issued in one State relating to a child's custody is relied upon in a different State, or when the question is raised in one country of the content and extent of parental rights and duties to a child of foreign nationality.

Cross-border situations raise questions that do not appear in purely domestic cases. This reflects the diversity of States' legislation (substantive harmonisation is almost non-existent in family law), and the fact that, in principle, the measures taken by the authorities of a given State, such as termination of parental rights as a consequence of abuse, can only be relied upon in a different State where that State's rules so provide.

This is precisely where private international law comes into the picture. The task of its rules is to: (*a*) indicate whether the authorities of a particular State have the power to rule on a given cross-border matter (otherwise stated, whether they have jurisdiction over that matter); (*b*) identify the law governing that matter's substance, thereby solving a 'conflict of laws'; (*c*) determine whether, and by which means, State authorities are permitted or required to provide assistance to the authorities of another State; and (*d*) set out the conditions subject to which the judgments or other measures issued in one State qualify for recognition and enforcement in a different State.

Private international law rules vary, in principle, from one State to another. Over the last two decades, however, the European Union has deployed significant efforts towards the harmonisation of private international law, based on competences currently contemplated in Article 81 of the TFEU, on judicial cooperation in civil matters.

Specifically, the Union has enacted legislative measures establishing uniform rules on jurisdiction, the applicable law, international judicial assistance, and recognition and enforcement of judgments on a range of family and child-related issues. The measures concerned include Regulation No 2201/2003 on jurisdiction and recognition and enforcement of judgments in matrimonial matters and matters of parental responsibility (Brussels II *bis*),[8] soon to be replaced by Regulation 2019/1111,[9] Regulation 4/2009 on jurisdiction, applicable law, recognition and enforcement of decisions and cooperation in matters relating to maintenance obligations[10] and Regulations 2016/1103 and 1104 on jurisdiction, applicable law and the recognition and enforcement of

8 [2003] OJ L 338/1.
9 [2019] OJ L 178/1.
10 [2009] OJ L 7/1.

decisions in matters of matrimonial property regimes and property consequences of registered partnerships.[11]

Furthermore, the Union has resorted to its external competence to conclude (or authorise the Member States to conclude in its interest) international conventions serving basically the same purposes. This occurred, among others, with the Hague Convention of 23 November 2007 on the international recovery of child support and other forms of family maintenance, with the Hague Protocol concluded on the same day regarding the law applicable to maintenance obligations, and the Hague Convention of 19 October 1996 on jurisdiction, applicable law, recognition, enforcement, and co-operation in respect of parental responsibility and measures for protection of children.[12]

The purpose of this chapter is to provide a brief illustration of the different ways in which the fundamental rights that the Union aims to safeguard and promote affect the action of the Union's institutions taken towards the harmonisation of private international law in family and child-related matters. This influence is threefold. The concern for the protection of fundamental rights is, first, one reason why the Union involved itself in the harmonisation of private international law in family and child-related matters; second, that concern is a key to understanding the design of the Union's rules of private international law in the fields above; and third, it serves as a guideline for the interpretation of such rules.

2. HARMONISATION AS A WAY TO ENHANCE THE PROTECTION OF FUNDAMENTAL RIGHTS

Effectiveness is a constant concern for human rights law. Fundamental rights, as the European Court of Human Rights frequently puts it, are intended to be practical and effective, not theoretical and illusory.[13] Their mere assertion is insufficient: to be meaningful, the law of human rights must be interpreted and applied so as to enable the persons concerned to enjoy in fact the benefits to which they are entitled.

Cases exist in which the effective protection of a right is at risk because the situation features a cross-border element. Take guardianship, for example. The appointment of a guardian, officially charged with caring for the interests of an orphan child, is one way to ensure that the child's fundamental rights – such as the right to education or the right not to be exposed to abuse and exploitation – enjoy effective protection. Now, if the child happens to spend several weeks

11 [2016] OJ L 183/1 and 30, respectively.

12 For the three instruments see <http://hcch.net>.

13 See generally D. J. Harris, M. O'Boyle et al., *Law of the European Convention on Human Rights* (3rd ed.), Oxford University Press, Oxford 2014, p. 18.

in a country other than the country where he normally lives (for instance, at some relatives' house during school holidays), the question arises of whether the guardian may discharge his duties in that country and provide the child with the protection or assistance he may need while there.

The private international law rules of the country where the child has moved determine whether the foreign judgment that appointed the guardian can be relied upon there. The scope of the guardian's powers will normally depend on the law specified for that purpose by the conflict-of-law rules of the same country. In the end, it is for the private international law of the State concerned to decide whether the guardian can conduct his tasks in a spatially continuous way, that is, without such interruptions or other hindrances as may arise because of the internationality of the case. Should the guardian's authority prove discontinuous (e.g. because recognition of the appointing judgment is impossible, and reappointment by local courts becomes necessary), the protection afforded the child may be less intense or not as timely as the circumstances would require. For example, due to his powers' foreign origin, the guardian could be prevented from representing the child in a situation calling for urgent action on his part, such as where parental permission is required prior to a particular medical treatment following an accident.

Ensuring the cross-border continuity of a person's rights and status is very much in the nature of private international law. One may say that the purpose of private international law consists in creating bridges between legal orders. Recognising a foreign judgment or instructing courts to apply, where appropriate, a foreign law, amounts, in fact, to opening the legal system of the forum to the 'products' of other legal systems, so that those products (a court decision, a substantive right existing under a given law, etc.) may be relied upon before local authorities, in spite of their foreign origin.

Each State is free, in principle, to determine whether a foreign judgment deserves recognition, and in which circumstances foreign law, rather than the law of the forum, ought to apply. Otherwise stated, it is for each State to decide whether, in a given set of circumstances, the rights asserted in a foreign judgment or resulting from a foreign law should be enforceable locally. That said, failure to ensure continuity amounts to an interference by the 'receiving' State in the enjoyment of the rights in question. And, absent appropriate justification, that interference may amount, in turn, to a violation of the fundamental rights of the individuals concerned.[14]

---

[14] See generally on the relationship between the law of human rights and private international law, L. R. Kiestra, *The Impact of the European Convention on Human Rights on Private International Law*, T.M.C. Asser Press, The Hague 2014, and J. J. Fawcett, M. Ní Shúilleabháin and S. Shah, Human Rights and Private International Law, Oxford University Press, Oxford 2016.

The European Court of Human Rights followed this approach, for example, in *Negrepontis-Giannisis*, a case concerning an order for adoption issued by a Michigan court. It held that the Greek authorities, by refusing to recognise that order, had violated Article 8 of the ECHR, for they had prevented the adoptee from asserting in Greece the family ties thus created.[15] In the Court's view, the grounds on which Greek authorities had come to that conclusion were not compelling enough to justify their interference with the adoptee's right to respect for family life.

Lack of appropriate interstate coordination may undermine human rights' effectiveness in other ways as well. The authorities of a State may need the assistance of another's authorities to discharge their functions effectively in cases with cross-border implications. This may occur, for instance, when a country's courts, charged with supervising a child's guardianship, seek assistance in a country where the child is believed to be present, in order to discover his whereabouts, in particular when it appears that he may need protection. Here too, it is for the private international law rules of the requested State to establish whether, and subject to which conditions, the authorities of that State are permitted or required to comply with the request. If the request were declined, the ability of the guardian and the supervising court to protect the child would be undermined.

All in all, private international law is a tool that States might need to use in order to ensure the effective realisation of fundamental rights.

The European Union lacks, in general, the power to regulate family and child-related matters substantively. Rather, as mentioned, it has the power to address those matters from the standpoint of private international law. By establishing uniform rules on jurisdiction, the recognition and enforcement of judgments, the applicable law and interstate cooperation, the Union purports to improve the mobility of individuals across borders. This way, harmonisation of private international law rules minimises the risk that, because of mobility, Member States could find themselves unable to safeguard effectively the fundamental rights of those concerned.

As a matter of fact, legal security is better served under harmonised rules of private international law, rather than under rules that vary from one State to another. Where regional (as opposed to national) rules apply, the legal implications of mobility become easier to manage, at least within Europe, and the protection of the relevant fundamental rights becomes stronger.

Consider, for instance, a marriage annulled by the courts of a Member State on grounds of invalidity. An obvious corollary of the annulment is each spouse's ability to enter into a new marriage. In fact, they have a fundamental right to do so since they enjoy the right to marry and found a family, as stated, in particular, in Article 12 of the ECHR and Article 9 of the CFREU. This right

15 Judgment of 5 December 2013, ECLI:CE:ECHR:2013:1205JUD005675908.

can only be meaningfully exercised in a cross-border scenario if the authorities before which the new marriage is to be celebrated are instructed to consider the previous marriage as annulled: the non-recognition of the judgment whereby the marriage has been annulled would prevent the spouses to marry again.

The Brussels II *bis* Regulation harmonises the rules that govern recognition of judgments relating, inter alia, to the annulment of marriage. By harmonising those rules, the Union has created a situation in which the right to marry can be exercised, in circumstances as those considered above, in the same manner and based on the same conditions throughout Europe, that is, irrespective of the Member State where the annulment was declared and of the Member State before whose authorities the new celebration is to take place. This state of affairs makes respect for the right to marry more secure and predictable. It also avoids discrimination between former spouses, since each will be able to rely on the judgment anywhere in Europe under the same conditions. The fundamental right to marry and form a family would hardly be as effective without a uniform body of rules providing for European-wide enforcement of annulment decisions.

3. THE IMPACT OF HUMAN RIGHTS ON THE DESIGN OF PRIVATE INTERNATIONAL LAW RULES

The concern for effective protection of fundamental rights may affect the design of private international law rules. These rules can be shaped in various ways. Choosing the appropriate design may advance the realisation of the human rights of the persons concerned.

Actually, the policies underlying the Union's action in family law and the law of children affect the content and operation of private international law rules in a variety of ways. In some cases, a concern for fundamental rights translates into rules that require States to adopt a particularly open attitude towards foreign law and foreign judgments. In other cases, fundamental rights have a bearing on how a cross-border matter is localised, that is, on the factors that define the 'centre of gravity' of a given situation and that identify the court(s) with jurisdiction and the applicable law. These two patterns are analysed below.

3.1. FUNDAMENTAL RIGHTS AS A FACTOR OF OPENNESS TOWARDS FOREIGN JUDGMENTS AND FOREIGN LAW

Private international law rules, as noted above, can be seen as gateways through which the legal order of a State 'receives' products of other legal orders, be they court judgments, court settlements, administrative decisions, authentic instruments or substantive rules of a general and abstract character.

The gateway thus realised may be more or less broad, depending on requirements the legislator decides to establish for these purposes.

Openness, by definition, makes it easier to ensure the protection of rights across borders. Admittedly, situations may arise in which a foreign judgment or rules of foreign law should be disregarded (including, of course, where enforcement of that judgment or application of those rules would undermine the fundamental rights of the persons concerned). But an open attitude towards foreign legal products is, as a matter of principle, the most practical way to provide rights resulting from those products with spatially continuous protection.

Thus, one way to enhance the effective protection of a right consists in providing that recognition and/or enforcement of a judgment asserting such right is only subject to few requirements. For example, Article 41 of the Brussels II *bis* Regulation provides that rights of access to a child, where granted in a Member State's enforceable judgment, may be enforced in another Member State 'without the need for a declaration of enforceability and without any possibility of opposing its recognition', provided only that the judgment has been certified in the State of origin in accordance with the Regulation itself.[16] This provision is intended to make the movement of access judgments across Europe as swift and secure as possible, thereby contributing to the effective realisation of fundamental rights of parents and their children to enjoy their mutual company, as regulated by the relevant court decisions.

Similar remarks apply to the rules set forth in Regulation No 4/2009 governing the recognition and enforceability of judgments relating to family maintenance. Those rules aim at enabling the maintenance creditor to enforce his or her claims rapidly and inexpensively across borders.[17] This goal, where it refers to claims brought in the interest of a child, underlies a concern for the actual realisation of that child's fundamental right to a standard of living adequate for his or her physical, mental, spiritual, moral and social development. Actually, to preserve the latter right, Article 27(4) of the UNCRC requires State parties to take 'all appropriate measures to secure the recovery of maintenance for the child from the parents or other persons having financial responsibility for the child, both within the State Party and from abroad' through international agreements or other appropriate arrangements. Facilitating the recognition of foreign support orders is, arguably, one such measure.

---

16 See generally on the enforcement of access judgments U. Magnus, 'Article 41 – Right of Access', in U. Magnus and P. Mankowski (eds.), *Brussels II bis Regulation*, Sellier, Munich 2012, p. 350.

17 See generally, and for further references, L. Walker, 'New (and Old) Problems for Maintenance Creditors Under the EU Maintenance Regulation' in P. Beaumont, M. Danov, K. Trimmings and B. Yüksel (eds.), *Cross-border Litigation in Europe*, Hart Publishing, Oxford/Portland 2017, p. 771.

3.2. THE RELEVANCE OF HUMAN RIGHTS TO THE CHOICE OF CONNECTING FACTORS

Private international law rules typically build on geographical considerations. Most perform their function by determining where a particular case should have its 'centre of gravity' for the purpose of identifying the court with jurisdiction or of determining the applicable law.

When choosing the relevant connecting factors, legislators are normally guided by a broad range of policies. Some reflect a concern for the proper functioning of private international law rules themselves (such as ensuring that the applicable law can be easily established in advance and remains the same over time, whenever stability is an asset). Others, instead, refer to objectives of a substantive nature (such as providing the weaker party with special protection *vis-à-vis* the other party or advancing the realisation of a collective interest).

As far as family and child-related matters are concerned, the policy considerations that underlie the Union's legislation generally include a concern for the protection of fundamental rights of the persons involved. This concern may affect the design and operation of connecting factors in a variety of ways. Some rules are primarily designed with human rights concerns in mind. Other rules mirror policies of a different kind, but come with 'correcting' devices which can be triggered whenever the risk arises of the non-realisation (or insufficient realisation) of the pertinent fundamental rights.

3.2.1. Rules Primarily Reflecting a Concern for Fundamental Rights

Article 8 of the Brussels II *bis* Regulation provides an example of the first type of rules. According to Article 8, jurisdiction in matters of parental responsibility lies, in principle, with courts of the Member State where the child habitually resides.[18] This provision makes the child and the social environment where he or she is growing up the centre of gravity of litigation. This option reflects, in turn, some key tenets of the Union's approach to the law of child protection.

To begin with, Article 8 refers specifically to the child and his or her environment. Where the parents or the holders of parental responsibility live or work is immaterial, and so is the place where any connected matrimonial matter is being litigated. By taking into account nothing more than the child's situation, Article 8 translates the principle, enshrined in Article 3(1) of the UNCRC and in Article 24(2) of the CFREU, according to which, in all actions concerning children, the best interests of the child represent 'a primary consideration'. Localising a child-related matter otherwise than referring primarily to the child

---

18 See, in general, A. Borrás, 'Article 8 – General Jurisdiction' in U. Magnus and P. Mankowski, above n. 16, p. 109.

concerned would hardly be consistent with the above principle and might result in the child himself being insufficiently protected.

Secondly, Article 8 of the Brussels II *bis* Regulation merely refers to the child's 'habitual residence', that is, where the child's interests are most significantly located. No weight is given to other personal connections, such as the child's domicile (which may be legally presumed to be the same as his or her parents) or nationality. One explanation for that is precisely the concern for the child's well-being. The needs of a child are normally best assessed by a court sitting near the environment where the child himself is growing up, that is, in practice, where he goes to school and where he primarily entertains his social and affective relations. The court identified on that ground is presumably in the best possible position to get in touch with those taking care of the child, and, more generally, those aware of his actual living conditions. Furthermore, the court near the child's habitual residence is, in principle, thanks to its direct knowledge of the surrounding social environment, better placed than others to conduct a proper and reliable assessment of the child's actual situation and needs. Conferring jurisdiction on that court is thus one way to ensure that, as a matter of principle, the decisions concerning the interests of a child provide the child in question with appropriate protection, based on his or her actual needs and his or her specific situation, as the UNCRC and the CFREU require.

3.2.2. 'Corrections' Aimed at Ensuring the Protection of Human Rights in Particular Circumstances

Designing a connecting factor having a particular substantive goal in mind is not always enough to ensure that such goal can be reached. Situations may occur where a private international law rule does not lead, in fact, to the practical result that the legislator intended to promote. Similar shortcomings may be avoided, or mitigated, by a provision that corrects the rule in particular circumstances.[19]

Several examples of such corrections can be found in the Union's legislation on the private international law of family and child-related matters. The Brussels II *bis* Regulation provides, again, an interesting illustration. According to Article 15(1) of the Regulation, the courts of a Member State having jurisdiction as to the substance of a matter of parental responsibility may, by way of exception, transfer the case to a court of a different Member State with which the child concerned has a 'particular connection', where the court in question appears to be 'better placed' to decide the matter in light of the best interests of the child. Article 15 presents itself as an exception to Article 8, but it ultimately serves

---

19 See, in general, on the kind of corrections examined in these pages, S. M. Bouyahia, *La proximité en droit international privé de la famille*, L'Harmattan, Paris 2015, especially at p. 325 ff.

the same policy, namely the realisation of the fundamental rights of the child. Article 15 builds on the assumption that, in the majority of cases, the courts of the Member State where the child is habitually resident are the courts best placed to rule on the interests of the child in question. Still, it acknowledges that in particular circumstances things may be otherwise, and allows the case to be transferred to the courts of another State, thereby preventing Article 8 from producing an unfortunate practical result. A different correcting device features in the Hague Protocol of 23 November 2007 on the law applicable to maintenance obligations. Pursuant to Article 3 of the Protocol, maintenance obligations are governed, in general, 'by the law of the State of the habitual residence of the creditor'. This provision, which is based on a concern for the protection of the creditor, may, in special circumstances, fail to meet its purpose. Article 4 aims to avert this risk by introducing special rules for cases raising a particularly acute concern for the effective realisation of the (fundamental) right to maintenance, as it occurs, such as where maintenance is claimed by a child towards his or her parents. Specifically, according to Article 4(2), '[i]f the creditor is unable, by virtue of the law referred to in Article 3, to obtain maintenance from the debtor, the law of the forum shall apply. In addition, pursuant to Article 4(4), if the creditor is still unable to obtain maintenance from the debtor, 'the law of the State of their common nationality, if there is one, shall apply'.

In practice, Article 4(2) and (4) correct the operation of Article 3 and Article 4(2), respectively, whenever their practical result departs from the result pursued by the Protocol. The correction, where it refers to child support, ultimately reflects a concern for the fundamental right of a child to a standard of living adequate for his development, examined above.

4. A HUMAN RIGHTS-ORIENTED INTERPRETATION OF THE UNION'S PRIVATE INTERNATIONAL LAW

The concern for the effective protection of fundamental rights also affects interpretation of the rules of private international law of the European Union in family law. This is, in fact, a rather straightforward implication of the instrumental character of the Union's provisions in this area. Since the provisions in question aim to enhance protection of human rights, they should be interpreted in a manner that maximises their ability to serve that purpose.

Human rights concerns may guide the purposive interpretation of the Union's rules of private international law in various ways. Two scenarios are considered here, namely, the impact of fundamental rights on the scope of 'autonomous' Union notions and the role of fundamental rights in the exercise of discretion under regional rules.

4.1. HUMAN RIGHTS AS A KEY TO THE INTERPRETATION OF THE UNION'S AUTONOMOUS NOTIONS

The European Court of Justice has stated on numerous occasions that the need for uniform application of its legislative measures and the principle of equality require that the terms of Union's legislation which makes no express reference to the law of the Member States for the purpose of determining its meaning and scope must normally be given an autonomous and uniform interpretation throughout the European Union, having regard to the context of the provision and the objective pursued by the legislation in question.[20]

When it comes to family relations or child protection, this exercise involves, inter alia, a reference to the rules that protect the relevant human rights.

The Court followed this approach in *J. McB.*[21] The case turned on the interpretation of the provisions in the Brussels II *bis* Regulation that provide for the return of children who have been wrongfully removed to or retained in a Member State other than the Member State where they habitually resided. Those provisions apply where the removal occurred in violation of custody rights, but fail to determine which person must have such rights of custody as may render a child's removal wrongful for the purposes of the Regulation, and rather refers to the law of the Member State where the child was habitually resident immediately before its removal or retention the question of who has such rights of custody. This implies that it is for the law of the latter Member State to determine the conditions under which the natural father of a child acquires rights of custody in respect of that child, and to specify whether the acquisition of those rights is dependent, or not, on a national court awarding such rights to him.

In the circumstances, the Court was asked whether such an apparently clear interpretation ought to be reconsidered in light of Articles 7 and 24 of the CFREU, which refer, as noted, to the right to respect for family life and the rights of the children. The Court agreed that the scrutiny was indeed pertinent, but found that the latter provisions did not preclude the above interpretation. The Court in fact acknowledged that the natural father of a child must be given the opportunity to apply to the national court with jurisdiction, before the removal, in order to request that rights of custody in respect of his child be awarded to him, and conceded that, in a similar context, this would in fact constitute the very essence of his right to private and family life. However, the Court also observed that, unlike the mother, the natural father is not a person who automatically possesses rights of custody in respect of his child. This circumstance, the Court added, does not affect as such the essence of his right to private and family life,

20 See, for instance, Case C-393/18 PPU, *U.D. v. X.B.*, ECLI:EU:C:2018:835, para. 46.

21 Case C-400/10 PPU, *J. McB. v. L.E.*, ECLI:EU:C:2010:582.

as protected under the CFREU, provided that his right to apply to the court with jurisdiction for rights of custody is safeguarded.

The Court went on to say that, having regard to the great variety of extramarital relationships and consequent parent-child relationships, Article 24 of the CFREU, read in conjunction with Article 7, does not preclude a situation where, for the purposes of the Brussels II *bis* Regulation, rights of custody are granted, as a general rule, exclusively to the mother and a natural father possesses rights of custody only as the result of a court judgment. Such a requirement enables the national court with jurisdiction to take a decision on custody of the child, and on rights of access to that child, while taking into account all the relevant facts, and in particular the circumstances surrounding the birth of the child, the nature of the parents' relationship, the relationship of the child with each parent, and the capacity of each parent to take the responsibility of caring for the child. Giving consideration to those facts, the Court concluded, is apt to protect the child's best interests, in accordance with Article 24(2) of the CFREU.

4.2. HUMAN RIGHTS AS A GUIDELINE IN THE EXERCISE OF JUDICIAL DISCRETION

Some of the Union's rules of private international law concerning family and child-related matters vest national courts with a significant measure of discretion in deciding what steps should be taken to ensure that the interests of the individuals involved are adequately protected. Determining that discretion's scope and how it should be used depends on the interpretation of rules that provide for such discretion. Concern for effective protection of human rights is often a key to interpretation of the rules in question.

This holds true, in particular, for provisions in the Brussels II *bis* Regulation which refer to the 'best interests' of the child concerned. For example, according to Article 12, on prorogation of jurisdiction, the courts of a Member State seised of divorce proceedings are entitled to hear any matter relating to parental responsibility connected with those proceedings where the jurisdiction of such courts has been accepted by the spouses 'and is in the superior interests of the child'. Similarly, as seen above, Article 15 allows the transfer of a parental responsibility case from the courts of one Member State to the courts of another, which are believed to be better placed to rule on the matter, provided, inter alia, that the transfer 'is in the best interests of the child'.

As stated by the European Court of Justice, the best interests of the child need to be taken into consideration in the context of the Brussels II *bis* Regulation 'to ensure respect for the child's fundamental rights'.[22] In light of this, the Court

22 Case C-403/09 PPU, *Jasna Detiček v. Maurizio Sgueglia*, ECLI:EU:C:2009:810, para. 53.

stated in *Child and Family Agency* that the national court envisaging a transfer in accordance with Article 15 must determine whether, in the circumstances, the transfer would be 'such as to provide genuine and specific added value, with respect to the decision to be taken in relation to the child, as compared with the possibility of the case remaining before that court'.[23]

The Court explained that various factors may need to be considered for the purposes of the latter assessment, including 'the rules of procedure in the other Member State, such as those applicable to the taking of evidence required for dealing with the case'.[24] For the same reasons, the national court in question must determine whether the envisaged transfer would be detrimental to the situation of the child, assessing 'any negative effects that such a transfer might have on the familial, social and emotional attachments of the child concerned in the case or on that child's material situation'.[25]

In practice, according to the Court, the discretion that Article 15 vests in national authorities should be exercised in such a way as to enhance the protection of the fundamental rights of the child. Otherwise stated, a transfer can only be envisaged where it would result in a better realisation of those rights.

5. CONCLUDING REMARKS

The rules of private international law of the Union concerning family law and child-related matters are among the tools that the Union itself employs to make sure that the fundamental rights of children and other family members enjoy appropriate protection in cases with a cross-border element. The concern for the full realisation of the above rights is a driving force behind the harmonisation of private international law at the regional level in this area. It also affects the design of several rules which resulted from the harmonisation process, and guides the interpretation of those same rules.

The relationship between private international law and the law of human rights is a complex one. As outlined above, the impact of human rights on the rules that govern jurisdiction, the applicable law, the recognition and enforcement of judgments and international judicial assistance may take different forms.

It is primarily the task of judicial and administrative authorities in individual Member States to exploit, in this respect, the potential of the regional rules of private international law, and to translate into practice the commitment of the Union to ensuring the effective protection of human rights.

---

23 Case C-428/15, *Child and Family Agency v. J.D.*, ECLI:EU:C:2016:819, para. 57.

24 Ibid.

25 Ibid., para. 59.

THE BEST INTERESTS OF THE CHILD PRINCIPLE AT THE INTERSECTION OF PRIVATE INTERNATIONAL LAW AND HUMAN RIGHTS

Marcella DISTEFANO

1. The Relationship between Private International Law and Human Rights 157
2. The Best Interests Principle in International Human Rights Law: Three Concepts in One 162
3. Best Interests of the Child and Private International Family Law: Towards a Convergence 165
4. Concluding Remarks 169

1. THE RELATIONSHIP BETWEEN PRIVATE INTERNATIONAL LAW AND HUMAN RIGHTS

Private international law and international human rights law intersect whenever the solution of cases with international aspects endangers the enjoyment of a fundamental right or freedom, or when the protection of human rights, as ensured by international judicial mechanisms, risks jeopardising the normal functioning of the rules governing the conflict of laws.

Scholarship, albeit inspired by a variety of legal perspectives, has attempted to theoretically frame these potential points of friction, basically referring to the idea that, directly or indirectly, the way the rules governing the conflict of laws function are by now influenced and conditioned by the pervasive nature of rules protecting human rights. It should thus be remembered that many authors have for some time been aware of, if not actually predicted, in regulatory and social contexts different from ours, the complex legal issues we are dealing with here.[1]

1 See, among others, P. LEREBOURS-PIGEONNIÈRE, La Déclaration universelle des droits de l'homme et le droit international privé français, in Le droit privé français au milieu du XXe siècle. Études offertes à Georges Ripert, LGDJ, Paris 1950, 255; B. GOLDMAN, La protection

In fact, in an era in which the fragmentation of regulatory regimes prevails,[2] in which the stratification of international, European and national sources results in complex dynamics of coordination and balancing of the legal values underlying the various disciplines;[3] at a time when international jurisdictions themselves,

internationale des droits de l'homme et l'ordre public international dans le fonctionnement de la règle de conflit des lois, in R. Cassin, Amicorum discipulorumque liber, vol. I, Pédone, Paris 1969, pp. 449–466; D. Cohen, 'La Convention européenne des droits de l'homme et le droit international privé français', Revue critique DIP (1989), 451; P. Mayer, 'La Convention européenne des droits de l'homme et l'application des normes étrangères', ibid. (1991), 651. See also the various attempts at a systematic organisation of the issue in P. Hammje, La contribution des principes généraux du droit à la formation du droit international privé, thèse dactyl., Paris I, 1994; E. Jayme, Identité culturelle et intégration: le droit international privé postmoderne, in *Recueil des Cours*, 1995, t. 251; F. Matscher, Le droit international privé face à la Convention européenne des droits de l'homme, in Travaux du Comité français de droit international privé, LGDJ, Paris 1996–97, 211; L. Gannagé, La hiérarchie des normes et les méthodes du droit international privé. Étude de droit international privé de la famille, LGDJ, Paris 2001; P. Kinsch, Droits de l'homme, droits fondamentaux et droits international privé, in Recueil des Cours, 2005, t. 318; B. Juratowitch, 'The European Convention on Human Rights and English Private International Law', (2007) *Journal of Private International Law*, 173; M. Hunter-Hennin, 'Droits des personnes et droits de l'homme: combination ou confrontation?', Revue critique DIP, (2007) 743; F. Marchadier, Les objectifs généraux du droit international privé à l'épreuve de la Convention européenne des droits de l'homme, Bruylant, Bruxelles 2007; L. R. Kiestra, *The Impact of the European Convention on Human Rights on Private International Law*, T.M.C Asser, The Hague 2014; J. Fawcett, M. N. Shúilleabháin and S. Shah, *Human Rights and Private International Law*, Oxford University Press, Oxford 2016. In Italian scholarship there has been no lack of studies on the relationship between international sources on human rights and rules governing the conflict of laws. See, among the many, L. Picchio Forlati, 'Critères de rattachement et règles d'applicabilité à l'heure de la protection des droits de l'homme en Europe', Rivista di diritto internazionale (2005), 907; G. Carella, 'Sistema delle norme di conflitto e tutela internazionale dei diritti umani: una rivoluzione copernicana?', Diritti umani e diritto internazionale (2014), 523; F. Salerno, 'Il vincolo al rispetto dei diritti dell'uomo nel sistema delle fonti del diritto internazionale privato', ibid., 549; ibid., 'I diritti fondamentali della persona straniera nel diritto internazionale privato: una prospettiva metodologica', Rivista di diritto internazionale privato e processuale (2014), 773.

2 The debate on the fragmentation of international law has not spared private international law. Many authors have highlighted its peculiar characteristics, linking it to the phenomenon of economic globalisation that would bring with it the disarticulation of national legal systems, the overcoming of the distinction between public and private law and the creation of a new governance of law. Among the many writings on the issue by H. Muir Watt see, 'Private International Law as Global Governance: Beyond the Schism: From Closet to Planet', (2011) *Transnational Legal Theory*, 347; ibid., Concurrence ou confluence? Droit international privé et droits fondamentaux dans la gouvernance globale, in Le droit entre tradition et modernité. Mélanges à la mémoire de Patrick Courbe, Dalloz, Paris 2012, 459; with Diego P. Fernández Arroyo (eds.), *Private International Law and Global Governance*, Oxford University Press, Oxford 2014; La globalisation et le droit international privé, in V. Heuzé and R. Libchaber and P. de Vareilles-Sommières (sous de la direction de), Mélanges en l'honneur du Professeur Pierre Mayer: Liber amicorum, LGDJ, Paris 2015, 607. See also R. Libchaber, L'avenir d'un paradoxe, ibid., 533.

3 See H. Gaudemet-Tallon, Le pluralisme en droit international privé: richesses e faiblesses. (Le funambule et l'arc-en-ciel), in Recueil des Cours, 2005, t. 312; S. Vrellis, Conflit ou coordination de valeurs en droit international privé. A la recherche de la justice, ibid., 2007, t. 328, 175.

starting with the ECtHR, are struggling to keep up with 'new' demands for the protection of individuals; private international law, by its nature an expression of the will to go beyond the normative divergences between systems, is undergoing a profound transformation and experiencing rediscovered vitality, having to reconcile public and private, general and particular interests under the 'watchful eye' of internationally recognised standards of human rights.

Without in these few introductory lines going into the merits of issues that would require much deeper analysis of the scholarship,[4] we here start with the assumption that the current rules governing the conflict of laws, by their nature and characteristics based on a plurality of methods of coordination between systems,[5] have among their many objectives also that of avoiding the occurrence of situations that are harmful to human rights. This is achieved sometimes by encouraging the integration of different legal cultures, at others by preserving national identities, or pursuing a specific material interest. The adoption of one criterion of connection rather than another responds to these multiple visions: thus, the criterion of nationality is perceived as a bulwark of a State's inalienable interests, while the propensity to use habitual residence is more closely linked to the idea of fostering integration between peoples and their cultures. Therefore, the two perspectives, one underlying private international law and the other inherent to the international protection of human rights, are not antithetical, but can coexist and, in some cases, work in unison.

Now, the assessment of conformity with the rules governing the conflict of laws established by international mechanisms guaranteeing human rights, especially as far as concerns the ECHR's system of jurisdictional protection for the purpose of this study, has different connotations according to whether priority is given to the rule governing the conflict of laws or to the

---

4 The basic philosophy underlying the rules of private international law has always been a 'puzzle' for those interested in the subject: the international harmony of solutions, coordination between systems, defence of the public order of the court, pursuit of material interests, and the unilateral or bilateral nature of the rules governing the conflict of laws are just some of the general questions that have always aroused the curiosity of scholars: see, for example, T. Azzi, O. Boskovic, Quel avenir pour la théorie générale des conflits de lois? Droit européen, droit conventionnel, droit commun, Bruylant, Bruxelles 2015. In national manuals, especially Italian and French, this aspect has always been considered as introductory to the study of rules governing the conflict of laws. See, among others, D. Bureau, H. Muir Watt, Droit international privé, PUF, Paris 2014; P. Mayer, V. Heuzé, Droit international privé, LGDJ, Paris/Montchrestien 2014; Y. Loussouarn, P. Bourel, P. de Vareilles-Sommières, Droit international privé, Dalloz, Paris 2013; with some differences M. L. Niboyet, G. de Geuoffre de la Pradelle, Droit international privé, LGDJ, Paris 2017; F. Mosconi, C. Campiglio, Diritto internazionale privato e processuale, Vol. I. Parte Generale e Obbligazioni, Utet Giuridica, Milano 2017; B. Barel, S. Armellini, Manuale breve. Diritto internazionale privato, Giuffré, Milano 2017; G. Carella, Fondamenti di diritto internazionale privato. Tra sovranità, cooperazione e diritti umani, Giappichelli, Torino 2018.

5 See P. Picone, Les méthodes de coordination entre ordres juridiques en droit international privé, in Recueil des Cours, 1999, t. 276.

material rule.[6] In the former case, it will be the judge of the court who has to exclude the application of a rule governing the conflict of laws that, for example, discriminates against the enjoyment of a fundamental freedom. On the other hand, when the application of the material rule is destined to result in a potential violation of human rights, it will be the instruments of private international law that intervene, to mitigate or exclude its effects in the legal system of the court. Therefore, we move according to the approach that attributes to the national judge (the judge of the court) the task, in the main, of dealing with potential conflicts with rules on human rights: such rules constitute, in fact, in national legal systems an unavoidable legislative parameter.[7]

On the basis of these methodological premises, and turning attention to the specific problems raised by private and procedural international family law, it should first be remembered that this is a field which has undergone profound transformations: once exclusively a legislative prerogative of States, today it is a complex set of international, European and national rules, on which there is copious case law of the ECtHR and the CJEU.[8]

The result of this melting pot of rules and case law, as some scholars have effectively highlighted, has been the development of two main legal approaches that seem to inform the discipline as a whole: on the one hand, the promotion of the individual in family relationships, due to the universal affirmation of human rights and, at the European level, fundamental rights; on the other, the internationalisation of these relationships, due to the mobility of individuals.[9]

While the latter is one of the most evident effects of economic globalisation and the breaking down of borders, the former seems to direct the legislative policy decisions of States towards the gradual overcoming of traditional linking criteria, such as nationality and habitual residence, to the advantage of the criterion of the autonomy of the will (or rather, of the individual choices of the protagonists in family relationships).[10]

---

6 See G. Carella, above n.1, 526; M. L. Niboyet, G. de Geuoffre de la Pradelle, above, n. 4, pp. 294–96.

7 See F. Salerno, Il vincolo al rispetto, above n. 1, p. 550.

8 On the development of private international and family law see, among others, Y. Lequette, Le droit international privé de la famille à l'épreuve des conventions internationales, in Recueil des Cours, 1994, t. 246; pp. 19–233; H. Stanford, 'Concepts of Family under EU Law: Lessons from the ECHR', (2002) *International Journal of Law, Policy and the Family*, 410; H. Fulchiron, J. Sosson, Parenté, filiation, origines. Le droit à l'engendrement à plusieurs, Larcier, Bruxelles 2013; B. Bourdelois, La famille du XXIe siècle et problématiques de conflits de lois, in Mélanges Mayer above n. 2, 91; A. L. Estin, *International Family Law: Volume I*, Elgar, Cheltenham/Northampton 2016.

9 See. H. Gaudemet-Tallon, Individualisme et mondialisation: aspects de droit international privé de la famille, in *A Commitment to Private International Law: Essays in Honour of Hans van Loon*, Intersentia, Cambridge 2013, p. 181.

10 There has been talk of the autonomy of the will as the best way to achieve the so-called 'right to mobility': J. Guillamé, L'affaiblissement de l'État-Nation et le droit international privé, LGDJ, Paris 2011, p. 284.

In particular, we are witnessing a phenomenon that has been defined as a *fait accomplis* in international family relations.[11] The judge of the court is increasingly obliged to decide on the validity of legal situations 'packaged elsewhere', even if such situations are unprecedented or even explicitly prohibited in the legal system of that court.

Attributing or denying effects to these family statuses clearly implies the need to examine the respect for the human rights of the individuals involved,[12] and in particular, of the weak subject *par excellence* of family relations, the child, for whom international human rights law now provides increasingly marked and detailed protection. It is worth mentioning, as a simple example, the difficulty encountered by national judges today in ascertaining the *status filiationis* in cases of transnational commercial heterologous surrogate motherhood.

By adhering to a strictly private international law reasoning, the protection of the child in international family relationships has been increasingly achieved by adopting various methods that largely reflect the evolution of society and law. These include, first of all, the *a priori* identification of a criterion of connection or jurisdiction, deemed suitable to ensure protection; and secondly, the private international law limit of public order, whose content has been extended to include international legislation on the rights of the child. Furthermore, and to combat transnational phenomena such as international child abduction, mechanisms of international judicial cooperation have been created in the civil sphere based on a single jurisdiction criterion, the habitual residence of the minor, before moving on to the adoption first of international treaties and then of European regulations, with a view to standardising private international law regulations.

All these distinct attempts to provide child protection within the discipline of international family relationships are, in our opinion, united by the direct or indirect recognition of the normative value of the principle of the best interests of the child. In some cases, taken as a presupposition, in others explicitly

11 See Y. Lequette, De la « proximité » au « fait accomplis », in Mélanges Mayer above n.2, 519.

12 This is a line of research which is of particular interest to scholars: see, among others, A. Bucher, La famille en droit international privé, in Recueil des Cours, 2000, 9; P. Lagarde, 'Développements futurs du droit international privé dans une Europe en voie d'unification', RabelsZ (2004), 225; P. Mayer, Les méthodes de la reconnaissance en droit international privé, in B. Ancel, B. Audit, T. Ballarino and G. P. Romano, Le droit international privé: esprit et méthodes. Mélanges en l'honneur de Paul Lagarde, Dalloz, Paris 2005, 547; G. P. Romano, 'La bilatéralité éclipsé par l'autorité: développements récents en matière d'état des personnes', Revue critique DIP (2006), 467; S. Bollée, 'L'extension du domaine de la méthode de la reconnaissance unilatérale', ibid. (2007), 307; R. Baratta, 'Problematic Elements of An Implicit Rule Providing for Mutual Recognition of Personal and Family Status in the EC', (2007) *IPRax*, 4; ibid., La reconnaissance internationale des situations juridiques personnelles et familiales, in Recueil des Cours, 2010, 253; ibid., 'Recognition of Foreign Personal and Family Status: A Rights Based Perspective', Rivista di diritto internazionale privato e processuale (2016), 413.

mentioned, the principle has shrugged off its image as an unknown magic formula,[13] to take the form of a legal rule with multiple contents. This chapter aims to investigate the systemic role and versatile function of the best interests of the child principle in contemporary private international family law.

2. THE BEST INTERESTS PRINCIPLE IN INTERNATIONAL HUMAN RIGHTS LAW: THREE CONCEPTS IN ONE

As codified in Article 3 of the CRC and then transposed into Article 24 of the EU Charter, the principle envisages the obligation to ensure that the best interests of the child are assessed and taken as a primary consideration in all actions affecting children by public and administrative authorities and legislative bodies.[14]

Despite the constant reluctance of scholars to consider it an effective instrument for the protection of children, it represents, like the principle of non-discrimination, that of the right to life and of listening to the child, the international standard of reference for the protection of minors. The strongest criticisms have always focused on the vague, almost programmatic nature of the rule.

---

13 This is the classic criticism of the principle formulated by J. Carbonnier, Droit civil, t. 2, Les personnes, 20e éd., PUF, Paris 1996, p. 175 and taken up by other authors such as Parker, 'The Best Interests of the Child. Principles and Problems', (1994) *International Journal of Law and The Family*, 38, contra P. Alston, 'The Best Interests Principle: Towards a Reconciliation of Culture and Human Rights', in P. Alston (ed.), *The Best Interests of the Child. Reconciling Culture and Human Rights*, Oxford University Press, Oxford 1994, pp. 1–25.

14 The international legislative movement concerning the principle has its origins in the adoption of two separate declarations on the rights of the child, the first in 1924 under the auspices of the League of Nations, the second in 1959, unanimously adopted by the General Assembly of the United Nations. In the latter, the second principle and para. 2 of the seventh principle respectively envisage that 'The child shall enjoy special protection, and shall be given opportunities and facilities, by law and by other means, to enable him to develop physically, mentally, morally, spiritually and socially in a healthy and normal manner and in conditions of freedom and dignity. In the enactment of laws for this purpose, the best interests of the child shall be the paramount consideration'; 'The best interests of the child shall be guiding principle of those responsible for his education and guidance; that responsibility lies in the first place with his parents'. The preparatory work of the CRC is resumed and illustrated in OHCHR, *Legislative History of the Convention on the Rights of the Child*, New York/Geneva 2007. For a detailed reconstruction of the prescriptive content of the Convention, see, within the extensive literature, P. E. Veerman, *The Rights of the Child and The Changing Image of Children*, Martinus Nijhoff, Dordrecht/Boston/London 1992; S. Detrick, *The United Nations Convention on the Rights of the Child*, Martinus Nijhoff, Dordrecht/Boston/London 1992; G. Van Bueren, *The International Law on the Rights of the Child*, Martinus Nijhoff, Dordrecht/Boston/London, 1998; Y. Kolosov, 'The Rights of the Child', in J. Symonides (ed.), *Human Rights: Concepts and Standards*, Ashgate, Aldershot 2000; M. Freeman, 'The End of the Century of the Child?', (2000) *Current Legal Problems*, 505–558; P. Alston and J. Tobin (eds.), *Laying the Foundations for Children's Rights*, The Unicef Innocenti Research Centre, Florence 2005, pp. 1–104, particularly pp. 1–8.

In reality, such a flexible formula not only reflects the difficult negotiating equilibrium achieved by the drafters of the CRC, but is useful for affirming the rights of the child. It reflects an attempt to balance, on a general level, the cultural, social and religious identities of the States with the universal nature of the rights of the child.[15] On the level of interpersonal relationships, the protection to be afforded to children should be compared to the rights of the other subjects involved: there is no doubt that the recognition of the paramount importance of the principle might conflict with other interests or rights, such as parental rights.[16]

Its prescriptive force, accompanied by the search for the multiple meanings that the principle is bound to assume, is now confirmed by the constant references made to it in national and international case law.[17]

Restricting ourselves to the latter, it is, first of all, the ECtHR which should be given merit for having acknowledged the central value of the principle, thus filling a significant legislative gap in the European system. The ECHR does not in fact include any provisions dedicated to the protection of minors, with the exception of Article 2 of Protocol I. Through the reference to the systemic value of the principle the Court has supported a child-oriented interpretation of many provisions contained in the Convention. With particular reference to the

---

15 See P. Alston, 'The Best Interests Principle', above n. 13, passim. However, this cannot disregard some values considered fundamental. In other words, a culturally oriented interpretation of the best interests of the child must not threaten the child's physical and psychological integrity; it cannot justify forced marriages at a young age, female genital mutilation or corporal punishment for 'educational' purposes; it cannot endorse discrimination based on belonging to an ethnic or religious minority; it cannot tolerate international crimes such as trafficking in human beings, the recruitment of children as soldiers, or the exploitation of child labour.

16 See J. Tobin, 'Understanding a Human Rights Based Approach to Matters Involving Children: Conceptual Foundations and Strategic Considerations', in A. Invernizzi and J. Williams (eds.), *The Human Rights of Children: From Vision to Implementation*, Ashgate Publishing, Farnham 2011, pp. 61–98. The author highlights that an overly generalised and theoretical use of this approach may end up nullifying the legislative effort that accompanied the adoption of the New York Convention, aimed at achieving compromises in order to fully involve all those who, in various ways and at various levels, interact with and condition the life of a child.

17 On the application of the principle see Hodgkin and Newell, *Implementation Handbook for the Convention on the Rights of the Child*, Unicef, New York 1998, pp. 39–51; UNICEF, *Protecting the World's Children: Impact of the Convention on the Rights of the Child in Diverse Legal Systems*, Cambridge University Press, Cambridge 2007; M. Freeman, *Article 3. The Best Interests of the Child, A Commentary on the United Nations Convention on the Rights of the Child*, Martinus Nijhoff, Dordrecht/Boston/London 2007, pp. 1–75; J. Zermatten, 'The Best Interests of the Child Principle: Literal Analysis and Function', (2010) *International Journal of Children's Rights*, 483–499; T. Lieefard and J. E. Doek, *Litigating the Rights of the Child: The UN Convention on the Rights of the Child in Domestic and International Jurisprudence*, Springer, Dordrecht/Heidelberg/New York/London 2015; D. Prabhat and J. Hambly, 'Bettering the Best Interests of the Child Determination: Of Checklists and Balancing Exercises', (2017) *International Journal of Children's Rights*, 754.

protection of family life, it has given States precise obligations of a negative and positive, substantial and procedural nature that aim at encouraging the pursuit of the material and relational well-being of the child. These range from ascertaining the relationship of filiation to the right of a child to know his origins; from the right to a name to the protection of a two-parent upbringing; from the right to grow and remain in the family of origin to the right to be reunited with it in case of a move abroad; from protection in the event of international abduction to the removal from the family for proven safety reasons; from educational choices to the recognition of an adoptive relationship or other forms of protection.[18]

The Inter-American Court of Human Rights also extolled its systemic value in its 2002 Opinion on the legal status of the minor, stating that '... the phrase "best interests of the child", set forth in Article 3 of the Convention on the Rights of the child, entails that children's development and full enjoyment of their rights must be considered the guiding principles to establish and apply provisions pertaining to all aspects of children's lives'.[19]

The CJEU has mentioned the principle, including it among the general principles of EU law, both in cases relating to the interpretation of specific provisions, such as those on family reunification or the management of migration, and in the framework of the private international law aspects of the Regulations. With particular reference to the Brussels II *bis* Regulation, the principle is explicitly referred to as the general objective of the Regulation, as an interpretative criterion and as a link to the EU Charter. Implicitly, then, it is found in many urgent preliminary ruling procedures relating to cases of international child abduction (*Rinau*, *Povse*, *Deticek*, *J. McB* and *Zarraga*).[20]

Taking its cue from these case law orientations, scholarship has examined distinct legal dimensions of the principle, at times emphasising its procedural

---

18 It is impossible here to give an account of all the ECtHR case law on the principle. For general aspects see F. Sudre, Rapport introductif. La « construction » par le juge européen du droit au respect de la vie privée, in F. Sudre (dir.), Le droit au respect de la vie privée au sens de la Convention européenne des droits de l'homme. Actes du colloque des 26 et 27 novembre 2004, Bruylant, Bruxelles 2005, 27; ibid., Droit européen et international des droits de l'homme, PUF, Paris 2011, pp. 534–563. For a detailed examination of the meaning of the principle of best interests in ECtHR case law, see K. Turković and A. Grgić, 'Best Interests of the Child in the Context of Article 8 of the ECHR', in J. Casadevall et al. (eds.), *Liber Amicorum Dean Spielmann*, WLP 2015, p. 629.

19 See Inter-American Court of Human Rights, Advisory Opinion OC-17/2002, 28.08.2002, requested by the Inter-American Commission on Human Rights, 'Juridical Condition and Human Rights of the Child' para. 137. For a precise reconstruction of the subjectivity of the minor, see the Concurrent Opinion of Judge Cançado Trindade. See also Inter-American Court of Human Rights, case of the 'Street Children', (*Villagran-Morales et al. v. Guatemala*), Judgment of November 19, 1999, (Merits).

20 See N. Bareït, 'La Cour de Justice de l'Union européenne artisane de la lutte contre les enlèvements d'enfants', Revue trimestrielle de droit européen (2011), vol. 4, pp. 537–559; B. Ancel, H. Muir Watt, 'L'intérêt supérieur de l'enfant dans le concert des juridictions: le Règlement Bruxelles II bis', Revue Critique DIP (2005), pp. 569–605.

character, at others focusing on its substantial value, or specifying its interpretative scope.[21]

These interpretations of the three-pronged meaning of the principle were taken up and clearly developed by the CRC Committee in General Comment No. 14 dedicated to Article 3 of the CRC.[22]

Regarding one meaning, the Committee emphasises the substantial nature of the principle, which binds the State to the implementation of legislative, administrative and judicial measures that take into account the interests of the minor. The self-executing nature of Article 3 of the CRC is emphasised and, consequently, the fact that it may be invoked in judicial procedures a consideration which, as is known, is not unanimously acknowledged by national courts.

In its second meaning the Committee aims to enhance its interpretative-systematic value pursuant to Article 31 para. 3(c) of the VCLT. The principle thus acts as a kind of 'legislative glue' that unites the relevant international rules, ensuring effectiveness for the individual rights attributed to the child.

In its third and last dimension, the principle assumes yet another value, embodying the obligation to provide precise procedural guarantees to evaluate the positive or negative impact of the measure adopted for the individual minor involved. Elements of various kinds thus assume importance, such as the child's opinion, his cultural, religious and social identity, the maintenance of family ties, taking care of his health, the particular situation of vulnerability in which he may find himself, but also parental affection and care, and school-based and social integration. The particular evaluation of the situation in which the minor is found therefore becomes a prerequisite for making a decision.

While today, therefore, there seem to be few doubts about the special significance of the principle in international human rights law, let us now see how, in the specific field of international family relations, it has been achieved.

3. BEST INTERESTS OF THE CHILD AND PRIVATE INTERNATIONAL FAMILY LAW: TOWARDS A CONVERGENCE

The principle of the best interests of the child affects private international family law in particular ways, at times assuming the appearance of a connecting or jurisdictional criterion, at others informing the limits of public policy, and at others becoming a material objective, achieved through the technique of renvoi

21 See Zermatten, 'The Best Interests of the Child Principle', above n. 17, 48.

22 See General Comment no. 14 (2013) on the right of the child to have his or her best interests taken as a primary consideration (Article 3 para. 1), CRC/C/GC/14, 29.05.2013.

in favorem, of the combination of laws, of the overriding mandatory rules, or through mechanisms of international judicial cooperation. Whether covertly or explicitly, the use of any one of these methods reveals an intent to apply the best interests principle of.[23]

Considering these criteria, the choice has always fluctuated between nationality and habitual residence, except for in common law systems, where importance is given to domicile. All these criteria respond to a need for proximity, in the sense that they express a special link between the child and the State, according to the traditional approach based on the spatial location of a given case.

The clear preference for the principle of nationality, typical of the period of national codification, has given way to the factual criterion of the child's habitual residence. This occurred as a result of a substantial assimilation of jurisdictional and connection criteria. Once the criterion of habitual residence has been selected to establish jurisdiction, there has been a tendency to also use it establish the applicable system of law, in order to ensure certainty and speed in the resolution of cases concerning children.[24]

The so-called 'conflictual' interest of the principle has therefore been manifested in the concept of proximity, in the sense that the criteria of jurisdiction and connection express *a priori* (or rather, abstractly) the 'best' spatial placement of the child, presuming that the court appealed to is the most suitable to protect his rights.

The sudden social changes affecting family relationships of an international nature, the consequent evolution of family law and, above all, the universal affirmation of the principle of best interests in the triple dimension mentioned above, have led to a partial change in perspective: from the protection of children we have moved on to the protection of the individual child, from the merely 'conflictual' value of the principle we have arrived at its substantial and procedural value.[25]

---

23 See for example the Italian Legislation on Private International Law of 1995 (no. 218), as reformed in 2012 with law no. 219, which provides for the combined application of several laws with a view to aiding the ascertainment of filiation; the use of the renvoi *in favorem* technique to pursue the same objective; the application of Italian law, as an overriding mandatory rule, to guarantee various rights of the child (the unique nature of the status of son/daughter, the attribution to both parents of parental responsibility, the duty of both parents to provide for the maintenance of their child, the power of the courts to take measures that remove or restrict parental responsibility); without forgetting the role of the best interests as a principle of public policy.

24 See the Hague Convention of 19 October 1996 on jurisdiction, applicable law, recognition, enforcement and co-operation in respect of parental responsibility and measures for the protection of children.

25 See C. Chabert, L'intérêt de l'enfant et les conflits de lois, PUAM, Aix-en-Marseille 2001; P. Hammje, L'intérêt de l'enfant face aux sources internationales du droit international privé, in Mélanges Lagarde, above n. 12, pp. 365–381.

This new way of looking at the interests of the child originated in the ECtHR. The ECtHR, first with the *Wagner* judgment, challenged the public policy limitation by using the principle of higher interest as a counter-limitation.[26] Then, in the *Neulinger* case, the Court re-examined the 1980 Hague Convention on international child abduction,[27] recognising the procedural and substantial value of the principle.

From the procedural point of view, the ECtHR introduced an exception to the existing mechanism, underlining the importance assumed in the individual case by a particular evaluation of the conditions in which the child finds himself before the decision ordering return is taken. With regard to the substantial nature, the court attached a precise meaning to the principle, that of achieving the physical, psychological and relational well-being of the child.[28]

---

26 See Case of *Wagner and J.M.W.L v Luxembourg*, No. 76240/01, ECtHR 2007. For a comment see F. Marchadier, 'La protection européenne des situations constituées à l'étranger', Recueil Dalloz (2007), 2700; P. Franzina, 'Some Remarks on the Relevance of Article 8 of the ECHR To the Recognition of Family Status Judicially Created Abroad', Diritti umani e diritto internazionale (2011), 609. In our preferred sense, also extended to the analysis of cases of surrogate motherhood, see P. Kinsch, L'article 8 de la Convention et l'obligation de reconnaître les situations familiales constituées à l'étranger: à la recherche du fondement d'une solution jurisprudentielle, in Mélanges Spielmann, above n. 18, pp. 273–282.

27 Some authors, starting with the value attributed to the principle in international human rights law, had long emphasised the need to re-read the rules contained in the 1980 Hague Convention on the civil aspects of international child abduction, in the light of this new legislative benchmark and, more generally, of the internationally recognised rights of the child. See, among others, C. Bruch, 'The Hague Child Abduction Convention: Past Accomplishments, Future Challenges', in S. Detrick and S. Vlaardingerbroek (eds.) *Globalization of Child Law: The Role of the Hague Conventions*, Brill, Netherlands 1999, p. 33; ibid., 'Religious Law, Secular Practices, and Children's Human Rights in Child Abduction Cases under the Hague Child Abduction Convention', (2000) *New York University Journal of International Law and Politics*, 49–58; J. Lewis, 'The Hague Convention on the Civil Aspects of International Child Abduction: When Domestic Violence and Child Abuse Impact the Goal of Comity', (2000) *The Transnational Lawyer*, 391–449; M. H. Weiner, 'International Child Abduction and the Escape from Domestic Violence', (2000) *Fordham Law Review*, 593–706; A. Schulz, 'The 1980 Hague Child Abduction and the European Convention on Human Rights', (2002) *Transnational Law and Contemporary Problems*, 356; R. Schuz, 'The Hague Child Abduction Convention and The United Nations Convention on the Rights of the Child', in P. Lødrup and E. Modvar (eds.), *Family Life and Human Rights: Papers Presented at the 11th World Conference of the International Society of Family Law*, Gyldendal Akademisk, Oslo 2004, pp. 721–755; A. Fiorini, 'Enlèvements internationaux d'enfants: solutions internationales et responsabilités étatiques', Revue de droit de McGill (2006), 51, pp. 279–326; A. Bucher, L'intérêt de l'enfant pénètre la convention sur l'enlèvement, in Vers de nouveaux équilibres entre ordres juridique. Liber amicorum Hélène Gaudemet-Tallon, Dalloz, Paris 2008, 683; T. Kruger, *International Child Abduction Cases: The Inadequacies of the Law*, Oxford University Press, Oxford 2011.

28 See *Neulinger and Shuruk v Switzerland* (GC), No. 41615/07, ECtHR 2010. See D. Stoeger, 'International Child Abduction and Children Rights: Two Means and The Same Ends', (2011) *Michigan Journal of International Law*, 511–552; M. Distefano, Interesse superiore del minore e sottrazione internazionale di minori, Cedam, Padova 2012; Criticisms of the approach adopted by the Court, due to the negative impact it could have on the functioning

Returning to the issue a few years later, the ECtHR toned down and refined its orientation in the *X. v. Latvia* case, pointing out that in the *Neulinger* test ruling it did not intend to dismantle the Hague Convention, but rather to take a further step towards effective protection of the child. National courts will no longer be able to mechanically apply the Hague Convention, but must adequately justify any decision ordering return, taking into account the circumstances of the case.[29]

The change in the Court's perspective compared to the past is clear: the procedural obligations deriving from Article 8 ECHR, interpreted in the light of the Hague Convention of 1980, implemented the mechanism, meaning that the ECHR had been infringed only in cases where the State had not promptly enforced the return order.[30] After *Neulinger*, as specified in *X v. Latvia*, the substantial and procedural value of the best interests principle is also promoted,

---

of the mechanism, as a result of time passing, have been levelled by: P. Beaumont, 'The Art. 8 Jurisprudence of the European Court of Human Rights on the Hague Convention on International Child Abduction in Relation to Delays in Enforcing the Return of a Child, in G. Venturini and S. Bariatti (eds.), Nuovi strumenti del diritto internazionale privato. Liber Fausto Pocar, Giuffrè, Milano 2009, pp. 75–94; P. Beaumont, K. Trimmings, L. Walker and J. Holliday, 'Child Abduction: Recent Jurisprudence of the European Court of Human Rights', (2015) *International and Comparative Law Quarterly*, 39–63; N. Lowe, 'A Supra-National Approach to Interpreting the 1980 Hague Child Abduction: A Tale of two European Courts. Part 1: Setting the Scene and Part 2: the Substantive Impact of the Two European Courts' Rulings upon the Application of the 1980 Convention', (2012) *International Family Law*, 48–52 and 170–179.

29 See the case of *X. v Latvia* (GC), no. 27853/09, §107, ECtHR 2013: 'the Court considers that Article 8 of the Convention imposes on the domestic authorities a particular procedural obligation in this respect: when assessing an application for a child's return, the courts must not only consider arguable allegations of a "grave risk" for the child in the event of return, but must also make a ruling giving specific reasons in the light of the circumstances of the case. Both a refusal to take account of objections to the return capable of falling within the scope of Articles 12, 13 and 20 of the Hague Convention and insufficient reasoning in the ruling dismissing such objections would be contrary to the requirements of Article 8 of the Convention and also to the aim and purpose of the Hague Convention. Due consideration of such allegations, demonstrated by reasoning of the domestic courts that is not automatic and stereotyped, but sufficiently detailed in the light of the exceptions set out in the Hague Convention, which must be interpreted strictly, is necessary'. See L. Garlicki, 'Two Conventions and one Regulation (on Human Rights Aspects of International Child Abduction)', in *Liber Amicorum Dean Spielmann*, above n. 17, 217–227; P. McEleavy, 'The European Court of Human Rights and The Hague Convention On International Child Abduction: Prioritising Return or Reflection?', (2015) *Netherlands International Law Review*, 365–405; H. Keller and C. Heri, 'Protecting the Best Interests of the Child: International Child Abduction and the European Court of Human Rights', (2015) *Nordic Journal of International Law*, 270–296.

30 For a reconstruction of European case law prior to *Neulinger*, see P. Beaumont, 'The Jurisprudence of the European Court of Human Rights and the European Court of Justice on the Hague Convention on International Child Abduction', in Recueil des Cours, 2008, t. 335, pp. 9–103; F. Marchadier, La contribution de la Cour européenne des droits de l'homme à l'efficacité des conventions de la Haye de coopération judiciaire et administrative, Revue Critique DIP (2007), pp. 677–715.

to ensure the effectiveness of the internationally recognised rights of the child. We should consider the value of such an approach in cases where abduction is a result of episodes of domestic violence and is made by the primary caregiver.

The best interests principle thus allows us to modernise the extraordinary mechanism embodied in the Hague Convention, adapting the system for the protection of abducted children to respond to changing sociological factors.

By extending these considerations to other subjects and to other legal disciplines of international family relationships involving the protection of children – in particular of measures to protect minors, matters relating to the exercise of parental responsibility and cases of surrogate motherhood – the principle of the child's best interests is not at all an element of regulatory instability, but rather a factor in the development and implementation of the rights internationally attributed to the child.

The CJEU itself, called upon to interpret the meaning of the key notions of 'habitual residence of the child' and 'parental responsibility', has adopted a factual and substantial approach, with a view to aiding the effective protection of the individual child involved.[31]

Recently, in the *Child and Family Agency* case, the CJEU found the need to assess the negative impact on the well-being of a child that could result from the transfer of jurisdiction, pursuant to Article 15 of the Regulation.[32]

4. CONCLUDING REMARKS

As mentioned in the introductory paragraph, this chapter is based on the premise that private international law and international human rights law are regulatory systems of a complementary nature.

In the former, its technical nature has for some time made space for the material value of the instruments of private international law. In the latter, the

31 The use of the criterion of habitual residence of the child does not always promote his substantial protection: see E. Gallant, Réflexions sur la résidence habituelle des enfants de couples désunis, in Mélanges Mayer, above n. 2, pp. 255–272.

32 See case C/428-15, *Child and Family Agency v J.D.*, ECLI:EU:C2016:819, para. 58: 'the requirement that the transfer must be in the best interests of the child implies that the court having jurisdiction must be satisfied, having regard to the specific circumstances of the case, that the envisaged transfer of the case to a court of another Member State is not liable to be detrimental to the situation of the child concerned'. For a comment see N. Lowe and H. Setright, 'Transferring the Problem: How Article 15 of the Revised Brussels II Regulation operates in a public context', (2017) *International Family Law*, 18; R. Lamont, 'The Development of Child Protection Across International Borders for Children at Risk of Harm', in G. Douglas, M. Murch and V. Stephens (eds.), *International and National Perspectives on Child and Family Law: Essays in Honour of Nigel Lowe*, Intersentia, Cambridge/Antwerp/Portland, 2018, pp. 233–245.

specific aims of systems for protecting human rights, in particular the ECHR, mandate the pursuit of justice in individual cases.

Since national courts have the task of reconciling these different approaches aimed at the protection of children, the principle of best interests, in its threefold conflictual, substantive and procedural dimension, will be of great use.

Returning to Chabert's clear words: 'sous un vêtement unitaire, la notion de l'intérêt supérieur de l'enfant est une notion plurale qui demande une approche unitaire'.[33]

---

33 See Chabert, above n. 24, p. 93.

RECOGNITION OF A FOREIGN STATUS *FILII*

Pursuing the Best Interests Principle

Roberto Baratta

1. Introduction 171
2. ECtHR Activism as to the *Ordre Public* Exception 174
3. Outlining the Best Interests Test.. 178
4. Conclusion.. 184

1. INTRODUCTION

Recognising a status *filii* duly acquired abroad can be seen as a ground for legitimising family models capable of adversely affecting the notion of a traditional family. A bibliography on international family law indicates that the 'family,' conceptualised as a mere unit of society, is a constantly changing area of study, a 'moving target', as it were.

Legal analysis, through the prism of international law, is not called to ideologically endorse notions of the 'traditional' family or 'untraditional' family. Respect for both human and children's rights, as defined by international instruments, unavoidably impacts national family law, including its private international law (PIL) system, and national communities' basic ethical principles. As long as international agreements are binding, they are part of academic legal research, which also must consider how international courts apply these agreements. However, as suggested elsewhere, a human rights-based perspective on the recognition of foreign family status does not necessarily lead to a unique or universal concept of the family.[1] As seen throughout this chapter,

1 *La reconnaissance internationale des situations juridiques personnelles et familiales*, Recueil des cours de l'Académie de droit international de La Haye, tome 348 (2010), 2011 Martinus Nijhoff Publ., Leiden/Boston, *passim*; 'Recognition of Foreign Personal and Family Status – A Rights Based Perspective', in *Rivista di diritto internazionale privato e processuale*, 2016, pp. 413–443.

international human rights standards do not prevent States from enjoying some space for *manoeuvre* insofar as national legal orders do not share the same foundational values. It still holds true that the international judiciary instituted by human rights treaties, in principle, allows domestic law to protect the family in the traditional sense, a weighty and legitimate reason that may justify differences in treatment.[2] Striking a balance between the role of the traditional family and international human rights standards is a delicate and difficult exercise. In this respect, critically evaluating both PIL systems and the international case law is necessary.

To begin with, under any system of conflict of laws, a foreign judgement or public act concerning a status *filii* can be prevented from producing effects in the forum if its recognition would be contrary to some predetermined requirements of the requested State. This is usually the case when the foreign authority (i.e. that of the State of origin) has not: (i) exercised jurisdiction according to the same criteria adopted by the national system of PIL (i.e. the national rules on jurisdiction); (ii) complied with the conflict of law rules of the forum; or (iii) issued a decision inconsistent with the forum doctrine of *ordre public* to cause manifest and serious harm to the fundamental principle of justice or morals characterising the requested State.

From the forum standpoint, the key issue is to assess whether it is possible not only to let a foreign decision produce effects in the domestic legal order but also to declare it enforceable. For that ultimate objective, quite often an order is obtained for entering the status *filii* duly acquired in the State of origin into the public registry of the State in which that status is expected to produce legal effects. Enforcement of a foreign civil status seeks not only to establish

---

2 *Ex plurimis* European Court of Human Rights (ECtHR) *Karner v. Austria* (Application no 40016/98) judgment of 24 July 2003, §40. Further, States are free, under Articles 8 and 14, to restrict access to marriage to different-sex couples (*Schalk and Kopf v. Austria* (Application no 30141/04), judgment of 22 June 2010, §108); *Chapin and Charpentier v. France* (Requête no 40183/07), arrêt du 9 juin 2016, §48). Yet the case law of the ECtHR is multifaceted. It has decided for instance that there is no majority of States providing for legal recognition of same-sex couples. Consequently, States enjoy a margin of appreciation in the timing of the introduction of legislative changes (*Petrovic v. Austria* (156/1996/775/976) judgment of March 27, 1998, §§36–43). In any case, States are still free, under Article 14 taken in conjunction with Article 8, to restrict access to marriage to different-sex couples (*Schalk and Kopf v. Austria*, cit. §108; *Chapin and Charpentier v. France*, cit., §48). However, the Court has found a violation of Article 14 taken together with Article 8 where a law barred same-sex couples from entering into civil unions (*Vallianatos and Others v. Greece* [GC] (Applications nos 29381/09 and 32684/09), judgment of 7 November 2013, §§91–92). Moreover, considering the continuing international movement towards legal recognition and taking into account the specific circumstances in Italy, the Court found that the Italian authorities failed to comply with the positive obligation under Article 8 to ensure same-sex couples have available a specific legal framework providing for the recognition and protection of their unions (*Oliari and Others v. Italy*, Applications nos 18766/11 and 36030/11, judgment of 21 July 2015, §§178 and 180–185).

a personal tie or to integrate a child into a family group but also to secure inheritance rights between the individuals concerned and to permit a child to acquire the parent's nationality to obtain inter alia a definitive leave to remain in the requested State.[3]

From a human rights perspective, the problem is that refusing recognition of a foreign act due a to conflict of laws can represent interference with an individual fundamental right insofar as it amounts to conduct that impairs the same right's enjoyment.[4] In fact, the impact of fundamental rights on family PIL concerns methodologies for securing recognition of foreign judgements and public acts. Parents can create a valid status *filii* abroad to demand its recognition and enforcement in their national or habitual residential State. This is problematic, particularly when they aim to circumvent prohibitions or restrictions of the *lex fori* that would have prevented them from acquiring the same filiation status through the application of domestic law, including its conflict of law rules.[5] This may happen when the requested State's law does not provide for the examination of the merits of the application submitted to the foreign court but restricts itself to verifying that the decision delivered abroad satisfies some international procedural requirements.

As a matter of principle, international obligations in regard to family law and related domestic provisions deserve to be reconciled if only to absolve

3 As a part of the legal system of the requested State, the normative approaches to the civil law effects accorded to foreign judgments or acts issued by an external authority, may vary from one country to another. As is known, they may be automatic or, as they often do, provide for judicial proceedings charged to assess whether some requirements for recognition and enforcement have been met. Under a conflict of laws perspective, procedures aimed at securing civil effects to foreign decisions ought to be conceived as alternative *conflict techniques* with respect to the traditional choice of law approach, which determine, first, the jurisdiction of the national court and, second, the law which it will apply. Such procedures do also seek to solve antinomies between different legal orders. It is self-evident that the failure to recognise e.g. a decree concerning a family status granted in another State, creates inevitably a *limping* family relationship, validly established in the State of origin but not existing in the forum, with all the related inconveniences for the persons concerned. Broadly speaking the overarching objective of PIL techniques, including recognition methods, is to address and solve such problems.

4 *Ex plurimis* HCtHR *Hussin v. Belgium* (Application no 70807/01) judgment of 6 May 2004, §5; *Negrepontis-Giannisis c. Grèce* (Application no 56759/08) judgment of 3 May 2011, §§58–60.

5 In this respect the *Wagner* case is illustrative (ECtHR, *Wagner and J.M.W.L. v. Luxembourg* (Application no 76240/01) judgment of 28 June 2007; the case is partially reported also in *Rev. crit. dr. int. privé*, with a comment by P. Kinsch). Ms Wagner could not adopt a child in Luxembourg, the State of her nationality, since, being not married, she could not fulfil the conditions to adopt set forth in the national civil code that was applicable under the Luxembourg system of PIL. Therefore, she chose to adopt a child in Peru because this country permitted adoptions by an unmarried woman. Hence, she aimed to indirectly obtain abroad what was unable to achieve directly through an application to adopt in Luxembourg (see in particular the judgment of the Luxembourg District Court of 2 June 1999, quoted in *Wagner*, at p. 8).

the relevant contracting party from responsibility. In short, this explains the consistent interpretation approach, i.e. PIL provisions regulating the recognition of a filiation relationship legally acquired abroad should be interpreted and applied consistently with the legal obligation to respect the right to family life, as well as the best interests of the child. For non-recognition of a foreign status *filii* is capable under certain conditions of adversely affecting the 'respect for the right to family life' and the 'best interests of the child' since these fundamental rights are guaranteed by international human rights standards, Article 7 of the European Charter of Fundamental Rights (ECFR), and Article 8 of the European Convention on Human Rights (ECHR).[6]

This approach does not necessarily imply an absolute obligation to recognise a foreign status *filii*, but it does entail the need to consider the child's fundamental rights, which are a set of common principles leaving some margin of appreciation to national authorities.[7] Assessing the impact of international human rights standards on the recognition of a foreign status *filii* is essential.

2. ECtHR ACTIVISM AS TO THE *ORDRE PUBLIC* EXCEPTION

Since PIL provisions on recognition and enforcement of a foreign judgment or public act fall under the scrutiny of international human rights bodies,[8] States are not free to rely on national provisions when deciding proceedings on whether to confer effects to a child status duly acquired abroad. A glance to international jurisprudence is illustrative.

---

6 The rights set forth in Article 7 of the ECFR broadly correspond to those guaranteed by Article 8 ECHR (see Explanations on Article 7 relating to the Charter of Fundamental Rights (2007/C 303/02), OJ 14.2.2007 C 303, p. 20). Insofar as the former corresponds to the latter, the meaning and scope of the Charter rights are the same as those laid down by the ECHR, though the Charter does not prevent the Union from providing more extensive protection (Article 52(3) ECFR).

7 The 'margin of appreciation' doctrine mirrors the subsidiary nature of the international protection of human rights, and it is usually conceived as an interpretative instrument deferring to areas of national self-determination (Y. Arai-Takahashi, *The Margin of Appreciation Doctrine and the Principle of Proportionality in the ECHR*, Intersentia, Cambridge, 2002, *passim*; M. Lugato, *Sulla sussidiarietà in diritto internazionale*, in *Archivio Giuridico*, 2011, p. 3 ff.; ibid., 'The Margin of Appreciation and Freedom of Religion: Between Treaty Interpretation and Subsidiarity', (2013) *Journal of Catholic Legal Studies*, vol. 52, 49; S. Bartole, P. De Sena and V. Zagrebelsky, *Commenario breve alla CEDU*, Cedam, Padue, 2012, p. 308; A. Legg, *The Margin of Appreciation in International Human Rights Law. Deference and Proportionality*, OUP, Oxford, 2012, p. 58).

8 It suffices to look at international judicial practice. For instance, in *Wagner* (cit.) the ECtHR held that the national decision dismissing enforcement of a Peruvian order of full adoption had not demonstrated that such a result was necessary in a democratic society. Highlighting that

The *ordre public* exception, which is specific to any system of PIL, is particularly affected by the functioning of international human rights provisions. By considering the activism of the European Court of Human Rights (ECtHR) in this respect, at least two elements are worth noticing.

First, States are required to ensure the identity rights of individuals concerned. The *Negrepontis-Giannisis* and *Mennesson* cases are important in this respect. In *Negrepontis-Giannisis*, the Strasbourg Court held that the grounds for invoking the *ordre public* exception, claimed by the Greek Court of Cassation to refuse recognition of an American adoption, 'ne répondent pas à un besoin social impérieux. Ils ne sont donc pas proportionnés au but légitime poursuivi en ce qu'ils ont eu pour effet la négation du statut de fils adoptif du requérant.'[9] Likewise, in *Mennesson*, the same Court indicated that 'regard should also be had to the fact that an essential aspect of the identity of individuals is at stake where the legal parent-child relationship is concerned. The margin of appreciation afforded to the respondent State in the present case therefore needs to be reduced.'[10]

As a result, according to the ECtHR, the role of the *ordre public* exception shrinks because this exception comes squarely under the international judge's scrutiny. The ECtHR held that the national judiciary has to strike a fair balance between national public interests – such as, in particular, the rights and freedoms of the persons concerned, health and morals and public policy – and the individual entitlement to respect for private and family life. The point of equilibrium is shifted toward the need to guarantee the existence of status *filii*, considered to be an inherent and crucial part of individual personal identity. From this perspective, the protection of national legitimate aims is downgraded.[11]

---

the margin of appreciation was limited by the fact that adoption by unmarried persons was permitted without restriction in most of the contracting States (ibid., §129), the Court held that relying on the application of the Luxembourg rules on the conflict of laws and, on that very basis, refusing enforcement, was inconsistent with the right to family life of the persons concerned. In the Court's eyes, that typical PIL approach failed 'to take account of the social reality of the situation'; therefore, the applicants' right to a family life encountered 'obstacles in their daily life and the child is not afforded legal protection' making it impossible to be fully integrated into the adoptive family (ibid., §132). In addition, it disregarded the best interests of the child and unduly let the conflict rules take precedence over the social reality and the situation of the persons concerned (ibid., §133. D. Bureau and H. Muir Watt, *Droit international privé*, tome II, Partie Spéciale, PUF, Paris, 2007, p. 171, admit that respect for national conflict rules cannot impeach the recognition of a family status concerning a child).

9 *Negrepontis-Giannisis c. Grèce*, cit., §§72–76.

10 Ibid., cit. §80.

11 In the ECtHR's reasoning, to define the margin of appreciation – as a notion instrumental to what is necessary in a democratic society – States enjoy a discretion according to the circumstances, the subject matter, as well as the context. It also admits that in this respect one of the relevant factors may be the existence or non-existence of common ground between the laws of the States of the Council of Europe. Hence, it is wide when there is no consensus between them and the case raises sensitive moral or ethical issues. However, that margin is to

Second and more importantly, the national legal order ought to safeguard the 'best interests of the child'.[12] According to the ECtHR case law, States' margin of appreciation in construing a national *ordre public* exception is constrained by this principle. In fact, the importance that the notion of a child's best interests is crucial whenever a child's situation is at issue. Decisions that impact the recognition of adoptions or filiations duly acquired abroad must strike a fair balance between State interests and those of the individuals that would be affected by a refusal: in assessing the situation of a child, national authorities are also expected to let his/her best interests prevail.[13]

The ECtHR's emphasis on the best interests of the child – a principle set out in numerous international instruments and primarily in the UN Convention on the Rights of the Child – is not a surprise.[14] Several cases provide high-profile illustrations. In *Wagner*, the ECtHR appreciated that a Luxembourg court recognised a Peruvian decision producing the effect of a full adoption in Luxembourg. Yet, the ECtHR did not welcome the fact that another national court had disregarded the same legal status, which – as the ECtHR highlighted – falls within the meaning of family life under Article 8. It noticed that the best interests of the child ought to be considered, as well as the need to give the child the most favourable status. This conclusion, the ECtHR indicated, would not have been 'prejudicial to Luxembourg's international public policy,'[15] provided that in a similar case, another national judge recognised a foreign adoption.

---

be restricted when a basic facet of an individual's existence or identity is at stake (*Labassee c. France* (Requête n° 65941/11) arrêt du 26 juin 2014, §56; *Mennesson v. France* (Application no 65192/11) judgment of 26 September 2014, §77). Denying recognition of a filiation tie affects the identity of the person involved, namely the child concerned. Consequently, the margin of appreciation is reduced (*Labassee*, cit. §58; *Mennesson*, cit. §80; and, respectively, §§60 and 81). See also *Foulon et Bouvet c. France* (Requête n°s 9063/14 et 10410/14) arrêt du 21 juillet 2016.

12 See the leading case *Neulinger and Shuruk v. Switzerland* [GC] (Application no 41615/07) judgment of 6 July 2010, §135.

13 *E.B. c. France* [GC] (Application no 43546/02) judgment of 22 January 2008, §§76 and 95.

14 Indeed, the Strasbourg Court has emphasised in its decisions that it has never considered the ECHR provisions as the only legal reference framework. On the contrary, it has focused on its obligation to also consider all available provisions and principles of international law applicable to the contracting States. This approach is clear since it held that the ECHR should not be interpreted in isolation and must be applied in accordance with the principles of international law. Indeed, according to its case law under Article 31(3)(c) of the Vienna Convention on the Law of Treaties of 1969, it points out the need to take into account any relevant rules of international law applicable in relations between the parties, including those relating to the international protection of human rights (see *Golder v. the United Kingdom* (Application 4451/70) judgment of 21 February 1975, §29; *Streletz, Kessler and Krenz v. Germany* [GC] (Application no 34044/96, 35532/97 and 44801/98) judgment of March 22, 2001, §90 ff.; and *Al-Adsani v. United Kingdom* [GC] (Application no 35763/97) judgment of November 21, 2001, §55).

15 See *Wagner*, cit., §134.

Moreover, in *Labassee*, the ECtHR admitted that non-recognition in France of a status *filii* amounts to an ethical choice, which results in the use of the exception of international public policy. Furthermore, it stated that France may wish to deter national citizens from going abroad to benefit from methods of assisted reproduction prohibited in its own territory.[16] Nonetheless, the implications of this approach concern 'the children themselves, whose right to respect for their private life … is substantially affected. Accordingly, a serious question arises as to the compatibility of that situation with the children's best interests, respect for which must guide any decision in that regard.'

Albeit within a different factual background, even the *Paradiso and Campanelli* judgement amounts to shrinking the scope of the public order exception.[17] In the ECtHR's vision, *ordre public* cannot represent a *carte blanche* to justify, *vis-à-vis* obligations imposed by Article 8 ECHR, any measure concerning a child without having first considered his/her *particular* best interests.[18] The ECtHR found a violation of Article 8 because the Italian authorities decided to remove a child from a host family. Such an order is, according to the Court, a measure of last resort that State authorities may adopt only to protect the child from immediate danger. The Court highlighted the necessity 'to ensure that a child is not disadvantaged on account of the fact that he or she was born to a surrogate mother, especially in terms of citizenship or identity, which are of crucial importance.'[19]

Strasbourg Court case law impacts the functioning of PIL systems. In other words, the ensuing result in terms of continuity between the status *filii* created abroad and the domestic legal order seems hardly questionable. If the requested State is to act in a manner so as to enable a status *filii* to be recognised in the forum as it stands abroad, the underlying rationale is that there should be, at least in principle, a line of *continuity* between the legal situation created in the State of origin and the domestic legal order[20] irrespective of whether requirements for

---

16 See *Labassee*, cit., §62 and 63.

17 *Paradiso and Campanelli v. Italy* (Application no 25358/12) judgment of 25 January 2015. The case concerned a violation of Article 8 ECHR because Italian authorities first refused recognition of the Russian birth certificate establishing the legal parent-child relationship entered in the civil status registers; secondly, they suspended parental rights; and finally ordered the removal of the child from the applicant's household. In that case, an Italian married couple had entered into a gestational surrogacy agreement with a Russian company, but no genetic link between the couple and the child was established.

18 Ibid., §80.

19 Ibid., §85.

20 According to the principles set out by the ECtHR in its case law, where the existence of a family tie with a child has been established, the State is bound to allow that tie to be developed and to establish legal provisions that render possible the child's integration in his family (see, *mutatis mutandis*, the *Marckx v. Belgium* (Application no 6833/74) judgment of 13 June 1979, p. 15, §31; *Kroon and Others v. The Netherlands* (Application no 18535/91) judgment of 27 October 1994, §32 and 36–40).

recognition laid down in the latter point in the opposite direction. International protection of human rights as imposed by the international judiciary is emerging as a standard-harmonising approach in family PIL. The room for legal relativism, which is typical of conflict of laws, is reduced insofar as international standards operate as a source of unity. This holds true whenever a status *filii* duly created abroad is characterised by a solid element of effectiveness. PIL procedures – measured through the prism of ECtHR jurisprudence – should also consider the social reality of the situation in which recognition (or enforcement) is sought.[21] International courts do not consider that applicants have recourse to recognition or enforcement techniques to circumvent domestic law prohibitions or restrictions. Criticisms in terms of *fraude à la loi*, although theoretically conceivable under a typical PIL reasoning, are downgraded *vis-à-vis* the obligation to preserve human rights as internationally guaranteed.

3. OUTLINING THE BEST INTERESTS TEST

As discussed, the principle of continuity is characterised by a crucial element that has been strongly emerging from international practice, i.e. the 'best interests of the child.' This test entails assessing the real and genuine interest of the child in any specific situation whenever a form of international filiation comes under national authorities' scrutiny. Actually, any decision on the care of a child must be based on pragmatic evaluation of the child's particular well-being while considering every element of the case, as even some national case law indicates.[22] The best interests test remains a complex paradigm. Against the

---

21 See *Wagner*, cit., §132.

22 For instance, English judges have granted a parental order in favour of a British couple that had entered into a motherhood surrogacy contract with a Ukrainian woman. Two children were born and conceived by the husband's gametes and the eggs of an anonymous donor. The English Court, despite the fact that the contract did not respond to the gratuity requirement imposed by UK legislation in such situations, focused on the welfare of the children and on the negative consequences to which both would have been exposed in the event of a negative ruling. It held that 'What the court is required to do is to balance two competing and potentially irreconcilably conflicting concepts. Parliament is clearly entitled to legislate against commercial surrogacy and is clearly entitled to expect that the courts should implement that policy consideration in its decisions. Yet it is also recognized that as the full rigor of that policy consideration will bear on one wholly unequipped to comprehend it let alone deal with its consequences (*i.e.* the child concerned) that rigor must be mitigated by the application of a consideration of that child's welfare. That approach is both humane and intellectually coherent. The difficulty is that it is almost impossible to imagine a set of circumstances in which by the time the case comes to court, the welfare of any child (particularly a foreign child) would not be gravely compromised (at the very least) by a refusal to make an order' ([2008] EWHC 3030 (Fam), *Re: X & Y (Foreign Surrogacy)*, http://www.bailii.org/ew/cases/EWHC/Fam/ 2008/3030.html). Further, 'given the effect of a parental order is to confer status

background of judicial practice, when considering recognition of the status *filii*, the national authority should assess *ex officio* the child's interests in each case with regard to the following three elements: i) all circumstances, including the need to secure the physical, emotional, material, educational development and safety of the child, for his/her benefit in society; ii) the proportionality of making a positive or negative ruling in light of the child's well-being and any related risk; and iii) the interests of other individuals concerned. Despite the need to prioritise the child's rights, this does not prevent a judge from considering other concerned individuals' legitimate needs.[23]

Finally, given that consideration of what is actually in the best interests of the child is always crucial, there is no need to emphasise that the national authority has to provide reasonable and detailed justifications as to why the child's interests have been assessed and satisfied in a specific case.

The national authority is expected to assess the child's best interests by the standard of a 'reasonable parent,' with regard not only to the social community's needs but also the period of time that has passed since the child was first declared to enjoy a status *filii* in the State of origin.

In this context, appropriateness of recognition may still vary from one State to another depending on factors such as traditions relating to the family's role and State intervention in family affairs. States enjoy a certain margin of appreciation. International human rights standards do not impose a unique notion of family and marriage, as these standards do not purport to create a uniform law.[24] Even though the definition of family life and the meaning of family as endorsed

---

for life, it is difficult to see how applying any principle other than welfare with a 'lifelong' perspective would be apt in deciding the final discretionary stage of a Section 30 application. I am wholly satisfied on that approach that the welfare of these children will best be served by the making of the parental order sought by these applicants' (ibid., §24). Even an Italian judge recognised English parental orders with which an Anglo-Italian couple had been assigned in England a parenting status in relation to two children born in 1997 and 2000 through a surrogate motherhood practice. The intended parents had concluded contracts providing for no compensation, according to which a woman became pregnant with a fertilised embryo with the husband's gametes of the same couple. The issue concerning recognition was raised many years after birth when the Italian woman returned to her home country following the dissolution of the marriage. The relationship between the children and the mother therefore presented, in this case, also a solid character of effectiveness according to the Court of Appeal of Bari, 13 February 2009, *I.M.* c. *G.A.J.R.*, in *Rivista di diritto internazionale privato e processuale*, 2009, 698, with comment of C. Campiglio, *Lo stato di figlio nato da contratto internazionale di maternità*, p. 599.

23 Belgium Constitutional Court ruling 30/2013 March 7, 2013, www.const-court.be, p. 13, point B. 10. In other words, although the child's best interests may, depending on their nature and seriousness, override those of the parents (*Sahin v. Germany* [GC] (Application no 30943/96) judgment of 8 July 2003, §66), the latter remain a factor when balancing the various interests at stake (*Neulinger and Shuruk v. Switzerland*, cit. §134).

24 R. Baratta, 'Recognition of Foreign Personal and Family Status: A Rights Based Perspective, cit., 414–415.

by the ECtHR are extremely broad,[25] this test is purely to determine whether Article 8 applies and is not used to appraise contracting parties' conduct. Likewise, human rights standards do not guarantee the right to adopt or to have a child.[26] Consequently, different regimes for traditional married couples and non-traditional families as regards adoption and filiation are not prohibited[27] provided that any difference in treatment is legitimate, proportionate and not discriminatory. Protection of the traditional family is a weighty and legitimate reason that can justify difference in treatment[28] despite quite a clear tendency to reduce the scope for *manoeuvre*.[29] However, if difference in treatment is based on sex or sexual orientation, States enjoy a narrow margin of appreciation[30] and none in some cases.

Sometimes, legitimising non-traditional family models is debatable from a human rights perspective based on the child's best interests. For instance, in the case of a second-parent adoption between two Austrian women who lived in a stable homosexual relationship together with the son of one of them, the ECtHR indicated that the non-discrimination principle affects the margin of appreciation with regard to the application of the proportionality principle. Accordingly, in the ECtHR's vision, proportionality does not require that the measure chosen be suitable to achieve the aim to exclude same-sex couples from the second-parent adoption sought (suitability test), but it is necessary to achieve the aim sought (necessity test). In its judgment, the Court held that the

25 *Marckx*, cit. §31; *Olsson v. Sweden (no. 1)* (Application no. 10465/83) judgment of March 24, 1988, §59.

26 For instance, according to Article 8 ECHR the right to respect for 'family life' does not safeguard the mere desire to found a family; it presupposes the existence of a family tie between a child born out of wedlock and his or her natural father, or the relationship that arises from a genuine marriage, or the relationship between a father and his legitimate child even if it proves, years later, to have had no biological basis (*Paradiso and Campanelli v. Italy* [GC], cit., §141).

27 ECtHR *Gas and Dubois v. France*, (Application no 25951/07) judgment of March 15, 2012, §69; *X and others v Austria* (Application no 19010/07) judgment of February 19, 2013, §§109 and 110.

28 ECtHR *Karner v. Austria* (Application no 40016/98) judgment of July 24, 2003, §40.

29 In *Kozak v. Poland* (Application no 13102/02) judgment of March 2, 2010, the ECtHR highlighted that the protection of family in the traditional sense is countered by the need to consider that 'given that the Convention is a living instrument, to be interpreted in the light of present-day conditions (see *E.B.* cit., §92), the State, in its choice of means designed to protect the family and secure, as required by Article 8, respect for family life must necessarily take into account developments in society and changes in the perception of social, civil-status and relational issues, including the fact that there is not just one way or one choice in the sphere of leading and living one's family or private life' (§98). As to same-sex couples, even though the ECtHR seems to have attached some importance to the continuing international movement towards the legal recognition of same-sex unions (*Oliari and Others v. Italy*, cit. §§178 and 180–185), it has left open the option for States to restrict access to marriage to different-sex couples (*Schalk and Kopf v. Austria*, cit., §108).

30 *Karner*, cit., §41; *Kozak*, cit. §98; *X and others v Austria*, cit., §99.

Austrian legislation contained an absolute prohibition, lacked coherence and did not allow the national judge to conduct an examination of each individual case[31] in terms of the interests of the child.[32]

The ECtHR's *ratio decidendi* is unconvincing. As discussed, the best interests principle implies the need to consider inter alia the interests of the biological father in not severing his legal tie with the son. In *X and another*, the biological father fairly refused his consent to adoption because he did not agree to be replaced by an adoptive parent. This is not *per se* a discriminatory step, as long as the father valued the relationship with his child, regardless of the mother's homosexuality. Moreover, the biological tie between the son and his father amounts to an 'identity element' of the personal and family life of both individuals, which judges should not neglect or put aside lightly. Finally, since there is no consensus among the Council of Europe's contracting parties about adoption by same-sex couples, national legal orders should, in principle, enjoy a reasonable margin of appreciation.

Moreover, from a wider perspective, the best interests principle may reasonably vary according to different filiations. As to access of same-sex couples to adoption, there seems to be a favourable trend in Italy. The Italian Court of Cassation has recently recognised not only marriage between two Frenchwomen, even though one of them also enjoyed Italian nationality and this kind of marriage cannot be celebrated in Italy. The Italian Court of Cassation has also recognised the status *filii* of a full adoption order made by a French court, according to which a partner adopted the biological child of the other partner and vice-versa. Basically, grounds for this recognition were based on both the long and solid relationship between them and the best interests principle as an important element of the *ordre public* exception.[33]

Let us briefly consider filiation through surrogacy practices, an area that is highly questionable ethically and legally. Medical science here has likely gone

---

31 *X and others v Austria*, cit. pp. 32–34. In this case, wishing to create a legal relationship between one of the applicants and the child, the mother and her partner concluded an adoption agreement and submitted it to the competent district court for approval. Being aware that the relevant provisions of the Civil Code could be understood to exclude the adoption of the child of one partner of a homosexual couple by the other partner, the applicants requested the Constitutional Court to declare those provisions unconstitutional as discriminating against them on account of their sexual orientation. The Constitutional Court rejected the request as inadmissible, pending the decision of the district court. National judges ultimately rejected the adoption agreement. Thus, the applicants complained under Article 14 (prohibition of discrimination) of the European Convention on Human Rights taken in conjunction with Article 8 (right to respect for private and family life) that they were being discriminated on their sexual orientation.

32 Ibid., p. 34.

33 See Cass. civ., sez. I, ord. 13 aprile 2018 – 31 maggio 2018, n. 14007, in www.dirittifondamentali.it.

too far since a child born through that practice may have up to six parents – i.e. biological, gestational and legal and intended parents.[34] No internationally agreed upon norms exist in this area of filiation and, consequently, there is hardly a European consensus on children born through (international) surrogacy arrangements and on the lawfulness of such a controversial practice.[35] One may even argue that in many States, surrogacy arrangements are rightly prohibited or limited. As the ECtHR case law shows, in principle States enjoy broad discretion.[36]

From this perspective, the need to respect the best interests principle may reasonably prevent the recognition of the related civil status established in the country of origin, at least whenever international surrogacy is considered as a means to circumvent national rules on international adoptions. Likewise, that practice may also turn out to be inconsistent with several legal requirements if the application is downgraded to one for the recognition of a foreign adoption.[37] Again, it would be highly questionable to recognise and enforce a biological parenthood relationship acquired abroad through surrogacy if both the biological and intended parents are elderly or had recourse to such practice for purely selfish motives. Even a genetic link *per se* may not establish a sufficient reason

---

34 R. Baratta, 'Diritti fondamentali e riconoscimento dello status *filii* in casi di maternità surrogata: la primazia degli interessi del minore' in *Diritti umani e diritto internazionale*, 2016, p. 312.

35 Some European countries are averse to couples travelling abroad with the purpose of entering a surrogacy arrangement and returning home with a child, deeming surrogacy as incompatible with national public policy. National attitudes towards surrogacy arrangements are different. These are prohibited, sometimes even via criminal sanctions (France, Switzerland and Italy). In other countries surrogacy practices are lawful under strict legal conditions, even imposing the necessity for an altruistic purpose (The Netherlands and United Kingdom). Sometimes they are tolerated (Poland and Belgium). In some legal orders surrogacy arrangements are exploited for commercial goals (Georgia, Ukraine and Russia): see the Hague Conference on Private International Law, *A Preliminary Report on the Issues Arising from International Surrogacy*, No. 10 of March 2012, p. 9; K. Trimmings and P. Beaumont (eds.), *International Surrogacy Arrangements: Legal Regulation at the International Level*, Hart Publ., Oxford 2012, *passim*. Thus, international surrogacy arrangements have been increasingly challenging PIL systems with respect, in particular, to the recognition of the civil status of the surrogate child within the State of origin of the intended parents. Indeed, the number of cross-border arrangements concluded in surrogacy-friendly jurisdictions has been increasing.

36 In *Mennesson*, cit., the ECtHR held that 'States must in principle be afforded a wide margin of appreciation regarding the decision not only whether or not to authorize this method of assisted reproduction but also whether or not to recognise a legal parent-child relationship between children legally conceived as a result of a surrogacy arrangement abroad and the intended parents' (§79; see also §78). See H. Fulchiron and C. Bidaud-Garon, 'Reconnaissance ou reconstruction? A propos de la filiation des enfants nés par GPA, au landemain des arrêts Labassée, Mennesson et Campanelli-Paradiso de la Cour européenne des droits de l'homme.' in *Rev. crit. dr. int. privé*, 2015, p. 1; R. Baratta, 'Diritti fondamentali.' cit., p. 309.

37 M. Vonk and K. Boele-Woelki, *Surrogacy and Same-sex Couples in The Netherlands*, in *Legal Recognition of Same-Sex Relationships in Europe. National, Cross-Border and European Perspectives*, Intersentia, Cambridge-Antwerp-Portland 2012, p. 123.

to comply with the best interests of the child criterion unless it is accompanied by a serious commitment to advance the child's welfare throughout his/her life. Parents' interests alone, though based on a genetic link, seem weaker and secondary from a perspective of enhancing the child's best interests. Parents' interests may be personal and legitimate human aspirations; yet, they should be considered a lesser element in relation to the beneficial effects for the child concerned. In any case, in international commercial surrogacy, the fundamental rights of other persons may be affected since these arrangements can imply the sale of a child under Article 35 of the Convention on the Rights of the Child and exploitation of surrogate mothers.[38] Moreover, a surrogate mother's rights to be informed and to give the necessary consent for medical procedures (which may be freely withdrawn at any time) must be respected.[39] Thus, it is necessary that *de iure condendo*, a large multilateral international convention, conveniently addresses these issues.[40]

---

38 J. Tobin, 'To Prohibit or Permit: What is the (Human) Rights Response to the Practice of International Commercial Surrogacy?' (2014) *Int. Comp. Law Quart.*, 317; G. Puppinck and C. de la Hougue, 'Quelles voies de droit international pour interdire la maternité de substitution.' 2015, *passim*; B. Barel and S. Armellini, *Manuale breve di diritto internazionale privato*, Giuffré, Milano, 2015, p. 163; S. Allan, 'The Surrogate in Commercial Surrogacy: Legal and Ethical Considerations, in Surrogacy, Law and Human Rights', in P. Gerber and K. O'Byrne (eds.), *Surrogacy, Law and Human Rights*, Routledge, London and New York 2015, p. 113; A. Vettorel, 'International Surrogacy Arrangements: Recent Developments and Ongoing Problems' in *Rivista di dritto internazionale private e processuale*, 2015, p. 526.

39 See the so-called Oviedo Convention (1997), the Convention for the protection of Human Rights and Dignity of the Human Being with regard to the Application of Biology and Medicine: Convention on Human Rights and Biomedicine, Articles 5 and 10.

40 It should not only be capable of addressing the *international market of surrogacy* (which is growing: see the Hague Conference on Private International Law, *A Preliminary Report on the Issues Arising from International Surrogacy*, cit., p. 8, and C. Hausammann, and N. Hitz Quenon, 'Maternité de substitution: la perspective des droits humains' in *Centre suisse de compétence pour les droits humains*, Newsletter CSDH of 11 May 2014) but it could also conveniently address the need to protect the fundamental rights of all the persons. It could possibly prohibit any forms of international commercial surrogacy so as to block 'the practice of gestational surrogacy which involves reproductive exploitation and use of the human body for financial or other gain' (*Report on the Annual Report on Human Rights and Democracy in the World 2014 and the European Union's policy on the matter* (2015/2229(INI)), para. 114. Indeed, the European Parliament has condemned 'the practice of surrogacy, which undermines the human dignity of the woman since her body and its reproductive functions are used as a commodity; considers that the practice of gestational surrogacy which involves reproductive exploitation and use of the human body for financial or other gain, in particular in the case of vulnerable women in developing countries, shall be prohibited and treated as a matter of urgency in human rights instruments.' See however, for a different approach, K. Trimmings and P. Beaumont (eds.), *International Surrogacy Arrangements: Legal Regulation at the International Level*, cit., p. 647 (which supports the idea of regulating international commercial surrogacy, this being more pragmatic). See also M. Wells-Greco, *The status of Children Arising from Inter-Country Surrogacy Arrangements*, Eleven Int. Publ., The Hague 2015, *passim*.

Another delicate issue concerns the recognition of the status *filii* in favour of same-sex couples having become parents through international surrogacy arrangements. States that prevent access to parenthood in such situations, including through adoption, should enjoy a wide margin of appreciation. Certainly, further elaboration on these matters will require assessments from the viewpoint of social dignity and the principle of non-discrimination based on sexual orientation. Again, national case law is varied, and no clear trend is so far emerging.[41] Yet, filiation through surrogacy methods raises serious ethical issues that should not be neglected even for same-sex couples.

4. CONCLUSION

When recognising a foreign status *filii*, the principle of the best interests of the child should prevail and guide national courts' administration of justice. Thus, judicial decisions are expected to value the child's best interests, as well as his/her identity, as primary criteria. If refusing the recognition of a filiation acquired abroad adversely affects the child, a national court is, in principle, expected to uphold the legal status validly created abroad since it falls within the notion of family life captured by Article 8 of the ECHR.[42] As discussed, respect for family and private life, as internationally guaranteed, requires also the consideration of the situation's social reality, considering the child's best interests. However, this approach does not entail the need to recognise a foreign status *filii* as long as it fits the best interests principle as outlined above.

41 In Belgium, a male same-sex couple had twin babies through surrogacy in California and returned home with a birth certificate naming both of them as parents. The Belgian registry office refused to register the US birth certificates. In the first instance the Belgian Court determined that the recognition of the US birth certificates violated the national *ordre public*, focusing also on the fact that circumvention of Belgian parentage and adoption laws could not subsequently be legitimised. Non-recognition of the twins' US birth certificates meant that in Belgium the US surrogate mother is regarded as the child's legal parent, whereas in the US the Belgian fathers are regarded as the child's legal parents. On appeal, the Liège Court of Appeal ordered that the birth certificates be recognised and registered at the civil registry, but only as far as the legal relationship with the biological father was concerned. The registration of the legal parenthood of the biological father's husband was not possible, as he was not a biological parent (see M. Vonk and C. Boele-Woelki, *Surrogacy and Same-Sex Couples in The Netherlands*, cit., p. 137). Likewise, see Tribunal Supremo (Sala de lo Civil) No de recurso 245/2012, 02/02/2015, http://www.poderjudicial.es,with interesting arguments concerning how to strike a right balance between the respect for fundamental rights and the prohibition of surrogacy in Spain and comments by P. A. de Miguel Asensio, 'El nuevo Auto del Tribunal Supremo sobre gestación por sustitución y la evolución de la jurisprudencia europea' in http://pedrodemiguelasensio.blogspot.com.es/2015/03/el-nuevo-auto-del-tribunal-supremo.html#more.

42 See *Wagner*, cit., §133. See also the Italian case law mentioned by C. Tuo, 'The Italian Regime of Recognition of Intercountry Adoption of Children in Light of the ECHR: What About Singles?' in *Cuadernos de Derecho Transnacional* (Octubre 2015), vol. 7, n. 2, p. 357.

Under this approach, a 'child first' judicial policy valuing the primacy of a child's rights is the ultimate solution given that the child is the most vulnerable person. The UN Convention on the Rights of the Child has proclaimed a child's right to preserve his/her identity, including nationality, name and family relationships.[43] In filiation and adoption cases, the leitmotiv is primarily the child's interests, not the parents'. Yet, the best interests principle does not imply an absolute obligation to recognise a status *filii* duly acquired abroad insofar as the requested State enjoys a margin of appreciation founded on basic ethical principles and values.

One may wonder whether a national judge may dismiss an application aimed at recognising a status *filii* on the basis of the constitutional limits doctrine, i.e. a legal device that might also protect the core of domestic family values – which mirror national identity concerns – from external interference. This author would suggest that, in principle, there is no need to turn to this doctrine. First, national courts should not lightly uphold domestic law's primacy over international obligations because such an approach exposes the forum State to international accountability. A constructive dialogue between international and national courts is a useful means to possibly reconcile constitutional values with international obligations. Second, the classical PIL objection of *ordre public* covers the core of national constitutional limits. In this respect, the normative value of a child's rights is not only a 'bridge principle' capable of initiating harmonisation and constructive dialogue between courts but also a normative tool that confers upon contracting States a margin of appreciation when assessing a child's best interests. As seen above, when there is no consensus within the Member States of the Council of Europe and the case raises sensitive moral or ethical issues, the margins of appreciation for protecting the child's rights and core family values are wider inasmuch as the requested State provides a minimum standard of guarantees as set forth by international instruments.

43 For a telling example of dialogue between the British Supreme Court and the ECtHR see M. Lugato, 'Considerazione dei "processi interni" e "dialogo" fra Corti supreme', in Triggiani et al (eds.), *Dialoghi con Ugo Villani*, Cacucci editore, Bari, II, 2017, p. 999.

SURROGACY ARRANGEMENTS AND THE BEST INTERESTS OF THE CHILD

The Case Law of the European Court of Human Rights

Katarina TRIMMINGS

1. Introduction 187
2. Case Law Overview 188
 2.1. Recognition of a Legal Parent-Child Relationship Established Abroad 188
  2.1.1. *Mennesson v France* and *Labassee v. France*. 188
  2.1.2. *Laborie v. France* 190
  2.1.3. *Foulon and Bouvet v. France*. 191
 2.2. Travel Restrictions on Children Born through Cross-Border Surrogacy: *D. v. Belgium* 192
 2.3. Removal of the Child from the Intending Parents: *Paradiso and Campanelli v. Italy*. 194
3. Recognition of the Legal Parent-Child Relationship 198
 3.1. Genetic Link and Legal Parentage 198
 3.2. Commercial vs Altruistic Surrogacy 203
4. Conclusion. 207

1. INTRODUCTION

The chapter begins with a comprehensive albeit brief overview of the case law of the European Court of Human Rights (ECtHR) on cross-border surrogacy (section 2). This is followed by a detailed analysis of the ECtHR's approach to the recognition of the legal parent-child relationship established abroad as a result of cross-border surrogacy (section 3). The focus of the chapter is on the problem of legal parenthood in the cross-border surrogacy context, with a particular emphasis on two key themes that arise in this context: the link between legal parentage and genetics, and the distinction between altruistic and commercial surrogacy. Throughout the analysis, the role of the best interests of the child principle in the specific context of the recognition of legal parentage established abroad through cross-border surrogacy is explored. The chapter concludes that, by prioritising the best interests of the individual child concerned, the ECtHR's recognition of legal parenthood in cross-border surrogacy undermines the principle of the best interests of the child generally.

2. CASE LAW OVERVIEW

Existing case law of the ECtHR on cross-border surrogacy can be placed into three broad categories, depending on the core legal issue that was dealt with in the particular case: (1) recognition of a legal parent-child relationship established through surrogacy abroad; (2) removal of the child from the intending parents; and (3) travel restrictions on children born through cross-border surrogacy.

2.1. RECOGNITION OF A LEGAL PARENT-CHILD RELATIONSHIP ESTABLISHED ABROAD

2.1.1. Mennesson v France *and* Labassee v. France[1]

The ECtHR addressed the issue of the recognition of a parent-child relationship established abroad in the context of cross-border surrogacy for the first time in the joint cases of *Mennesson v. France* and *Labassee v. France*. The cases concerned

[1] *Mennesson v France*, no. 65192/11, 26 June 2014, *Labassee v. France*, no. 65941/11, 26 June 2014. Judgments of the Fifth Section of the European Court of Human Rights sitting as a Chamber. The two cases were conducted simultaneously. *Mennesson*, para. 3. For a detailed analysis of these cases see P. Beaumont and K. Trimmings, 'Recent Jurisprudence of the European Court of Human Rights in the Area of Cross-Border Surrogacy: Is There Still a Need for Global Regulation of Surrogacy?' in F. Ippolito and G. Biagioni (eds.), *Migrant Children in the XXI Century: Selected Issues of Public and Private International Law*, Editoriale Scientifica, Italy 2016, pp. 109–136. Available also as a Centre for Private International Law Working Paper No 2016/4, <http://www.abdn.ac.uk/law/documents/CPIL_2016-4.pdf> accessed 31.07.2018. See also G. Puppinck and C. de la Hougue, 'ECHR: Towards the Liberalisation of Surrogacy: Regarding the Mennesson v France and Labassee v France Cases', <http://papers.ssrn.com/sol3/papers.cfm?abstract_id=2500075> accessed 23.03.2017 (originally published in French in *Revue Lamy de Droit Civil*, 2014, p. 78); M. Wells-Greco and H. Dawson, 'Inter-Country Surrogacy and Public Policy: Lessons from the European Court of Human Rights' (2014/2015) 16 *Yearbook of Private International Law*, 315, 330–33; C. Fenton-Glynn, 'International Surrogacy before the European Court of Human Rights' (2017) 13 *Journal of Private International Law*, 546, 552–54; M. Welstead, 'Parented at Last: *Mennesson v France* (65192/11); *Labassee v France* (6594/11)', (2014) *International Family Law*, 270; I. R. Lescastereyres, 'Recognition of the Parent-Child Relationship as a Result of Surrogacy and the Best Interest of the Child' (2015) 16 *ERA Forum*, 149; Hague Conference

the refusal to grant legal recognition in France to parent-child relationships that had been legally established in the United States between children born as a result of cross-border surrogacy and their intending parents. In both cases the intending parents were a married heterosexual couple. The children were conceived using the intending fathers' sperm and donor eggs. Court orders made in California and Minnesota respectively ruled that the intending parents were the children's legal parents.[2] The surrogacy arrangement that had been entered into by the Mennessons resulted in the birth of a set of twins[3] and the surrogate mother that had been hired by the Labassees gave birth to a baby girl.[4] Upon the birth of the children, birth certificates were drawn up in the United States to reflect the terms of the court orders.[5] The French authorities, however, refused to enter the particulars of the birth certificates in the French civil status register.[6] The couples then took the matter to court. Their claims were dismissed at the final instance by the French Court of Cassation,[7] which held that the California and Minnessota court judgments were incompatible with French international public policy as they contained provisions which conflicted with fundamental principles of French law, in particular the principle of inalienability of civil status.[8] The Court also held that recording the particulars of the birth certificates would give effect to a surrogacy agreement which was null and

on Private International Law, 'The Parentage/Surrogacy Project: An Updating Note', February 2015, paras. 5–9, <http://www.hcch.net/upload/wop/gap2015pd03a_en.pdf.> accessed 31.07.2018. For an explanation of the French approach to surrogacy, including cross-border surrogacy, see M. Meilhac-Perri, 'National Regulation and Cross-Border Surrogacy in France' (2014/2015) 16 *Yearbook of Private International Law*, 275; and L. Perreau-Saussine and N. Sauvage, 'National Report on Surrogacy: France', in K. Trimmings and P. Beaumont (eds.), *International Surrogacy Arrangements: Legal Regulation at the International Level*, Hart Publishing, Oxford 2013, Chapter 7.

2 In *Mennesson* the judgment was made in the form of a pre-birth order by the Supreme Court of California on 14.07.2000: *Mennesson*, para. 9. In *Labassee* two judgments were made on 31.10.2001 (i.e. four days after the child's birth) by the Court of the State of Minnessota. In the first judgment, the court abolished the parental status of the surrogate mother, and in the second judgment the court, having noted that the intending father was the biological father of the child, granted legal parentage and custody of the child to the intending father and allowed him to return to France with the child. The court also ruled that no access to the child was to be granted to the surrogate mother, who had renounced all her rights to the child: *Labassee*, para. 9.

3 The children were born on 25.10.2000: *Mennesson*, para. 10.

4 The child was born on 27.10.2001: *Labassee*, para. 8.

5 *Mennesson*, para. 10, and *Labassee*, para. 10.

6 *Mennesson*, para. 11, and *Labassee*, para. 11.

7 Court of Cassation, First Civil Decision, 06.04.2011, per *Mennesson*, para. 27, and *Labassee*, para. 17.

8 Per *Mennesson*, para. 27, and *Labassee*, para. 17. On a more philosophical level, in the context of surrogacy the principle of the inalienability of civil status (*l'indisponibilité de l'etat des personnes*) reflects the view that biological mothers should not be contractually bound to give up their children. See 'Family: Foreign Surrogacy Arrangement – Child Conceived Using Father's Sperm and Donor Egg' (Case Comment) (2014) *European Human Rights Law Review*, 547, 549.

void on public policy grounds under the French Civil Code.[9] The couples then brought the case before the ECtHR. The applications were lodged jointly by the intending parents (the Mennessons and Labassees respectively) and the children (Valentina and Fiorella Mennessons and Juliette Labassee respectively).[10] The applicants relied primarily on the right to respect for their private and family life guaranteed by Article 8 of the European Convention on Human Rights (ECHR).[11] In both cases the Court held that there had been no violation of Article 8 of the Convention concerning the intending parents' right to respect for their family life; however, there had been a violation of Article 8 of the Convention concerning the children's right to respect for their private life.[12]

The problem of non-recognition of a legal parent-child relationship established abroad as a result of a cross-border surrogacy arrangement returned before the ECtHR in 2016[13] in the joint cases of *Foulon and Bouvet v. France*,[14] and in 2017 in the case of *Laborie v. France*.[15] The cases involved surrogacy arrangements entered into in India[16] and Ukraine[17] respectively.

2.1.2. Laborie v. France[18]

The factual matrix in *Laborie v. France* was similar to that of *Mennesson* and *Labassee* in that the intending parents were a married heterosexual French

---

9 *Mennesson*, para. 27, and *Labassee*, para. 17; the relevant provisions of the French Civil Code being Articles 16-7 and 16-9. Article 16-7 states: 'All agreements relating to procreation or gestation for the benefit of another are null.' Article 16-9 clarifies that 'The provisions in this chapter are of public order': French Civil Code, consolidated version of 02.03.2017, English translation ('French Civil Code' or 'Civil Code') <www.wipo.int/wipolex/en/details.jsp?id=17359> accessed 02.07.2018.

10 *Mennesson*, para. 1, and *Labassee*, para. 1.

11 *Mennesson*, para. 43, and *Labassee*, para. 34. Article 8 (titled 'Right to respect for private and family life') states: '1. Everyone has the right to respect for his private and family life, his home and his correspondence. 2. There shall be no interference by a public authority with the exercise of this right except such as is in accordance with the law and is necessary in a democratic society in the interests of national security, public safety or the economic well-being of the country, for the prevention of disorder or crime, for the protection of health or morals, or for the protection of the rights and freedoms of others.'

12 *Mennesson*, para. 102, and *Labassee*, para. 81. See section 3 below for more details.

13 A prior unsuccessful request to have a refusal by national authorities to recognise a legal parent-child relationship established through surrogacy abroad adjudicated on by the ECtHR was made in the case of *Paradiso and Campanelli v Italy*, No. 25358/12. See section 2.3. below.

14 *Foulon and Bouvet v. France*, Nos. 9063/14 and 10410/14, 21 July 2016, judgment of the Fifth Section of the European Court of Human Rights sitting as a Chamber.

15 *Laborie v. France*, No. 44024/13, 19 January 2017, judgment of the Fifth Section of the European Court of Human Rights sitting as a Chamber.

16 *Foulon and Bouvet v. France*, paras. 6 and 20.

17 *Laborie v. France*, para. 6.

18 *Laborie v. France*, No. 44024/13, 19 January 2017, judgment of the Fifth Section of the European Court of Human Rights sitting as a Chamber.

couple (although resident in Dubai since 2007).[19] Twins were born as a result of the arrangement,[20] and birth certificates issued by the Ukrainian authorities listed the intending parents as the legal parents.[21] The French authorities refused to transcribe the birth certificates into the French civil status register.[22] The intending parents then brought the matter before French courts, but without any success.[23] When the case reached the ECtHR, the applicants complained of the violation by the French authorities of their right to respect for private and family life under Article 8 of the ECHR.[24] The ECtHR reached the same outcome as in *Mennesson* and *Labassee* – i.e. that there had been no violation of the intending parents' right to respect for their family life, but that the French authorities had violated the children's right to respect for private life.[25]

2.1.3. Foulon and Bouvet v. France[26]

In contrast to *Mennesson*, *Labassee* and *Laborie*, *Foulon and Bouvet* involved single French men[27] as intending parents who had had recourse to commercial surrogacy in India.[28] The birth certificates issued in India listed the intending father and the surrogate mother as the legal parents.[29] However, the French authorities, suspecting recourse to surrogacy, refused to transcribe the birth

19 Ibid., paras. 1 and 12.

20 Ibid., para. 1.

21 Ibid., para. 6.

22 Ibid., para. 8.

23 Judgment of the Court of first instance (Nantes), 10.11.2011, and judgment of the Court of appeal (Rennes), 08.01.2013, per *Laborie*, paras. 9–14. The applicants did not appeal to the Court of Cassation as they felt that a complaint to the French Supreme Court was doomed to failure due to three judgments of 06.04.2011 in which the Court held that the refusal to transcribe particulars of a foreign birth certificate in the context of surrogacy was justified. Interestingly, this argument was accepted by the ECtHR. Although the applicants had not exhausted available domestic remedies, the ECtHR was willing to depart from the admissibility criteria set out in Article 35(1) of the ECHR, and declared the application admissible: per *Laborie*, paras. 17–22.

24 Ibid., para. 23.

25 Ibid., para. 32.

26 *Foulon and Bouvet v. France*, Nos. 9063/14 and 10410/14, 21 July 2016, judgment of the Fifth Section of the European Court of Human Rights sitting as a Chamber.

27 Although Mr. Foulon was a US-resident: Gènéthique, 'Gestational Surrogacy: the ECHR Supports Child Purchase for All', <http://www.genethique.org/en/gestational-surrogacy-echr-supports-child-purchase-all-65999.html#.W0J7UjpKjIV> accessed 24.07.2018.

28 *Foulon and Bouvet*, paras. 1, 6 and 20.

29 Ibid., paras. 6 and 20. The surrogate mother who had been hired by Mr Foulon gave birth to a baby girl (Emilie Sanja Lauriane) on 31.07. 2009. The surrogate mother who had acted for Mr Bouvet delivered twin boys (Adrien and Romain) on 26.04.2010. Ibid., paras. 5 and 19. It is, however, unclear from the ECtHR decisions or the relevant French Court of Cassation judgments (Court of Cassation (First Civil Chamber) Nos. 1091 and 1092 of 13.09.201) whether the genetic material originated from the surrogate mother or an egg donor had been used.

certificates into the French civil status register.[30] The French Court of Cassation held that the refusal by the authorities to transcribe the children's birth certificates was justified as the applicants had been involved in a 'fraudulent process' when they concluded a gestational surrogacy arrangement, which was contrary to French law.[31] Before the ECtHR, relying on Article 8 of the ECHR, the intending fathers alleged a breach of their and the children's right to respect for their private and family life.[32] The Court noted that the situation of the applicants in this case was similar to that of the applicants in the *Mennesson* and *Labassee* cases and reached the same conclusion as in those cases.[33] The Court held that there had been a violation of the right to respect for private life of the children concerned, although the parents' right to respect for family life had not been violated.[34]

2.2. TRAVEL RESTRICTIONS ON CHILDREN BORN THROUGH CROSS-BORDER SURROGACY: *D. v. BELGIUM*[35]

In September 2014, the ECtHR was called upon to adjudicate on a different facet of cross-border surrogacy, namely the acceptability of travel restrictions on children born through cross-border surrogacy arrangements. This issue arose in the case of *D. v. Belgium*, which concerned the Belgian authorities' initial refusal to issue a travel document for a child who had been born in Ukraine as a result of a surrogacy arrangement entered into by two Belgian nationals, one of which (the intending father) was also the child's biological parent.

Following the birth of the child the intending parents obtained a Ukrainian birth certificate where they were both recorded as the child's legal parents.[36] The intending parents then approached the Belgian embassy in Kiev with the request for a Belgian passport for the child.[37] This was refused on the ground

30 Ibid., paras. 8–11 and 22–24.

31 Ibid., paras. 17 and 32. Judgment of the Court of Cassation (First Civil Chamber) of 13 September 2013, per *Foulon and Bouvet*, paras. 17 and 32. The Court of Cassation held that 'In the presence of this fraud, neither the best interests of the child guaranteed by Article 3(1) of the United Nations Convention on the Rights of the Child (UNCRC) nor the respect for private and family life within the meaning of Article 8 of the ECHR could be successfully invoked […].' Per *Foulon and Bouvet*, para. 17.

32 Ibid., para. 45.

33 Ibid., para. 55.

34 Ibid., para. 58.

35 *D. v Belgium*, No. 29176/13, 11 September 2014, judgment of the Second Section of the European Court of Human Rights sitting as a Chamber. For comments on the case see, for example, M. Wells-Greco and H. Dawson, above n. 1, p. 333; C. Fenton-Glynn, above n. 1, pp. 548–9; Hague Conference on Private International Law, above n. 1, para. 9.

36 *D. v Belgium*, para. 6. The child was born on 26.02. 2013, ibid., para. 5.

37 Ibid., para. 7.

that the applicants were unable to provide 'certain documents making it possible to confirm the family relationship with the child.'[38] The intending parents applied to the President of the Brussels Court of First Instance (the President), sitting as the urgent applications judge, asking him to order the embassy to issue them with a travel document for the child so that they could bring the child to Belgium.[39] The President declared the urgent request admissible but unfounded on the ground that the intending parents' file 'left many questions unanswered concerning the surrogate mother and the method of procreation used.'[40] In particular, there was insufficient evidence as to the biological relationship between the child and at least one of the applicants.[41] The President held that, as Belgian law established maternity on the basis of childbirth, the intending mother was unable to prove a family relationship with the child.[42] As regards the father, the President refused to accept that the results of the DNA test carried out via an Internet site had any probative value.[43] The intending parents appealed against that decision. However, shortly after filing the appeal their residence permit in Ukraine expired and they had to return to Belgium, leaving the child in Ukraine in the care of a nanny.[44] The intending parents remained separated from the child for the period of three months, until the Brussels Court of Appeal reached its decision on the matter. The Court of Appeal found that since the submission of the file at first instance the applicants had submitted a large number of additional documents which confirmed the intending father's status as the biological father.[45] Consequently, the Court of Appeal ordered the Belgian authorities to issue appropriate travel documents for the child in order to enable the child to travel to Belgium with the intending father.[46]

In their complaint to the ECtHR, the intending parents alleged that their separation from the child due to the Belgian authorities' refusal to issue a travel document to the child violated their right to respect for their family

38 Ibid., para. 8.

39 Ibid., para. 9. Before the President could decide on the application, the intending parents, accompanied by the child, attempted to board a flight at Kiev airport, relying on the child's birth certificate. They were, however, turned away by the airline. Ibid., para. 11.

40 Ibid., para. 12.

41 Ibid.

42 Ibid.

43 Ibid.

44 Ibid., para. 14.

45 Ibid., para. 16. The Court then listed several additional reasons that militated in favour of the intending parents' application. These were as follows: first, the recognition of the legal parent-child relationship between the child and the intending father would 'pose no serious threat to law and order in Belgium'; second, the surrogacy agreement was valid under Ukrainian law; and third, the intending father's right to a family life with the child and the child's right to become attached to the intending father 'without awaiting the outcome of the proceedings on the merits' had to be considered by the Court when balancing the competing interests at stake.

46 Ibid.

life guaranteed by Article 8 of the ECHR.[47] The Court refused to adjudicate on the compatibility of the initial refusal by the Belgian authorities to issue travel documents for the child with the ECHR as this issue had been resolved by the time the case reached the Court. However, the Court did examine the complaint concerning the separation of the intending parents and the child while waiting for the travel document. The Court acknowledged that the separation amounted to interference in their right to respect for their family life.[48] Nonetheless, such interference was justified by the legitimate aim of the prevention of crime, in particular, the need to prevent trafficking in human beings, and by the aim of protecting the rights of other persons, specifically, the surrogate mother and the child.[49] The Convention could not oblige the States to authorise entry to their territory of children born to a surrogate mother without the national authorities having a prior opportunity to conduct certain legal checks.[50] Consequently, the application was dismissed as manifestly unfounded.[51]

Importantly, the ECtHR also noted that the issue of the recognition of the child's Ukrainian birth certificate was not the subject of the complaints submitted to the Court by the applicants.[52] At the time of the application these proceedings were pending before the domestic courts.[53]

2.3. REMOVAL OF THE CHILD FROM THE INTENDING PARENTS: *PARADISO AND CAMPANELLI v. ITALY*[54]

In January 2017, the Grand Chamber of the ECtHR reached its decision in a rather complex case of *Paradiso and Campanelli v. Italy*. The case concerned

47 Ibid., para. 37.
48 Ibid., para. 49.
49 Ibid., paras. 52–53.
50 Ibid., para. 59.
51 Ibid., para. 64. See Article 35 of the ECHR and below n. 56.
52 Ibid., para. 48.
53 Ibid.
54 *Paradiso and Campanelli v. Italy*, No. 25358/12, ECHR 2015/12. The Grand Chamber decision reversed the Chamber decision from 27.01.2015 (Judgment of the Twelfth Section of the European Court of Human Rights sitting as a Chamber). For an analysis/comments on the Chamber decision see P. Beaumont and K. Trimmings, above n. 1, pp. 116–136; C. Fenton-Glynn, above n. 1, pp. 555–59; ECtHR, 'Questions and Answers on the *Paradiso and Campanelli v. Italy* Judgment (27 January 2015)' <https://www.echr.coe.int/Documents/Press_Q_A_Paradiso_and_Campanelli_ENG.pdf> accessed 02.06.2018; M. Wells-Greco and H. Dawson, above n. 1, pp. 334–36; G. Puppinck, 'Comments on the ECHR case of Paradiso and Campanelli v. Italy', 30.01.2015, <http://eclj.org/Releases/Read.aspx?GUID=ec4d5af3-db22-4b01-8b44-2ab3846b770e&s=eur> accessed 31.07.2018; S. Florescu, 'What about Children? Critical Perspectives in the Light of a New European Judgment on Surrogacy', 28.04.2015, <http:/leidenlawblog.nl/articles/what-about-

the refusal by Italian authorities to register a Russian birth certificate of a young child who had been born through gestational surrogacy in Russia, and the subsequent physical removal of the child by the Italian authorities from the intending parents, after it transpired that they had no biological relationship with the child.[55] So, importantly, unlike in the cases set out in sections 2.1. and 2.2. above, the child in *Paradiso* was biologically unrelated to either of the intended parents.

The applicants' complaint concerning the refusal by Italian authorities to register the details of the Russian birth certificate which listed Mr Campanelli and Ms Paradiso as the child's legal parents was declared inadmissible at the first instance by the Chamber.[56] This conclusion was reached on the ground that the intending parents had not exhausted the available domestic remedies as they had not appealed to the Italian Court of Cassation against the decision of the Italian court[57] which had confirmed the refusal to register the birth certificate.[58] As this complaint was resolved by the Chamber, it fell outside the scope of examination by the Grand Chamber.[59]

The applicants' main complaint, however, concerned the actions of the Italian authorities which culminated in the physical removal of the child from the intending parents and his placement in the care of the social services without contact with and in a location unknown to the intending parents.[60] The Italian court had declared the child to be the son of unknown parents, born on 27 February 2011 in Moscow, and ordered that a new name be given to the child and a new birth certificate be issued accordingly.[61] By the time the case came before the ECtHR where the applicants complained of the violation of their right to respect for private and family life under Article 8, the child had been adopted by third persons.[62]

---

the-children> accessed 15.06.2018. For a detailed analysis of the Grand Chamber decision see P. Beaumont and K. Trimmings, 'The European Court of Human Rights in Paradiso and Campanelli v. Italy and the Way forward for Regulating Cross-Border Surrogacy' in J. Scherpe, C. Fenton-Glynn and T. Kaan (eds.), *Eastern and Western Perspectives on Surrogacy*, Intersentia, Cambridge 2019.

55 Although the intending parents unsuccessfully submitted that they had been unaware that Mr. Campanelli's sperm was not used for the purposes of the IVF procedure, and that an error was made by the Russian IVF clinic during the medical procedure. *Paradiso*, para. 31.

56 *Paradiso and Campanelli*, para. 84. The admissibility criteria are set out in Article 35 of the ECHR. On admissibility see, for example, F. de Londras and K. Dzehtsiarou, *Great Debates on the European Convention on Human Rights*, Palgrave, London 2018, pp. 49–69.

57 Decision of the Campobasso Court of Appeal of 03.03.2013. Per *Paradiso and Campanelli*, para. 83.

58 *Paradiso and Campanelli*, para. 84.

59 Ibid.

60 Ibid., para. 49.

61 Ibid., para. 48.

62 Ibid., para. 53.

Central to the primary issue of the Italian authorities' decision to remove the child and to place him under guardianship was the question whether family life had been established between the intending parents and the child.[63] The majority of the Grand Chamber acknowledged that in certain situations *de facto* family life can exist between an adult and a child 'in the absence of biological ties or a recognised legal tie, provided that there are genuine personal ties'.[64] Nevertheless, on the facts of the present case the Grand Chamber held that family life did not exist between the intending parents and the child, meaning that there was no *de facto* family life to be protected by the Convention.[65] In reaching this conclusion, the Grand Chamber had regard to three factors: first, the absence of a biological link between the child and the applicants; second, the short duration of their relationship with the child (the couple had spent about 6 months together with the child in Italy and the intending mother had spent about 2 months

---

63 See, more generally, F. Banda and J. Eekelaar, 'International Conceptions of the Family' (2017) *International & Comparative Law Quarterly*, 833, for a detailed analysis of the evolving way the 'family' and 'family life' have been interpreted in human rights instruments and in the case law of the relevant institutions; and L. Bracken, 'Challenging Normative Constructions of Parentage in Ireland' (2017) 39 *Journal of Social Welfare and Family*, 316.

64 *Paradiso and Campanelli*, para. 148.

65 Ibid., para. 158. In their joint concurring opinion, judges De Gaetano, Pinto De Albuquerque, Wojtyczek and Dedov agreed with the outcome of the case, but expressed serious reservations as to the manner in which the judgment was reasoned. The judges criticised the majority's analysis for determining the existence or non-existence of family life, which they described as follows: 'According to the judgment, the existence or non-existence of family life is essentially a question of fact, depending upon the existence of close and constant personal ties (see, in particular, paragraph 140). In our view, the proposed formula is simultaneously both too vague and too broad. The approach seems based on the implicit assumption that existing interpersonal ties should enjoy at least prima facie protection against State interference. We note in this respect that close and constant personal ties may exist out of the scope of any family life. The reasoning does not explain the nature of those specific interpersonal ties which form family life. At the same time, it seems to attach great importance to emotional bonds (see paragraphs 149, 150, 151 and 157). However, emotional bonds per se cannot create family life.' Instead, judges De Gaetano, Pinto De Albuquerque, Wojtyczek and Dedov proposed the following reasoning: 'Family life can either be formalised under domestic law or not. In case of de facto interpersonal ties which are not formalised under the domestic law, several elements have to be assessed before one can determine whether family life exists. First, as the concept of family requires the existence of stable ties, one must examine 'the nature and stability of the interpersonal links'. Second, one must scrutinise 'the manner in which the interpersonal links have been established'. This element has to be examined both from a legal and moral perspective, in order to avoid protecting faits accomplis in violation of legal rules or fundamental moral principles.' In the view of the four judges, in *Paradiso and Campanelli*, the links between the intending parents and the child were established in violation of both Italian law and international adoption law.

before that with the child in Russia);[66] and, third, the uncertainty of the ties between the applicants and the child from a legal perspective.[67] This was so regardless of 'the existence of a parental project and the quality of the emotional bonds' that the intending parents had forged with the child in the first stages of his life.[68]

Although the Grand Chamber found that the contested measures did not fall within the scope of the applicants' family life, it determined that the measures fell under the second limb of Article 8, i.e. within the scope of the applicants' private life.[69] Nevertheless, the Grand Chamber concluded that the removal of the child from the intending parents was 'in accordance with the law',[70] pursued a legitimate aim, i.e. preventing disorder and protecting the child's rights and freedoms,[71] and was 'necessary in a democratic society'.[72] Accordingly, the Grand Chamber found, by eleven votes to six, that there had been no violation of Article 8 of the ECHR in the present case.[73] It is believed here that this was the correct conclusion as, otherwise, States would be encouraged to condone illegal conduct at the expense of the protection of the public interest,[74] which could have resulted in the resistance on the part of Italy and other contracting parties to implement the judgment.[75] In terms of the substance of the decision, it has been rightly suggested that, indeed,

> [i]t is not for the European Court of Human Rights to effectively create "family rights" for any couple in Europe who want to have a baby by hiring a surrogate mother anywhere in the world even when neither intending parent has a genetic relationship with the child. This has to be a matter on which countries in Europe are allowed to have different views.[76]

66 The majority refused to define a minimum period of shared life which would be required to constitute *de facto* family life. It held instead that 'the assessment of any situation must take account of the "quality" of the bond and the circumstances of each case.' *Paradiso and Campanelli*, para. 153.

67 Ibid., para. 157.

68 Ibid.

69 Ibid., para. 166.

70 Ibid., paras 174. See also the analysis at paras. 168–173.

71 Ibid., para. 178. See also the analysis at paras. 175–177.

72 Ibid., paras. 179–214.

73 Ibid., para. 216. In concluding that there had been no violation of Article 8, the Grand Chamber reversed the first instance judgment which was given by the Chamber on 27.01.2015. See above n. 54.

74 See P. Beaumont and K. Trimmings, above n. 54. See also 'Adopted Embryos Born by Surrogate Women' (Case Comment) (2017) *European Human Rights Law Review*, 323, 326.

75 Implementation of the ECtHR judgments depends largely on the goodwill of the contracting parties despite some diplomatic pressure from the Committee of Ministers. When reaching its judgments, the Court is cautious not to overstep 'its legitimacy wall – an imaginary boundary beyond which it could not go.' See F. de Londras and K. Dzehtsiarou, above n. 56, p. 34.

76 P. Beaumont and K. Trimmings, above n. 1, p. 123.

3. RECOGNITION OF THE LEGAL PARENT-CHILD RELATIONSHIP

This section examines in detail the ECtHR's approach to the recognition of the legal parent-child relationship in the context of cross-border surrogacy. It builds on the case law overview in section 2.1, namely the cases of *Mennesson v. France*,[77] *Labassee v. France*,[78] *Laborie v. France*,[79] and *Foulon and Bouvet v. France*,[80] and explores two key themes that arise from these judgments: the link between legal parentage and genetics, and the significance of distinguishing between altruistic and commercial surrogacy. The role of the principle of the best interests of the child as expounded in the above case law is explored throughout the analysis.

3.1. GENETIC LINK AND LEGAL PARENTAGE

In reaching its decision in *Mennesson v. France* (which, as explained in sections 2.1.2. and 2.1.3. above, was followed in the subsequent cases of *Labassee v. France*, *Laborie v. France*, and *Foulon and Bouvet v. France*), the ECtHR considered that a person's identity was intrinsically linked with biological parentage,[81] and that the right to establish one's identity was in turn connected with the right to respect for private life under Article 8.[82] In the words of the Court, the right to respect for private life under Article 8 'implies that everyone must be able to establish the substance of his or her identity, including the legal parent-child relationship'.[83] In particular, the Court observed that 'an essential aspect of one's identity is at stake' where legal parentage is concerned,[84] implying that when it comes to legal parentage, the margin of appreciation afforded to the State must be reduced.[85] The refusal to recognise in France the legal parent-child relationship that had been established under Californian

---

77 *Mennesson v France*, No. 65192/11, 26 June 2014, 26 June 2014, judgment of the Fifth Section of the European Court of Human Rights sitting as a Chamber.

78 *Labassee v. France*, No. 65941/11, 26 June 2014, judgment of the Fifth Section of the European Court of Human Rights sitting as a Chamber.

79 *Laborie v. France*, No. 44024/13, 19 January 2017, judgment of the Fifth Section of the European Court of Human Rights sitting as a Chamber.

80 *Foulon and Bouvet v. France*, Nos. 9063/14 and 10410/14, 21 July 2016, judgment of the Fifth Section of the European Court of Human Rights sitting as a Chamber.

81 *Mennesson*, para. 100. In the words of the Chamber, 'biological parentage' is 'a component of identity'.

82 Ibid., para. 99.

83 Ibid.

84 Ibid., para. 96.

85 Ibid., para. 80.

law 'undermined the children's identity within French society'.[86] Such refusal was considered particularly worrying where, as in the present case, 'one of the intended parents is also the child's biological parent.'[87]

The Court then identified nationality and the right to inheritance as the relevant elements of identity. Although the children's biological father was French, they were unable to obtain French nationality.[88] In addition, the children's inheritance rights were 'less favourable' as they could only inherit from the intended parents as legatees.[89]

The Court then explored whether French law afforded the intending parents an alternative remedy such as allowing them to establish the legal parent-child relationship under domestic law, for example by means of a declaration of paternity or adoption.[90] This line of inquiry, however, led to the conclusion that not only did the French authorities refuse to register the details of the US birth certificates, but other avenues such as a declaration of paternity or adoption were incompatible with the case law of the Court of Cassation.[91]

Following this analysis the Court held that by preventing the recognition and establishment under domestic law of the relationship between the twins and their biological father, France 'overstepped the permissible limits of its margin of appreciation'.[92] Consequently, the children's right to respect for their private life had been violated.

Significantly, this situation was irreconcilable with the children's best interests.[93] The Court pointed out that respect for the child's best interests must 'guide any decision',[94] including, as in the present case, a decision concerning the recognition of legal parentage established abroad through cross-border surrogacy. This leads to the conclusion that the principle of

---

86 Ibid., para. 96.

87 Ibid., para. 100.

88 Ibid., para. 97.

89 Ibid., para. 98. This meant that the inheritance tax would be calculated as if the child was a third party.

90 Ibid., para. 100. For a critique of the application of such alternative solutions in surrogacy cases see S. Sucker, 'To Recognise or Not to Recognise ? That is the Question!' (2015) 17 *European Journal of Law Reform*, 257, 260–65.

91 Ibid., para. 100. On this point see also *Laborie*, para. 31, and *Foulon and Bouvet* para. 56, where the ECtHR noted that since its decisions in *Mennesson* and *Labassee* the French domesic law had evolved in that on 03.07.2015 there was a 'reversal of jurisprudence' of the Court of Cassation, which resulted in alternative avenues of establishing the legal parent-child relationship being made available to biological fathers in cross-border surrogacy cases (by means of the recognition of paternity under Article 316 of the Civil Code or the *de facto* enjoyment of civil status under Article 317 of the Civil Code; *Foulon and Bouvet* paras. 53 and 56). The utility of these remedies for cases decided prior to July 2015 was, however, uncertain.

92 *Mennesson*, para. 100.

93 Ibid., para. 99.

94 Ibid.

the best interests of the child must prevail over public policy considerations concerning surrogacy.[95]

This conclusion, however, does not seem to be of universal application. Indeed, a variety of scenarios may arise in surrogacy cases depending on the existence or non-existence of the biological link between the child and the intending parent(s). The child may be genetically linked with one, both or none of the intending parents. Similarly, the surrogate mother may or may not be also the genetic mother of the child, depending on whether her ovum was used for the child's conception. The above analysis and conclusion clearly apply to situations where the intending father is also the biological father, as was the case in all the relevant ECtHR decisions considered thus far.[96] It is irrelevant whether the intending father is heterosexual[97] or homosexual.[98] Indeed, the *Foulon and Bouvet* case resolved previous ambiguity as to whether the Court's reasoning in *Mennesson* would extend to same-sex applicants. Nevertheless, it ought to be pointed out that both Mr Foulon and Mr Bouvet were in effect single men,[99] and that the birth certificates issued in India listed the surrogate mother as the legal mother. Would the outcome be different if the birth certificate listed a same-sex couple as the legal parents? Would a non-recognition of the legal parenthood of the biologically unrelated intending father constitute a violation of the ECHR?

The same question arises also in relation to heterosexual couples and the position of the biologically unrelated intending mother, as was the case in *Mennesson*, *Labassee* and *Laborie*. As the judgments are unclear in this respect, the question whether the imperative to recognise the legal parent-child relationship covers also the relationship between the child and the biologically unrelated intending parent remains for now unanswered.[100]

---

95 This appears to conflict with the freedom of a State to outlaw surrogacy domestically, which was acknowledged by the ECtHR. See *Mennesson*, para. 62 and *Paradisso and Campanelli*, para. 100. Although States are allowed to ban surrogacy within its territory, the ECtHR's jurisprudence compels them to accept the effects of surrogacy arrangements commissioned by their nationals abroad. This approach is likely to encourage potential intending parents to circumvent domestic legislation prohibiting surrogacy.

96 *Mennesson*, *Labassee*, *Laborie*, and *Foulon and Bouvet*.

97 See *Mennesson*, *Labassee* and *Laborie*.

98 See *Foulon and Bouvet*.

99 Although Mr. Bouvet was living as a couple with another man, he commissioned the surrogacy arrangement as a sole intending parent. Apparently, Mr. Bouvet's partner had previously hired a surrogate mother through the same clinic (Hiranandani clinic in Mumbai) to have twins. GÈNÉTHIQUE, above n 27.

100 It has been suggested that to treat the second intending parent differently with regard to the acquisition of parental status would negatively impact 'the child's sense of identity and security as a person who has assumed the role of parent would not be legally recognised as such.' See M. WELLS-GRECO, above n. 1, p. 338. Wells-Greco likens the situation of the intending mother (or indeed the second intending parent in homosexual relationships, see *Foulon and Bouvet* above) to the historical position of the unmarried father. Ibid., p. 339.

Nevertheless, it is expected that the uncertainty concerning the parental status of the biologically unrelated intending mother will be resolved when the ECtHR reaches its decisions in the currently pending cases of *Saenz and Saenz Cortes v. France*[101] and *Braun v. France*.[102] In the former case, the intending parents had entered into a surrogacy arrangement in Ukraine; in the latter, surrogacy was commissioned in the US State of Florida. The factual background of both cases was similar to that of *Mennesson*, *Labassee* and *Laborie* – i.e. the cases involved heterosexual French couples[103] and the children were conceived using the intending fathers' sperm and donor eggs. The birth certificates issued in Ukraine and Florida respectively listed both intended parents as the child's legal parents. The French authorities, however, recognised only the parentage of the intending father by permitting only a partial transcription of the birth certificate. The authorities refused to recognise the intending mother as the child's legal mother, arguing that, according to French law,[104] legal motherhood was based on the reality of childbirth.[105] A departure from the *mater semper certa est* principle was allowed only in cases of full adoption.[106] The French Court of Cassation observed that its case law had developed since the ECtHR decisions in *Labassee* and *Foulon and Bouvet* by allowing that a child born as a result of cross-border surrogacy be adopted by the spouse of the biological father. Such adoption provides a means of establishing under domestic law a legal parent-child relationship between the child and the intending mother. Despite that, in their applications to the ECtHR, the applicants argue that the refusal by the French authorities to transcribe the entirety of the birth certificate has resulted in the violation of the child's right to respect for his/her private life under Article 8 of the Convention, and in the discrimination of the child on the grounds of birth under Article 14 of the Convention. The outcome of the *Saenz* and *Braun* cases is eagerly awaited.

Another question that remains unanswered is whether the obligation to recognise the legal parentage of the biologically-related intending parent would apply also to situations where the known source of the genetic material was the intending mother rather than the intending father. Indeed, would

---

101 *Saenz and Saenz Cortes v France*, No. 11288/18.

102 *Braun v France*, No. 1462/18.

103 At the time of the surrogacy arrangement and the application to the ECtHR the Brauns, like the Labories were resident outside of France, in Thailand (Bangkok). See section 2.1.2 above.

104 Civil Code, Article 47.

105 See K. Trimmings and P. Beaumont, 'Parentage and Surrogacy in a European Perspective', in J. Scherpe (ed.), *European Family Law*, vol. III, Edward Elgar, Cheltenham 2016, pp. 232–283, for analysis of the different approaches to legal parenthood (i.e. the gestational test, the genetics test and the intent test).

106 Civil Code, Article 356(1).

the Court in *Mennesson*, *Labassee* or *Laborie* have taken the same view if the biologically-related intending parent had been the mother?[107] Interestingly, the Chamber did not expressly discuss whether there is a difference between legal fatherhood and legal motherhood, and, instead, referred to a single concept of legal parenthood. It would not, however, be straightforward to analogically apply the Court's reasoning in *Mennesson* to a biologically-related intending mother. This is in particular because the *Mennesson* approach would be contrary to the gestational test on which the establishment of legal motherhood is traditionally based.[108] This ties up with another open question – i.e. what approach would the Court take if the surrogate mother sought to establish or preserve her parental status in the face of the opposition of the intending parent(s), and would the outcome differ if the child was born as a result of a traditional surrogacy arrangement, i.e. where the surrogate mother was also the genetic mother of the child?[109] Rather confusingly, the existing ECtHR case law on surrogacy refers to 'biological' parentage, the meaning of which is clear in the context of a male but less so in the context of a female. Indeed, 'biological' parentage, when used in relation to a male, refers to genetics as the sole 'biological' element that men contribute to procreation. However, when used in relation to a female, the term 'biological' parentage ordinarily comprises both genetics and gestation. As stated above, it is unclear whether the Court's view that 'biological parentage' is 'a component of identity' would apply equally to a genetically-related intending mother. It is similarly uncertain whether the Court's reasoning would be applicable to a traditional surrogate on account of her genetic and gestational connection with the child, or indeed, to a gestational surrogate on account of her gestational link with the child.[110] Would the position of a traditional surrogate mother be stronger than the position of a gestational surrogate mother if seeking to establish or preserve her parental status against the will of the intending parents?

---

107 Hague Conference on Private International Law, above n. 1, para. 8.

108 See K. Trimmings and P. Beaumont, above n. 105. See also the analysis of the *Saenz* and *Braun* cases above.

109 A traditional surrogacy arrangement can be defined as a surrogacy arrangement where the surrogate provides her own genetic material and thus the child born is genetically related to her. Such an arrangement may involve natural conception or artificial insemination. See Hague Conference on Private International Law, 'The Desirability and Feasibility of Further Work on the Parentage / Surrogacy Project', Prel. Doc. No 3 B of March 2014, Annex A, <https://assets.hcch.net/docs/6403eddb-3b47-4680-ba4a-3fe3e11c0557.pdf> accessed 20.07.2018; and K. Trimmings and P. Beaumont, above n. 105.

110 See J. Fawcett, M. Ní Shúilleabháin and S. Shah, *Human Rights and Private International Law*, Oxford University Press, Oxford 2016, para. 14.43.

3.2. COMMERCIAL vs ALTRUISTIC SURROGACY[111]

Another area that received insufficient attention in the ECtHR's case law on surrogacy is the distinction between commercial and altruistic surrogacy. Worryingly, when reaching its conclusion on the obligation of State authorities to recognise a legal parent-child relationship that has been established abroad as a result of surrogacy, the Court in *Mennesson* or *Labassee* made no differentiation between relationships established through cross-border commercial and altruistic surrogacy. It was hoped that this issue would be addressed in *Foulon and Bouvet* and/or *Laborie* as these cases differed from *Mennesson* and *Labassee* in that they involved economically less developed countries as the countries of birth[112] where concerns over the exploitation of women hired as surrogate mothers are more prevalent than in relation to the United States where the Mennesson and Labassee children were born.[113] It is disappointing that the Court did not address this important aspect of cross-border surrogacy and thus implicitly approved of commercial surrogacy in the cross-border context.

The failure to distinguish between commercial and altruistic surrogacy is disturbing in particular[114] because the current practice of commercial surrogacy undermines well-established standards of international human rights law – women's rights and children's rights alike.[115] In terms of relevant international instruments in the children's rights context, the starting point is the

---

111 See K. Trimmings and P. Beaumont, above n. 105.

112 See sections 2.1.2 and 2.1.3 above.

113 See European Parliament, 'Annual Report on Human Rights and Democracy in the World 2014 and the European Union's Policy on the Matter', 30.11.2015, <http://www.europarl.europa.eu/sides/getDoc.do?pubRef=-//EP//TEXT+REPORT+A8-2015-0344+0+DOC+XML+V0//EN> accessed03.07.2019, para. 114: '[...] the practice of gestational surrogacy [...] involves reproductive exploitation and use of the human body for financial or other gain, in particular in the case of vulnerable women in developing countries [...].' See also Hague Conference on Private International Law, above n. 1, para. 18 and Annex II; and K. Trimmings and P. Beaumont, 'General Report', in K. Trimmings and P. Beaumont (eds.), *International Surrogacy Arrangements: Legal Regulation at the International Level*, Hart Publishing, Oxford 2013, pp. 528–531.

114 Mandating States to recognise legal parent-child relationships established through cross-border surrogacy, without differentiating between altruistic and commercial surrogacy is alarming also on other grounds. For examination of these reasons see P. Beaumont and K. Trimmings, above n. 1, pp. 130–32.

115 See, for example, United Nations Special Rapporteur on the Sale and Sexual Exploitation of Children, 'Annual Thematic Report 2017', A/HRC/37/60, 15 January 2018; and United Nations Committee on the Rights of the Child, 'Concluding Observations on the Combined Third and Fourth Periodic Reports of India', 13.06.2014, UN Doc CRC/C/IND/CO/3-4, para. 57.

United Nations Convention on the Rights of the Child (the UN Convention).[116] The UN Convention is silent on surrogacy and when examining the applicability of the Convention provisions to surrogacy, the outcome is ambiguous. On one hand, Articles 2,[117] 3[118] and 7[119] provide some support for the ECtHR's reasoning in *Mennesson* concerning the children's right to private life.[120] Also, it can be argued that as the UN Convention contains frequent references to the child's parents, cross-border recognition of legal parenthood is an inevitable pre-requisite to the enjoyment of the UN Convention rights generally.[121] One the other hand, however, commercial surrogacy, with its related concerns over commodification of children and inherent potential for abuse, infringes several articles of the UN Convention. These provisions include in particular Article 21(d), which seeks to prevent commercialisation of international adoption, and Article 35, which imposes on the contracting parties the obligation to prevent 'the sale of or traffic in children for any purpose or in any form'. The sale of children is defined in the Optional Protocol on the Sale of Children, Child Prostitution and Child Pornography[122] as 'any act or transaction whereby a child is transferred by any person or group of persons to another for remuneration or any other consideration.'[123] This definition is undoubtedly

---

116 United Nations Convention on the Rights of the Child, 2 September 1990, <http://www.ohchr.org/EN/ProfessionalInterest/Pages/CRC.aspx> accessed 31.07.2018.

117 Article 2(1) prohibits discrimination against the child, including on grounds of 'birth or other status.' Article 2(2) mandates contracting parties to ensure that 'the child is protected against all forms of discrimination or punishment' on the grounds of 'the status, activities [...] of the child's parents, legal guardians, or family members.'

118 Article 3 requires that the child's best interests be a primary consideration in all actions concerning children.

119 Article 7(1) requires that the child be registered immediately after birth, and guarantees a right from birth to a name and nationality.

120 Hague Conference on Private International Law, 'Private International Law Issues Surrounding the Status of Children, Including Issues Arising from International Surrogacy Arrangements', Prel. Doc. No 11, March 2011, para. 25 <https://assets.hcch.net/docs/f5991e3e-0f8b-430c-b030-ca93c8ef1c0a.pdf> accessed 04.08.2018.

121 J. Fawcett, M. Ní Shúilleabháin and S. Shah, above n. 110, para. 14.57.

122 Optional Protocol to the Convention on the Rights of the Child on the Sale of Children, Child Prostitution and Child Pornography, 18 January 2002 <http://www.ohchr.org/EN/ProfessionalIntrest/Pages/OPSCCRC.aspx> accessed 31.07.2018. See, for example, G. Puppinck and C. de la Hougue, above n. 1; and D. Smolin, 'Surrogacy as the Sale of Children: Applying Lessons Learned from Adoption to the Regulation of the Surrogacy Industry's Global Marketing of Children', Stanford University, Selected Works, 2015 <https://works.bepress.com/david_smolin/19/> accessed 31.07.2018. More generally, see UNICEF, 'Handbook on the Optional Protocol on the Sale of Children, Child Prostitution and Child Pornography', 2009 <https://www.unicef-irc.org/publications/pdf/optional_protocol_eng.pdf> accessed 05.04.2017.

123 For a detailed analysis of the applicability of this definition to commercial surrogacy see United Nations Special Rapporteur on the Sale and Sexual Exploitation of Children, 'Annual Thematic Report 2017', A/HRC/37/60, 15 January 2018.

wide enough to cover commercial surrogacy.[124] Other relevant provisions concern the child's right to know[125] and maintain contact with his/her parents[126] and to preserve his/her identity.[127] The preservation of identity under Article 8 clearly suggests 'a prioritisation of the child's initial identity', which is at odds with the current practice of cross-border commercial surrogacy.[128]

The obligation to recognise a legal parent-child relationship established as a result of a cross-border surrogacy arrangement, including a commercial surrogacy arrangement, contradicts the findings of the United Nations Special Rapporteur on the Sale of the Child set out in her recent report on surrogacy.[129] The Report was presented to the UN Human Rights Council in March 2018. Given the risk of sale of the child in commercial surrogacy,[130] the document makes the following recommendation:

> States generally should not automatically recognize parentage orders or birth records from foreign States in respect of commercial surrogacies, but should review carefully the proceedings abroad. The State of the intending parents is responsible for conducting post-birth best interests determinations, protecting the child's identity rights and access to origins, and making independent assessments as to parentage, and also for inquiring into the treatment and post-birth consent of the surrogate mother. The State of the intending parents should only grant parentage and parental responsibility to intending parents after such evaluations, based on the best interests of the child.[131]

The ECtHR approach is based on the premise that it is in the best interests of the child born through cross-border surrogacy, including commercial surrogacy, to have a secure upbringing, through recognising the intending parent(s) as that child's legal parents. Contrary to this approach, the Special Rapporteur,

---

124 J. Fawcett, M. Ní Shúilleabháin and S. Shah, above n. 110, para. 14.58.

125 Article 7(1): 'The child shall be registered immediately after birth and shall have the right from birth to a name, the right to acquire a nationality and. as far as possible, the right to know and be cared for by his or her parents.'

126 Article 9(3): 'States Parties shall respect the right of the child who is separated from one or both parents to maintain personal relations and direct contact with both parents on a regular basis, except if it is contrary to the child's best interests.'

127 Article 8: '1. States Parties undertake to respect the right of the child to preserve his or her identity, including nationality, name and family relations as recognized by law without unlawful interference. 2. Where a child is illegally deprived of some or all of the elements of his or her identity, States Parties shall provide appropriate assistance and protection, with a view to re-establishing speedily his or her identity.'

128 J. Fawcett, M. Ní Shúilleabháin and S. Shah, above n. 110, para. 14.58.

129 Report of the United Nations Special Rapporteur on the Sale and Sexual Exploitation of Children, A/HRC/37/60, 15 January 2018.

130 The report refers expressly to 'regulated and unregulated commercial surrogacies', ibid., para 70.

131 Ibid.

although acknowledging the importance of the security of legal parentage for the child, believes that the best interests of the child principle does not demand automatic recognition of the parent-child relationship established abroad as a result of commercial surrogacy. Instead, the principle requires that the State of the intending parents reviews the foreign proceedings, and grants legal parentage to the intending parent(s) only if the best interests of the child in question justifies such an outcome. This approach is more in line with viewing the best interests principle as a group rather than an individual right.[132] It may be suggested that the underlying premise of this approach in the context of cross-border commercial surrogacy is that commercial surrogacy, through commodifying children, undermines the best interests of children generally and, therefore, should be discouraged and requires a more cautious approach when it comes to dealing *ex post facto* with the legal consequences of the practice. The intending parents should not be 'rewarded' by automatic recognition of the parental status they acquired in exchange of a payment in the country of birth.

The Special Rapporteur warns against normalising the sale of children and other human rights violations when regulating surrogacy at domestic or international level,[133] and describes the shortcomings of the 'recognition approach' advocated by the ECtHR as follows:

> The demand that domestic parentage orders be recognized globally without appropriate restrictions and without consideration of human rights concerns raises the related risk that a minority of jurisdictions with permissive approaches to commercial surrogacy, and with regulations that fail to protect the rights of vulnerable parties against exploitation, could normalize practices globally that violate human rights. [...] [I]f this type of governing legal regime becomes accepted, whether as international or national law, or through recognition principles, it would undermine established human rights norms and standards.[134]

Indeed, in relying solely on the recognition method, the ECtHR approach, although displaying a child-centred method,[135] fails to satisfactorily address

---

132 On the difference between the best interests principle as a group right and the best interests principle as an individual right see, for example, UNHCR, 'UNHCR Guidelines on Determining the Best Interests of the Child', May 2008, pp. 20–22 <http://www.unhcr.org/4566b16b2.pdf> accessed 04.08.2018; and N. Cantwell (UNICEF), 'The Best Interests of the Child in Intercountry Adoption', 2014, p. 16 <https://www.unicef-irc.org/publications/pdf/unicef%20best%20interest%20document_web_re-supply.pdf> accessed 04.08.2018.

133 Report of the United Nations Special Rapporteur on the Sale and Sexual Exploitation of Children, above n. 129, para 23.

134 Ibid., paras 23 and 24.

135 See C. Achmad, 'Children's Rights to the Fore in the European Court of Human Rights' (2014) *European Human Rights Law Review*, 638, 642; A. Gouttenoire, 'Surrogacy Arrangements: At Last, the Primacy of the Child's Interests' (2015) 1 *Montesquieu Law Review*, 103; and M. Wells-Greco, above n. 1, p. 339, who rightly describes the ECtHR decisions in *Mennesson* and *Labassee* as 'landmarks for the rights of surrogate-born children'.

the legal and ethical complexities of commercial surrogacy.[136] The recognition method, though capable of reducing limping relationships, offers only an *ex post facto* solution to the problem of legal parenthood. It does not address other serious issues, including serious human rights concerns that surround cross-border commercial surrogacy.[137] Not less importantly, the automatic recognition approach advocated by the ECtHR is to be criticised also for undermining domestic constraints on surrogacy and encouraging recourse to cross-border commercial surrogacy.[138]

It is suggested here that the recognition approach should be substituted by a global multilateral solution which would address the problem of legal parentage alongside other private and public law considerations, in particular the human rights of all concerned.[139]

4. CONCLUSION

The ECtHR approach towards recognition of the parent-child relationship established abroad through cross-border surrogacy means that a parental status acquired abroad, whether through a judgment or otherwise, is entitled to protection under Article 8 of the ECHR[140] as long as the intending father is biologically linked to the child and the parental status was acquired by the intending parent(s) legally and in good faith under the foreign legal system.[141] Hence, once the surrogacy has taken place in the foreign jurisdiction and the child has been legally relinquished to the intending parents, recognition of the parent-child relationship between the child and the biologically related intending father cannot be denied in the recognising state.[142] The fact that

---

136 See G. Puppinck and C. de la Hougue, above n. 2; Hague Conference on Private International Law, above n. 1, para. 11; and J. Fawcett, M. Ní Shúilleabháin and S. Shah, above n. 110, para. 14.43; P. Beaumont and K. Trimmings, above n. 1, pp. 125–126; M. Welstead, above n. 1, pp. 272–73; and C. Fenton-Glynn, above n. 1, pp. 564–66.

137 See P. Beaumont and K. Trimmings, in J. Scherpe, C. Fenton-Glynn and T. Kaan (eds.), above n. 54.

138 See for example J. Fawcett, M. Ní Shúilleabháin and S. Shah, above n. 110, para. 14.43; P. Beaumont and K. Trimmings, above n. 1, pp. 125–126; and M. Welstead, above n.1, pp. 272–73.

139 See P. Beaumont and K. Trimmings, in J. Scherpe, C. Fenton-Glynn and T. Kaan (eds.), above n. 54; Hague Conference on Private International Law, above n. 1, para. 12; and K. Trimmings and P. Beaumont, above n. 113, pp. 531–549.

140 See M. Wells-Greco, above n. 1, p. 341.

141 See P. Franzina, 'Some Remarks on the Relevance of Article 8 of the ECHR to the Recognition of Family Status Judicially Created Abroad', (2011) 5 *Diritti Umani e Diritto Internazionale*, 609.

142 See C. Fenton-Glynn, above n. 1, p. 555.

such a parental status 'could not have been acquired under the recognising forum's own system of law or public policy will not, in itself, be enough.'[143] In other words, Article 8 is to remedy the operation of the forum's private international law rules on recognition whenever the latter bring about an unlawful limitation on the child's right to respect for their private life.[144] Unfortunately, this approach amounts to compromising the best interests of children in general, i.e. the requirement to tackle the commodification of children as imposed by the Optional Protocol on the Sale of the Child, through favouring the individual child and his/her immediate need for a secure legal parent-child relationship.[145]

---

143 P. Kinsch, 'Recognition in the Forum of a Status Acquired Abroad – Private International Law Rules and European Human Rights Law', in K. Boele-Woelki et al. (eds.), *Convergence and Divergence in Private International Law – Liber Amicorum Kurt Siehr*, Eleven International Publishing, The Hague 2010, p. 272.

144 H. Muir Watt, 'Concurrence d'Ordres Juridiques et Conflits de Lois de Droit Privé', in M. Lagarde, *Vers de Nouveaux Équilibres Entre Ordres Juridiques: Mélanges en l'honneur d'Hélène Gaudemet-Tallon*, Dalloz 2008, p. 617, per M. Wells-Greco, above n. 1, p. 341.

145 See K. Norrie, 'Surrogacy in the United Kingdom: An Inappropriate Application of the Welfare Principle', in E. Sutherland and L. Barnes Macfarlane, *Implementing Article 3 of the United Nations Convention on the Rights of the Child: Best Interests, Welfare and Well-Being*, Cambridge University Press, Cambridge 2018, pp. 165–179.

CROSS-BORDER RECOGNITION OF ADOPTION

Rethinking Private International Law from a Human Rights Perspective

Chiara Ragni

1. Lack of Harmonisation of Family Law in Europe and its Impact on Recognition of Foreign Adoptions 209
2. The International Legal Framework: The 1993 Hague Convention and its Limits 211
3. The Right to the Continuity of Family Status: Social Reality and Legitimate Expectations v. Legal Relationships 215
4. Reconciling Human Rights and Private International Law 220

1. LACK OF HARMONISATION OF FAMILY LAW IN EUROPE AND ITS IMPACT ON RECOGNITION OF FOREIGN ADOPTIONS

The practice of adoption was largely viewed as a strictly national procedure for a long time, and as such, it was regulated by domestic rules. The international dimensions of this phenomenon have emerged as a relatively recent occurrence. These include both the movement of children across international borders for adoption and the possibility of obtaining the recognition of *status filiation* is duly acquired abroad through adoption. As we will see, notwithstanding their cross-border implications, these matters are only partly covered by international rules. Questions regarding issues such as the criteria that prospective parents should meet to be eligible for adoption or the legal effects of adoption are still mostly regulated by domestic legislation; States remain in fact reluctant to refrain from exercising their exclusive jurisdiction in family matters.

Even in the EU context, notwithstanding the entry into force of an increasing number of rules defining key aspects of jurisdiction, applicable law and recognition and the enforcement of judgments in the fields of divorce, maintenance obligations, parental responsibility, among others,[1] substantive aspects of family law are still regulated by national legislation. The failure to pass uniform rules on family issues demonstrates the cautious attitude of States in this regard.

For example, the limited number of ratifications alleged to the 1967 European Convention on the Adoption of Children, and even fewer to the revised version of the treaty, which was adopted in 2008 to account for legal and social developments in the European framework,[2] can be read as proof of the aforementioned reluctance of States to cede their exclusive jurisdiction in family matters. This approach is due to the continuing influence on family law of moral, religious or political beliefs, which often vary across States.

Against this background, cross-border recognition of the parental status arising from foreign adoptions has encountered obstacles. In some cases, orders duly entered into in one country may be considered contrary to the public policy of another country (such as in the case of adoptions pronounced in favour of same-sex couples). In others such orders may be recognised with different – and generally more limited – effects than those produced in the country of origin (as in the case of single adoption). Furthermore, they could be deemed as not valid under the law, according to the conflict-of-law rules of the concerned State (such as in the case of *kafalah*, the alternative care option in Islamic law for children deprived of a family environment).

At the international level, the only legal instrument that addresses the matters under consideration is the Hague Convention of 29 May 1993, which

---

1 On the harmonisation of EU private international law in family matters, see K. Boele-Woelki, *Perspectives for the Unification and Harmonisation of Family Law in Europe*, Intersentia, Cambridge 2003.

2 It is worth recalling, even if the topic will be addressed in section 3, that the 2008 European Convention on the Adoption of Children (Revised – Strasbourg, 27.11.2008) was elaborated also in order to take into account developments that occurred in the European context with regard to adoption. It particularly highlights the need to acquire the consent of the father to the adoption, even in the case of children born out of wedlock (Council of Europe Treaty Series – No. 202. Explanatory Report, CETS 202, Adoption of Children (Revised Convention), §27 ff.), and it also stresses the importance of considering the opinion of the child when he or she is considered by law as having sufficient understanding. This reflects the emphasis placed at both the international and EU levels on the importance of giving the child an opportunity to be heard in proceedings affecting him or her unless such hearing is inappropriate. Finally, considering the legal and social developments in most CoE Member States with regard to the regulation of family matters, the Convention envisages the possibility of opening adoption to 'same sex couples who are married to each other or who have entered into a registered partnership together'. It also leaves States 'free to extend the scope of [the] Convention to different sex couples and same sex couples who are living together in a stable relationship'. For more details on the Convention and, more broadly, on the regulation of adoption in Europe see C. Fenton-Glynn, *Children's Rights in Intercountry Adoption: A European Perspective*, Intersentia, Cambridge 2014.

provides for the automatic recognition of intercountry adoption orders.[3] However, notwithstanding its relevance, this treaty only covers situations when the parents and the child are resident in two different Member States. Outside its scope, recognition of foreign adoptions is subject to domestic rules, with no legal guarantee that the situation lawfully acquired in one country and its legal consequences will be recognised in another.

This matter has been broadly addressed by national courts. It has also been the object of some relevant cases brought before the European Court of Human Rights (ECtHR), which was called upon to pronounce on whether the lack of recognition of a foreign adoption violated family rights under Article 8 of the European Convention on Human Rights (ECHR), as well as minors' rights. As stated by the 1989 UN Convention,[4] and, accordingly, by the EU Charter of Fundamental Rights,[5] the child's best interests should in fact be a primary consideration in all decisions affecting minors.[6]

Assuming, also in the light of the analysis of the jurisprudence of the ECtHR, that the recognition of *status filii* (as well as the individual status of the child) should be considered a means to protect family rights and pursue the best interests of the child, the aims of this chapter are as follows: i) to frame the rules aimed at regulating the recognition of foreign adoptions in the European context; ii) to identify (also in the light of existing practice) possible gaps in EU, international and national legislations regarding these matters; and iii) to assess how conflict-of-law rules on the recognition of *status filii* duly acquired abroad should be reshaped in light of human rights standards and social developments in family relationships. The underlying idea is that a line of continuity between the legal situation created in the State of origin and the domestic legal order should be guaranteed as a matter of principle, even if limited exceptions should be available to fulfil the best interests of the child in any particular case.

2. THE INTERNATIONAL LEGAL FRAMEWORK: THE 1993 HAGUE CONVENTION AND ITS LIMITS

Beginning in the 1960s, the growth in international adoptions with the increasing number of orphan children made States aware of the need to cooperate and

3 The Hague Convention on the Protection of Children and Cooperation in Respect of Intercountry Adoption (29.05.1993). Other Conventions that are relevant in this area (such as the aforementioned CoE European Convention on the Adoption of Children) limit themselves to providing some general standards that parties should comply with to safeguard the child's best interests; however, they do not address recognition issues, nor do they include conflict-of-laws rules.

4 Convention on the Rights of the Child (New York, 20.11.1989), Article 3.

5 Charter of Fundamental Rights of the European Union (Nice, 2000), Article 24.

6 On the child's best interests principle and its relevance with regard to transnational families, see M. Distefano in this volume.

embrace a multilateral approach to the phenomenon; their first aim was to define common shared standards to protect children against abduction, human trafficking or any other form of abuse. To that end, the Convention on the Protection of Children and Co-operation in Respect of Intercountry Adoption was finally concluded at the 17th session of the Hague Conference on Private International Law. The treaty, which only applies in cases where the adoptive parents and the child reside in different Member States, aims at establishing 'safeguards to ensure that intercountry adoptions take place in the best interests of the child and with respect for his or her fundamental rights as recognised in international law'. It provides procedural standards for courts, administrative authorities and private intermediaries to guarantee that the best interests of the child principle is the guiding standard in all decisions regarding the adoption of minors, as is also stated by the aforementioned 1989 New York Convention.

Based on the premise that the best interests of minors are served by growing up with their own parents or at least maintaining his or her cultural, linguistic, religious and ethnic identity, as appropriate, the 1993 Hague Convention considers that adoption should be pronounced only in cases where it is the only means of ensuring 'a permanent family to a child for whom a suitable family cannot found in his or her State of origin'.[7] The underlying idea is therefore that intercountry adoption should be considered a last resort and that it only serves the purpose of providing a family to abandoned children.

In line with its stated objective, the Convention does not apply to simple adoption and only covers adoptions that create a permanent parent-child relationship.[8] Single adoption might therefore be a viable option under the treaty,[9] provided that it is likely to produce the same legal consequence of creating a parentage link or where it can be converted into an adoption having such an effect in the receiving State.[10] With regard to other conditions that an order should fulfil to benefit from the Convention's regime, Chapter V lists some procedural safeguards aimed at ensuring the protection of children's rights against any possible abuse.

Like other treaties and legal instruments adopted in the field of private international law, to ensure internal consistency and the protection of national fundamental principles, Article 24 provides that 'the recognition of an adoption

---

7 See 1993 Hague Convention, Preamble, which reproduces the idea expressed in Article 21, sub-paragraph (b) of the United Nations Convention on the Rights of the Child.

8 See Article 2 of the 1993 Hague Convention.

9 Notwithstanding references to adoptive parents, the possibility that intercountry adoption may also be pronounced in favour of a single person is clearly envisaged by Article 2 of the Convention.

10 This hypothesis is regulated by Article 27, which permits the receiving State to convert simple adoption into a full adoption, provided that the law allows it and the consents that are necessary for the purpose of such an adoption have been given. On this point, see P. H. Pfund, 'Intercountry Adoption: The 1993 Hague Convention: Its Purpose, Implementation, and Promise', (1994) *Family Law Quarterly*, 53–88.

may be refused in a Contracting State only if the adoption is manifestly contrary to its public policy, taking into account the best interests of the child'. As is further clarified in the Explanatory Report, the specification that the safeguarding of national interests and values should necessarily be balanced against the protection of the best interests of the child means that the mere existence of large-scale differences among domestic legislation with regard to the regulation of minors' adoption is not a sufficient ground to refuse the recognition of foreign decisions.[11] In addition, to affirm the continuity of parental bonds and thereby avoid limping situations, the Convention provides a preventive mechanism of coordination between the child's State of origin and the State of destination.[12]

However, this mechanism does not preclude the possibility that adoption is refused to same-sex couples or to unmarried persons in accordance with domestic rules. According to Article 5, the eligibility requirements are in fact subject to national legislation and the recognition of foreign decisions might be denied on the grounds of their alleged contravention of the fundamental principles of the requested State.[13]

---

11 According to the Explanatory Report annexed to the 1993 Hague Convention: 'neither Article 24 nor any other articles of the Convention provides for the exception of the unknown institution as a ground to refuse recognition of the adoption granted in a Contracting State, ... Thus, the solution is the same and the fact that the recognizing State does not have the institution of adoption, or a particular form of adoption, cannot be used as a ground to deny recognition to foreign adoptions' (para. 428).

12 See R. Baratta, 'La reconnaissance internationale des situations juridiques personelles et familiales', (2010) *Collected Courses of the Hague Academy of International Law*, 348, 271, at 343, where the author indicates that the Convention should therefore be capable of avoiding *a priori* the creation of limping adoptions in concerned States.

13 In Italy, see for example, Law No. 476 of 31.10.1998, which authorises the ratification and implementation of the 1993 Hague Convention, as amended by Law No. 149 of 28.03.2001, which provides that only married couples are entitled to intercountry adoption and foreign decisions should comply with fundamental principles of Italian law in family matters. According to this rule, the well-established jurisprudence of the Italian Supreme Court (*Corte di Cassazione*) decided that adoptions pronounced abroad in favour of single persons only produce in Italy the limited effects of the so called adoption in particular cases as envisaged by Article 44 of the Italian Law on adoption: 'This approach rests on the adoption in particular cases being conceived as not capable of interrupting the relationship between the child and his/her family of origin and giving rise to parental links between the former and the family of the adoptive parent'. On this issue, see C. E. Tuo, 'The Italian Regime of Recognition of Intercountry Adoptions of Children in Light of the ECHR: What about Singles?' (2015) *Cuadernos de Derecho Transnacional* 7, 357–68. On the specific issue of the recognition of foreign adoptions under the 1993 Hague Convention also see L. Carpaneto, 'Recognition of Protection Measures affecting Migrant Children' in F. Ippolito and G. Biagioni (eds.), *Migrant Children: Challenges for Public and Private International Law*, 419–53, n 25. However, the best interests of the child principle should also take precedence over fundamental principles of domestic legislation, due to it being, according to some scholars, a limit that prevails over the public policy exception. See F. Mosconi and C. Campiglio, *Diritto internazionale privato e processuale*, II, Torino 2014, p. 229.

Nonetheless, the safeguarding of national public concerns encounters a limitation in the need to protect the best interests of the child, which should take precedence over any other consideration.

Since the term 'family' is not defined under the Convention, which only makes reference to spouses or persons habitually resident in a State party, the possibility that intercountry adoption is pronounced in favour of same-sex married parents is not *per se* ruled out. The reasons why this scenario was left uncovered are in fact traceable to historical conditions. When the Convention was being drafted from 1988 to 1993, no country allowed same-sex couples to adopt. The question was still being debated even in States such as Denmark or the Netherlands, which pioneered same-sex partnerships or marriages. Against this background, negotiators abstained from specifically addressing the matter, thus leaving States free to decide for themselves whether the intended parent is qualified to adopt according to Article 5, if all the other conditions required by the treaty are fulfilled. In the light of the Convention, what instead is more questionable is the eligibility of *de facto* couples unless the decision concerns only one of the partners and/or is likely to produce the effects of a full adoption.

Beyond the discretion that States still enjoy regarding the interpretation of the concept of family under the Convention, a further and more important limit of the treaty concerns its scope of application. As anticipated above, Article 2 postulates that for the international discipline to be applied, the intended parents and the adoptive child must be resident in different Member States. Although all the EU Member States are parties to the 1993 Hague Convention, outside the European context, about half of the world's countries have never ratified the treaty. In such cases as well as in all the situations not covered by the Convention, the recognition of adoptions pronounced abroad is still entirely subject to domestic legislation unless bilateral agreements exist. Thus, foreign adoptions of children may not be recognised or may be given limited effects in the State where the parents reside, in cases when they do not meet domestic – both substantive and procedural – requirements[14] which, as well as conceptions of public policy, often vary from one country to another.

Under traditional methods of private international law, the recognition of legal parentage established abroad through adoption may prove to be hard given the lack of international or uniform conflict-of-law rules. The application of traditional methods could therefore result in the spread of limping situations.

---

14 Even countries where the 1993 Hague Convention is in force might require additional conditions not provided by the treaty for the recognition of intercountry adoptions. See in this regard the report '20 Years of the 1993 Hague Convention Assessing the Impact of the Convention on Laws and Practices Relating to Intercountry Adoption and the Protection of Children', Preliminary Document No 3 of May 2015, drawn up by the Permanent Bureau for the attention of the Special Commission of June 2015 on the practical operation of the Hague Convention of 29.05.1993 on Protection of Children and Co-operation in Respect of Intercountry Adoption.

This means that a status, though validly acquired under one State's system of private international law, is not recognised as valid under that of another. Such situations are not only undesirable but might also breach the family rights of the people involved.[15]

However, the margin of discretion that States enjoy in regulating family matters remains subject to the limits deriving from human rights law. In this regard, a distinction should be traced between purely internal situations, which fall within the scope of domestic legislation, and cross-border relationships, including both intercountry adoption and situations whereby a State is required to recognise status acquired abroad in accordance with the national legislation of a different country. While, as concerns the former, States are free to decide how to regulate the right to adopt, with regard to the latter, national values concerning for example the protection of traditional family must be balanced against the need to protect the social reality of situations already existing abroad.

This issue was brought before the ECtHR, where the refusal by national authorities to recognise foreign adoption orders was actually challenged on the ground of its incompatibility with the right to family life.

3. THE RIGHT TO THE CONTINUITY OF FAMILY STATUS: SOCIAL REALITY AND LEGITIMATE EXPECTATIONS v. LEGAL RELATIONSHIPS

Notwithstanding their falling within the domain of domestic law, family relationships are also protected under international law by human rights treaties. For example, the 1989 New York Convention, which is focused on minors, emphasises both the importance of the child growing up in a family environment and the role played to that end by intercountry adoption (Article 21(b)). It also places upon party States an obligation to protect family life from any kind of unlawful or arbitrary interference (Article 16). The right of individuals to have their family life protected is also enshrined at the international level in many human rights legal instruments, starting with the 1948 UN Declaration for Human Rights (Articles 12 and 29(2))[16] as well as the International Covenant on Civil and Political Rights (Article 23). In the European context, the same rights are protected by Article 8(1) of the ECHR and by Article 7 of the EU Charter of Fundamental Rights.

---

15 On the impact of human rights considerations on the functioning of PIL mechanisms, see R. Baratta, 'Recognition of Foreign Personal and Family Status: A Rights Based Perspective' (2016) *Rivista di diritto internazionale privato e processuale*, 413.

16 The Declaration was proclaimed by the United Nations General Assembly in in General Assembly Resolution No 217 Paris on 10.12.1948 (UN Doc. A/RES/217 – III). Although the Declaration is not able to produce legally binding effects, its adoption made a fundamental contribution to the promotion of human rights and the adoption of treaties that are modelled on it.

The question is whether these norms also imply an obligation for States to recognise family *status* acquired abroad or, more specifically, if they also enshrine a right to adopt children.

While the right to adopt is not included, as such, among those guaranteed by the ECHR,[17] the relationship between the adoptive parents and the adoptee child is nonetheless considered to be a family tie for the purposes of Article 8.[18] Accordingly, as it was stated for the first time in *Hussin v. Belgium*, the refusal to give effect to a family relation or a *status* legally acquired abroad in principle amounts to an interference with protected rights.[19] Although the judges dismissed the application in the aforementioned case on the ground that the justification given by the State for validating the refusal appeared to be well-founded under the conflict-of-law rules governing the competence to declare a foreign order enforceable, the reasoning of the Court regarding the obligations of State parties in matters of recognition of a family *status* obtained abroad are of utmost importance for tracing the subsequent development of its jurisprudence on the matter.

Some years later, in *Wagner v. Luxembourg*, the Court had to pronounce on whether the failure of Luxembourg authorities to recognise a full adoption order issued by a Peruvian court in favour of a single person as valid in domestic law, which had been justified on the grounds of its allegedly being against public policy, had violated Article 8 of ECHR.[20]

After explaining that *de facto* 'family life' existed between the adoptive mother and the child even in the absence of a legal tie resulting from the enforcement of the foreign order, the judges considered that the refusal to recognise the Peruvian decision amounted to an interference with the right to family life of both the adoptive mother and the child. In assessing whether the interference was in breach of the rights protected by the Convention, the Court followed a consolidated approach. It first verified whether the cumulative conditions provided by Article 8(2) were fulfilled. According to the norm, for a domestic

---

17 In this regard the ECtHR has already explained that this right cannot be inferred from the Convention, in which Article 8 only protects existing relationships. Therefore, States enjoy a broad margin of the discretion concerning the regulation of the requirements for adoption: ECtHR, *Frettè v. France*, No. 36515/97, 26.02.2002, ECHR 2002-I, §29.

18 'It must be pointed out that the adoption orders conferred on the applicants the same rights and obligations in respect of their adopted children as those of a father or mother in respect of a child born in lawful wedlock, while at the same time ending any rights and obligations existing between the adopted children and their biological father or mother or any other person or body': ECtHR, *Pini and Others v. Romania*, Nos. 78028/01 and 78030/01, 22.09.2004, §§140–142, ECHR 2004-V; the same concept was reiterated in more recent cases. See for example *Frettè v. France*, §32 and in the same vein *EB v. France*, in which the Court insisted that 'the provisions of Article 8 do not guarantee either the right to found a family or the right to adopt' [GC] *E.B. v. France*, No. 43546/02, 22.01.2008, §41.

19 ECtHR, *Hussin v. Belgium*, No. 70807/01, 06.05.2004.

20 ECtHR, *Wagner and J.W.M.L. v. Luxembourg, No.* 76240/01, 28.06.2007, ECHR 2007-VII.

restrictive measure to be considered legitimate under the Convention, national authorities should demonstrate that the limitation on the relevant rights was in accordance with the law (or prescribed by the law) as well as necessary in a democratic society and proportionate to the pursuit of specific legitimate aims set out by the treaty. Insofar as family relations are concerned, these include both safeguards for public health and morals and the protection of the fundamental rights of other persons. In *Wagner v. Luxembourg*, the Court first noted that the measure had been taken by French authorities in accordance with the law, namely with Article 367 of the Civil Code. The Article limited full adoption to married couples based on traditional notions of child-raising by a mother and father. However, most European states permit adoption by unmarried persons without any restriction, so that it was hardly proved that the denial of full adoption effects to the Peruvian order was also strictly necessary in a democratic society.

The Court further indicated that in cases involving children, their best interests – including the right to have the most favourable status recognised as well as the protection of their emotional and affective ties – should prevail over all other considerations. It then noted that in allowing the Luxembourg conflict-of-law rules to take precedence over the social reality of the situation, domestic authorities had precluded the adoptive child and her mother from being afforded legal protections granted by the law and from living their daily lives in the absence of insurmountable obstacles. Accordingly, the Court concluded that in the specific case at issue, the Luxembourg courts 'could not reasonably disregard the legal status validly created abroad and corresponding to a family life within the meaning of Article 8 of the Convention'.[21] It then reiterated its view of the Convention as follows:

> a living instrument and must be interpreted in the light of present-day conditions' … the Court considers that the reasons put forward by the national authorities – namely, the strict application, in accordance with the Luxembourg rules on the conflict of laws, of Article 367 of the Civil Code, which permits adoption only by married couples – are not 'sufficient' for the purposes of paragraph 2 of Article 8.[22]

Reference was therefore made to factual elements such as 'de facto family ties', 'day-by-day life' and 'social reality' that should take precedence over the strict application of legal rules in cases when this leads to an unjustified restriction of human rights, particularly when minors' interests are concerned.[23]

---

21 *Wagner v. Luxembourg*, §133.

22 Ibid., §135.

23 The same approach was taken some years later with regard to the recognition of family ties deriving from recourse to surrogacy. In *Paradiso Campanelli v. Italy*, for example, the Court stated that 'la référence à l'ordre public ne saurait toutefois passer pour une carte blanche

The same approach was taken some years later in *Negrepontis-Giannissis v. Greece*, in which the Court considered the compatibility with Article 8 ECHR of the refusal of the Greek authorities to recognise an adoption order made in 1984 by a court in the American state of Michigan in favour of the uncle of a Greek citizen.[24] As the adoptive father was an orthodox bishop, and as such prohibited under Greek canon law from carrying out secular acts, including adoption, the recognition was refused on public policy considerations, which according to the Greek Supreme Court should be understood in Greece as embodying the aforementioned canon rules.

In finding a violation of Article 8, the ECtHR held that the refusal did not answer to a pressing social need. Even in a case when there should have been a legitimate aim worthy of protection, the measure taken by the Greek Supreme Court was disproportionate, as it completely denied the 'social reality' of a relationship that had existed for more than 20 years and which should have been properly considered.

Notwithstanding the differences between the two cases, the decisions of the ECtHR in *Wagner* and *Negrepontis* appear to point to the same conclusion. By making reference to factual elements or situations, the Court clarifies that Article 8 requires that domestic legislation provide a possibility of recognition of a legal parent-child relationships established abroad regardless of their validity under private international law.[25] Such an obligation depends on two main circumstances. The first and most important one is that the situation has been effectively created and actually exists within the legal order of a given country,[26] and has been developed and consolidated during a significant period of time, and the relationship has all the characteristics to be considered as a family tie for the purposes of Article 8.

---

justifiant toute mesure, car l'obligation de prendre en compte l'intérêt supérieur de l'enfant incombe à l'État indépendamment de la nature du lien parental, génétique ou autre' ECtHR [GC], *Paradiso and Campanelli v. Italy*, No. 25358/12, 24.01.2017, §80.

24 ECtHR, *Negrepontis-Giannisis v. Greece*, No. 56759/08, 03.05.2011. For a comment, see P. Franzina, 'Some Remarks on the Relevance of Article 8 of the ECHR to the Recognition of Family Status Judicially Created Abroad', (2011) *Diritti umani e diritto internazionale* 5, 609–16.

25 In the same vein, see the recent Advisory Opinion, delivered upon the request of the French Court of Cassation, regarding the recognition in domestic law of a legal parent-child relationship between a child born through a gestational surrogacy arrangement abroad and the intended mother. ECtHR [GC], Advisory Opinion, No. P16-2018-001, 10.04.2019.

26 In this context, it has been correctly pointed out that 'for this condition to be met, both formal and substantial standards may have to be looked at. In *Wagner* and in *Negrepontis-Giannisis* the ECtHR referred to the fact that the foreign judgments at issue had *validly* created a family relationship in the country of origin and to the fact that each of these relationships had since become a *social reality*': P. Franzina, above n. 24, p. 612. It should be noted however that in *Pini* v. *Romania*, the ECtHR also envisaged the possibility that family life might arise from a 'lawful and genuine adoption order', despite the absence of any affective ties between the adopters (based in Italy) and the adoptees (residing in Romania). Ibid., §148.

Secondly, the recognition of the status should correspond with a legitimate expectation of the people concerned. According to the jurisprudence of the ECtHR, the concept of 'legitimate expectation' includes both that the status was validly acquired abroad without recourse to fraud and that the parties could expect to have their relationship recognised in light of the practice followed in similar cases. This last element clearly emerges from *Wagner*, in which the ECtHR noted that the adoptive mother acted in good faith (in reliance on a previously established practice of Luxembourg courts whereby Peruvian judgments pronouncing full adoption in favour of unmarried women were recognised by operation of law) and had a legitimate expectation of recognition.[27] According to some scholars, legitimacy also depends 'upon the intensity of the links the situation has with the foreign legal system under which the status was acquired'.[28]

The above suggested reading of the jurisprudence of the ECtHR finds support in the reasoning made *a contrario* in cases regarding surrogacy agreements, with particular reference to the recent decision rendered by the Grand Chamber in *Paradiso and Campanelli v. Italy*. The refusal to recognise the relationship between the intended parents and the child was mainly justified on the grounds of the illegality of the couple's conduct, whereby they circumvented Italian legislation which expressly prohibits surrogacy, and had recourse to this practice in Russia. The Italian government moreover alleged that the relation with the child did not possess the characteristics of stability and continuity necessary for it to qualify as a family tie. The Court agreed with the reasons invoked by the State: on the one hand, it rejected the argument made by the parties that a family tie effectively existed between the intended parents and the baby;[29] on the other, with regard to the alleged violation of the right to private life, which entails both the expectation of the intended parents and the right of the child to have his or her status recognised, the Court considered the measure taken by the Italian government as legitimate and proportionate under Article 8(2) of the Convention.[30]

The idea that seems to emerge is that no valid or legitimate expectation of the parties existed in this case that was likely to be perturbed and that might have justified a different conclusion. In a previous stage of the case, notwithstanding that it found that the measure taken by the Italian government violated Article 8

27 *Wagner v. Luxembourg*, §130. For a more in-depth analysis of the last point see *infra*, section 4.

28 P. Kinsch, 'Recognition in the Forum of a Status Acquired Abroad – Private International Law Rules and European Human Rights Law' in K. Boele-Woelki et al. (eds.), *Convergence and Divergence in Private International Law – Liber Amicorum Kurt Siehr*, Eleven International Publishing, The Hague 2010, p. 259–75, specifcally p. 273.

29 In order to reach this conclusion, the Court took into consideration 'the absence of any biological tie between the child and the intended parents, the short duration of the relationship with the child and the uncertainty of the ties from a legal perspective': [GC], *Paradiso and Campanelli*, §157.

30 [GC] *Paradiso and Campanelli v. Italy*, §199–211.

of the Convention, the Chamber noted that because the child had 'undoubtedly developed emotional ties with the foster family with whom he was placed' after being removed from the applicants, the 'finding of a violation in the applicants' case cannot therefore be understood as obliging the State to return the child to them'.[31] In other words, and coherently with the suggested reading, the legitimate expectations to be safeguarded in the case were those of the foster family who took care of the baby and had developed an affective bond with him.

4. RECONCILING HUMAN RIGHTS AND PRIVATE INTERNATIONAL LAW

Notwithstanding that States enjoy a broad margin of appreciation concerning the determination of the requirements that adoptive parents should meet to be eligible for adoption, the above analysis of the jurisprudence of the ECtHR reveals that when it comes to the recognition of a situation that already exists, domestic rules will attract close scrutiny by the Court.

In a situation that is dependent on foreign judgments or that was legally created abroad, the review of the Court on the legitimacy of the State's denial to give it effect will therefore necessary imply a scrutiny of domestic conflict-of-law rules.

The question of the impact of human rights on private international law is not a new one; for many years, both domestic courts and doctrine have explored viable solutions to reconcile these two areas of law.[32] States enjoy broad discretion in the regulation of private international law, particularly in the field of family law, as noted above. The exercise of such discretion cannot override the limits imposed by human rights standards and obligations. A compromise between the two areas must therefore be achieved in situations susceptible to a potential conflict between them.[33]

Such a compromise should be reached by starting from the assumption that private international law and human rights rules somehow pursue similar goals. Ensuring the cross-border continuity of a person's rights and status is one of

---

[31] ECtHR, Second Section, No. 25358/12, *Paradiso and Campanelli v. Italy*, 27.01.2015, §88.

[32] See, inter alia, L. R. Kiestra, *The Impact of the European Convention on Human Rights on Private International Law*, Springer, The Hague 2014; J. J. Fawcett, M. N. Shúilleabháin, and S. Shahm, *Human Rights and Private International Law*, OUP, Oxford 2016; and in this volume, P. Franzina, 'The Place of Human Rights in the Private International Law of the Union in Family Matters'.

[33] In this vein, see P. Kinsch, 'The impact of Human Rights on the Application of Foreign Law and on the Recognition of Foreign Judgments – A Survey of the Cases Decided by European Human Rights Institutions' in T. Einhorn and K. Siehr (eds.), *Intercontinental Cooperation Through Private International Law–Essays in Memory of Peter E. Nygh*, TMC Asser Press, The Hague 2004, p. 197, pp. 202–05; J. J Fawcett et. al., above n. 32, p. 49.

the purposes of conflict-of-law rules, which – as suggested in this book – aim at creating bridges between legal orders and serve as a means of safeguarding family rights under Article 8.[34] The jurisprudence of the ECtHR should not be read as if it points to the 'indiscriminate displacement of conflict of laws rules';[35] rather, the idea that emerges is that a strictly formalistic approach to the question of the recognition of family *status* acquired abroad should be set aside in cases when it results in the complete frustration of legitimate expectations of the persons concerned, with a special regard to situations in which a child's interests are at stake. A right balance of all the concerned interests cannot be struck but on a case-by-case basis.

An analysis of the jurisprudence of the ECtHR moreover suggests that private international law might also synergistically contribute to human rights protection. For example, in *Harroudi v. France*, the Court was called upon to pronounce on the question of whether a French choice-of-law rule giving effect to a prohibition on adoption of the child under the national law was compatible with Article 8.[36] Specifically, the applicant complained of the refusal of domestic courts to grant her a full adoption of an Algerian child that she had taken into her legal care three years previously by way of the Islamic institution of *kafalah*.[37] The refusal was justified on the grounds of the provisions of the French Civil Code, which prohibit full adoption of children in cases where such is not provided by their national law.

On the premise that French law provides the means to alleviate the effects of that prohibition, the Court concluded that 'the respondent State, which seeks to encourage the integration of children of foreign origin without cutting them off immediately from the rules of their country of origin, has shown respect for cultural pluralism and has struck a fair balance between the public interest and that of the applicant'. In other words, the choice-of-law rule under question was regarded as a means of protecting cultural rights while simultaneously providing the child with the possibility of enjoying similar protections to those accorded by the law to adoptive children.[38]

Even if they do not specifically address adoption, it is worth mentioning that in other cases the Court considered that human rights law and conflict-of-law

---

34 In this vein, see Fawcett et al., above n. 32.

35 P. Kinsch, above n. 28, p. 266.

36 ECtHR, *Harroudj v. France*, No. 43631/09, 04.10.2012.

37 On matters regarding the recognition of *kafalah* in European Countries, see A. Lang in this volume.

38 The decision was criticised on the grounds of the deference that the Court 'accords to legal formalism and to the use of rigid juridical 'nationality' as a connecting factor in regulating a child's personal status': J. J. Fawcett et al., above n. 31, p. 775. More generally, on the balance between the need for safeguarding cultural interests and the need to grant a secure parent-child relationship, see E. Bartholet, 'International Adoption: Thoughts on the Human Rights Issues', (2007) *Buffalo Human Rights Law Review* 13, 180, 191–92.

rules can work together towards the same purpose. For example, in most cases regarding child abduction, the return of the child, which is the main object of the 1980 Convention on the Civil Aspects of Child Abduction, was considered as being the means of ensuring the maintenance of family ties with both parents, as well as (more broadly) of responding to the general public interest of protecting the best interests of children, by discouraging future kidnapping.[39]

Also in the case of adoption, the jurisprudence of the ECtHR clearly indicates that human rights law and private international law can support each other in the pursuit of common objectives. Fundamental rights are at the heart of all international rules dealing with international adoption, which are aimed at ensuring that this practice shall never be used as a means of perpetrating human trafficking, abduction, or other forms of exploitation. Accordingly, starting from the 1993 Hague Convention on Intercountry Adoption, international rules require that the recognition of adoption orders is subject to a procedure that ensures minors' protection against all possible forms of abuse with a view to granting children the possibility of growing up in a wholesome family environment. Moreover, as indicated in the 2008 European Convention on the Adoption of Children, international rules also insist on the importance of perceiving adoption as a last resort for resolving cases whereby there are no alternative options for providing a child with a family. In accordance with the goals pursued, international rules also recognise the need to seek the opinion of the child of a sufficient age and maturity,[40] as well as the necessity that the adoption order is pronounced by a competent entrusted authority acting in compliance of fundamental procedural safeguards.

The promotion of minors' best interests, which is a shared goal of both human rights and private international law, not only requires that they be granted protection against abuses, but also the right to have their family ties recognised and protected by the State. This does not necessarily postulate an obligation to recognise all of the legal effects of adoption orders. Rather, it points to a duty to ensure that the child is not deprived of family situations or relationships duly

---

39 On this issue see in this volume, R. Lamont.

40 The 1967 Convention did not take a strong position on the child's consent to an adoption (see Articles 5 and 9(9)(f)). The right of the child to be heard is rather protected by all international treaties concerning children's rights: see Article 12 of the 1989 New York Convention; Article 3(b) of the European Convention on the Exercise of Children's Rights (1996, ETS No. 160); Article 4(d) of the 1993 Hague Convention on Inter-Country Adoption; Article 13 of the 1980 Convention on the Civil Aspects of International Child Abduction; Article 23 of the Convention of 19.10.1996 on Jurisdiction, Applicable Law, Recognition, Enforcement and Cooperation in Respect of Parental Responsibility and Measures for the Protection of Children. Within the EU context, also see Article 24(1) of the Charter of Fundamental Rights of the EU (2012/C 326/02) and Article 11(2) of the Regulation (EC) 2201/2003 (see, in this volume, L. Carpaneto).

established abroad that contribute to the development of his/her personality. The refusal to recognise an existing parent-child link arising from a foreign adoption should be pronounced only after a careful assessment of the situation. Furthermore, the impact of restrictive national measures on the right of children to have their identity guaranteed must be assessed, in addition to the legitimate expectation that the social reality of their emotional bonds is safeguarded. As was recently pointed out by the ECtHR in its Advisory Opinion of 10 April 2019: 'Article 8 of the Convention does not impose a general obligation on States to recognise *ab initio* a parent-child relationship ... What the child's best interests – which must be assessed primarily *in concreto* rather than *in abstracto* – require is for recognition of that relationship, legally established abroad, to be possible at the latest when it has become a practical reality. It is in principle not for the Court but first and foremost for the national authorities to assess whether and when, in the concrete circumstances of the case, the said relationship has become a practical reality' (*ivi*, para. 52).[41]

A human rights-based attitude to private international law should therefore necessarily imply rethinking traditional methods based on strict applications of conflict-of-law rules in favour of a more flexible approach to the recognition of *status* acquired abroad.[42] As suggested by the relevant literature, to settle possible normative conflicts, private international law 'should be shaped and understood as a means to pursue the fundamental rights of the individuals concerned'.[43] Positive obligations descending from human rights treaties and Article 8 ECHR do not in fact entail a general duty for the State to remove all obstacles to recognition, but rather an obligation to 'forge its PIL provisions so as to make them *result-oriented*'.[44] This means that domestic legislation should be able to ensure that, far from being the results of an automatic and rigid application of internal rules, decisions on recognition should be the results of a careful assessment of all the interests involved.

41 Above n. 25.

42 It has been correctly suggested in this regard that, according to this approach, public policy could be for example conceived – and applied – as a means of providing private international law with the inherent flexibility to ensure the protection of human rights: F. Salerno, 'Il vincolo al rispetto dei diritti dell'uomo nel sistema delle fonti del diritto internazionale privato', (2014) *Diritti umani e diritto internazionale*, 549.

43 In this context, see R. Baratta, above n. 15, p. 426 ff.

44 Ibid.; for an assessment of possible solutions, see P. Lagarde, 'La reconnaissance, mode d'emploi' in *Vers de noveaux équilibres entre ordre juridiques, Liber Amicorum Héléne Guaudemet-Tallon*, Paris, Dalloz 2008, p. 481; I. Thoma, 'The ECHR and the *Ordre Public* Exception in Private International Law', (2011) *Netherlands International Privaatrecht (NIPR)*, 13; P. Kinsch, above n. 27, 273 ff.

PROTECTING CHILDREN'S RIGHTS AFTER CHILD ABDUCTION

The Interaction of the CJEU and ECtHR in Interpreting Brussels II *bis*

Ruth LAMONT

1. Introduction 225
2. International Child Abduction: The Legal Framework within the EU 226
   2.1. Protecting Children's Rights 226
   2.2. Remedying Child Abduction 228
3. Protecting Children's Rights on Child Abduction in the Supranational Courts.. 231
   3.1. Child Abduction and Children's Rights in the CJEU and ECtHR 231
   3.2. The Role of Supranational Courts in Applying Children's Rights ... 240
4. Conclusions.. 242

1. INTRODUCTION

International parental child abduction represents a fundamental breakdown of family relationships. It has the potential to severely affect or destroy the relationship between the child and one parent, and to affect the child's welfare into adulthood.[1] As the subject of child abduction proceedings, the child's rights should be protected, particularly their right to have decisions taken in their best interests, and their right to be heard in decisions affecting their interests.[2]

In the European Union (EU), the Hague Convention on the Civil Aspects of International Child Abduction 1980 (Hague Abduction Convention) and the

---

1 M. FREEMAN, 'Parental Child Abduction: The Long Term Effects' (2015) *International Family Law*, 54, 57.

2 Article 3(1) and Article 12 CRC.

Brussels II*a* Regulation[3] both seek to remedy an abduction by returning the child to their habitual residence prior to the abduction. Despite the importance of protecting the rights of abducted children, the law on child abduction does not make direct reference to the best interests of the child. The interpretation and application of the return remedy and the protection of children's rights in this context has been subject to litigation in the two supranational European courts: the European Court of Human Rights (ECtHR), and the Court of Justice of the European Union (CJEU). This chapter will explore the problems and challenges that have developed in the jurisprudence of these two supranational courts in attempting to protect children's rights on child abduction. In particular, the patchwork of children's rights instruments and the relationship between the ECtHR and the CJEU have resulted in inconsistencies in approach. It will be suggested that the supranational context is a difficult environment to further develop children's rights, given the spatial and temporal distance of the courts from the dispute. Whilst these courts are important to the promotion of children's rights, it will be suggested that the domestic courts remain the key forum for the protection of children's rights on child abduction.

The first section will examine the children's rights framework and the range of children's rights instruments applied within Europe. The legal framework remedying international child abduction within the EU will also be outlined. The key case law of the ECtHR and the CJEU will be analysed in the third section for their interpretation and application of children's rights on child abduction.

2. INTERNATIONAL CHILD ABDUCTION: THE LEGAL FRAMEWORK WITHIN THE EU

2.1. PROTECTING CHILDREN'S RIGHTS[4]

Children living in Europe are formally protected by, and derive rights from, a number of rights documents binding on the Member States of the EU: the European Convention on Human Rights 1950 (ECHR), the UN Convention on the Rights of the Child 1990 (CRC), and the EU Charter of Fundamental Rights 2012 (Charter).[5] Each of these documents protects children's rights, although the nature, scope and enforceability of the rights vary.

3 Council Regulation (EC) 2201/2003 of 27 November 2003 concerning jurisdiction and the recognition and enforcement of judgments in matrimonial matters and the matters of parental responsibility (2003) OJ L338.

4 For more detail see H. Stalford, *Children and the European Union*, Hart, Oxford 2012.

5 Charter of Fundamental Rights of the European Union (2012) OJ C 326/391.

All EU Member States are signatories to the ECHR, although the EU is not a signatory at the current time.[6] The ECHR is not a children's rights document and does not address children directly. However, as a 'living instrument', the European Court of Human Rights (ECtHR) has sought to interpret the Convention, and particularly Article 8(1), the right to respect for private and family life, in accordance with children's rights.[7] The ECtHR will attach particular importance to the best interests of the child as a primary consideration in determining the balance of rights between family members under Article 8 ECHR.[8] There is increasing evidence of a child-centred approach emerging in the ECtHR, as it shows greater willingness to refer to other, more child-centred instruments, such as the CRC.[9] Where judicial remedies have been exhausted in the national courts, individuals may petition the ECtHR alleging a breach by the State of their rights under the ECHR.

The CRC is a global rights document drafted by the United Nations, specifically directed at protecting and promoting children's rights. It is a comprehensive document containing a broad range of rights interpreted with guidance from the UN Committee on the Rights of the Child which also monitors the performance of State parties in compliance with the rights protected. All EU Member States are parties to the CRC.[10] There are four core principles in the CRC forming the basis of interpretation of the other rights in the Convention: the child's right to life, survival and development,[11] non-discrimination,[12] promotion of the best interests of the child,[13] and respect for the views of the child.[14] The CRC also protects children from illicit transfer and non-return from abroad,[15] requires State parties to take measures against child abduction,[16] and protects the right of the child to have a relationship with both parents, unless this is contrary to their best interests.[17] The CRC may be justiciable in the national courts of the Member State, and there is an

---

6 Accession under Article 6(2) of the Treaty on European Union (TEU) has been prevented by the CJEU in Opinion 2/13, ECLI:EU:C:2014:2454.

7 See U. Kilkelly, *The Child and the European Convention on Human Rights*, Ashgate, Farnham 1999.

8 ECtHR, *Johansen v. Norway*, No. 17383/90, 17.01.1995, paras. 23–33, 1996-III.

9 A. F. Jacobsen, 'Children's Rights in the European Court of Human Rights: An Emerging Power Structure' (2016) 24 *International Journal of Children's Rights*, 548, 545.

10 The UK is a signatory to the Convention, but has not ratified it, though the Supreme Court has indicated that it is a source of guidance in interpretation of provisions affecting children where Article 8 ECHR is engaged: see *ZH (Tanzania) v. Secretary of State for the Home Department* (2011) UKSC 4.

11 Article 6 CRC.

12 Article 2 CRC.

13 Article 3(1) CRC.

14 Article 12 CRC.

15 Article 11 CRC.

16 Article 35 CRC.

17 Article 9 CRC.

individual complaints procedure to the Committee.[18] Both the CJEU[19] and the ECtHR[20] have referred to the CRC in judgments as a source of guidance and interpretation in considering children's rights in the context of the ECHR or the Charter.

The rights expressed in the CRC are to some extent reflected in the EU Charter. Article 24 of the Charter specifically protects children's rights, protecting the right of the child to be heard in decisions affecting them where the child is of an appropriate age and maturity; the right of the child to have decisions made in his or her best interests; and the right of the child to have contact with both parents, unless this is contrary to their best interests. This is an unusual mixture of rights that do not exactly reflect the core principles of the CRC, but are a specific recognition of children's rights in the cross-border context.[21] The protection of the child's right to maintain a relationship with both parents reflects concerns generated by the free movement of persons disrupting family relationships across national borders. This right in particular has been referred to by the CJEU in its judgments on cases of international child abduction.[22] Article 7 of the Charter also protects the right to respect for private and family life in the same terms of Article 8 ECHR.[23] The Charter applies when the Member States are implementing EU law,[24] limiting the applicability of Article 24 to cases where European law is engaged.

The framework for children's rights protection is multi-layered and the applicable rights may vary depending on whether national law or EU law is engaged. There is significant potential for the development of arguments based on the protection of the rights of a child, but this form of reasoning is only beginning to develop in the supranational courts. International child abduction is one context in which rights have been used to question and potentially disrupt the existing legal frameworks in pursuit of compliance with children's rights obligations.

2.2. REMEDYING CHILD ABDUCTION

The legal framework governing child abduction between Member States of the EU is a combination of EU law and international law. The Hague Convention

---

18 Rules of Procedure under the Optional Protocol to the Convention on the Rights of the Child on a communications procedure, 2013. Available at <http:/www.ohchr.org/EN/HRBodies/CRC/Pages/CRCIndex.aspx> accessed 10.10.18.

19 Case C-540/03, *European Parliament v. Council*, ECLI:EU:C:2008:85, para. 39.

20 ECtHR, *X, Y and Z v. United Kingdom*, No. 21830/93, 22.04.1997, para. 24, 1997-II.

21 R. Lamont, 'Article 24' in S. Peers et al. (eds) *The EU Charter of Fundamental Rights: A Commentary*', Hart, Oxford 2014.

22 Case C-403/09 PPU, *Jasna Detiček v. Maurizio Sgueglia*, ECLI:EU:C:2009:810, para. 53.

23 Article 52(3) of the Charter states that the meaning and scope of rights reflected in the ECHR are the same, unless the EU provides a greater level of protection.

24 Article 51(1) of the Charter.

on the Civil Aspects of International Child Abduction 1980 (Hague Abduction Convention 1980) aims to ensure that a child that has been wrongfully removed or retained from their habitual residence[25] is returned[26] as quickly as possible to their home State. This remedy of return is subject to limited exceptions within the Convention, including the objections of the child to return and return placing the child at grave risk of physical or psychological harm.[27] This Convention is global in scope, and is generally regarded as highly successful in responding to the difficult situation arising after a child has been unlawfully removed or retained by limiting the role of the court in the country where the child is now present to deciding whether to return the child or not. This approach effectively limits the conflicts between substantive national laws regarding custody and access to the child since the focus is on whether the child should be returned or not, and the circumstances in which return may be refused are highly circumscribed. In only 12% of cases globally is return of the child refused following a summary judicial hearing.[28]

Despite the existence of the Hague Abduction Convention 1980, the law was supplemented by the EU in the Brussels II *bis* Regulation.[29] This Regulation governs jurisdiction and recognition of judgments over divorce and parental responsibility disputes within the EU. As one aspect of the issues relating to parental responsibility, the EU sought to regulate the situation where a child was abducted between two EU Member States. It was suggested that, as a consequence of the free movement of persons within the European space, it would be a more common problem between the Member States that should attract a specific legal framework within the EU.[30] However, the Hague Abduction Convention's return remedy remains the remedy where a child has been unlawfully removed or retained between two EU Member States.[31] The Brussels II *bis* Regulation contains rules to modify the operation of the Convention, notably requiring Member States to hear the child during return proceedings if they are old and mature enough,[32] which is not an obligation of the Hague Abduction Convention 1980, although the child's objections to returning to their habitual residence may form the basis for the refusal of a return application.[33]

---

25 Article 3, Hague Abduction Convention 1980.

26 Article 12, Hague Abduction Convention 1980.

27 Article 13, Hague Abduction Convention 1980.

28 N. Lowe and V. Stephens, 'A Statistical Analysis of Applications Made in 2015 under the Hague Convention on the Civil Aspects of International Child Abduction – Global Report' available at <https://assets.hcch.net/docs/d0b285f1-5f59-41a6-ad83-8b5cf7a784ce.pdf>.

29 Council Regulation (EC) 2201/2003 concerning jurisdiction and the recognition and enforcement of judgments in matrimonial matters and the matters of parental responsibility, repealing Regulation 1347/2000, (2003) OJ L338.

30 See P. McEleavy, 'The Brussels II *bis* Regulation: How the European Community has Moved into Family Law' (2002) 51 *International and Comparative Law Quarterly*, 883.

31 Article 11(1), Brussels II *bis*.

32 Article 11(2), Brussels II *bis*.

33 Article 13(2), Hague Abduction Convention 1980.

In addition, where the return of the child is initially refused, under the Brussels II *bis* Regulation, the court with jurisdiction in the child's habitual residence prior to the abduction has the opportunity to determine whether the child should be returned home, despite the initial refusal, in a substantive hearing to determine the child's welfare.[34] If the return of the child is ordered following this substantive hearing and the judgment is certified, the judgment is automatically enforceable in the State to which the child was abducted.[35] This mechanism has caused some controversy, given the ability of the court in the child's habitual residence to effectively override the initial refusal to return the child, and the fact that no defence to enforcement of this judgment is available.[36] In Case C-491/10 PPU *Aguirre-Zarraga*, despite the child's objections to returning to Spain from Germany, the Spanish court ordered the child's return in a full custody hearing. The German court sought to refuse enforcement of the judgment on the ground of non-compliance with Article 24 of the Charter and the obligation to hear a child in proceedings, but as no defence is available to enforcement, the CJEU found that the custody order would have to be appealed in Spain to prevent return.

The process of returning the child is widely regarded as a successful method of resolving cases of child abduction. It avoids conflicts of jurisdiction over the child by awarding primacy to the country of the child's habitual residence,[37] presuming that the majority of evidence remains in that jurisdiction and that this is the place of the child's 'home'. The use of only summary proceedings, focused only on whether the conditions for return are made out, rather than on the overall welfare of the child, mean that a wider assessment of the best interests of the child is not possible or desirable in the forum of refuge. The aim is to enable the courts in the State to which the child has been abducted to act quickly to restore the environment prior to the abduction. The presumption that the child will be returned, and the circumstances in which the child will not be returned are highly restrictive, further reinforcing this aim. The exceptions to return under Articles 12 and 13 of the Hague Abduction Convention 1980 are designed to reflect circumstances where the child's rights would otherwise be at risk or infringed, for example, where there is a serious risk of harm to the child on return.[38] The principle of returning the child in almost all cases is also said to deter other parents from abduction by restoring the *status quo*. The reality is often that most parents are unaware of the restrictions on moving their child abroad without the appropriate permissions, and the existence of the Hague

---

34 Articles 11(6)–(8), Brussels II *bis*.

35 Article 42(2), Brussels II *bis*.

36 Case C-491/10 PPU, *Aguirre-Zarraga v. Simone Pelz*, ECLI:EU:C:2010:828.

37 Article 10, Brussels II *bis* defines when jurisdiction is transferred from the court of the child's habitual residence following a refusal to return the child.

38 R. Schuz, *The Hague Child Abduction Convention: A Critical Analysis*, Hart, Oxford 2013, p. 26.

Abduction Convention 1980 and the return remedy come as a severe shock to the abducting parent.

The Hague Abduction Convention 1980 states that a child should not be returned in breach of their fundamental rights under Article 20, although this provision is rarely used.[39] Recital 33 of the Brussels II *bis* Regulation states that the Regulation … seeks to ensure respect for fundamental rights of the child as set out in Article 24, Charter.' The operation of the return remedy will always represent a potential breach of the right to respect for private and family life since the child will be returned to their habitual residence and there is no obligation on the abducting parent to return with them, affecting the relationship. The summary nature of return proceedings is specifically designed to avoid a full assessment of the best interests of the child and their circumstances prior to the abduction in any court other than that of their habitual residence. The breach in the relationship between the child and the left behind parent anticipated by the Convention is intended to be remedied by the return remedy, although in some circumstances undertakings or orders may be made to restrict contact on return.[40] The return remedy is designed to secure the best interests of the child without an individualised assessment of the child's circumstances, apart from those falling within the specific exceptions to return.[41] It is to some extent assumed that an almost automatic process of return will secure the best interests of the child. This approach has been questioned, for example, where there are allegations of domestic violence against the father seeking the return of a child.[42] The limitations of the return remedy in assessing individual circumstances of children would appear inimical to the best interests of the child and the protections provided by the CRC and the Charter.

3. PROTECTING CHILDREN'S RIGHTS ON CHILD ABDUCTION IN THE SUPRANATIONAL COURTS

3.1. CHILD ABDUCTION AND CHILDREN'S RIGHTS IN THE CJEU AND ECtHR

Cases of child abduction have been referred to both the ECtHR and the CJEU to consider whether the rights of children have been infringed in a range of

39 Ibid., p. 79.

40 Article 11(4), Brussels II *bis*.

41 V. Stephens and N. Lowe, 'Children's Welfare and Human Rights under the 1980 Hague Abduction Convention – the Ruling in *Re E*' (2012) 34:1 *Journal of Social Welfare and Family Law*, 125, 128.

42 M. Weiner, 'International Child Abduction and the Escape from Domestic Violence' (2000) 69 *Fordham Law Review*, 593, 706.

circumstances. The ECtHR has heard petitions from individuals involved in return proceedings alleging various breaches by the State of their rights under the ECHR. The CJEU has heard cases referred under the preliminary reference procedure regarding the interpretation of the provisions of Brussels II *bis*,[43] including compliance with the terms of the Charter. The two courts have adopted different approaches to assessing children's rights in the context of child abduction, with the ECtHR initially prepared to encourage consideration of the individual child's circumstances, and the CJEU seeking to reinforce the application of the return remedy.

In *Maumousseau v. France*,[44] the ECtHR heard the case of a child retained from the USA in France. The French court ordered the return of the child to the USA, but enforcement of the order was physically resisted. It was argued that enforcement of the decision by the French State authorities would breach the mother and child's Article 8 ECHR rights by affecting their relationship. This is indubitably the case, but the ECtHR regarded the breach of Article 8 through enforcement of the return remedy as being justified by the need to restore the relationship with the left behind parent in the USA. The Court stated that it was … entirely in agreement with the philosophy underlying the Hague Convention.[45] It regarded the return remedy as a proportionate response to child abduction and the enforcement of the return remedy as necessary to protect the right of the child to a relationship with both parents, and to vindicate the Article 8 ECHR rights of the left behind parent. The State was under a positive obligation under Article 8 ECHR to take expeditious measures to ensure reunification of the child with their parent through rapid consideration of the application for return and enforcement if an order is made.[46]

By contrast, and more controversially, the ECtHR in *Neulinger v. Switzerland*[47] appeared to suggest that, despite the summary nature of the return proceedings, consideration had to be given to the individual child's welfare in the context of the Hague Abduction Convention 1980. In this case, a child had been removed from Israel to Switzerland by his mother, who was concerned that his father would raise him in an ultra-orthodox Jewish community. The father succeeded on appeal in obtaining an order for the return of the child. The mother and child argued that the return would cause the child severe psychological harm and enforcement of the order would represent a breach of Article 8 ECHR. The ECtHR upheld the complaint on the grounds that return could not be

---

43 Article 267 of the Consolidated Version of the Treaty on the Functioning of the European Union (2012) OJ C 326/1.

44 ECtHR, *Maumousseau and Washington v. France*, No. 39388/05, 06.12.2007.

45 Ibid., para. 69.

46 ECtHR, *Iosub Caras v. Romania*, No. 7198/04, 27 July 2006; *Raban v. Romania*, No. 25437/08, 26.10.2010.

47 ECtHR, *Neulinger and Shuruk v. Switzerland*, No. 41615/07, 06.07.2010.

automatic on the application of the Hague Abduction Convention 1980,[48] and the child's best interests had to be assessed by the domestic authorities in each case.[49] Return in this case would be harmful to the child and was not in his best interests, so enforcement of the order would be in breach of Article 8 ECHR. The Court stated that:

> ... an in-depth examination of the entire family situation and of a whole series of factors, in particular of a factual, emotional, psychological, material and medical nature ... with a constant concern for determining what the best solution would be for the abducted child ...

was required for the domestic authorities to be in compliance with Article 8 ECHR.[50] This element of the judgment caused significant concern since it suggested that a fully individualised welfare assessment was required before a return order could be issued, contrary to the underlying approach of the Hague Abduction Convention 1980.[51] The ECtHR seemed prepared to abandon the enforcement of a return order where delay and circumstances affected the child's best interests, irrespective of whether an exception to return had been made out before the domestic court. Anxiety was expressed over whether the normal approach to summary proceedings in Hague Abduction Convention 1980 cases was compliant with Article 8 ECHR.[52]

However, the ECtHR subsequently retreated from the controversial implications of the judgment in *Neulinger* in *X. v. Latvia*.[53] The mother was a Latvian national who was living in Australia and unlawfully removed her daughter to Latvia. She argued that returning the child to Australia would cause severe psychological harm, contrary to Article 13(b) of the Hague Abduction Convention 1980, and that the Latvian authorities had not taken the circumstances into account fully, failing to consider relevant reports on the child's psychological state and of the father's mistreatment of the mother in Australia. The Court upheld these failures in the domestic court's application of the Convention as a breach of Article 8 ECHR. The factors capable of constituting an exception to return under Article 13 Hague Child Abduction

48 Ibid., paras. 137–138.

49 Ibid., para. 139.

50 Ibid., para. 39.

51 L. Walker and P. Beaumont, 'Shifting the Balance Achieved by the Abduction Convention: The Contrasting Approaches of the European Court of Human Rights and the Court of Justice', (2011) 7 *Journal of Private International Law*, 231, 233.

52 V. Stephens and N. Lowe, 'Children's Welfare and Human Rights under the 1980 Hague Abduction Convention – the Ruling in *Re E*', (2012) 34:1 *Journal of Social Welfare and Family Law*, 125, 129. In the English courts see *Re E (Children)(Abduction) (Custody Appeal)* (2011) UKSC 27.

53 ECtHR, *Neulinger* in *X v. Latvia*, No. 27853/09, 26.11.2011.

Convention 1980 must be considered by the domestic court in the light of the best interests of the child as a primary consideration in the light of Article 8 ECHR, and give reasons for the decision made. The mother had suffered a disproportionate interference with her right to respect for her family life because there was a failure in the procedural guarantees of Article 8 ECHR. The ECtHR made it clear that it was the responsibility of the domestic court to consider any safeguards available for the child on return.

In its judgment in *X. v. Latvia*, the ECtHR also took the opportunity to consider the effect of the judgment in *Neulinger*, stating that:

> ... the Court considers it opportune to clarify that its finding in the *Neulinger* judgment does not in itself set out any principle for the application of the Hague Convention by the domestic court.[54]

Despite the suggestion that the individual child's welfare should be the focus of all return applications, the ECtHR in *X. v. Latvia* restricts these considerations to the exceptions to return already in existence in the Hague Abduction Convention 1980, in accordance with the normal approach to such applications. The Court has subsequently reiterated that the overall framework of the Hague Abduction Convention 1980 itself is compliant with the ECHR, but that the Convention must be correctly interpreted and applied by the domestic court to avoid a breach of Article 8 ECHR. In *Ferrari v. Romania*,[55] the ECtHR considered that a harmonious interpretation of the Hague Abduction Convention 1980 and the ECHR could be maintained if the exceptions to return are genuinely considered and reasons are given in accepting or rejecting an exception when it is argued before the domestic court. The factors forming the basis of the argued exception to return have to be assessed in the light of Article 8 ECHR and the primary consideration of the child's best interests. This attaches great importance to the role of the exceptions to return as a protection against the automatic issuance and enforcement of return orders, making the order proportionate, even though it potentially affects one parent's relationship with their child.

This approach was most recently reiterated by the ECtHR in *Severe v. Austria*[56] following an abduction from France to Austria. The father had not seen his twin sons for more than seven years. The Court considered that the decisive issue was whether domestic courts in choosing and implementing enforcement measures had struck a fair balance between the child, the parents and public order, taking account of the best interests of the child as a primary consideration.[57] In taking this approach, it referred to the obligation under the

---

[54] Ibid., para. 105.

[55] ECtHR, *Ferrari v. Romania*, No. 1714/10, 28.04.2010.

[56] ECtHR, *Severe v. Austria*, No. 53661/15, 21.09.2017.

[57] Ibid., para. 101.

CRC to attach primary importance to the best interests of the child.[58] Whilst in this case the return order and first attempt at enforcement were expeditious, it subsequently took the Austrian courts over five years to decide against the enforcement of the return order. The change in circumstances affecting the children was primarily determined by the passage of time and was attributable to the conduct of the Austrian authorities in breach of the father's Article 8 ECHR rights.[59] However, given the change in circumstances, it was not appropriate to impose an obligation to return the children to France, but the Austrian authorities were obligated to address the breach of Article 8 ECHR.[60]

In its judgments considering the impacts of the Hague Abduction Convention 1980, the ECtHR has emphasised the primary importance of the child's best interests in decision-making in child abduction cases. This is potentially highly disruptive to the underlying philosophy of the Convention, as illustrated by the anxieties surrounding the *Neulinger* judgment, where the individual best interests of the child appeared to be emphasised over the enforcement of an order to return the child. The Court has adopted the position that the Convention as a whole is compliant with the ECHR and protects children's rights on child abduction, if it is correctly applied and the exceptions to return are given their true role in allowing for consideration of the child's individual circumstances and welfare. This can be difficult for the returning court to achieve in a summary hearing, with limited evidence and arguments that protection will be more effectively provided when the child is returned, particularly where the existence of a grave risk of harm to the child is suggested. The highly restrictive interpretation of Article 13(b), Hague Child Abduction Convention 1980 and the emphasis on returning children as a deterrence and to enable consideration of welfare in the habitual residence court could also undermine this approach. However, it is a realistic approach where individual welfare assessments between countries may vary significantly and the abduction occurred only a short time before the return application is heard.[61] It does however intimate a more nuanced and considered approach to the interpretation of the Convention in the light of children's rights and, in particular, the importance attached to the primacy of the child's best interests.

The approach of the ECtHR may be contrasted with that of the CJEU.[62] Despite the specific protection for children made available in the EU Charter under Article 24, the CJEU has proved much less willing to focus on child

---

58 Ibid., para. 99.

59 Ibid., para. 166.

60 Ibid., para. 122.

61 R. Schuz, 'The Hague Abduction Convention and Children's Rights Revisited', (2012) *International Family Law*, 35, 36.

62 For more detail see: L. Walker and P. Beaumont, 'Shifting the Balance Achieved by the Abduction Convention: The Contrasting Approaches of the European Court of Human Rights and the Court of Justice', (2011) 7 *Journal of Private International Law*, 231.

welfare and autonomy. The CJEU has been asked in a number of preliminary references to consider the interpretation of the child abduction rules contained within Brussels II*a* and the impact of Article 24 of the Charter on these rules. The focus of the CJEU has been on Article 24(3) of the Charter, the right of the child to have a relationship with both parents, rather than on the right of the child to have decisions made in their best interests, or the right of the child to be heard in decisions affecting their interests.

In Case C-403/09 PPU *Detiček v. Sgueglia*,[63] the child was removed in breach of a custody order from Italy to Slovakia by her mother. The mother issued proceedings in Slovakia to obtain custody of the child, but the father sought to enforce the Italian custody order in Slovakia. The mother argued that the child would face severe psychological harm on return to Italy and the child had expressed a wish to remain in Slovakia with her mother. The CJEU was asked whether the Slovakian court could use emergency protective measures[64] to prevent the return of the child to Italy. The Court emphasised the obligation in the EU legal order of mutual recognition of judgments between Member States and the trust that exists between the Member States' legal systems. The Slovakian court could not use emergency measures to prevent the enforcement of the Italian custody judgment and the return of the child to Italy. In considering the impact of Article 24 of the Charter, the CJEU emphasised Article 24(3) and the right of the child to have a relationship with both parents,[65] unless there are '... objective considerations relating to the actual person of the child and his or her social environment ...'.[66] These considerations should be deliberated by the court with jurisdiction, in this case the Italian court. The CJEU did not consider in detail the fact that the child had objected to being sent back to Italy, despite the guarantees in Article 24(1) of the Charter, and the child's situation was considered in the context of the parental relationship.

The emphasis on mutual trust between the Member States and the allocation of jurisdiction was again in evidence in Case C-491/10 PPU *Aguirre-Zarraga v. Pelz*.[67] The child had been retained by her mother in Germany from her father in Spain. The German court refused to return the child to Spain because of her objections to returning to Spain under Article 13(2) of the Hague Abduction Convention 1980. The father issued proceedings for a full custody hearing in Spain under Articles 11(6)–(8), Brussels II*a*. In the course of the Spanish proceedings the child was offered the opportunity to be heard by the court but was not in fact heard. The Spanish court in giving judgment on custody ordered

63 ECLI:EU:C:2009:810.
64 Article 20, Brussels II*a*.
65 Ibid., para. 59.
66 Ibid., para. 60.
67 ECLI:EU:C:2010:828.

the return of the child from Germany under Article 11(8) of the Brussels II*a*. This judgment was automatically enforceable,[68] but the German court sought to resist enforcement on the grounds that Article 24(1) of the Charter had been breached and the child had not been heard in the Spanish proceedings. The CJEU rejected this argument, stating that any appeal against the Spanish order should be heard in the court with jurisdiction.[69] In relation to the right of the child to be heard, the CJEU stated that the Spanish court, as the court with jurisdiction, held responsibility for protecting this right.[70] The Court argued:

> … the systems for recognition and enforcement of judgments handed down in a Member State which are established by that regulation are based on the principle of mutual trust between Member States in the fact that their respective national legal systems are capable of providing an equivalent and effective protection of fundamental rights, recognised at European Union level, in particular, in the Charter of Fundamental Rights.[71]

The Brussels II*a* Regulation has recently been recast, with the new Regulation 2019/111 applying from 2022, but there is unlikely to be any shift in the importance attached to return of abducted children between the Member States in the interpretation of the new Regulation.[72]

The ECtHR and the CJEU both considered the child abduction framework in the same factual circumstances in the case of *Povse*. The CJEU heard a preliminary reference from the Austrian courts in Case C-211/10 PPU *Povse*[73] regarding the return of a child removed from Italy to Austria by her mother and the enforcement of an Italian custody judgment favouring the left behind father. In interpreting the provisions of Brussels II*a*, the CJEU again emphasised the importance of Article 24(3) of the Charter over concerns relating to the child's best interests given changed circumstances since the abduction:

> … the importance of delivering a court judgment on the final custody of the child that is fair and soundly based, the need to deter child abduction, and the child's right to maintain on a regular basis a personal relationship and direct contact with

68 Article 42, Brussels II*a*.
69 Ibid., para. 69.
70 Ibid., para. 66.
71 Ibid., para. 70.
72 European Commission proposal for a Council Regulation on jurisdiction, the recognition and enforcement of decisions in matrimonial matters and the matters of parental responsibility, and on international child abduction COM (2016) 411 final, 30.06.2016. Council Regulation 2019/1111 on jurisdiction, the recognition and enforcement of decisions in matrimonial matters and the matters of parental responsibility, and on international child abduction (recast) [2019] OJ L178/1, 02.07.2019.
73 Case C-211/10, *Doris Povse v. Mauro Alpago*, ECLI:EU:C:2010:400.

> both parents, take precedence over any disadvantages moving [from Austria to Italy] might entail.[74]

Subsequent to the abduction, the mother had formed a further relationship and had another child, the child subject to proceedings had lost her Italian language skills and had had no meaningful contact with the father. Following the CJEU judgment which required the return of the child to Italy, the mother resisted the enforcement of the return order and argued that the Austrian courts were breaching her Article 8 ECHR right in seeking to enforce the order.[75] She petitioned the ECtHR on the grounds that the substantial time delays in decision-making, now nearly seven years, meant that the circumstances had changed for the child to such an extent that it was contrary to her best interests to enforce her return to her father in Italy. The ECtHR considered the fact that the CJEU had already examined the mother's application and the Austrian court's interpretation of the Brussels II*a* provisions.[76] The Austrian court was complying with the mandatory requirements of European law and was not therefore in breach of Article 8 ECHR in enforcing the return order, despite the changed circumstances of the child. The protection of children's rights is restricted in both courts to considering in which national court the rights should be vindicated, rather than interrogating the substantial elements of the application in the light of the best interests of the child.[77]

The ECtHR approach in *Povse* minimised the impact of changing circumstances subsequent to the abduction on the child and their best interests. The fact that the CJEU had previously considered the case and the Brussels II*a* Regulation required enforcement of the custody judgment shielded the Austrian courts from a full review by the ECtHR. The ECtHR assumed that the CJEU judgment and interpretation of the Brussels II*a* Regulation was compliant with human rights obligations because of the existence of the Charter. However, the Charter was used to justify the strict interpretation of the Regulation and obligations to enforce judgments and return the child. Rather than considering the impact of the passage of time on the child's best interests, the focus of the CJEU was on the right of the child to a relationship with both parents. The ECtHR has accepted that change of circumstances over time may constitute a breach of Article 8 ECHR where the national authorities fail to implement and enforce return orders expeditiously. However, return may

---

74 Ibid., para. 63.

75 ECtHR, *MA/Sofia Povse* and *Doris Povse v. Austria*, No. 3890/11.

76 ECtHR, *Bosphorous Hava Yollari Turizm ve Ticaret Anonim Sirketi v. Ireland*, No. 45036/11, 30.06.2005, 2005-VI.

77 R. Lamont, 'Commentary on *Povse v. Austria*' in H. Stalford, K. Hollingsworth and S. Gilmore (eds.), *Re-writing Children's Rights Judgments*, Hart, Oxford 2017, pp. 513–516.

not be required if circumstances have changed to such an extent that it would impact on the best interests of the child.[78]

The two supranational courts appear to have a very different approach to the application of children's rights in child abduction cases.[79] The ECtHR has addressed the individualised assessment of a child's best interests in the context of the Hague Abduction Convention 1980 and the exceptions to return.[80] By contrast, the CJEU has been concerned to ensure that return of the child takes place and that the jurisdictional rules contained within Brussels II*a* are correctly applied. There has been no overall reassessment of the legal framework addressing child abduction in the light of children's rights in either court, but reinforcing the requirement to return in the CJEU risks minimising the rights of individual children. Despite the specific inclusion of children's rights within the EU Charter, the ECtHR has been more sensitive to an analysis of the law that accounts for the interests of the individual abducted child.

The adoption of the CRC has encouraged greater consideration of the individual interests of children, although signatory States are required to adopt measures combating child abduction.[81] Drawing the balance between a rapid effective return mechanism to combat child abduction and the individual interests of the child who has been abducted is delicate[82] because it relies on two different analyses of the problem of child abduction. Focusing on the individual best interests of the abducted child may fully protect their welfare, but it may inhibit the relationship with the left behind parent and allow the abducting parent to bring about an otherwise unlawful action in moving the child abroad. Yet focusing solely on return in allocating the jurisdiction for a full custody assessment to the habitual residence risks ignoring pertinent circumstances that may harm the child concerned. The EU attempted to address this conundrum in Brussels II*a* by allowing the court of the child's habitual residence to retain jurisdiction over custody proceedings even after return of the child is refused.[83] However, this has enabled the CJEU's approach of emphasising return of the child, whilst at the same time the ECtHR is shifting in favour of an explicit

78 *Severe v. Austria*, No. 53661/15.

79 P. Beaumont, K. Trimmings, L. Walker and J. Holliday, 'Child Abduction: Recent Jurisprudence of the European Court of Human Rights', (2015) 64 *International and Comparative Law Quarterly*, 39, 51.

80 P. McEleavy, 'The European Court of Human Rights and the Hague Child Abduction Convention: Prioritising return or reflection', (2015) 62 *Netherlands International Law Review*, 365, 400.

81 Article 35 CRC.

82 R. Schuz, 'The Hague Child Abduction Convention: Family Law and Private International Law', (1995) 44 *International and Comparative Law Quarterly*, 771, 780.

83 Article 10, Brussels II*a*. See P. McEleavy, 'The New Child Abduction Regime in the European Union: Symbiotic Relationship or Forced Partnership?', (2005) 1 *Journal of Private International Law*, 1, 5.

analysis of the exceptions to return in the Hague Abduction Convention 1980 as a form of best interests assessment.

3.2. THE ROLE OF SUPRANATIONAL COURTS IN APPLYING CHILDREN'S RIGHTS

The approach of the CJEU and the ECtHR in relation to child abduction demonstrates the open and flexible nature of children's rights obligations. Each court has a developed a slightly different approach and emphasis in their analysis of rights in relation to child abduction. The legal environment in which the analysis of rights takes place is highly pertinent. In the circumstances of international child abduction, there is global agreement that States must seek to combat it in the interests of children,[84] and legal obligations between States to enforce the return of abducted children. The rights protections the ECtHR and the CJEU are responsible for upholding are subtly different. The ECtHR has emphasised the importance of individualised assessments of child abduction cases and the role of the exceptions to return in protecting the best interests of abducted children. Despite the specific guarantees contained in Article 24 of the Charter, the CJEU has focused on interpretation of the EU's legal framework on child abduction, as it is obligated to by the preliminary reference procedure. In terms of children's rights protection, the position of the child within the parental relationships and the maintenance of those ties, rather than the individual circumstances or the opinion of the child heard in proceedings, have been the key concerns of the Court. This is a legitimate approach to the analysis of child abduction disputes but the differences in approach potentially send a confused message to domestic courts across Europe. The underlying role of the CRC has not provided consistency, despite providing a point of reference for both supranational courts.

Where the two courts have interacted on international child abduction, this has provided no solution. In *Povse*,[85] where both courts had the opportunity to consider factual basis of the same case, the circumstance that the CJEU had first considered the case effectively shielded the Austrian court from further interrogation because it was carrying out its obligations in EU law to enforce the return order.[86] The legal relationship between the two courts affected the nature of the legal analysis conducted by the ECtHR of the circumstances affecting the

---

84 Article 35 CRC.

85 Case C-211/10, *Doris Povse v. Mauro Alpago*, ECLI:EU:C:2010:400; ECtHR, *MA/Povse v. Austria*, No. 3890/11.

86 ECtHR, *Bosphorous v. Ireland*, No. 45036/11.

child. Despite its competence under the EU Treaty,[87] the EU's accession to the ECHR as a signatory has not taken place, partly because the CJEU has ruled that accession would be 'liable adversely to affect the specific characteristics and the autonomy of EU law'.[88] This limits the extent of the true dialogue that can be developed between the courts on areas such as children's rights.

Most return applications are heard entirely by domestic courts. The supranational courts in Europe hear very few child abduction cases, only those where a petition is made to the ECtHR, or there is a question of interpretation of EU law referred from the domestic court to the CJEU.[89] The supranational courts can give a uniform interpretation of key terms, such as habitual residence, which can aid the consistency and uniformity in application of the return remedy.[90] It has not provided uniformity of approach to children's rights in this context. The supranational courts rely on the previous evidence gathered by the domestic courts and do not hear directly from the child concerned, since neither court provides for this opportunity in their rules of procedure. The time taken over applications to the supranational courts further delays decision-making, despite the need for rapidity if return is to be successfully achieved. The child will grow and develop in the time taken to hear the application, even if it is expedited. The supranational courts in child abduction cases are asked highly contextual questions about the abduction and the protection of children's rights in this context. It is inevitable that both courts are so remote from the dispute itself that they struggle to engage with fact-dependent family issues. This can cause difficulties for the courts, such as those in *Neulinger*, where the outcome for the child in protecting their best interests as perceived by the ECtHR was regarded as affecting the application of the return remedy overall.

The application of children's rights in the context of international child abduction has demonstrated the limits of the supranational courts in determining and promoting children's rights obligations. The patchwork of children's rights obligations does not provide consistency in application and the CJEU in particular has been selective in determining which rights are most relevant to child abduction. The requirement to maintain the operation of the return remedy globally, and the distance from the dispute in question, limits the scope for analysis by supranational courts' in relation to the Hague Abduction Convention 1980 as a children's rights instrument.

---

87 Article 6(2) TEU, Protocol 8 TEU.

88 Opinion 2/13, 14 December 2014, ECLI:EU:C:2014:2454.

89 Article 267 TFEU.

90 R. Lamont, 'Habitual Residence and Brussels II *bis:* Developing Concepts for European Private International Family Law', (2007) 3 *Journal of Private International Law*, 261, 280.

4. CONCLUSIONS

Since the agreement of the Hague Abduction Convention 1980, the adoption of the CRC has changed the global children's rights landscape. The protection of the best interests of the individual child has become a more central feature of family law and this is to some extent reflected in the case law of the ECtHR on child abduction. The exceptions to return and the obligation on the State to effectively enforce the return order once made have become important to the protection of the rights of the child under Article 8 ECHR. By contrast, the CJEU has focused on reinforcing the return of children and the allocation of jurisdiction between the Member States. This may shift with the adoption of the recast Brussels II*a* Regulation 2019/1111, but the emphasis on returning abducted children between EU Member States is unlikely to be significantly disrupted. The inconsistencies in the approach of the supranational courts highlights that the most important forum for the protection of children's rights remains the domestic courts. The majority of decisions in relation to child abduction are taken at this level, and the proper assessment of the factual matrix of the case and the child's opinion can only be ascertained by the domestic court. The supranational courts have an important role in identifying the significance of children's rights but the practical application and realisation of children's rights for individual children remain the primary responsibility for the domestic courts of the Member States.

CROSS-BORDER PARENTAL CHILD ABDUCTION IN THE EU

Is there Room for a Human Rights Exception?

Costanza Honorati

1. Article 20 of the 1980 Hague Convention: Between Public Policy and Fundamental Rights 243
2. The Difficulty of Framing the Scope of Article 20, Particularly with Regard to Article 13(1)(b). 246
3. Application of Article 20 in Purely Conventional Cases. 252
4. Is there a Use for Article 20 in EU Abduction Cases? 259

1. ARTICLE 20 OF THE 1980 HAGUE CONVENTION: BETWEEN PUBLIC POLICY AND FUNDAMENTAL RIGHTS

Article 20 of the 1980 Hague Convention resembles a ghost – although it is the subject of many rumours, it is nowhere to be seen. Metaphor aside, the provision has stimulated strong debate and discussion ever since its drafting; however, its application has remained limited, thereby resulting in only marginal practical relevance. Nonetheless, the importance of this rule far exceeds the number of decisions that have been expressly determined by it. In a time characterised by the growing relevance of human rights and increasing violations of the same, the potential and the implicit effects of this rule outweigh the doubts and justify a short comment with regard to where we stand.

Article 20 of the 1980 Hague Convention provides for an additional reason to those listed in Article 12 for refusing the return of an abducted child, namely when such return

> would not be permitted by the fundamental principles of the requested State relating to the protection of human rights and fundamental freedoms.

The drafting history of the provision calls for a strict interpretation of its scope of application.[1] After a long debate, the rule was accepted only because the delegations refused to insert a public policy clause – a must-have provision at the time – and feared that this could lead some States to make reservations to the Convention.

Accordingly, the threshold for the operation of Article 20 should be higher than what would amount to a 'simple' public policy clause. As the Vera Perez Explanatory Report asserted, to trigger the provision and refuse return on this basis

> it will be necessary to show that the fundamental principles of the requested State … do not permit it; it will not be sufficient to show merely that return is incompatible, even manifestly incompatible, with these principles.[2]

Although the distinction between what is 'not permitted' by fundamental principles and what is 'manifestly incompatible' with those principles offers no clear guidance, situations that might be incompatible with the public policy of the requested State could nonetheless fall out of the scope of application of Article 20 and thereby not justify a refusal of return on such grounds.

As the following section will demonstrate, national courts have generally upheld a strict interpretation of this provision and allowed little room for such an exception, thus confirming its purpose and rationale as imagined by the drafting committee.[3] However, this situation might change in the future. Although public policy exceptions have lost much of their strength in recent times – certainly within EU Member States and possibly also in more general terms – the impact of human rights has risen dramatically. Paradoxically, while the reference to fundamental principles 'relating to the protection of human rights and fundamental freedoms' was meant to restrict the scope of application of

---

1 However, see M. H. Weiner, 'Strengthening Article 20' (2004) *U.S.F. Law Review* 38, 701, 708–10 for an opposite construction of the *Travaux Preparatoires* of the Convention, arguing that such was not the real intention of the States' delegates. The author claims that the current strict interpretation of Article 20 is the result of: a) the statement made by the Special Rapporteur Perez-Vera cited below; b) the interpretation provided by the US State Department according to which the violation of human rights must 'utterly shock the conscience'; and c) the court's application of such a rule, which is primarily based on the former two elements. The author investigates each of these factors and concludes that a wider application of the rule is quite legitimate and appropriate in light of the need for an effective protection of human rights.

2 *Actes et Documents de la Quatorzième Session de la Conference de la Haye de droit international privé* (1980), III, Discussions, pp. 337–39; also reporting the same, see K. Trimmings and P. Beaumont 'Article 20 of the 1980 Hague Abduction Convention' (2014) *Journal of Comparative Law* 9, 70.

3 For an overall positive assessment of how (little) Article 20 has been working, see R. Schuz, *The Hague Child Abduction Convention. A Critical Analysis*, Hart Publishing, Oxford 2013, p. 369.

public policy, as the operation of such exceptions was considered to be a major risk in the 1980s, the same reference could become the Trojan horse for a wider application of Article 20 in modern times.

A sign of such a possible trend can be identified in the decision *X. v. Latvia*, given by the European Court of Human Rights (ECtHR) in 2013.[4] In an obiter comment, the Grand Chamber of the ECtHR held that national courts incur an obligation to scrutinise the circumstances of the case (and of course to do so in the light required by the Court) because

> the rights safeguarded by Article 8 of the Convention … represent 'fundamental principles of the requested State relating to the protection of human rights and fundamental freedoms' within the meaning of paragraph 20 of the Hague Convention.[5]

The relation between the scope of application of Article 20 and of Article 8 of the European Convention on Human Rights was clearly mistaken and has been rightly criticised on multiple grounds.[6] Furthermore, the decision opens the way to a possible (mis)use of Article 20, particularly due to the authoritativeness of the source offering the interpretation. It is to be welcomed that this hint has thus far remained unprecedented and has not been followed by further developments of the ECtHR.

The reference to the protection of human rights as an extreme ground to refuse return could become crucial within the Area of Freedom, Security and Justice, whereby Member States share the same catalogue of mandatory fundamental rights as enshrined in and commanded by the EU Charter of Fundamental Rights. Indeed, investigating the scope of application of Article 20 within the EU could turn out to be particularly delicate because of the latter peculiar legal context.

Article 20 was framed to operate within an international convention aimed at the widest possible multilateral application. This goal has been fully accomplished, as the 1980 Hague Convention is currently binding in 100 States, thus making it one of the most successful Hague Conventions.[7] The increasing number of Contracting States inevitably based on different legal, social and cultural values supports the need to establish safeguards – and probably to begin operating them over a wider extent – to protect both internal consistency and the most fundamental principles in the domain of family rights. In other words, it is precisely because of the increasing success of the Convention, which now

---

4 ECtHR (Grand Chamber), *X. v. Latvia*, No. 27853/09, 26.11.2013.

5 Ibid., §117.

6 For example, see K. Trimmings and P. Beaumont, above n. 2, p. 70.

7 Guyana, acceding in February 2019, was the hundredth State, see https://www.hcch.net/en/instruments/conventions/status-table/?cid=24 (as per March 2019).

encompasses States with widely different traditions, that the relevance of such a provision might be getting stronger.

As is well known, the 1980 Hague Convention has a special application within the EU. When drafting Regulation (EC) No. 2201/2003 on jurisdiction, recognition and enforcement of judgments in matrimonial matters and parental responsibility (the so-called Brussels IIa Regulation), the European legislator considered that the general principles of the Convention should be upheld and confirmed. At the same time, they believed that the special relation of mutual trust and unity of aims among EU Member States should strengthen the international obligations binding upon them. This view of common values and mutual trust underlying an Area of Security, Justice and Freedom resulted in a partial modification of the Convention to enhance its efficacy when applied between two EU Member States.

It is here submitted that Article 20's rationale and scope of application strongly depends on the overall structure of the Convention and the balance it achieves in each specific legal context. As such, it receives a different understanding depending on the legal environment in which it is called upon to operate. This calls for adopting a different approach when it is applied by virtue of the reference made by Regulation No. 2201/2003 (i.e. between two EU Member States) versus when it is applied by its own force (i.e. to 'purely conventional' cases).[8]

After a brief analysis of the scope of application of Article 20 (Section 2) and its application to international cases (Section 3), this chapter investigates the impact of the Article 20 defence in EU cases (Section 4), i.e. in cases whereby the abduction results in the removal of a child from one EU Member State to another.

2. THE DIFFICULTY OF FRAMING THE SCOPE OF ARTICLE 20, PARTICULARLY WITH REGARD TO ARTICLE 13(1)(b)

Defining the correct scope of application of Article 20 has always been difficult due to its vague framing, which was the outcome of a political compromise as seen above. The rule offers no clear direction with regard to determining the 'fundamental principles relating to the protection of human rights and fundamental freedoms'. It does not specify the person whose rights are at stake. Furthermore, its relation to other provisions of the Convention is ambiguous and problematic.

---

8 This includes cases in which a child is abducted to an EU Member State from a non-EU country. In such situations, the Brussels IIa Regulation does not apply and one should revert to the 'normal' Convention.

With regard to the first point, the referred principles envisage the widest spectrum and are potentially unlimited.[9] The rule encompasses not only those human rights that are recognised and well-established by international conventions but also principles and standards that are enshrined in each national legal system (possibly at the constitutional level). The only limitation for identifying such rules is the inherently vague one of referring to human rights and fundamental freedom.

Similarly as regards the operation of public policy, Article 20 aims to protect national values and principles that would be endangered by returning the child to his or her State of habitual residence. The provision thus serves and protects the internal coherence of States. Such a necessary unilateral approach is an important concern. Operating this provision runs counter to the general aim of the Convention and does so on a purely internal and unilateral consideration.

With regard to the subjective scope of application of the provision, the rights of the abducted child will certainly come into consideration. However, it is debatable if the rights of *other* children involved, such as the step siblings of the abducted child, have the same relevance.[10] It is even more questionable whether parents' rights are also encompassed by the rule. Considering the structure and the purpose of the Convention, it could be argued that parents' rights, and particularly those of the abducting parent, should not be covered. However, such a limitation does not appear convincing upon closer analysis. Indeed, while the rights of the child are expressly taken into account by the Convention (for example, by Articles 12 and 13), those of parents (and particularly the abducting one) are not considered at all, or are considered to a far lesser degree. Moreover, one can imagine situations in which the rights of the abducting parent might not coincide with those of the child. The practical implementation of an international convention, particularly when drafted and promoted by the Hague Conference on Private International Law, should not result in the violation of anyone's fundamental rights, even when that person is an abducting parent. Therefore, due to Article 20's purpose as a final safeguard, this provision should be construed as giving relevance to the fundamental principles related to the human rights of any and all parties involved in child abduction.

The second level of difficulty derives from Article 20's ambiguous relationship with other rules of the Convention that provide for the refusal of return. Because the Article sets an additional limit to the general obligation

---

9 See M. Everall, N. Lowe and M. Nicholls, *International Movement of Children*, 2nd ed., Lexis Nexis, Bristol 2016, p. 610, para. 26.10.

10 For example, see *A v. GS* (2004) 187 FLR 240 where an Australian court refused to apply Article 20 to a case in which a young girl argued that the return of her abducted stepsister would violate her own human rights. The court maintained that Article 20 was solely concerned with the rights of the abducted child and his/her custodial parents. The case is further discussed by K. Trimmings and P. Beaumont, above n. 2, p. 82.

to order return which is mandated by Article 12(1), problems of delimitation could theoretically arise with regard to *any* of the multiple grounds for refusing return considered by the Convention, including when these are based on the settlement of the child pursuant to Article 12(2) or on the opposition of the child by virtue of Article 13(2). Unquestionably, however, the major difficulties arise with regard to Article 13(1)(b), which allows the court to refuse return when the child is at a grave risk of physical or psychological harm or of enduring an otherwise intolerable situation.

Multiple commentators have indicated a clear overlapping of the two provisions. Many situations that could lead to a refusal of return on the basis of grave risk would likely violate a fundamental right under Article 20.[11] Likewise, a gross violation of the fundamental rights of each of the parties affected by the abduction would likely imply a grave risk of physical or psychological harm to the child. This theoretical overlapping is confirmed by what occurs in practice: parties plead on both legal grounds, shifting from one characterisation to the other without a clear line between the two hypotheses. Moreover, courts use both grounds if they feel they should refuse return but are uncertain of the most appropriate ground for doing so.

Depending on different factual circumstances, at least two major patterns might fall within one or the other provision. Domestic violence is one of the two. As Merle Weiner argued 15 years ago,[12] when a mother flees with her child to a different country to escape domestic violence, the return of the child should be refused based on Article 13 (whereby violence committed against the mother can be construed as a grave risk of a psychological harm to, or an otherwise intolerable situation for the child) and on Article 20 (whereby the former option is negated, as in cases when violence was suffered by the mother, but the father is loving and caring towards the child – albeit this situation may sound too theoretical and be unlikely in real life).

Similarly, when a mother or her child qualifies for refugee or humanitarian protection and applies for international protection in the State of refuge, the return of the child to the State of habitual residence should be refused because this would infringe an international obligation of the State of refuge, irrespective of any different consideration argued on the basis of the 1980 Hague Convention that might yield opposing results. This also means that even when return would not expose the child to a personal and direct grave risk of physical harm, returning to a State that is at war, where levels of internal unrest exceed a tolerable level or where fundamental rights cannot be protected in a reasonable way, would

---

11 P. Beaumont and P. McEleavy, *The Hague Convention on International Child Abduction*, Oxford University Press, Oxford 1999, p. 172; M. Everall, N. Lowe and M. Nicholls, above n. 9, p. 610, para. 26.9.

12 See two articles that were published in 2004, the first of which is cited above at n. 1, and the second is M. H. Weiner, 'Using Article 20' (2004) *Family Law Quarterly* 38, 583–622.

violate the fundamental principles of the requested State and should not be allowed. This latter case deserves special consideration and greater caution given the present situation of migration flows, including migrant children, in Europe.

It is thus acknowledged that some patterns could theoretically be characterised as falling under multiple provisions, especially under Article 13 and Article 20. However, blurring the scope of application of these two rules might not be conducive to an effective and consistent application of the Convention. Having two different provisions whose scopes of application are overlapping and which might come into consideration under similar circumstances contradicts the principle that all parts of the Convention should have an *effet utile*. Legal scholars should strive to construe the two set of rules in such a way that each will have a specific scope of application and thereby avoid overlapping and gaps.

Indeed, a tentative explanation has been proposed whereby Article 13 would offer a ground for refusal based on factual matters, whereas Article 20 would be applied when the refusal is based on the legal framework of the requesting State.[13] However, such a construction, albeit intriguing at a theoretical level, is probably of little practical help as it offers no clear way of distinguishing between one case and the other and *de facto* leads to potentially challenging both rules in courts.[14] A better approach seems to be one that relies on the argument wherein Article 13 prescribes a limited exception to the Convention by its own force, while Article 20 recognises an exception (primarily) grounded on national constitutions. Such a criterion emphasises the different rationale of the two provisions, stressing that

> Article 20 provides a mechanism whereby the necessary flexibility is built into the Convention to avoid a conflict between the international obligations imposed by the Convention and the dictates of the domestic Constitution.[15]

However, it again does not offer guidance on when to apply one or the other.

The rationale of Article 20 is thus to be an *ultimate safeguard clause* for cases in which return should not be ordered because other, more specific grounds for refusal were not applicable. Article 20 should thus be construed as a last resort

---

13 P. Beaumont and P. McEleavy, above n. 11, p. 174, referring to an interview with A. Dyer held in March 1995. Using such a criterion, Article 20 would only legitimate refusal of return when the incompatibility with national principles is the effect of the legal situation existing in the State of prior habitual residence. The said legal situation must however have arisen subsequently to the acceptance of the adhesion of the requesting State. In fact, it must be presumed that acceptance of adhesion implies acknowledging the compatibility of the legal framework in force in that State for the purpose of the application of the Convention.

14 M. Everall, N. Lowe and M. Nicholls, above n. 9, p. 610, para. 26.9.

15 For this stance, see the Supreme Court of Ireland, 15.12.2011, *Nottinghamshire County Council v. K.B. and K.B.* (2011) IESC 48, one of the very few cases that have been argued solely on Article 20. See further on the case below para. 4.

to which one should turn only in cases where more specific grounds for refusing return (i.e. the grave risk of harm as envisaged by Article 13(1), opposition of the child pursuant to Article 13(2), or the settlement of the child considered by Article 12(2)) have already been examined and deemed inapplicable.

In order to avoid a possible overlapping with Article 13, the two provisions should therefore be built as mutually exclusive. All cases that could fall within Article 13 should not be examined under Article 20. By contrast, the latter should apply (only) to cases that are different from those dealt with under Article 13, i.e. cases that infringe children's rights but do not amount to a typical case of grave risk.[16] Moreover, it should cover the possible violations of parents' rights or even State policies concerned with fundamental rights and freedom.

On a more general note, the scope of application of Article 20 is directly linked to the interpretations given to two other more specific provisions and, more generally, to the particular and evolving operation of the Convention in practice. The wider the application granted to Article 13, the narrower should be the operation of Article 20.

The case of domestic violence is a good example of the possible interaction between the two provisions.

Since 2011, the Hague Conference has undertaken – and is still undertaking – an enormous effort to investigate the issue of domestic violence in relation to the Article 13(1)(b) 'grave risk' exception.[17] In that year, at the Sixth Meeting of the Special Commission, a special body was set up in the framework of the Hague Conference to review the practical operations of the 1980 Hague Convention. Focus was then placed on the increasing allegations of domestic violence and the possible related risks for children. It was then determined to further investigate the scenario of domestic violence for the grave risk exception, considering the need to promote a consistent interpretation of the provision. This is particularly so with regard to the evaluation of evidence and the determination of the grave risk of harm in cases when domestic violence against the mother is alleged. The majority of experts, however, have considered that any future work should not be limited to allegations of domestic and family violence, but that should include

16 In other words, a situation that falls under Article 13 but does not rise to the standard of a grave risk could nonetheless be refused on the basis of Article 20 because it is considered to violate fundamental rights. Conversely, if the defence of grave risk is appropriate, there is no need to trigger Article 20 as this provision would be applied only *ad abundantiam*.

17 During the same time period, a number of articles have been written on the same topic, analysing the perceived difficulties across numerous jurisdictions. For an exhaustive bibliography, see the paper drawn for the attention of the Special Commission by the Hague Conference Permanent Bureau, *Domestic and Family Violence and the Article 13 'Grave Risk' Exception in the Operation of the Hague Convention of 25.10.1980 on the Civil Aspects of International Child Abduction: A Reflection Paper*, Prel. Doc. No 9, May 2011, p. 3, notes 2, 3, and 4. See also the annexes for a list of relevant cases.

the widest range of situations in which a 'grave risk of harm' could be asserted.[18] In 2012, a working group was established to develop a *Guide to Good Practice* on the interpretation and application of Article 13(1)(b). The working group met several times in 2014, 2016 and 2018 and produced a *Draft Guide* based on the meeting of the Seventh Special Commission in October 2017.[19]

It is beyond the scope of this discussion to examine the content of this *Guide*, which, albeit not yet final, is well-structured and complete and offers clear guidance for judicial handling of a grave risk defence. For the purpose of this chapter it is sufficient to stress the general understanding underscoring the *Guide*, according to which the term 'domestic violence' can encompass different facets of abuse within the family. This may include physical, psychological, sexual and/or financial abuse. Furthermore, it may be directed towards the child ('child abuse'), and/or towards a parent, or even towards other family members.[20] It is today beyond doubt that family or domestic violence falls within the scope of Article 13(1)(b) when directed against the mother, as the correlation between a child's exposure to domestic violence, whether direct or indirect, and later problems in adult life, is generally established.[21] Accordingly, many of the situations that some years ago could trigger Article 20 are plainly covered by Article 13 at present. A similar development might be currently on-going with regard to the return of a refugee child, as will be addressed in the next section.

More generally, the monitoring of the practical application of the Convention and its progressive development has resulted in a better understanding of the cases falling under Article 13(1)(b). And this impacts on the scope Article 20.

---

18 This choice was grounded on the note that an approach focusing only on domestic violence would lead to a different standard being applied to such cases, a conclusion not supported by the textual construction of Article 13(1)(b) and not favoured by the Commission.

19 See the Draft Guide to Good Practice on Article 13(1)(b) of the Hague Convention of 25.10.1980 on the Civil Aspects of International Child Abduction, Prel. Doc. No. 3 of June 2017 (available at https://assets.hcch.net/docs/0a0532b7-d580-4e53-8c25-7edab2a94284.pdf). The Seventh Meeting of the Special Commission, in its meeting on 10–17.10.2017 has invited the Working Group to finalise the Guide and recommended that priority is given to this work.

20 This definition is drawn from the *Draft Guide to Good Practice* cit., Annex 3, *Dynamics of Domestic Violence, International Norms Relevant to Domestic Violence and Violence against Children*, para. 10.

21 See for example the decision in *Re E (Children) (Abduction: Custody Appeal)* [2011] UKSC 27, where the court found that exposure to the harmful effects of witnessing by the child of physical or psychological abuse of his own parent can place the child in an 'intolerable situation' in light of Article 13(1)(b). In *Re S*, the Court addressed the issue of the abducting parent's perceptions, and went even further than in *Re E* by saying that it is irrelevant whether the risk is the result of objective reality or of the abducting parent's subjective perception of reality – *Re S (A Child) (Abduction: Rights of Custody)* [2012] UKSC 10.

3. APPLICATION OF ARTICLE 20 IN PURELY CONVENTIONAL CASES

Recent surveys on the present state of affairs have illustrated that although multiple attempts have been made to oppose the return of the child on the basis of Article 20, courts have rarely accepted this argument.[22] Case law is highly diversified, and the scope of the present chapter does not allow for an in-depth analysis of the different situations. However, the major patterns gleaned from previous analyses by authoritative scholars have been grouped to provide a general overview of the context.[23] Most of the cases considered were drawn from the practice of US courts or other common law countries; it is in fact comparatively less usual that Article 20 is pleaded in EU courts. Section 4 investigates whether a different application might be justifiable *within* the EU; however, in all cases when a child is abducted to the EU from a non-EU country, the 1980 Hague Convention applies by its own force (i.e. not because it is referred to by the Brussels IIa Regulation). Therefore, in such cases, EU courts should investigate, *ex officio*, if returning the child violates fundamental rights according to the following practice.

One of the most frequently invoked grounds to trigger Article 20 is the violation of fundamental principles that would arise from the *poor quality or the inefficiency of the judicial system of the requesting State*; however, this type of complaint has been generally refused by national courts. General remarks on the organisation, partiality, corruption or excessive length of the proceedings in the requesting State have generally been rejected by the courts of the requested State. Indeed, through ratification and acceptance thereof, States mutually show a general trust in the legal system of each contracting party, which deprives this ground of much force.[24] In some cases, the claim was dismissed because insufficient evidence of the alleged risk had been provided or because of procedural irregularities that should have been challenged in the requested State.

Similarly, no room has been allowed for challenges based on the constitutional rights of the requested State. In several cases, constitutional rights enshrined in the national fundamental charter of the requested State have been relied upon to argue that return of the child would not be permitted by national

---

22 Although the Hague INCADAT database (to be searched at www.incadat.com) shows the significant figure of 62 cases mentioning Article 20 as one of the grounds pleaded in courts, in most cases the fundamental rights defence is raised only *ad abundantiam* to reinforce a defence primarily based on Article 13. Cases in which Article 20 has been relied upon as an autonomous ground are quite rare, and only a small bunch of them have been successful.

23 This author has largely relied on the recent and complete analysis offered by K. Trimmings and P. Beaumont, above n. 2, and by R. Schuz, above n. 3, as well as the rich INCADAT database, above n. 21.

24 See P. Beaumont and P. McEleavy, above n. 11, p. 174.

principles. For example, cases have been disputed concerning the right to enter and remain in the country of citizenship under the Canadian Constitution; the right to travel, including the right to leave the requesting State, as granted by the US Constitution; the right of an Irish citizen to access Irish courts; the right to travel and relocate guaranteed under the Spanish legal system; and the right of parents to care for their children (and of children to be cared for by their parents) under the Czech Constitution.[25]

This line of reasoning has rightly been generally refused.[26] It has to be kept in mind that such an assessment has to be made a priori, on a purely prognostic appraisal of whether the requesting State is likely to violate the fundamental principles of the requested State. The compatibility of these (constitutional) rights with the Convention and its clear obligation to return the abducted child (solely to decide on his/her custody) is a pre-condition for the application of the Convention and is assessed in general terms before its ratification. In the absence of special circumstances, refusing return on one of the aforementioned grounds would violate the same *raison d'être* of the Convention.[27]

The same can be said with regard to the constitutional (and human) right prohibiting any discriminatory treatment (whether on gender, sexual,[28] racial or cultural grounds). This specific issue provides for a strong case for refusing return on a theoretical level, as non-discrimination is at the core of human rights doctrine. It might also seem particularly appropriate in light of the different standards of protection afforded to males and females in States which are parties to the Hague Convention, particularly in family law matters. Such a ground has indeed been upheld by some courts, although this has happened only rarely.[29]

---

25 For example, see a case whereby a Czech mother had abducted her child from Israel and sought to refuse return by alleging a violation of her and her child's rights as guaranteed by the Czech Constitution: Constitutional Court of the Czech Republic, 07.12.2000, III. ÚS 440/2000 DAOUD, also at www.incadat.com/en/case/468). For further references to the other cases mentioned herein, see K. Trimmings and P. Beaumont, above n. 2, p. 75–76, p. 79.

26 Indeed, even when such arguments were accepted and return refused, such as in the famous Spanish case *Carrascosa v. McGuire* (Spanish Appellate Court, 18.01.2006 n. 10), the interpretation given by the Spanish court was not appropriate. For a brief critical comment, see K. Trimmings and P. Beaumont, above n. 2, p. 79 (n. 86).

27 The relevance of constitutional rights as a benchmark to appraise the legitimacy of a return will also be analysed in section 4.

28 See the case decided by a Canadian court whereby a lesbian mother abducted her child to Canada from Mexico and then claimed that returning the child would violate her fundamental rights because of the homophobia in the latter State. The court rejected that argument, although return was ultimately refused based on Article 13(1)(b).

29 For one of the few cases in which a return was refused on the basis of prospective discrimination against the abducting mother, who was purportedly to be 'punished' by a rabbinical court, the Spanish case decided by the Audiencia Provincial Barcelona, 21.04.1997, *Re S*, is often cited (also at www.incadat.com/en/case/244). However, this decision does not provide a good example because the court refused return relying on false evidence provided in the first instance proceedings.

In fact, the decisions upholding such reasoning have been comparatively few, having regard to the number of times this ground has been – or could have been – raised. Possibly, difficulties in supplying evidence for the specific situation might have played a role in limiting such arguments and/or their success. In addition, the overlapping with the risk of physical or psychological prejudice envisaged by Article 13(1)(b) is more concrete in such cases. As explained above, when the facts of the case can be construed as meeting the grave risk standard, return should be refused on such grounds rather than those based on Article 20. Having said all this, it is here submitted that a complaint for a situation of – effective, although prospective – discrimination should require a clear and convincing in-depth assessment, particularly in regard to countries where pervasive religious laws and traditions influence family law,[30] thus commanding the courts to give due regard to the special circumstances of the case.

Challenges based on and around the *best interests of the child* are extremely delicate. This might appear to be a solid ground on which to trigger Article 20, given the common perception that the child's best interests amount to a general principle related to the fundamental rights of the child. Notwithstanding this growing awareness, only relatively few reported cases have raised this argument, none of which was successful. As a previous commentator has shown,[31] the best interests test is disputed based on two opposing scenarios. According to the first scenario, the child's best interests are prejudiced by the sole fact of returning him/her to the State of residence,[32] (a line of argument that was favoured in the ECtHR decision in the *Neulinger* case); under the second scenario, the argument is that the requesting State (i.e. the State of residence where the custody proceedings are to be held) would not offer a sufficient guarantee of applying the best interests standard to the substance of the case.

Both lines of argument have generally gained little success, as they run counter to the general principle according to which the State from which the return is requested (i.e. the State of refuge) should *not* enter into a best interests

---

30 Special focus must be placed on discrimination against women as a consequence of religious traditions and laws that could bias the custody proceeding in the State of habitual residence. Because of the dual system of competence (religious and civil) available in that country, this might not be a sufficient ground for refusing return to Israel, notwithstanding the competence of a rabbinical court. However, a stronger case might be made with regard to Muslim countries applying the Sharia, as these laws discriminate against mothers in several ways. On this point, see R. Schuz, above n. 3, p. 359 (and n. 38) citing A. Zahalka, *The Sharia Courts: Between Adjudication and Identity*, Israel Bar Association, Tel Aviv 2009, p. 66; U. Khaliq and J. R. Young, 'Cultural Diversity, Human Rights and Inconsistency in the English Courts', (2001) *Legal Studies* 21, 192, 217–19.

31 See R. Schuz, above n. 3, p. 355–56.

32 For example, in the US case *Kufner v. Kufner* (519 F.3d 33 (1st Cir. 2008)), the mother maintained that the grave risk of harm was unconstitutional because it did not lead to assessment of the best interests of the child, the latter being less demanding than the grave risk test. That argument was rejected by the court.

test on the substance of the case. As is well known, this issue was blurred by the European Court of Human Rights (ECtHR) in the famous *Neulinger* case. However, following the strong criticism of the ambiguous phrasing used therein, the ECtHR clarified in the subsequent case of *X. v. Latvia* that the State of refuge should limit its jurisdiction and investigation to the grounds for refusing return. While a best interests test must indeed be conducted in both proceedings, the object thereof is limited to the specific subject matter of the proceedings. Thus, the court of the State of refuge is to limit the assessment of the best interests of the child to the existence of a ground of refusal, including any objection based on Article 20, and it should not expand on where and with whom the child should live.[33]

Some chances of success emerged in a case alleging that immigration laws in the State of the child's habitual residence prevented the abducting mother from re-entering the State and from participating in person in the custody proceedings. In *Ardito*, an Australian court found that immigration rules precluded the abducting mother from re-entering the US, which was the child's State of residence. Therefore, should the child be returned, the mother would be unable to attend custody proceedings held there. The court held that denying the mother the right to appear in her child's custody proceedings would be 'contrary to all concepts of fairness' and refused to order the return of the child.[34] Although the refusal was also grounded on Article 13(1)(b) – arguing that returning without the mother would result into an intolerable situation for the child – the case is worth mentioning because the Article 20 defence was raised *ex officio*, by the court's own motion, thus illustrating a potential use of the provision that could be of further interest in forthcoming cases. It should be noted however, that in subsequent cases in which similar reliance on the impossibility of attending custody proceedings was invoked, the defence was rejected because the court valued differently the reasons alleged for that impossibility.[35]

33 The point was clearly made by the UK Supreme Court, 14.03.2012, in *Re S. (A Child) (Abduction: Rights of Custody)* (UKSC 10, (2012) 2 A.C. 257) whereby the Court emphasised that 'neither the Hague Convention nor, surely, Article 8 of the European Convention requires the court which determines an application under the [1980 Hague Convention] to conduct an in-depth examination [of the entire family situation and of a whole series of factors, in particular of a factual, emotional, psychological, material and medical nature, and a balanced and reasonable assessment of the respective interests of each person]'. A similar criticism had previously been made by the UK Supreme Court, 10.06.2011, *Re E. (Children) (Abduction: Custody Appeal)*, UKSC 27, ((2012) 1 A.C. 144. Both decisions can be found also at INCADAT, www.incadat.com/en/case/1147 and www.incadat.com/en/case/1068, respectively.

34 Family Court of Australia (Melbourne), 29.10.1997, *State Central Authority of Victoria v. Ardito*. To be found summarised on www.incadat.com/en/case/283.

35 For further considerations on this point, see K. Trimmings and P. Beaumont, above n. 2, p. 74–75.

A similar area of concern and of possible use of the Article 20 defence is that of an abducted child who has been granted asylum and refugee status in the State to which he/she has been abducted. Should the child nonetheless be returned? How should the investigation conducted by the authorities concerned with the asylum be considered by the judicial court assessing the existence of a ground for non-return under the Hague Convention?

Case law on this issue is quite ambiguous because of the various patterns considered. The possibility of varying outcomes is exemplified by two decisions given in recent times by Canadian and US courts in cases involving a similar pattern. Both cases concerned Mexican nationals abducted by relatives to Canada and the US. Shortly upon their arrival, the children applied for refugee protection on the basis of alleged physical and psychological abuse committed by the mother. Pending the Hague return proceedings filed by the left-behind Mexican mother, the administrative authority (respectively, the Canadian Immigration and Refugee Board and the US Department of Homeland Security (DHS)) granted the refugee status, thereby leaving the judicial authority to determine the delicate issues of whether such status compels – or at least amounts to a sufficient ground for discretion for – refusal of return under Article 20 or under Article 13(1)(b).

The final outcomes of the two cases diverge. The Canadian court, relying on the international obligation of *non-refoulement* derived from the 1951 Geneva Convention,[36] found that

> as in the extradition context, the principle of *non-refoulement* is directly implicated where the return of a refugee child under the Hague Convention is sought;[37]

hence, both Articles 13 and 20 of the latter were thereby construed so as to avoid violating such principle. The court also noted that

> given its expertise and specialised knowledge, the decision of the IRB on fact and credibility-driven issues are accorded a high degree of deference by the courts.[38]

It follows that, although the decision to refuse return is discretionary (and thus the court is not bound by the grant of a refugee status), the situation amounts to a rebuttable presumption that the grave risk of harm exception is engaged; thus, a refugee child is *prima facie* entitled not to be sent back. Furthermore, the child

---

36 According to Article 33(1) of the 1951 Geneva Convention, 'no Contracting State shall expel or return ('refouler') a refugee in any manner whatsoever to the frontiers of territories where his life or freedom would be threatened on account of his race, religion, nationality, membership to a particular social group or political opinion'.

37 Court of Appeal for Ontario, 02.06.2011, *A.M.R.I. v. K.E.R.*, 2011 *ONCA* 417, para. 67, published at www.incadat.com/en/case/1067. Also see the commentary to this decision in K. Trimmings and P. Beaumont, above n. 2, p. 80.

38 Decision last cited, para. 72.

should not carry the burden of proving that the conditions leading to a refugee protection have not changed.

On the contrary, the US Court appears to have attached less consideration to the assessment made by the national DHS, and stressed that

> despite similarities, the asylum finding that the children have a well-founded fear of persecution *does not substitute for* or control *a finding under Article 13(1)(b)* of the Hague Convention ... The judicial procedures under this Convention do not give to others, even a governmental agency, authority to determine such risks. ... The prior consideration of similar concerns in a different forum are relevant, but an asylum grant *does not remove from the district court the authority to make controlling findings* on the potential harm to the child.[39]

Although the appellate court in the given case ultimately decided to vacate the order for return and remand the case to a different district court for further consideration, its stance was that the asylum process should neither interfere with the Hague's return proceedings nor with the specific assessment made by judicial authorities.

Regardless of the difference between the approaches and outcomes of these courts, the pattern of the abduction of refugee children further exemplifies the problematic interference between Article 20 and Article 13(1)(b). Refugee status was in these cases granted in a situation that appears to border on what should be covered by Article 13(1)(b). A case in which the issue of domestic violence is at stake – a clear cause of risk of physical or psychological harm to the child – would probably require a more proper characterisation of the relevant facts under the latter provision. The different rules on the collection and testing of evidence before administrative bodies, as well as the lack of confrontation with the left-behind parent, gives rise to a potential for abuse of the asylum determination process by the abducting parent. As has already occurred with regard to situations of domestic violence (see above, section 2), it is likely that through Article 20 courts are paving the way for protecting refugee children who still face uncertainties in the light of the 'standard' application of the Convention. Article 20 is therefore used to reinforce a defence that would probably be more appropriately addressed under another ground (i.e. under Article 13). This is a path that could be followed until a better awareness of what is the most appropriate legal defence emerges.[40]

---

39 United States Court of Appeals for the Fifth Circuit, 01.08.2014, *Sanchez* v. *R. G. L.*, 2014 U.S. App. LEXIS 14849 (5th Cir. 2014), p. 21, also at www.incadat.com/en/case/1288 (emphasis added).

40 The reference to the international and constitutional principle of *non-refoulement*, which was pivotal to the legal reasoning of the Canadian decision and would be violated if the child were to be returned, appears to link the case to Article 20 in a more appropriate manner. On the contrary, such principle was not even mentioned in the US decision.

This approach might further vary if refugee status is granted to the child or the abducting parent on a ground encompassing a more general scope, such as persecution on account of race, religion, or nationality, or on humanitarian grounds. Such are cases in which the evidence of risk of persecution required for the grant of a refugee status does not directly and immediately amount to evidence of risk of physical harm to the specific child as required by Article 13. For example, a Syrian or a Yemenite mother flees abroad with her child due to the eruption and spread of civil war. If she is granted a refugee status and asylum, could she be forced to return to Syria or to Yemen under the Hague Convention because she left without her husband's consent and the court assessed that her child would not be at threat to his/her life? Civil wars and other internal conflicts in some countries are of such gravity, are so long-enduring and have such a destructive impact on people's everyday lives that returning a child there could violate the fundamental principles of the requested State, and thus justify a refusal of return.

Finally, another situation triggering Article 20 is when the return of an abducted child girl is opposed on the grounds of risk of a *forced marriage*. To the best of the author's knowledge, this kind of case has not yet arrived at the courts, but is likely to arise sooner or later. Under normal circumstances, a marriage, even when organised by the family without the minor spouse's consent, could not *per se* be seen as amounting to a risk of physical or psychological harm. Nonetheless, the idea that a young girl's freedom to make such a personal, life-affecting decision can be superseded contradicts the fundamental principles of Western countries and could potentially 'utterly shock the conscience of the courts'. A mother abducting her young daughter who is being forced to marry an older man she neither knows nor wants to marry and leaving a country where it is common and acceptable to do so (either by law or by social custom) should not be forced to return her. It is this author's view that such a situation would be a good case for refusing return under Article 20.

This short survey, albeit by no means complete or fully comprehensive, provides a general idea of the widely different patterns that might trigger the application of Article 20. Many more scenarios could be imagined and will occur in the future, as the range of 'fundamental principles ... relating to the protection of human rights and fundamental freedoms' is wide and continuously developing. Furthermore, the respective national perspectives underlying this provision – which aims to protect such principles as they are relevant 'in the requested State' – call for a unilateral interpretation of this ground.

As proposed at the beginning of this section, any EU court should investigate returning an abducted child to a non-EU State along these lines. As shall be illustrated in the following section, however, the situation might be different if the abduction involves two EU Member States.

4. IS THERE A USE FOR ARTICLE 20 IN EU ABDUCTION CASES?

Having this brief overview in mind, one should now turn to consider if there is room for a fundamental rights exception within the EU. It is here maintained that the scope of application of Article 20 is particularly delicate when it is challenged in abduction cases that concern only EU Member States due to the peculiar legal context that is binding on such States. The EU legal framework offers a different milieu in at least two respects: the first one pertains to a common and uniform procedural framework; the second one relates to the standard and content of the fundamental rights that might come into consideration.

Concerning the first point, mention must be made of the fundamental cornerstone of mutual trust in the efficiency and impartiality of the judiciary system of all Member States. Such a principle deprives of force any defence based on the ground of the requesting State's 'inability' to provide adequate protection to the abducted child and/or fair custody proceedings to the abducting parent.

Such a (mandatory) confidence in the Member State's judiciary and legal system has a special impact on return proceedings in abduction cases. As mentioned, the operation of the 1980 Hague Convention is reinforced among EU Member States through the Brussels IIa Regulation, which has partially modified some of its rules. Based on the principle of mutual trust and on the interests of the child to be assessed by its natural judge, the Regulation emphasises and strengthens the competence of the State of the child's habitual residence to hold custody proceedings. Article 10 reiterates the competence of such court in abduction cases by precluding jurisdiction on custody from being transferred to the State of refuge. The same rationale underscores the priority mechanism envisaged by Article 11, paras. 6–8 (also called the trumping order), the aim of which is precisely to uphold the competence of the court of habitual residence.

Enacting this same policy, Article 11(4) of the Brussels IIa Regulation currently prohibits a court from refusing the return of a child if adequate arrangements can be made to secure the child's safe return. On a literal interpretation, the rule currently appears to be limited to cases in which refusal of return is grounded on Article 13; however, it is submitted that it conveys a general policy. Regulation (EU) No 606/2013 on the mutual recognition of protection measures in civil matters establishes a special mechanism based on the issuance of a certificate and is aligned in the same direction in terms of enabling a speedy and automatic enforcement of all protection measures.[41]

---

[41] Further distinguishing features of the return procedure in abduction cases set by the Brussels IIa Regulation are the mandatory hearings of the child (Article 11(2)) and the applicant for return (article 11(5)) and the short timeframe set for decisions on return (Article 11(3)). For a broader discussion of the differences between the Brussels IIa

Although the decision to order or refuse return of the child must be left to a case-by-case assessment by the single court with regard to all factual circumstances, there is no doubt that the conditions for a legitimate refusal of return within the EU are even more restrictive than those – already restrictive and exceptional – that apply in pure conventional cases. This clearly imposes a further limitation on the application of the residual safeguard embraced by Article 20.

The second line of difference focuses on the content of the fundamental rights and freedoms that could be violated by returning the child. A relevant distinguishing feature is that EU Member States share common fundamental rights and freedoms, as enshrined in the EU Charter of Fundamental Rights; furthermore, they all are subject to the uniform application of the rights envisaged in the ECHR. Such a circumstance is of particular and two-fold importance with regard to the topic that is addressed here.

First, as repeatedly emphasised both by legal literature and the ECtHR, the Hague Convention must be interpreted in a manner that complies with the fundamental rights of the ECHR. Each and any ground for refusing return must be construed so as to respect the rights thereof. Accordingly, one could assume that there is no need to operate a 'special' safeguard to ensure the respect of fundamental rights, as these rights are already embodied within the normal operation of the Hague Convention through a proper construction of the other rules, specifically Article 13.[42]

Second, with specific reference to EU Member States, which are all under an obligation to guarantee the level of protection ensured by the EU Charter, which in turn largely recalls the ECHR (certainly so in regard of the present topic), the occasion to trigger Article 20 by alleging a possible violation of fundamental rights in the requesting State is reduced to cases whereby national (constitutional) rules offer a *higher* standard of protection in comparison to what is outlined in the EU Charter. Although such a situation is not impossible, it will occur only exceptionally. Conversely, given the approximation realised through EU and European rules, cases that entail a violation of fundamental rights or discriminatory treatment (see section 2) that are recognised by both the Constitution and the European Convention are likely to be deprived of substance. Indeed, Article 20 has an even more limited scope of application within the EU as it can be used only in defence of fundamental rights that receive a specific and higher protection by national constitutions.

Regulation and the 1980 Hague Convention, see, among others, M. Everall, N. Lowe and M. Nicholls, above n. 9, Chapters 4, 8, and especially 28; K. Trimmings, Child Abduction *within the European Union*, Hart Publishing, Oxford 2013.

42 This point is reinforced by the circumstance that when enacting implementing legislation to the 1980 Hague Convention, neither the UK nor Finland have incorporated Article 20 into domestic law. Subsequent case law in these jurisdictions show that the safeguards enshrined in this rule are considered already operating through other rules.

Furthermore, as in the case of the public policy exception, *mere differences* in the degree of protection offered by national constitutions might not be sufficient to meet the test required by Article 20 and ground a decision that return is not permitted by national principles.

A good example of such a problematic assessment can be observed in a case recently decided by the Irish Supreme Court.[43] Fearing that care proceedings in the UK could lead to adoption, a UK family relocated to Ireland with their two children. In the subsequent return proceedings, they argued that return would violate the protection of the family as guaranteed by the Irish Constitution.[44] This was because adoption without consent – one of the possible outcomes of care proceedings filed by social services in UK – would be in breach of their constitutional rights.

The decision given by the Irish Supreme Court in this case is quite relevant to our topic as it focuses exclusively on Article 20 and provides an accurate reconstruction of the rationale and application of the rule with regard to family rights.

First, the Court clarified that even constitutional differences between the laws of England and of Ireland do not suffice to refuse return, as one must demonstrate that

> the manner in which children would be dealt with in the requesting State ... would offend against the provision of the Irish Constitution if administered in an Irish court.[45]

Furthermore, even in this second case, the feared consequences must be closely and directly connected to the court's order; to justify refusal of return, the offence to the constitutional principles must be a direct and immediate consequence of such order rather than a mere possibility, i.e. one of various scenarios the child would face.[46]

The decision of the Irish Supreme Court thereby offers some guidance for situations where Member States have different views regarding rights

43 See Supreme Court of Ireland, 15.12.2011, above n. 15.

44 Reference is made to Articles 41 and 42 of the Irish Constitution, which read as follows: 'The State ... guarantees to protect the Family in its constitution and authority' (Article 41, para. 1) and 'The State acknowledges that the primary and natural educator of the child is the Family and guarantees to respect the inalienable right and duty of parents to provide, according to their means, for the religious and moral, intellectual, physical and social education of their children' (Article 42, para. 1).

45 Supreme Court of Ireland, 15.12.2011, para. 52.

46 See the decision last cited, para. 56. The Court thus found that the practice whereby English courts considering childcare application follow the so-called single track – according to which all issues, including adoption, are addressed in a single hearing – does not justify refusing return on the basis of Article 20. In fact, adoption would be no more than a possibility and was not even proposed at that given stage of the childcare procedure (see para. 67).

guaranteed at a constitutional level. Indeed, although the standard of human rights protection is higher and more comparable within the EU, one can imagine situations in which the application of Article 20 could be challenged.

A good case, for example, would be the return of a child in cases of maternal surrogacy and same-sex couples. It is well known how States have different views and policies in the area of maternal surrogacy and parenthood by same-sex partners. The majority of EU Member States grant same-sex couples the same rights as heterosexual couples. Some (such as Spain, the Netherlands, Sweden and others) also recognise the right to parenthood, others don't. However, even in these latter countries, that do not establish a right to parenthood (such as Italy), once a child is born abroad and registered to a same-sex couple in the State of birth, the principle of the best interests of the child commands that such status and the associated parental relations be fully recognised.

On the contrary, in other EU countries, the legal (and possibly the social) framework does not provide for the recognition of same-sex couples, and children of such couples will not be recognised as such, regardless of whether they are born abroad. Moreover, it is argued that issues concerning the status of citizens and family matters fall outside the scope of EU law, at least from a theoretical point of view. Therefore, imposing a common sharing of values is beyond the powers of the EU.

Such a situation could trigger Article 20 and the fundamental rights exception. No abduction case among same-sex partners is known to the present author. However, given the rising number of same-sex couples entering into parental relations, same-sex couples will sooner or later also experience problems arising out of the failure of a couple relationship, including the plague of child abduction. Thus, this issue will raise further unexplored questions.

For example, let us imagine the case of a same-sex couple of Hungarian nationality. They become parents to a child through maternal surrogacy in Canada and subsequently return to Hungary to settle as a family. Knowing the legal and political difficulties in having the birth deed recognised in Hungary, they initially request that the child is registered to only one of them, such as the man bearing a biological link to the child in the case of a male same-sex couple or the woman who delivered the child in the case of a female same-sex couple. Later, they ask the Canadian court to rectify the deed so as to include also the second (intended) parent; however, uncertain of the final outcome, the couple ultimately decides not to seek the recognition of this second document in Hungary. When the couple subsequently splits, the non-biological parent (a fully legitimate parent, according to the State of birth of the child) decides not to remain in a country that does not recognise his/her parental rights and flees to Spain with the child. The day after his/her arrival he/she asks for recognition of the second Canadian birth deed and initiates proceedings asking for full custody over the child. When the left-behind parent files a return application under the 1980 Hague Convention before the Spanish court, the abducting parent raises an Article 20 exception, arguing that he/she would not be considered a parent by the Hungarian court and that, should the child be returned, his/her right to family life (and the child's rights too) would be infringed.

In such a situation, one could imagine that the Spanish court might be tempted to refuse return on the basis that not recognising the abducting parent's status and that of the child would violate the fundamental rights of both child and parent. Such an issue involves constitutional rights and should be determined in the State of residence according to the standards set by the ECHR and EU Charter. However, could we really blame the State of refuge for not *taking the risk* of depriving a child of his/her *status filiationis* in relation to his/her 'intended' parent and thereby declining to send the child and parent back to a State where they would have to challenge the courts to see their rights recognised?

Opening the Pandora's box of Article 20 defences might however also turn into a double-edged sword. The interpretation offered in the aforementioned case leads to the full recognition of the *status filiationis*; however, one could also imagine the opposite situation whereby Article 20 is triggered to defend a State's interest over its specific view on parental rights, thus leading to non-recognition of same-sex parental rights.

Suppose a same-sex couple of Lithuanian and Hungarian nationality is habitually resident in Spain, where they become parents to a child born in Spain through maternal surrogacy. When the couple's relationship deteriorates, one of the two – either the women who actually delivered the child or the man who has a biological link to the child – abducts the child to Hungary. He/she then initiates custody proceedings in this State and requests sole custody. As is common among heterologous couples, the left-behind (intended or social) parent requests the return of the child to Spain and initiates parallel custody proceedings in that country. What would be the likely reaction of Hungarian courts? Could we imagine that Hungary, a State that does not recognise same-sex relations and the parental tie to children born to such relationships, would refuse to return the child to a country where such unions and relationships are recognised, arguing that such a situation would violate the general principles of the requested State?

No answer to these hypothetical cases is currently available. The primary aim in outlining them was to illustrate how the field of human rights and fundamental principles in family matters is still developing and remains far from settled. Article 20 could usefully play a role in such scenarios. Nonetheless, it should be emphasised that such a provision favours neither a uniform application nor a coordination of competence. On the contrary, it crystallises diversities and fosters forum shopping. Although the latter might be done for a just cause – i.e. the protection of internal consistency and standards of protection – operating this provision should not be encouraged within the EU legal system.

IMPACT OF THE BEST INTERESTS OF THE CHILD ON THE BRUSSELS II *TER* REGULATION

Laura CARPANETO

1. The Best Interests of the Child and the 'Brussels II System': Setting Terms of Reference 265
2. Impact of the BIC Principle: The Structure and Scope of Application 270
3. Rules on Jurisdiction 274
4. More Efficient Circulation of Decisions 277
5. The New Proactive Attitude Toward Hearing the Child and Mediation 279
6. Assessment of the Child's Situation in 'Moving' within the EU Judicial Area 281
7. Is the BIC Better Protected by the New Rules? 284

1. THE BEST INTERESTS OF THE CHILD AND THE 'BRUSSELS II SYSTEM': SETTING TERMS OF REFERENCE

The best interests of the child[1] (BIC) is the key principle of the 1989 CRC, one of most ratified treaties in the world. Article 3 of the CRC states that the best interests of the child shall be a primary consideration in all actions concerning children, and other Articles explain how the BIC shall be considered in specific

[1] On the notion of the BIC under Article 3 CRC, see Committee on the Rights of the Child, General Comment No. 14 (2013) on the right of the child to have his or her best interests taken as a primary consideration (Article 3 para. 1). On the notion in (public) international law, see C. FOCARELLI, 'La Convenzione di New York sui diritti del fanciullo e ilconcetto di 'best interest of the child', (2010) *Rivista di diritto internazionale*, 981. On the BIC in private international law, see M. DISTEFANO, *Interesse superiore del minore e sottrazione internazionale di minori*, CEDAM, Padua 2012; K. LENAERTS, 'The Best Interests of the Child Always Come First: The Brussels II bis Regulation and the European Court of Justice', (2013) *Jurisprudencija/Jurisprudence* (online), 1302–1328; J.M. POBJOY, 'The Best Interests of the Child Principle as an Independent Source of International Protection', (2015) *International and Comparative Law Quarterly*, vol. 64, 327–363; O. LOPES PEGNA, 'L'interesse superiore

situations.[2] As a well-established principle,[3] to what extent the BIC is an independent source of protection, for example, for migrant children, is widely debated.[4]

Today, the BIC principle surely plays a relevant and growing role in private international law, mainly due to increasing interaction between human rights and private international law: human rights protection strongly influences the functioning of private international law rules,[5] which are now not only interpreted coherently but also shaped to grant protection to human (and in particular children's) rights. On the other hand, the adoption of, as far as possible, uniform private international rules on matters concerning children is deemed in itself as facilitating the application and implementation of the BIC.[6]

---

del minore nel regolamento n. 2201/2003', (2013) *Rivista di diritto internazionale privato e processuale*, 357; R. Schuz, 'Influence of the CRC on Hague Conventions', (2010) *Journal of Family, Law and the Practice*, 48.

2 Reference is made to the situation of a child who might be separated from his/her parents (Article 9) to the situation of the common responsibilities of both parents for the upbringing and development of the child (Article 18), to adoption proceedings (Article 21), to the situation of children deprived of liberty being separated (Article 37) and to the situation of children accused of having infringed the criminal law. See C. Focarelli, above n. 1, p. 981 ff. and M. Zupan, *The Best Interests of the Child: a Guiding Principle in Administering Cross-Border Child-Related Matters*, in T. Liefaard and J. Sloth-Nielsen (eds.), *The United Nations Convention on the Rights of the Child. Taking Stock after 25 years and looking Ahead*, 2016, at 214, where the Author points out the importance of the above provisions for resolving cross-border cases.

3 This principle is recalled also in other instruments of (public) international law. Reference is made, for example, to the Convention on the elimination of all forms of discrimination against women, the African Charter on the rights and welfare of the child, the Charter of Fundamental Rights of the European Union. See J.M. Pobjoy, above n. 1, at 328. The impact of the best interests of the child in the Hague Conference on Private International Law's Conventions is expressly analysed by M. Zupan, above n. 2, at 215–219.

4 See J.M Pobjoy, above n. 1, at 328. In general, on the protection which instruments of public as well as private international law may grant to migrant children see F. Ippolito and G. Biagioni, *Migrant Children: Challenges for Public and Private International Law*, Editorialescientifica, Naples 2016.

5 See L.R. Kiestra, *The Impact of the European Convention on Human Rights on Private International Law*, 2013, https://rechercheisidore.fr/search/resource/?uri=10670%2F1.azcvbf; P. Kinsh, 'L'apport de la jurisprudence de la Court Européenne des droits de l'homme', in P. Lagarde (ed.), *La reconnaissance des situations en droit international privé*, Pedone, Paris, 2013, pp. 43–45; ibid., 'Recognition in the Forum of a Status Acquired Abroad – Private International Law Rules and European Human Rights Law', in K. Boele-Woelki, T. Einhorn, D. Girsberger and S. Symeonydes (eds.), *Convergence and Divergence in Private International Law – Liber Amicorum Kurt Siehr*, Eleven International, The Hague 2010, 272 ff.; P. Ivaldi and C.E. Tuo, 'Diritti fondamentali e diritto internazionale private dell'Unione europea nella prospettiva dell'adesione alla CEDU', (2012) *Rivista di diritto internazionale privato e processuale*, 736.

6 See UN Committee on the Rights of the Child, General Comment No. 14, para. 68, p. 15, where specific reference is made to the main instruments in force at that time (i.e. 1980 Convention on the Civil Aspects of International Child Abduction, 1993 Convention on the Protection of Children and Co-operation in Respect of Intercountry Adoption, the

A second reason possibly explaining the BIC's growing relevance in private international law is the 'irresistible extension'[7] of party autonomy to adults' relationships and their 'liberalisation', which needs to be counterbalanced by greater attention to the protection of the BIC, with the child considered a weaker party in family relationships. Consequently, family law tends today to focus not on marriage, but on parent-child relationships.[8]

EU private international law is developing coherently with these generally emerging global trends. Within the EU judicial area, interaction of private international law rules and fundamental freedoms makes it possible for adults to select a legal order that better satisfies their interests in personal and economic matters. Against this background, the EU's focus has shifted onto children's protection, in particular after the Lisbon Treaty: besides Member States' international obligations to protect the BIC derived from the CRC's ratification, today the EU itself is committed to pursuing the protection of children and their interests, as expressed in Article 3 TFEU and Article 24 of the European Charter of Fundamental Rights, which has achieved the same value as the fundamental Treaties.[9]

In particular, the BIC's increasing relevance clearly results from the evolution of the 'Brussels II system', the cornerstone rules of EU private international law in family matters, originally embodied in Regulation 1347/2000 (Brussels II), now in Regulation 2201/2003 (Brussels II *bis*) and, starting from the 01 August 2022, in Regulation 2019/1111 (Brussels II *ter*).[10] A few months after the adoption of the Brussels II Regulation, the need to grant equal protection to all children formed the basis of its first amendment,[11] which resulted not only in the

1973 Convention on Recognition and Enforcement of Decisions Relating to Maintenance Obligations and the 1973 Convention on the Law Applicable to Maintenance Obligations), which have been a primary source of inspiration for the EU instruments in the field. See also European Parliament Resolution of 28.04.2016 on safeguarding the best interests of the child across the EU on the basis of petitions addressed to the European Parliament (2016/2575(RSP)), para. 23, where Member States are called to encourage non-contracting States to join the 1993 Hague Convention 'which would guarantee that all children benefit from the same standards'.

7 See A.E. von Overbeck, 'L'irrèsistible extension de l'autonomie en droit international privé', in *Nouveaux itineraries en droit. Hommage à Francois Rigaux*, Bruylant, Bruxelles 1993, pp. 619–636.

8 See G. Douglas, '*Marriage, Cohabitation, and Parenthood – from Contract to Status?*', in S.N. Katz, J. Eekelaar and M. Macklean (eds.), *Cross Currents: Family Law and Policy in the US and England*, Oxford Scholarship Online, Oxford 2000, p. 212.

9 In this light, a new mechanism of surveillance and monitoring in respect of the best interests of the child has been set up, by virtue of the 'Eurochild report'. See COM (2014) 224 final, 2013 Report on the Application of the EU Charter of Fundamental Rights, and SWD (2014) 141 final – Commission Staff Working Document accompanying the Report. On this point, see M. Zupan, above n. 2, 220.

10 See art. 105 of Regulation 2019/1111.

11 See recital no. 5 of the Regulation 2201/2003.

enlargement of its scope to include children born outside of wedlock,[12] but also in the adoption of innovative solutions in the area of parental responsibility.[13] A few years later, the Commission embarked on the first recast, focusing on matrimonial matters,[14] resulting in no changes to the Brussels II *bis* Regulation, but in the adoption of a separate legal instrument applicable to cross-border divorces and separations (Regulation 1259/2012).

A novelty with an indirect, but crucial impact on the Brussels II *bis* Regulation's proper functioning in relation to the BIC is the urgent preliminary reference procedure (PPU).[15] After this fast track's introduction in 2008,[16] the Court of Justice has consistently recognised urgency in cases within the scope of application of the Brussels II *bis* Regulation and, in particular, in cases concerning a child's separation from one of the parents.[17] In 2016, a second recast started,[18]

---

12 See COM (2002). With specific reference to the enlargement of the scope of application of the Regulation, see O. Lopes Pegna, above n. 1, at 361.

13 Reference is made, in particular, to: (i) the introduction of special rules of international child abduction, supplementing those of the 1980 Hague Convention; (ii) the introduction of some space for party autonomy in choice of court; and (iii) the mechanism of the transfer of jurisdiction to a more appropriate forum.

14 See Proposal for a Council Regulation amending Regulation (EC) No. 2201/2003 as regards jurisdiction and introducing rules concerning the applicable law in matrimonial matters COM (2006) 399.

15 The urgent preliminary procedure (also known with the acronym 'PPU' deriving from the French translation '*procedure préjudicielle d'urgence*') is regulated by Article 23a of the Statute of the Court, Article 107 of the Rules of Procedure, paras. 39 and 40 of the Recommendations to national courts and tribunals in relation to the initiation of preliminary ruling proceedings, in OJ C 338 06.11.2012, pp. 1–6. See T. Kruger and L. Samyn, '*Brussels II bis: Successes and Suggested Improvements*', (2016) *Journal of Private International Law*, 146, where they point out how crucial this mechanism has been to adequate development of the law combined with respect of the rights of the children and families. On the relevance of the PPU mechanism in Brussels II *bis* proceedings, see K. Lenaerts, above n. 1, at 1303, and, with specific reference to child abduction proceedings, in particular where compared with the procedure *vis-à-vis* the European Court of Human Rights, see R. Schuz, *The Hague Child Abduction Convention: A Critical Analysis*, Hart Publishing, Oxford/Portland 2013, p. 28.

16 See Council Decision of 20 December 2007 amending the Protocol on the Statute of the Court of Justice, OJ L 24 of 29 January 2008, p. 42; Amendments to the Rules of Procedure of the Court of Justice, OJ L 24 of 29 January 2008, p. 39; and OJ L 92 of 13 April 2010, p. 12. The PPU is available from 1 March 2008.

17 See A. Dutta and A. Schulz, 'First Cornerstones of the EU Rules on Cross-border Child Cases: The Jurisprudence of the Court of Justice of the European Union on the Brussels IIa Regulation From C to Health Service Executive', (2015) *Journal of Private International Law*, 1–40, at 7.

18 On the recast procedure, see *Recasting the Brussels IIa Regulation. Workshop 8 November 2016*, PE 571.383; H. Van Loon, 'The Brussels IIa Regulation: Towards a Review?', *in Cross-Border Activities in the EU – Making Life Easier for Citizens*, PE 510.003, 2015, pp. 177–207; C. Honorati, 'La proposta di revisione del regolamento Bruxelles II bis: più tutela per iminori e più efficacia nell'esecuzione delle sentenze', (2017) *Rivista di dirittointernazionale privato e processuale*, 2–55; M.C. Baruffi, 'Uno spazio di libertà, sicurezza e giustizia a misura di minori: la sfida (in)compiuta dell'Unione europea nei casi di sottrazioneinternazionale', (2017) *Freedom, Security and Justice: European Legal Studies*, 2–25; Th. de Boer,

focusing on parental responsibility,[19] and aimed at better protecting the best interests of the child by simplifying the procedures and enhancing their efficiency.[20]

EU institutions have reviewed the existing rules in order to strike a new balance between the need to provide as clear-cut uniform rules of private (procedural) international law as possible based on abstract reasoning for the BIC involved in cross-border proceedings of parental responsibility and, conversely, the need to better protect the BIC in specific and concrete situations. Under the post-Lisbon legal framework, this is a challenging task that requires a more proactive approach to the protection of the BIC. The task is challenging also because the Brussels II *bis* Regulation, as previously mentioned, is the cornerstone of EU private international law instruments in family matters and, therefore, impacts other private international law rules concerning children.[21]

The importance of the revision of such a key instrument is also confirmed by the fact that, despite Brexit, the United Kingdom has participated in the recast and, up to now, is bound by Regulation 2019/1111.[22]

'What We Should Not Expect from a Recast of the Brussels IIbis Regulation', (2015) *Nederlands Internationaal Privaatrecht*, 10 ff.; T. Kruger and L. Samyn, above n. 14, pp. 132–168; E. Rodriguez Pineau, 'La refundición del Reglamento Bruselas II bis: de Nuevo sobre la function del derecho internacional privado europeo', (2017) *Revista Espanola de Derecho Internacional*, vol. 69, 139–165; B. Ubertazzi, 'The Hearing of the Child in the Brussels IIa Regulation and its Recast Proposal', (2017) *Journal of Private International Law*, 568–601; C. Honorati, 'La proposta di revisione del Regolamento Bruxelles II-bis: più tutela per iminori e più efficacia nell'esecuzione delle decisioni', (2017) *Rivista di diritto internazionale privato e processuale*, 247–282; J. Borg-Barther, *Jurisdiction in Matrimonial Matters – Reflections for the Review of the Brussels IIa Regulation*, PE 571.361, 2016.

19 See the Study on the assessment of Regulation (EC) 2201/2003 and the policy options for its amendment, (Final Evaluation Report) at https://publications.europa.eu/en/publication-detail/-/publication/463a5c10-9149-11e8-8bc1-01aa75ed71a1/language-en, in particular at p. 53.

20 See Commission Proposal for a Council Regulation on jurisdiction, the recognition and enforcement of decisions in matrimonial matters and the matters of parental responsibility and on international child abduction (recast), COM (2016), 411, 30.6.2016, p. 2.

21 In this regard, it should be considered that Regulation 4/2009 does not expressly mention the BIC among its leading principles and the European Court of Justice has missed the opportunity to consider them as a guiding principle for the interpretation of the rules on jurisdiction, although reference is made to it in the joint cases C-400/13 and C-408/13, *Sanders*, ECLI:EU:C:2014:2461. On this point, see M. Zupan, above n. 2, at 222. It should be also pointed out that no express reference exists in other EU private international law instruments on family matters to the need of applying them coherently with the Brussels II *bis* Regulation (whilst in the field of civil and commercial matters, it is imperative to interpret Brussels Ia, Rome I and Rome II Regulations as a 'system', see recital no. 7 of the Rome I Regulation stating that its substantive scope as well as the provisions should be consistent with Brussels I Regulation and, therefore, also with Brussels Ia, as well as with Regulation Rome II).

22 On this topic, see N. Bennet, 'The European Family in Crisis: The Consequences of Brexit on English Family Law', in *Family Law*, October 2018. On the effects of the Brexit on private international law instruments concerning children in the United Kingdom, see P. Beaumont,

In the following section, the amendments proposed by the institutions in the recast procedure and finally incorporated in the Brussels II *ter* Regulation are considered through the lens of the BIC.[23]

2. IMPACT OF THE BIC PRINCIPLE: THE STRUCTURE AND SCOPE OF APPLICATION

Crucial for swifter application of the 'Brussels II system' is clear determination of its (broad) scope of application and also clearer determination of its key notions (i.e. parental responsibility matters and habitual residence of the child). Under the current rules, parental responsibility matters are completely autonomous from matrimonial ones:[24] when dissolution of marriage jurisdiction is settled without clear evidence of prorogation in favour of that court under Article 12 of Brussels II *bis*, parental responsibility matters concerning a child born in wedlock shall be adjudicated by the court of her/his habitual residence.[25] In adopting Regulation 2019/1111, EU institutions have not taken the opportunity to create an independent instrument devoted only to issues of parental responsibility.[26] Even if that solution might have further increased the EU private international law instruments' fragmentation, practice has proved that in parental responsibility matters, the EU has been not only more successful in amending existing rules, but also in adopting innovative solutions. One might argue that a more precise determination of the Regulation's scope would have made its application easier not only internally (i.e. in relation to matrimonial matters), but also with regard to other EU instruments and other instruments in force globally.

'Private International Law Concerning Children in the UK after Brexit: Comparing Hague Treaty Law with EU Regulations', available at https://www.abdn.ac.uk/law/documents/CPIL%20Working%20Paper%20No%202017_2.pdf.

23 For information on the status of the ongoing recast procedure, see the following web-page: http://www.europarl.europa.eu/oeil/popups/ficheprocedure.do?lang=en&reference=2016/0190(CNS)#tab-0.

24 Brussels II *bis* (as well as Brussels II *ter*) Regulation has a double character: it provides rules on jurisdiction and recognition and execution, on one side, and autonomous rules concerning respectively matrimonial and parental responsibility matters, on the other.

25 Reference is made in C-184/14, *A v. B*, ECLI:EU:C:2015:479, where the Court confirmed that in the absence of prorogation of jurisdiction towards ongoing proceedings on matrimonial matters, the courts where the children have their habitual residence shall retain jurisdiction on parental responsibility matters. This also means that no *lis pendens* arises from the two proceedings mentioned. See I. Kunda and D. Vrbljanac, 'Lis Pendens' (Articles 16, 19), in C. Honorati (ed.), *Jurisdiction in Matrimonial Matters, Parental Responsibility and International Abduction*, Giappichelli, Turin 2017, pp. 227–231.

26 Despite authoritative suggestions in this regard, see A. Borràs, 'From Brussels II to Brussels II bis and Further', in K. Boele-Woelki and C. Gonzales Beilfuss (eds.), *Brussels II bis: Its Impact and Application in the Member States*, Intersentia, Antwerp 2007, pp. 3–22, at p. 21.

In relation to other EU instruments, the Brussels II *bis* (as well as *ter*) Regulation keeps its cornerstone position in family matters, for example, through Article 3 of Regulation 4/2009 and Article 5 of Regulation 2016/1103, which coordinate their rules on jurisdiction with those provided by the Regulation. When such coordination is not expressly established, the European Court of Justice tends to confirm the centrality of Brussels II system rules.[27]

Furthermore, incidental questions on parental responsibility arising before an authority of a Member State without jurisdiction under the Regulation are expressly addressed by the new Regulation, which states that the jurisdictional authority should solve the incidental question, with effects limited to the proceedings at stake.[28]

In external relations with instruments in force globally, a step forward in the BIC has been made by better clarifying the Brussels II *ter* Regulation's relationship with the 1996 Hague Convention (ratified by all EU Member States). More precisely, the 1996 Hague Convention conflict of law rules are expressly recalled as applicable by the Member States' authorities.[29] Such a step, even if it is not much celebrated, surely increases global uniformity and aligns the Brussels II system with modern EU Regulations on private international law matters, providing rules aimed at solving all private international law issues arising in cross-border situations. Furthermore, while confirming the Regulation's jurisdictional priority over that of the 1996 Hague Convention anytime the child concerned habitually resides in an EU Member State's territory, in specific circumstances, the new rules extend application of some 1996 Hague Convention jurisdictional rules to fill gaps in the BIC in practice.[30]

Practice shows that difficulties arise in establishing the scope of application *ratione materiae* and, in particular, whether a public law issue falls within the Brussels system.

The European Court of Justice case law has provided some guidance,[31] which has not been incorporated into new rules, for example, in the recitals.

In this regard, a most delicate issue which has been considered in the recast is whether to expressly extend the application of new rules to unaccompanied

27 Reference is made in the following Court of Justice case-law: C-404/14, *Matouskova*, ECLI:EU:C:2015:653, and C-565/16, *Saponaro*, ECLI:EU:C:2018:265. See M. Zupan, 'Scope of Application, Definitions and Relations to Other Instruments', in C. Honorati (ed.), *Jurisdiction in Matrimonial Matters, Parental Responsibility and International Abduction*, above n. 25, at 5.

28 See recital no. 32 of the Regulation 2019/1111, where the example of a succession dispute in which a child is involved and a guardian *ad litem* needs to be appointed is made.

29 See Recital 92 Regulation 2019/1111.

30 See art. 97 of Regulation 2019/111. On this topic, see M. Zupan, above n. 2, pp. 33–35, and T. Kruger and L. Samyn, above n. 14, pp. 151–154.

31 Reference is made to C-435/06, A, ECLI:EU:C:2007:714 and C-92/12 PPU, *Health Service Executive v. S.C. and A.C.*, ECLI:EU:C:2012:255.

minors.[32] With reference to the 1996 Hague Convention, the Brussels II system's primary source of inspiration, this issue was debated during a Special Session in October 2017.[33] The majority of States did not agree on possibly and expressly extending the Convention rules' application to unaccompanied minors, relying mainly on the Convention's exclusion from the scope of its application the rights of asylum and immigration under Article 4(j).[34] Under the Brussels II *bis* Regulation, the same exclusion is provided under recital 10. Furthermore, a specific ground of jurisdiction based on presence in case of refugee or internationally displaced children is expressly foreseen under Article 13(2). However, starting from the considerations above and taking into account, on the one hand, the European Court of Justice's approach, which tends to construe the scope of application of the Regulation as extending to all measures for the protection of minors, including those taken by public authorities,[35] and, on the other, the relevance of the BIC principle[36] and its interpretative function, there is little doubt that the Brussels II *bis* Regulation applies also to migration and asylum and, in particular, to unaccompanied minors.[37]

The new rules confirm the above approach and, in this light, references to decisions on rights of asylum and immigration have been removed. Furthermore, whilst, on the one hand, the proposal of a specific recital providing that jurisdiction rules should be applicable to refugee children and children who have been internationally displaced, not only by disturbances in their country, but also for socio-economic reasons, has not been accepted,[38] on the

32 Under EU law, the unaccompanied minors are those children who are not accompanied by adults who are responsible for them whether by law or by the practice of the Member State concerned and for as long as they are not effectively taken into the care of that adult (see article 2(j) Dublin Regulation).

33 See Prel doc special session no. 7.

34 In the Explanatory report (no. 36), with regard to the meaning of the above exclusion, Prof. Paul Lagarde pointed out that 'These are decisions which derive from the sovereign power of States. Only decisions on these matters are excluded: in other words, the granting of asylum or of a residence permit. The protection and representation of children who are applying for asylum or for a residence permit fall, to the contrary, within the scope of the Convention'.

35 See C-435/06, *C*, ECLI:EU:C:2014:2461, and C-523/07, *A*, ECLI:EU:C:2009:225; C-92/12 PPU, *Health Service Executive v. S.C. and A.C.*, ECLI:EU:C:2012:255.

36 Committee on the Rights of the Child, General Comment No. 6, 2005, CRC/GC/2005/6, paras. 19–21.

37 See S. Corneloup (coordinator), *Children On the Move: A Private International Law Perspective*, Study for the Juri Committee, PE 583.158 – June 2017, p. 13–14, where the group of researchers expressly suggests recalling Lagarde's explanations (see above n. 33) concerning the scope of application of the 1996 Hague Convention also within the context of the new Brussels II *bis* Regulation. Such an invitation has not been followed by the Commission in its proposal.

38 See European Parliament legislative resolution of 18 January 2018 on the proposal for a Council Regulation on jurisdiction, the recognition and enforcement of decisions in matrimonial matters and matters of parental responsibility, and on international child abduction (recast) (COM(2016)0411 – C8-0322/2016 – 2016/0190(CNS)) (Special legislative procedure – consultation – recast).

other, recital 25 of Regulation 2019/1111 introduces further guidance as to coordinate the application of the new rules with the analogous jurisdictional rules of the 1996 Hague Convention. More precisely, under the above recital, the rule on jurisdiction grounded on the presence of the child under Article 11 of the Regulation should be applied only to children who had their habitual residence in a Member State before the displacement and, therefore, assuming that children who had their habitual residence in a third State could be granted a *forum* under the relevant rules of the 1996 Hague Convention.

Further steps toward better assessment of the scope of application have been made. First, the new rules apply to children up to 18 years old (including those having acquired capacity before that age, through emancipation for example), but rules on child abduction, coherent with the 1980 Hague Convention, apply only to children under 16 years old.[39] The introduction of such a rule at EU level should surely be appreciated since it grants uniform interpretation of a key notion, avoiding any reference to national laws.

With regard to the scope of application *ratione personae*, the new Regulation has not taken the opportunity to provide guidance on the position of persons having *de facto* family ties with the child in cross-border proceedings concerning parental responsibility matters, even if some rules of Regulation 2019/111 expressly recognise the possibility for them, being interested parties, to act in the BIC.

On the other hand, the European Court of Justice has recently confirmed the trend toward extending the scope of application *ratione personae* in the *Valcheva* case, where a grandmother's right of visitation was recognised as falling within Brussels II *bis*' scope of application.[40]

Habitual residence is another key notion for determining the Brussels II *bis* Regulation's scope of application and its functioning. Notwithstanding its importance and difficulties in practical application, the new Regulation does not provide any further guidance in this regard.[41] Indeed, European Court of

---

See European Parliament legislative resolution of 18 January 2018 on the proposal for a Council Regulation on jurisdiction, the recognition and enforcement of decisions in matrimonial matters and matters of parental responsibility, and on international child abduction (recast) (COM(2016)0411 – C8-0322/2016 – 2016/0190(CNS)) (Special legislative procedure – consultation – recast).

39 See recital no. 17 of the Regulation 2019/111.

40 See C-335/17, *Neli Valcheva* v. *Georgios Barbanarakis*, ECLI:EU:C:2018:359, at para. 36, where the Court points out that in order to avoid the adoption of conflicting measures in the best interests of the child, the same court which has given the custody to the child to the father and has recognised the right to visit of the mother, shall deal also with the issue of the right to visit to a person different from the parents.

41 The European Parliament was in favour of the introduction of a definition, see European Parliament Resolution 28 April 2016 on safeguarding the best interests of the child across EU on the basis of the petitions addressed to the European Parliament (2016/2575(RSP)), but the Commission's proposal does not take into account this indication and the European

Justice case law has not only indicated the rationale underlying this notion and the elements considered for its assessment, but has also provided specific guidance in difficult cases, for example, concerning new born children in abduction proceedings.[42] The choice not to provide a specific definition of habitual residence in parental responsibility issues and, thus, not to transform a factual notion into a legal one, seems coherent with the overall purpose of facilitating free movement of persons and their integration into new countries; it also seems coherent with the approach adopted under the aegis of the Hague Conference on Private International Law. Given its crucial role, however, the introduction of a few recitals to synthesise the assessment method of the child's habitual residence, as indicated by European Court of Justice case law, would have surely aided the Regulation's swifter application.[43] Still, it is possible that the Commission will adopt an adjourned version of the Practice Guide, which, as happened for previous versions, and will provide specific guidance for the interpretation of such a notion.[44]

3. RULES ON JURISDICTION

Rules on jurisdiction now in force are shaped for the BIC following the criterion of proximity:[45] since citizenship no longer necessarily reflects the proximity of a child to a specific jurisdiction, the court of the child's habitual residence decides the case. Habitual residence is therefore *in abstracto* the ground that better grants protection to the BIC (*rectius* of all children) at the procedural level. Assigning jurisdiction to the court that effectively and *in concreto* is better placed to decide the specific case, makes it exceptionally possible to move from the general rule and to apply special ones, provided that such action serves the BIC. Besides the general rule of jurisdiction, holders of parental responsibility can prorogue jurisdiction in favour of courts exercising jurisdiction on matrimonial matters

---

Parliament has not reiterated it during the recast, see European Parliament Legislative Resolution 18 January 2018 on the proposal for a Council regulation on jurisdiction, the recognition and enforcement of decisions in matrimonial matters and matters of parental responsibility, and on international child abduction (recast) (COM(2016)411 – C8-0322/2016 – 2016/0190(CNS)).

42 Reference is made in case C-376/14 PPU, *C. v. M.*, ECLI:EU:C:2014:2268, at paras. 50–57.

43 Such a solution has been adopted in Regulation 650/2012 in recitals 24 and 25.

44 This approach has been recently followed by the Hague Conference of Private International Law for the 1993 Hague Convention on protection of children and co-operation in respect of inter-country adoption: given the challenges encountered by some contracting States in determining the habitual residence of the adoptive parents as well as of the adoptable children, a note has been recently published. The document is available at https://assets.hcch.net/docs/12255707-4d23-4f90-a819-5e759d0d7245.pdf.

45 See S. Cornelup, 'Les règles de compétence relatives à la responsabilité parentale', in H. Fulchiron and C. Nourissat (eds.), *Le nouveau droit communautaire du divorce et de la responsabilité parentale*, Dalloz, Paris 2005, pp. 79 ff.

or of courts of the State having a substantial connection with the child; on the other hand, transferring the case to a more appropriate *forum* is also possible.

This flexible structure of rules on jurisdiction[46] is not altered in the new Regulation. However, the important amendment proposed by the Commission that rules on jurisdiction will no longer refer to a court, but more generally to an authority, in order to encompass any judicial or administrative authority having jurisdiction on matters of parental responsibility, has not been included in the final version.[47]

The new Regulation not only confirms that rules on jurisdiction are shaped toward the BIC, but it also emphasises that such rules should be applied in compliance with the BIC, as defined by Article 24 of the Charter of Fundamental Rights and by the CRC.[48] Under the post-Lisbon legal framework, a general duty to interpret and apply any piece of EU law in light of the BIC arises; *a fortiori*, this shall be followed in applying the Brussels II system's rules concerning parental responsibility. Thus, any time a departure from the general rule of the child's habitual residence is established based on party autonomy or jurisdictional transfer, specific reasoning that justifies such a departure in light of the BIC should be provided.

In relation to the general rule establishing jurisdiction of the court of the child's habitual residence, Regulation 2019/1111 clarifies that, in case of the child's lawful relocation, jurisdiction should follow the child. For proceedings already pending, the rule is to maintain the existing jurisdiction until the proceedings come to an end. However, the courts are also allowed to transfer jurisdiction, which, therefore, may move with the child.[49] These clarifications do not affect, however, the rule establishing *perpetuation jurisdictionis* for three months for proceedings modifying a decision on access rights in the Member State where the child's former habitual residence was before lawful transfer, provided that the parent left behind still has her/his habitual residence in that State.[50] An important novelty is the enhancement of party autonomy in the choice of court and, given that the achievement of an agreement on jurisdiction reduces litigation, this is an important step forward in light of the BIC.[51]

---

46 Given that – as clearly stated by the CJEU in the case of *E v. B* – '(j)urisdiction in matters of parental responsibility must be determined, above all, in the best interests of the child', flexibility is crucial.

47 See Proposal for a Council Regulation on jurisdiction, the recognition and enforcement of decisions in matrimonial matters and the matters of parental responsibility, and on international child abduction (recast) – General approach, available at https://www.consilium.europa.eu/register/en/content/out?&typ=ENTRY&i=ADV&DOC_ID=ST-15401-2018-INIT.

48 See recital no. 19 of Regulation 2019/1111.

49 See recital no. 21 of Regulation 2019/1111.

50 See art. 8 Regulation 2019/1111.

51 See P. Beaumont, above n. 22.

Under Article 10 of Regulation 2019/1111, proceedings in parental responsibility can be initiated (i) before the courts of a Member State having a substantial connection with the child, (ii) provided that the exercise of jurisdiction is in the BIC, and (iii) anytime the parties, as well as any holder of parental responsibility, so agree, not only at the time the court is seised, but also in the course of the proceedings.

As with choice of court, the new regime proposed also emphasises the exceptional character of the rule providing for a case's transfer to a more appropriate *forum*, and thus also confirms the necessity not to transfer the case further. An important novelty is the 'bi-directional' character of the transfer: besides the transfer from the court having jurisdiction to a more appropriate forum, under Article 14 of Regulation 2019/1111 a court not having jurisdiction may request a transfer of jurisdiction to the court of habitual residence of the child. Such a transfer shall be exceptional in nature and justified by the existence of a particular connection with that court, which is considered to be better placed to assess the BIC in that particular case.

No further guidance for the application of the transfer mechanism is provided. However, the European Court of Justice has made important statements in this regard in the *Child and Family Agency* case,[52] where the Court has clarified not only the transfer mechanism's rationale, but also indicated elements relevant for assessing whether the transfer complies with the BIC. First, a transfer shall have a 'concrete and real added value' that must be evaluated *not* based on Member States' substantial laws, but on procedural ones. Second, the transfer will be deemed in the BIC any time it does not negatively affect the child's free movement or that of persons involved. Important novelties with regard to provisional measures have been proposed and these are of great importance for granting protection to children involved in cross-border disputes. Notwithstanding its clear wording,[53] the European Court of Justice has made many decisions on the Brussels II *bis* Regulation's Article 20, aimed at clarifying not only its scope of application, but also the effects deriving from the adoption of protective measures in other proceedings. Under the Court's interpretation of current rules, provisional measures adopted by a court not having jurisdiction on the merits shall have only territorial reach and, therefore, cannot circulate within the European judicial area. Consequently, such measures cannot grant effective protection to the child.

---

52 Reference is made in case C-428/15, *Child and Family Agency v. J. D and R.P.D*, ECLI: EU:C:2016:819.

53 See on this point T. Kruger and L. Samyn, above n. 14, at 148, who point out that the existing rule of Brussels II *bis* is very clear, compared to other rules existing in other Regulations where, for example, it has been necessary for the Court to clarify the scope of application of the rule.

In an attempt to strike a new balance between the need to grant immediate protection to the child and the need to prevent forum shopping,[54] it has been originally proposed that protective measures should 'travel' with the child and, therefore, that such measures should be automatically enforceable in all Member States and that they should automatically expire as soon as the authority of the competent jurisdiction has ruled on the matter's merits.

In the end, such amendments have not been included: as a general rule, only provisional measures adopted by the court having jurisdiction 'travel' with the child. However, as an exception, the same regime has been granted also to those provisional measures adopted by the courts of the State of refuge for the protection of children from the grave risk of being exposed to an intolerable situation in return proceedings.[55,56]

4. MORE EFFICIENT CIRCULATION OF DECISIONS

Major problems have been encountered concerning the execution of decisions in other Member States.[57] Thus, the recast's intervention was twofold: (i) abolition of the *exequatur* for all decisions concerning parental responsibility matters, as has recently been done in civil and commercial matters with the Brussels Ia Regulation;[58] and (ii) measures to enforce decisions more efficiently (despite States' well-known reluctance *vis-à-vis* the imposition of a standard affecting national procedural rules).[59]

In the new Regulation, the abolition of *exequatur*, already applying for decisions on visitation rights and on the child's return, has been extended to all decisions falling within the Regulation's scope of application, including custody rights, child protection orders and placement orders.[60] Consequently, a decision

54 See T. Kruger, 'Enhancing Cross-Border Cooperation', *in Recasting the Brussels IIa Regulation. Workshop 8 November 2016*, PE 571.383, p. 39.

55 See recital 30 of Regulation 2019/1111.

56 Recital no. 40 of the Commission's proposal points out that such measures, when ordered without the respondent being summoned to appear, should not be recognised and enforced under the Regulation. Unlikely under the regime concerning the execution of decisions, under Article 35.3, provisional and protective measures do not need to be notified or communicated, neither translated into the official language of the State of destination.

57 It resulted in decisions that are often not executed or executed with significant delays. Furthermore, the intervention of specialised lawyers is necessary, and costs may vary from €1000 to €4000.

58 See S.M. Carbone and C.E. Tuo, *Il nuovo spazio giudiziario europeo in materia civile e commerciale. Il Regolamento CE n. 1215/2012*, Giappichelli, Turin 2016.

59 On the proposed rules on abolition of *exequatur* and execution of decisions, see E. Rodriguez Pineau, above n. 17, at p. 146–152.

60 See art. 34 of Regulation 2019/1111. Even if the *exequatur* is abolished with regard to all decisions on parental responsibility matters, decisions on the rights of visit as well as those

can be immediately executed in the destination State, where, under recital 60, competent authorities are granted the possibility of ordering, taking or arranging for specific measures at the enforcement stage, such as non-coercive but also coercive measures.

Besides the possibility of starting an action for non-recognition of a foreign decision in parental responsibility matters, expressly envisaged by the new Regulation, incorporating the achievement of the *Rinau* decision,[61] it is now also possible to suspend, or even refuse, execution under specific circumstances: not only when execution is suspended in the State of origin, but also when there is still room for an appeal against the decision itself.

Temporary suspension of the enforcement of the decision is also possible in case of grave risk of physical or psychological harm to the child. Such a request shall be made not only by the person against whom enforcement is sought, as well as by any interested party acting in the BIC, but also by the child concerned (where applicable under national law). However, if the grave risk is of a lasting nature, enforcement shall be refused.[62]

As authoritatively observed,[63] the Commission has proposed the *exequatur*'s abolition as inevitable. However, whether such a step is justified on the ground of enhancing mutual trust and European integration, or on the ground of enhancing the BIC, remains an open question. Besides the *exequatur*'s abolition, further measures have been introduced in order to make execution of foreign decisions in Member States more efficient.[64] To start the execution, the interested person shall provide the certificate, accompanied by a copy of the decision before the authority that has been granted competence for execution by the Member State where the decision shall be executed.

A very important change has occurred with regard to the so-called 'privileged decisions' on rights of access and return of the child: while under the current rules there is no way to stop their recognition and enforcement, under Article 50 of Regulation 2019/1111, in compliance with the principle *rebus sic stantibus*, their recognition and enforcement shall be refused if and to the extent that it is irreconcilable with a later decision relating to parental responsibility and concerning the same child. The different positions mentioned confirm a common need to strike a new balance between competing purposes: on the one side, extending the *exequatur*'s abolition to all decisions covered by the Regulation coherent with the Stockholm Program and with results achieved in other fields of civil judicial cooperation is clearly a step forward in enhancing mutual trust;

---

on the return of the child still follow a special regime, as expressly provided by section II of Title IV of Regulation 2019/1111. See E. Rodriguez Pineau, above n. 17, at p. 146.

61 C-195/08 PPU.

62 See art. 56 of Regulation 2019/1111.

63 See E. Rodriguez Pineau, above n. 17, at p. 149.

64 Reference is made in Articles 30–36 of the Commission's proposal.

on the other side, making it possible under Article 56 to suspend or refuse enforcement of all decisions (included the 'privileged' ones) in case of grave risk for the child, as well as under Article 50 to refuse recognition and enforcement of the 'privileged' decisions (for which automatic execution has been working since the Brussels II *bis* Regulation) anytime they are 'irreconcilable' with a later decision, clearly shows a greater attention to BIC *in concreto*.

5. THE NEW PROACTIVE ATTITUDE TOWARD HEARING THE CHILD AND MEDIATION

One of the most significant improvements in procedures concerning children is the acknowledgment that offering the child a genuine opportunity to express her/his views freely is crucial for the BIC principle's effectiveness. Hearing the child not only empowers her/him through direct participation in procedures affecting her/him, but also better enables the judge or authority to assess the factual situation, a particularly difficult task in cross-border proceedings.[65] In Regulation 2201/2003, despite a commitment in recital 33 to respect for fundamental rights, hearing the child still plays a limited role. First, an explicit requirement to hear the child is limited to child abduction procedures: when the 1980 Hague Convention rules on the general obligation to return the child in case of abduction and on exceptions to the above obligation apply, it shall be ensured that the child is given the opportunity to be heard, unless this appears inappropriate having regard to his or her age or degree of maturity.[66]

Notwithstanding the absence of a general requirement, failure to hear the child may be a ground for non-recognition of judgments in parental responsibility matters. More precisely, under Article 23(b), a foreign decision on parental responsibility may not be recognised in another EU country any time a child capable of forming her/his own views, in the absence of reasons of urgency, has not been heard.

A third field in which hearing the child plays a role is the issuance of certificates under Article 41(2)(c) for decisions concerning access and under Article 42(2)(a)

---

65 In this regard, it should be considered that in all proceedings, it is of great importance to avoid the exercise of a basic right of the child becoming an excessively onerous responsibility and this is all the more important in cross-border cases 'since the consequences of the choice expressed by the child can have a far heavier impact on the child's environment compared to cases geographically circumscribed to a small area'. See I. Pretelli, 'Child Abduction and Return Proceedings', in *Recasting the Brussels IIa Regulation*, above n. 17, at pp. 10–11.

66 It should be noted that this is one of the rules supplementing the 1980 Hague Convention, where a general obligation to hear the child is not clearly stated, but derives implicitly from Article 13.2. On this point, see B. Ubertazzi, 'Hearing of the Child', in C. Honorati (ed.), *Jurisdiction in Matrimonial Matters, Parental Responsibility and International Abduction*, above n. 25, at p. 171.

for decisions concerning the child's return. As is well known, these decisions are the first in the EU judicial space benefiting from the special regime of direct enforceability, subject to the issue of specific certificates, on which the court must declare, by 'ticking' a specific box, that the child had an opportunity to be heard, unless doing so was considered inappropriate. As the European Court of Justice has clearly pointed out in the *Aguirre Zarraga* case, courts of the State of origin decide whether hearing the child is appropriate and, if so, for taking all measures appropriate to the hearing's arrangement, having regard for the BIC and each case's circumstances. The current rules do not provide methods and means by which national courts should hear the child; they just recommend the use of EU rules on the taking-of-evidence Regulation.

Regulation 2019/1111, while confirming the recommendation above, takes a significant step forward in enhancing the BIC by providing a general, but very detailed, duty to hear the child in all proceedings concerning parental responsibility. Under Article 21,[67] all authorities exercising jurisdiction in proceedings concerning parental responsibility will have a duty to: (i) ensure that a child capable of forming views is given the genuine, effective opportunity to express those views freely during the proceedings; (ii) give due weight to the child's views according to age and maturity; and (iii) document its consideration in the decision. Such a solution is unprecedented: neither the 1996 Convention nor the 1980 Convention require that a child capable of forming her/his own views have a genuine, effective opportunity to express those views freely in judicial and administrative proceedings.[68]

In addition, the new rules reiterate the duty to hear the child in abduction proceedings[69] and confirm EU institutions' desire to enhance further the child's fundamental right to be heard.

In the same vein, a new pro-mediation stance is present. Article 25 of Regulation 2019/1111 imposes on the competent court a duty to examine

---

67 Article 21 – Right of the child to express his or her views: '1. When exercising their jurisdiction under section 2 of this Chapter, the authorities of the Member States shall, in accordance with national law and procedure, provide the child who is capable of forming his or her views with a genuine and effective opportunity to express his or her views, either directly, or through a representative or an appropriate body. 2. Where the court, in accordance with national law and procedure, gives a child an opportunity to express his or her view in accordance with this Article, the court shall give due weight to the views of the child in accordance with his or her age and maturity.'

68 See Permanent Bureau of the Hague Conference on Private International Law, in Recasting the Brussels IIa Regulation – Workshop on 08.11.2016, p. 70. Clearly, the two relevant Hague Conventions do not prevent the contracting States from hearing children in proceedings affecting them in accordance with their national procedural rules regarding the hearing of the child (as is clearly confirmed in Article 23(2)(b) of the 1996 Hague Convention, which is directly inspired by Article 12 of the Convention on the rights of the child).

69 Article 26 – Right of the child to express his or her views in return proceedings – 'Article 21 of this Regulation shall also apply in return proceedings under the 1980 Hague Convention.'

whether parties are willing to engage in mediation to find, in the BIC, an agreed solution, provided this does not unduly delay child abduction proceedings.[70] Under the new rules, competent authorities have a duty to consider achieving an amicable solution through mediation and other appropriate means for all cases concerning children, in particular in international child abductions. Reference is also made to the possibility for competent authorities to be assisted, where appropriate, by existing networks and support structures for mediation in cross-border parental responsibility disputes.

The European Parliament resolution of 18 January 2018 has proposed a specific amendment imposing on competent authorities, after assessment of the parties' desires, to ask them to engage in mediation. The Parliament also proposed: (i) a few amendments to facilitate parties' access to mediation (including a mention of financial aid); and (ii) the introduction of a new provision[71] stressing the importance of mediators' specific education in cross-border family disputes. However, such proposals have not been included in the final version of the Regulation.

None of the institutions have proposed to include in the new rules a specific reference to the European Parliament Coordinator on children's rights (formerly Mediator for International Parental Child Abduction), which has the power to provide assistance and also to encourage parties to have access to mediation. A reference within a recital would surely have been useful to let people, and not just experts in the field, know of its existence.

6. ASSESSMENT OF THE CHILD'S SITUATION IN 'MOVING' WITHIN THE EU JUDICIAL AREA

Among the novelties proposed, particularly important are the possibilities of collecting information on the child and assessing the compliance of her/his situation. More precisely, under the new rules, central authorities of Member States have a general duty of cooperation not only to discover a child's whereabouts, but also to collect and exchange information (also concerning the situation of a parent, a relative or other person who may be suitable to care for the child), and, moreover, to provide a report (i) on the situation of the child,

70 On this topic, see I. Pretelli, 'Child Abduction and Return Proceedings, in Recasting the Brussels IIa Regulation', above n. 17, pp. 10–11. The Author also points out that the idea of compulsory mediation has been rejected during preparatory works, on the ground that mediation is based on the willingness of the parties to conclude an agreement under the guidance of experts, and it is very unlikely that a party who is forced to enter into mediation will cooperate. However, the article points out that it might be possible to consider the solution of a compulsory intervention of a mediator in relation to the compulsory hearing of the disputed child. This could also work as a first step of the two parents resuming dialogue.

71 See Recital no. 43 of Regulation 2019/1111.

(ii) on any procedures under way concerning the child, or (iii) on decisions concerning the child.[72]

Besides the general possibility of assessing, through cooperation and exchange of information between central authorities, a child's situation and reporting on the child, in order to better decide cross-border issues concerning parental responsibility and to facilitate adoption of decisions related to a child's moving within the EU judicial space, the new Regulation also introduces specific rules asking for an assessment of the child's situation for the purposes of placing her/him abroad or deciding on her/his return after an abduction.

Starting from the child's cross-border placement, the main criticisms of its functioning have been tackled. Under the new rules, the receiving State's consent is mandatory and it shall be provided before the child's placement. Furthermore, because placement as a measure of protection is generally urgent,[74] the proposed rules introduce a three-month time limit for the receiving State to decide on the placement, which, together with the *exequatur*'s abolition, surely enhances the mechanism's functioning. For the BIC, however, the most important novelty is the rule requiring the submission of a report on the child. Under Article 82 of Regulation 2019/1111, the requesting authority has a duty to transmit a report on the child, together with reasons for the proposed placement or provision of care. More precisely, the proposed rule asks the central authority of the Member State of origin to transmit to the central authority of the Member State where the child is to be placed 'a request for consent which includes a report on the child together with the reasons of the proposed placement or provision of care', and also to provide these documents with the necessary translation. In providing for the duty to transmit a report on the child, together with reasons justifying the measure of protection, the proposed rule aligns the new Regulation with rules provided by Article 33 of the 1996 Hague Convention.

No specific reference is made (i) to the need to safeguard the child's rights and, in particular, the right to maintain personal contacts with parents, or (ii) to the need to provide solutions of care granting, as much as possible, continuity in a child's upbringing and the child's ethnic, religious, cultural and linguistic backgrounds. Both of these suggestions, even without having binding character, should surely be considered and possibly followed in drafting the report to be transmitted to the central authority of the State where the child will be placed. Furthermore, given the proposed rules' lack of further indications as to the report's content, guidance provided by Lagarde's Explanatory Report in the 1996 Hague Convention shall surely be considered. More specifically, the Explanatory Report indicates that the requesting authority shall provide information

[72] See article 80 of Regulation 2019/1111.

on the child's situation and on reasons for the proposed placement or provision of care.[73]

As for the requested Member State's consent, the proposed rules take an important step forward not only by making consent necessary in all EU Member States, preliminary to a child's transfer, but also in providing a deadline of three months for the requested Member State to give consent or not. On the other hand, unfortunately, the new rules do not make any reference to the grounds on which the requested Member State may deny consent and reject a child's placement. This is clearly regrettable considering that placement is a measure of protection for children in need of care and, consequently, denial of consent opposes the BIC *in abstracto* and in the specific situation. Lack of guidance for solving a dialectic between the BIC justifying the consent request and the requested State's interests justifying denial is likely to affect good and uniform functioning of cross-border placement.

A 'substantial' assessment of the child's situation is also required in child abduction procedures. Deep, critical analysis of the proposed rules on child abduction procedures is provided in Ruth Lamont's contribution to this volume. For the present work's purposes, however, attention is paid to the 'overriding mechanism' or 'second chance procedure' and, in particular, to the need for the court of habitual residence, when deciding on whether to replace the non-return order provided by the court of the Member State where the child has been wrongfully removed with a decision of return, to examine questions of custody of the child by thoroughly examining all circumstances, including, but not limited to, the conduct of the parents and taking into account the best interests of the child.[74]

The duty to undergo such an assessment clearly finds inspiration from ECtHR case law and, in particular, from the *Neulinger* and *Kampanella* decisions, in which the Court asked for an 'in-depth examination of family life' in order to decide on the return of the children illicitly abducted. While such a thorough examination was not possible in a procedure focused on the child's return as in the Brussels II *bis* Regulation, the new rules now ask for it in the context of a broader procedure on the merits. Together with the opposition procedure considered in the previous section, the requested examination shifts the balance between the BIC *in abstracto* (i.e. immediate return to the habitual residence) and the BIC *in concreto* in favour of the latter.

---

73 See the Explanatory Report on the 1996 Hague Child Protection Convention, at 593, para. 143. The Explanatory Report is available at the following address: https://www.hcch.net/en/publications-and-studies/details4/?pid=2943.

74 See recital 48 of Regulation 2019/1111.

7. IS THE BIC BETTER PROTECTED BY THE NEW RULES?

The Commission's purpose was a 'prudent and focused' recast aimed at 'better protect[ing] the best interests of the child by simplifying the procedures and enhancing their efficiency'.[75] Balancing the need to provide clear-cut solutions, aimed at reaching the overall purposes of EU private international law coherently, with protection (*in abstracto* and in general) of the BIC, and the need to provide flexible devices granting *in concreto* the BIC's protection has proved to be no easy task. In assessing whether this aim has been reached, the BIC's three dimensions may be considered:[76] (i) substantive, i.e. the child's right to have her/his best interests assessed and taken as a primary consideration; (ii) interpretative, i.e. granting priority to the interpretation most effectively serving the child's best interests; and (iii) procedural, i.e. asking for a specific evaluation of the possible impact of a decision on the child or the children concerned.

In the new Regulation, clearly, the procedural dimension plays a primary role in the identification of the court best placed to adopt decisions and to circulate decisions, agreements or public acts on parental responsibility matters in the European judicial space. In both respects, the proposed rules try to strike a new balance between 'procedural values' and the BIC.

As far as jurisdiction is concerned, the general rule of the child's State of habitual residence is further strengthened by the new provision establishing that pending proceedings shall also follow the child's moves, thereby further enhancing predictability and certainty. On the other hand, small steps toward the enhancement of party autonomy and, therefore, of flexibility, have been taken by giving parties the possibility of agreeing on jurisdiction not only at the beginning, but also during proceedings (if the Member State's law so provides).

More significant changes occur with regard to the movement of decisions, where a step toward the enhancement of mutual trust has been made by virtue of the *exequatur*'s abolition for all decisions on parental responsibility. Such a change is counterbalanced by the possibility of suspending, or even refusing, the enforcement of a decision any time the enforcement of a decision would expose the child to a grave risk.

The BIC principle's interpretative dimension is significantly strengthened: such a principle, which traditionally has been the *fil rouge* of the Brussels II system,[77] is now expressly recalled under the new rules. Beside this, as previously

---

[75] See Commission proposal COM(2016)411, p. 8.

[76] See General Comment No 14, p. 4.

[77] See M.C. Baruffi, 'La responsabilità genitoriale: competenze e riconoscimento delle decisioni nel Regolamento Bruxelles II', in S.M. Carbone and I. Queirolo (eds.), *Diritto di famiglia e dell'Unione europea*, Giappichelli, Turin 2009, p. 262.

mentioned, the overall EU legal framework demands more proactive action for the protection of children's rights.

Relevant changes have also to do with the principle's substantial dimension: an assessment of a child's situation in light of the BIC principle is required under the proposed rules in child abduction and cross-border placement cases, to obtain a better picture of the child's situation and, therefore, decisions better tailored to the individual child.[78]

The adoption of Regulation 2019/1111 clearly shows EU institutions' efforts toward better protecting children's rights in cross-border parental responsibility procedures, the major difficulty being striking a balance between the BIC *in abstracto* and the BIC *in concreto*. While the new Regulation seems to take steps in both directions and grants sufficient flexibility to move from one notion to the other, the challenge will be to develop consistent practice within the EU judicial space when considering the BIC in *concreto*. Crucial, in this respect, will be the role of the European Court of Justice, benefiting the PPU's fast track.

---

[78] The new rules do not expressly specify how broad the assessment shall be. Such an assessment should take into consideration elements necessary for assessing the BIC: the child's views, the child's identity, the preservation of the family environment and maintenance of relations, the child's care, protection and safety, the situation of vulnerability, and the child's rights to health and education. See General Comment No. 14, above n. 1, at pp. 12–18.

PROVISIONAL MEASURES AND THE BEST INTERESTS OF THE CHILD IN THE FIELD OF PARENTAL RESPONSIBILITY

Lidia SANDRINI

1. Introduction 287
2. Jurisdiction on the Substance and Jurisdiction to Issue Interim Relief. . . . 289
3. The Presence of the Child or of the Child's Assets as a Ground of 'Interim' Jurisdiction 295
4. Coordination between Measures and Impact on the Notion of 'Provisional and Protective Measures'. 302
5. Conclusions 307

1. INTRODUCTION

It is unanimously acknowledged that speedy action by courts is crucial when it comes to protecting the legal rights of minors in disputes concerning them,[1] particularly where young children are involved.[2] Thus, we may certainly say that speed is an essential element of the adjudication process for pursuing the best interests of children, as a procedural rule.[3] On the other hand, the need

[1] See Committee on the Rights of the Child, General Comment No. 14 (2013) on the right of the child to have his or her best interests taken as a primary consideration (Article 3, para. 1), CRC/C/GC/14 of 29.05.2013, para. 93: 'The passing of time is not perceived in the same way by children and adults. Delays in or prolonged decision-making have particularly adverse effects on children as they evolve. It is therefore advisable that procedures or processes regarding or impacting children be prioritized and completed in the shortest time possible'; European Convention on the Exercise of Children's Rights, Strasbourg, 25.01.1996, ETS No. 160, Article 7- Duty to act speedily: 'In proceedings affecting a child the judicial authority shall act speedily to avoid any unnecessary delay and procedures shall be available to ensure that its decisions are rapidly enforced. In urgent cases the judicial authority shall have the power, where appropriate, to take decisions which are immediately enforceable'.

[2] CJEU, case C-195/08 PPU, *Rinau*, ECLI:EU:C:2008:406, para. 81; case C-296/10, *Purrucker II*, ECLI:EU:C:2010:665, para. 83.

[3] As is well known, the General Comment No. 14, above n. 1, para. 6, underscores that, 'the child's best interests is a threefold concept which includes: (a) a substantive right,

to analyse all the elements necessary in the particular case to determine the best interests of the child in the substantive sense inevitably affects the duration of proceedings, which can often become quite complex.[4] Moreover, the conflict between speed and thoroughness is heightened in matters of parental responsibility, and is balanced within domestic legal systems by procedural rules that provide for interim measures of protection. The provisions on provisional and protective measures found in Regulation (EC) No. 2201/2003 are intended to bring about the same result in cross-border controversies.[5] This chapter will investigate the ways in which this Regulation implements the principle of the superior interests of the child, as well as how this principle, as incorporated in EU law, may be perceived through it. This analysis is particularly timely today, in light of the recent recast of the Regulation, not least of all in order to verify if, and to what degree, the modifications that had been proposed by the Commission,[6] and those eventually adopted,[7] effectively move toward strengthening the protection of children.

(b) a fundamental legal interpretative principle, and (c) a rule of procedure'. Concerning this last function in particular, see, ibid. para. 85 ff.

4 See, e.g., European Convention on the Exercise of Children's Rights, above n. 1, Article 6 – Decision-making process.

5 Council Regulation (EC) 2201/2003 of 27 November 2003 concerning jurisdiction and the recognition and enforcement of judgments in matrimonial matters and the matters of parental responsibility, repealing Regulation (EC) 1347/2000 [2003] OJ L338/1 (hereinafter also: Brussels IIa).

6 The reformulation (that followed the previous attempt of 2006, focused on matrimonial matters) started three years ago with the proposal for a Council Regulation on jurisdiction, the recognition and enforcement of decisions in matrimonial matters and the matters of parental responsibility, and on international child abduction (recast), COM/2016/0411 final (hereinafter also: the proposal), on which see C. Honorati, 'La proposta di revisione del regolamento Bruxelles II-*bis*: Più tutela per i minori e più efficacia nell'esecuzione delle decisioni' (2017) *Riv. Dir. Int. Priv. Proc.*, 247–282. The proposal was preceded by the Report from the Commission to the European Parliament, the Council and the European Economic and Social Committee on the application of Council Regulation (EC) 2201/2003, COM/2014/0225 final. In light of this report, scenarios for the reform of the regulation of provisional measures were put forward by M. Mellone, 'Provisional Measures and the Brussels IIbis Regulation: An Assessment of the Status Quo in View of Future Legislative Amendments' (2015) *Nederlands Internationaal Privaatrecht* 1, 20–26; T. Kruger and L. Samyn, 'Brussels II bis: Successes and Suggested Improvements' (2016) *Journal of Private International Law*, 132–168. More recently, see L. Carpaneto, 'La ricerca di una (nuova) sintesi tra interesse del minore "in astratto" e "in concreto" nella riforma del regolamento Bruxelles II-*bis*' (2018) *Riv. Dir. Int. Priv. Proc.*, 945–977, who takes into account also the general approach on the above-mentioned proposal reached by the JHA Council at its meeting held on 7 December 2018.

7 After this chapter had been completed, Council Regulation (EU) 2019/1111 of 25 June 2019 on jurisdiction, the recognition and enforcement of decisions in matrimonial matters and the matters of parental responsibility, and on international child abduction (hereafter also: the Recast) has been published in [2019] OJ L178/1. According to its Article 105, the new Regulation shall enter into force on the twentieth day following that of its publication in the Official Journal of the European Union, *i.e.* 22 July 2019. However, Article 100 establishes that it shall apply only to legal proceedings instituted, to authentic instruments formally drawn up

2. JURISDICTION ON THE SUBSTANCE AND JURISDICTION TO ISSUE INTERIM RELIEF

As well known, Article 20 of the Brussels IIa Regulation contains a rule that specifically addresses provisional and protective measures and allows them to be established even by the judicial authorities of Member States different from the one with jurisdiction over the substance of the matter.[8] Nevertheless, the Regulation first and foremost confers jurisdiction to adopt provisional measures on the latter courts. As is the case with other European Union Regulations that regulate jurisdiction, this is not stated explicitly in any particular rule,[9] and yet it has never been called into question.[10] This is also supported by the precedent established by the 1968 Brussels Convention:[11] the CJEU, albeit without any textual support, has not hesitated to declare that the same court identified as having the jurisdiction on the substance of the matter, 'also has jurisdiction to order any provisional or protective measures which may prove necessary'.[12] Such

---

or registered and to agreements registered on or after 1 August 2022, while Regulation 2201/2003 shall continue to apply to decisions given in legal proceedings instituted, to authentic instruments formally drawn up or registered and to agreements which have become enforceable in the Member State where they were concluded before that date and which fall within the scope of that Regulation. Given the timing, it is not possible to proceed here with an in-depth analysis of the final text of the Recast. However, a first-reading overview of the main differences among the current text, the Commission's proposal and such final text, as far as provisional measures are concerned, will be provided.

8 The text of Article 20 reads: 'Provisional, including protective, measures. 1. In urgent cases, the provisions of this Regulation shall not prevent the courts of a Member State from taking such provisional, including protective, measures in respect of persons or assets in that State as may be available under the law of that Member State, even if, under this Regulation, the court of another Member State has jurisdiction as to the substance of the matter. 2. The measures referred to in paragraph 1 shall cease to apply when the court of the Member State having jurisdiction under this Regulation as to the substance of the matter has taken the measures it considers appropriate.' Article 20 of Brussels IIa has been preceded by Article 12 of the Brussels II Regulation (Council Regulation (EC) 1347/2000 of 29 May 2000 on jurisdiction and the recognition and enforcement of judgments in matrimonial matters and in matters of parental responsibility for children of both spouses, [2000] OJ L160/19) and Article 12 of the Brussels II Convention (see Council Act of 28 May 1998 drawing up, on basis of Article K.3 of the TEU, the Convention on Jurisdiction and the Recognition and Enforcement of Judgments in Matrimonial Matters [1998] OJ C221/1).

9 According to M. Pertegás Senders and C. Mariottini, 'Article 20: Provisional, Including Protective, Measures' in U. Magnus and P. Mankowski (eds.), *European Commentaries on Private International Law, vol. IV, Brussels IIbis Regulation*, Sellier European Law Publishers, Köln, 2017, pp. 269-281, p. 269, n. 1, 'the formulation of Recital 16 … reflects that other head of jurisdiction, besides Article 20, are also relevant for applications for interim relief'.

10 See, e.g., CJEU, case C-256/09 *Purrucker I*, ECLI:EU:C:2010:437, para. 63 ff.; case C-92/12, *Health Service Executive*, ECLI:EU:C:2012:255.

11 Convention on Jurisdiction and the Enforcement of Judgments in Civil and Commercial Matters, Brussels, 27 September 1968 [1972] OJ L299/32.

12 CJEU, case C-391/95, *Van Uden Maritime BV v. Firma Deco Line*, ECLI:EU:C:1998:543, para. 19.

an interpretation now finds confirmation in the Recast, precisely where it specifies the notion of 'decision' for the purposes of the recognition and enforcement regime, dealt by in Chapter IV, and, to that aim, includes therein 'provisional, including protective, measures ordered by a court which by virtue of this Regulation has jurisdiction as to the substance of the matter'.[13]

Thus, under the current Article 8 (as well as under Article 7 of the Recast), the courts of a Member State in which a child is habitually resident will generally be authorised to adopt appropriate protective measures, both during proceedings and *ante causam*.[14] This choice by the EU legislator reveals a specific view of the 'best interests of the child', which manifests in the form of a procedural rule.[15] Indeed, habitual residence is favoured as an expression of the 'criterion of proximity',[16] since the judge nearest to 'the place which, in practice, is the center of that child's life'[17] appears to be best positioned to access all the elements important for reaching a decision that effectively reflects the child's concrete needs and, therefore, to proceed more quickly to a ruling.[18] By contrast, different kinds of ties, like the child's nationality, his or her cultural ties to the Member State of the parents' origin, or the intention of one or both parents to take up residency in a given country, amount to mere indicators that identify the location of the habitual residence.[19]

Nonetheless, the Regulation provides for exceptions to the proximity criterion, through which it gives more weight to the interests of minors in the substantive sense, as preordained in a general and abstract way by the legislator.[20] These include the continuing jurisdiction of the authorities of the State of former habitual residence, provided by Article 9,[21] in keeping with the child's right to maintain relationships with both parents under Article 24(3) of

---

13 See Article 2 para. 1(b); see also article 59 and, in the preamble, recitals 30 and 31.

14 On the notion of 'habitual residence' for purposes of this Regulation, see, among many, CJEU, case C-523/07, *A*, ECLI:EU:C:2009:225, paras. 35-42; case C-497/10 PPU, *Mercredi*, EU:C:2010:829, paras. 44 and 47-49; case C-111/17 PPU, *OL v PQ*, ECLI:EU:C:2017:436, paras. 42 and 43; and, finally, case C-393/18 PPU, *UD v. XB*, ECLI:EU:C:2018:835, para. 45 ff., with extensive references to previous case law.

15 See General Comment No. 14, above n. 1, paras. 6 and 85 ff.

16 See Brussels IIa, recital No. 12.

17 CJEU, case C-512/17, *HR*, ECLI:EU:C:2018:513, para. 42.

18 See CJEU, case C-403/09 PPU, *Detiček*, ECLI:EU:C:2009:810, para. 36; case C-256/09, above n. 10, para. 91, as well as case C-499/15, *W and V*, ECLI:EU:C:2017:118, paras. 51 and 52. On the appropriateness of the criterion of proximity for facilitating the collection of evidence, see CJEU, case C-111/17 PPU, above n. 14, para. 59. According to CJEU, case C-512/17, above n. 17, para. 54, the need to conduct an investigation that is specific to the circumstances of each case also has consequences for interpretation, as indications given in one case may only be applied to another case with due precaution.

19 CJEU, case C-512/17, above n. 17, paras. 57-65. See also case C-111/17 PPU, above n. 14, paras. 47 and 51.

20 General Comment No. 14, above n. 1, para. 6.

21 See, in the Recast, Article 8.

the EU Charter, and the extension of the competence of those authorities even when a child's place of residence has changed following an abduction (Article 10)[22]. From this perspective the rule on residual jurisdiction (Article 14)[23] is particularly important. Allowing for the exercise of jurisdiction by EU Member States in cases of minors who habitually reside in third countries reveals how the choice to protect the interests of the minor at the procedural level of proximity to the court is closely connected to broad agreement on the contents of these interests at the level of substantive law.[24]

The best interests of the child principle as a procedural rule, as well as its weight at the substantive level as an abstract matter, may yield priority following an evaluation of the circumstances of the particular case, as Article 15[25] provides for the transfer of the case to a court better placed to hear it.[26] This reveals how the legislator gives primacy to individual needs over the pursuit of general goals. The prioritisation of the interests of the child in the particular case is also in evidence in the rules on prorogation of jurisdiction, this time *vis-à-vis* the interests of other subjects involved in the dispute (Article 12).[27]

The general rule and its exceptions make for a regulatory framework that is sufficiently flexible, and well-suited to ensure that, in the majority of cases, the court with jurisdiction over the substance of the matter will also be the one best positioned to adopt provisional and urgent measures.[28] However, the reasons that support this conclusion differ according to the position of the court with regard to the child. Indeed, the criterion of proximity, manifested in the grant of jurisdiction to the courts of the State of habitual residence, is sufficient in and of itself, in many cases, to ensure the immediate effectiveness of the measures

---

22 Corresponding to Article 9 of the Recast.

23 It remains Article 14 in the Recast.

24 Article 12(4) establishes a similar rule for the extension of jurisdiction.

25 The current provision is split into Articles 12 and 13 of the Recast.

26 See CJEU, case C-428/15, *D.*, EU:C:2016:819, para. 58. See E. Gallant, 'Le Forum Non Conveniens de l'Article 15 du Règlement Bruxelles II Bis' (2017) *Revue critique de droit international privé*, 464.

27 CJEU, case C-215/15, *Gogova*, EU:C:2015:710, para. 41; case C-565/16, *Alessandro Saponaro and Kalliopi-Chloi Xylina*, ECLI:EU:C:2018:265, paras. 27 and 33. Nevertheless, it is interesting to note that, in this final decision, in light of circumstances that favoured linking the child to the chosen forum, the child's best interest requirement was considered to be satisfied, since 'the referring court has given no indication that might suggest that seizure of the court chosen by the parents would in any way prejudice the interests of the child' (ibid. para. 38), so that it appears that the existence of a connection between the child and the Member State to which the judicial authority that has been seised belongs effects a sort of presumption in favour of extending its competence to include the superior interests of the child. Article 12 of Regulation Brussels IIa finds equivalence in Article 10 of the Recast, despite the Correlation table (annex X to the Recast) not highlighting it, probably because of the substantial changes brought to the provision.

28 See B. Ancel and H. Muir Watt, 'L'intérêt Supérieur de l'Enfant dans le Concert des Juridictions: Le Règlement Bruxeels II Bis', (2005) *Revue critique de droit international privé*, 581.

adopted and, therefore, makes protection of the child more effective. The same cannot be said for the criteria for establishing jurisdiction that overlook the child's presence in the country, or which treat this as only one of many elements to take into consideration.[29] Concerning these, as well as under Article 8, in the event that the child is temporarily located in a country other than that of residence,[30] the competence of the court that has jurisdiction over the substance of the matter is justified not only as the natural outcome of the general character of the power of *ius dicere* attributed to it, but it is also appropriate in light of specific ways in which provisional protection is provided in family law disputes.[31] Despite the significant differences between the different national systems, the very nature of rights and protected interests involves agreement in moving toward measures anticipatory in nature, which are intended to set up provisional parameters for the family situation until a judgment is reached.[32] On the one hand, this feature of the measures makes it more difficult to assimilate them to enforcement procedures, a phenomenon which has regarded protective measures through the prioritisation of the enforcement phase over the adjudication phase.[33]

29 Moreover, precisely because the presence of the child may have a bearing on the application of these rules, the possibility may not be ruled out that, in particular cases, they may create the need for protections that have immediate effect.

30 On the importance of the physical presence of the child in a State for purposes of determining habitual residence, see, most recently, CJEU, case C-393/18 PPU, *UD v. XB*, ECLI:EU:C:2018:835, para. 52 ff., and the cases cited therein.

31 On the importance of the features of interim measures in family matters with respect to establishing jurisdiction, see P. Picone, 'Le Misure Provvisorie nel Diritto Internazionale Privato' in Id., *La Riforma Italiana del Diritto Internazionale Privato*, CEDAM, Padua 1998, p. 563 ff.

32 This trend is particularly clear where measures concern the children themselves, and their placement with one of the parents or elsewhere, or else the specific rules related to exercising visitation rights. Moreover, even where property rights are at issue, despite the usefulness of purely precautionary measures such as the seizure of assets, provisional decisions more often deal with the administration of the assets themselves or set a payment schedule for maintenance obligations. Concerning this it is important to bear in mind that maintenance obligations are not included within the scope of application of the Brussels IIa Regulation, but fall under Regulation (EC) 4/2009 of 18 December 2008 on jurisdiction, applicable law, recognition and enforcement of decisions, and cooperation in matters relating to maintenance obligations [2009] OJ L7/1. Nevertheless, practical application demonstrates that, very often, child support issues arise in connection with matters concerning parental responsibility, and for these cases Article 3(d) of Regulation (EC) 4/2009 applies. For more on this, see CJEU, case C-604/17, *PM v. AH*, ECLI:EU:C:2018:10, para. 32; case C-499/15, above n. 18, para. 47 ff., and the commentary by N. Joubert, 'La Résidence de l'Enfant du Divorce Face à la Demande de Modification de la Décision Relative à la Garde et aux Aliments', (2018) *Revue critique de droit international privé*, 138.

33 With regard to Article 24 of the 1968 Brussels Convention, traces of this orientation may be found in CJEU, case 125/79 *Denilauler v. snc Couchet Frères*, ECLI:EU:C:1980:130, para. 16: 'the contracting State, where the assets subject to the measures sought are located, are those best able to assess the circumstances which may lead to the grant or refusal of the measures sought or to the laying down of procedures and conditions which the plaintiff must observe in order to guarantee the provisional and protective character of the measures ordered'.

On the other hand, it leads to favouring the attribution of the authority to adopt provisional measures to the court with jurisdiction over the substance of the matter, due to the greater likelihood of consistency between the assessments made in the two phases of proceedings. Thus, concentrating the jurisdiction into one supports, among other things, the goal of achieving continuity in regulating the rights linked to parental responsibility.

Nevertheless, it is clear that, to meet this goal in cases where the measure adopted by the court with jurisdiction over the substance of the matter calls for forced execution, it is crucial that the measure benefit from the streamlined recognition and enforcement described in Chapter III of the Regulation,[34] so that it may be enforced in the different Member State where the child is actually living. This possibility, which is a consequence of the broad notion of 'judgment' adopted by the Regulation, becomes important in disputes concerning parental responsibility in a situation somewhat symmetrical to the one we have already considered, in which the competent judge orders, as a provisional measure, that a child be moved to a different Member State to better assure his or her protection.[35] The CJEU has dealt with the relationship between the interests of the child and rules on the circulation of provisional measures in precisely this context: a provisional measure was adopted by an Irish court which had jurisdiction over the substance of the matter, with the intention of bringing about the result described. In *Health Service Executive*, the CJEU explained how the urgent need to ensure effective protection of the child (a need that was particularly clear in that case) requires a teleologically-oriented interpretation of the procedural rules for obtaining a declaration of enforceability, in order to ensure the speediness of the procedure, which is essential in order to achieve the very purpose of the Regulations on parental responsibility.[36]

On the other hand, the overriding importance of the interests of the minor did not allow for bypassing the letter of the law or overlooking the need for a declaration of enforceability in order for the Irish measure to be enforced in England, despite the referring court's concerns about the risk of delay associated with obtaining the declaration.[37] Indeed, the CJEU held that only the legislator could make this possible, by modifying the regulatory scheme, underscoring that it falls to the legislator to establish effective procedural mechanisms to deal with the protection of minors.[38]

The CJEU's remarks on this point did not go unobserved, and, indeed, one of the central elements of the proposed revision of Brussels IIa advanced by the

---

34 Chapter IV of the Recast.

35 See Article 2(4).

36 Case C-92/12, above n. 10, paras. 127 and 133.

37 Ibid., paras. 114, 115.

38 Ibid., para. 121.

Commission was the elimination of the *exequatur* procedure.[39] In the proposal the Commission suggested to adopt a model already tested in other sectors,[40] and opened the possibility of giving weight to the grounds of refusal at the enforcement stage.[41] But this guarantee was deemed insufficient in the area of parental responsibility, and so a further proposal had been made to bolster the oversight of compliance with public policy, by verifying that the enforcement of decisions corresponded to the superior interests of the child where the child had objected to it, or where the circumstances had significantly changed since the time the decision was handed down.[42] It is likely that the latter situation would have arisen only rarely with regard to rulings adopting provisional measures,[43] and it is surely the assessment of the child's opinion that most frequently could have proved an obstacle to enforcement, because of the well-known differences in how Member States treat the rights of children to express their opinions in proceedings concerning them.[44] Moreover, with specific reference to proceedings to adopt protective measures, the urgent need to reach a decision and the resulting brevity of the proceedings often lead courts to omit such a step. These omissions are not currently considered grounds for another Member

39 See Article 30 ff. of the proposal, above n. 6.

40 See Article 39 ff. of Regulation (EU) 1215/2012 of the European Parliament and of the Council of 12 December 2012 on jurisdiction and the recognition and enforcement of judgments in civil and commercial matters [2012] OJ L351/1.

41 Article 40 of the proposal, above n. 6.

42 Ibid., para. 2. It is clear that this regulatory option aims to avoid any automatism that could be struck down by the European Court of Human Rights, as has already happened to the enforcement of decisions relating to returning minors who have been illegally abducted. For more on this, see L. Carpaneto, 'In-Depth Consideration of Family Life v. Immediate Return of the Child in Abduction Proceedings within the EU' (2014) *Riv. Dir. Int. Priv. Proc.*, 931–958.

43 Nonetheless, in CJEU case C-403/09 PPU, above n. 19, this exact situation was brought before a Slovenian court, and served as the grounds for its refusal to enforce an Italian provisional measure granting a father exclusive custody of a child.

44 A comparative look at Germany and Italy can be found in T. Pfeiffer, M. Escher and J. Wittmann, 'The Fragmentation of Recognition and Enforcement Regimes' in I. Viarengo and F. Villata (eds.), *Planning the Future of Cross-Border Families: A Path through Coordination. Final Study*, (EUFam's, Project JUST/2014/JCOO/AG/CIVI/7729) <www.eufams.unimi.it> accessed 20.10.2018, pp. 221 ff. In light of the need this study shows to identify standards shared by the Member States, the suggestion found in the European Parliament's Resolution on the Commission's proposal (P8_TA(2018)0017, 18.01. 2018), to recall at Rec. No. 23 – naturally along with Article 24(1) of the EU Charter and Article 12 of the United Nations Convention on the Rights of the Child – the Council of Europe Recommendation on the participation of children and young people under the age of 18 (CM/Rec(2012)2 of 28 March 2012) could surely be appreciated, as the indications contained therein could contribute to the adoption of a more uniform approach among Member States. Unfortunately, eventually the EU legislator did not consider such reference necessary and omitted it. In general, on Regulations providing for listening to the child and proposed modifications, see B. Ubertazzi, 'The Hearing of the child in the Brussels IIa Regulation and its Recast Proposal' (2017) *Journal of Private International Law*, 568–601.

State's refusal to enforce the measures, since Article 23(1)(b) of the Regulation allows for an exception to the duty to hear the child in urgent cases. By contrast, there was no room for exceptions in the proposal, and this could have potentially created an important obstacle to the circulation of provisional and protective measures.[45] The question arose whether such an inflexible approach was really necessary, and whether it was in line with the child's interests. Thoughtfully, the Recast answers these doubts in the negative: the final text retains the current exception for reasons of urgency to the rule that impose hearing the child, and reformulates in a restrictive way the ground for the refusal of the enforcement related to a change of circumstances after the decision has been given.[46] One cannot but welcome such an outcome, which, together with the abolition of the *exequatur*, results in a much more effective solution than the one envisaged by the Commission to the need of ensuring a timely and continuous protection of minors.

3. THE PRESENCE OF THE CHILD OR OF THE CHILD'S ASSETS AS A GROUND OF 'INTERIM' JURISDICTION

The decision of the EU legislator to reject the Commission's proposal to allow the Member State of enforcement a more extensive oversight over any provisional measures granted by the court with jurisdiction on the substance of the matter did not go without consequences for the recasting process. Because of that, a more far reaching reform of the rules governing protective measures taken by a court lacking such jurisdiction, particularly with regard to the circulation of these measures in the other Member States, has been avoided, yet, without forsaking the commitment to strengthen the effectiveness of provisional protection, even taking significant action concerning the existing limits on it.

Before looking at the revision process and at where it has eventually headed, it is worth recalling that the current text of Article 20 of the Regulation already contains notable differences with regard to the provisions with the same scope in other EU Regulations,[47] particularly because it does not exactly follow the

45 Urgency, as a factor which can justify not hearing the child's view, is not mentioned in the proposal, above n. 6, or in Article 20, the general rule governing the right of the child to express his or her opinion, and neither does it appear in Article 38, among the reasons not to enforce a measure. The choice is surprising, even in light of the case law of the CJEU, which has underscored the non-absolute nature of the right of the child to be heard. See, in particular, CJEU, case C-491/10 PPU, *Joseba Andoni Aguirre Zarraga v. Simone Pelz*, ECLI:EU:C:2010:828, para. 63.

46 See its Article 39 para. 2 and Article 56 para. 4.

47 See Council Regulation (EC) 44/2001 of 22 December 2000 on jurisdiction and the recognition and enforcement of judgments in civil and commercial matters (hereinafter: Brussels I) [2001] OJ L12/1, Article 31; Council Regulation (EC) 4/2009, above n. 32,

brief formula taken from the 1968 Brussels Convention.[48] Drawing on the 1961 and 1996 Hague Conventions on the protection of minors, the provision is completed by specifying the requirements for exercising this power, the first of which is the urgency of adopting measures.[49]

The urgency requirement relates both to the current circumstances of the child and to the practical impossibility of bringing the question of parental responsibility before the court with jurisdiction over the substance of the matter.[50] In other words, Article 20 assumes an instrumental and subsidiary role with regard to jurisdiction established on the basis of the criteria relating to the substance of the matter. This may even come out *ante causam* in cases in which the intervention by the judicial authority with jurisdiction over the substance would lack the necessary directness to be able to protect a child from the risk of serious harm. The urgency required by the rule may lie, therefore, in the need to ensure the immediate effectiveness of protective measures adopted by the court with jurisdiction to rule on the substance, hastening their ability to be enforced in the State where the child resides. Therefore, it appears that the English court in the *Health Service Executive* case mentioned above was correct to refer to Article 20.[51] While awaiting the declaration of enforceability of the Irish provisional ruling on the involuntary placement of the child in a residential institution in England, where she had been transferred in the meantime, the English court held that it was 'urgent that an interim order be made to allow for staff at the English [special care] Unit to detain and treat her'.[52]

On the other hand, the CJEU has refused to connect the urgency requirement with changes in the circumstances occurring after the court with jurisdiction

---

Article 14; Regulation (EU) 650/2012 of the European Parliament and of the Council of 4 July 2012 on jurisdiction, applicable law, recognition and enforcement of decisions and acceptance and enforcement of authentic instruments in matters of succession and on the creation of a European Certificate of Succession [2012] OJ L201/1, Article 19; Regulation (EU) 1215/2012, above n. 40, Article 35; Council Regulation (EU) 2016/1103 of 24 June 2016 implementing enhanced cooperation in the area of jurisdiction, applicable law and the recognition and enforcement of decisions in matters of matrimonial property regulation [2016] OJ L 183/1, Article 19; Council Regulation (EU) 2016/1104 of 24 June 2016 implementing enhanced cooperation in the area of jurisdiction, applicable law and the recognition and enforcement of decisions in matters of the property consequences of registered partnerships [2016] OJ L 183/1, Article 19.

48 See Article 24 of the 1968 Brussels Convention, above n. 11.

49 See Article 9 of the of the Convention concerning the powers of authorities and the law applicable in respect of the protection of infants, The Hague, 5.10.1961 (hereinafter: 1961 Hague Convention), and Article 11 of the Convention on jurisdiction, applicable law, recognition, enforcement and co-operation in respect of parental responsibility and measures for the protection of children, The Hague, 19.10.1996 (hereinafter: 1996 Hague Convention).

50 See P. Lagarde, Explanatory Report (1998) Proceedings of the Eighteenth Session (1996), tome II, 'Protection of children', <hcch.net> accessed 20.10.2018, 533–605, p. 567. See also CJEU, case C-523/07, above n. 14, para. 48; case C-403/09 PPU, above n. 18, para. 42.

51 Case C-92/12 PPU, above n. 10, paras. 51 and 130–132.

52 [2012] EWHC 1640 (Fam), para. 22.

over the substance of the matter has made a custody decision concerning the child, even on a provisional basis, whenever the alleged change derives from the fact that the child has become well-integrated into the environment where he or she lives following an illegal abduction. Indeed, intervention by the courts of the State where the child is living would amount to a substantive alteration of the determinations made by the competent court. More generally, '[i]f a change of circumstances resulting from a gradual process such as the child's integration into a new environment were enough ... any delay in the enforcement procedure in the requested Member State would contribute to creating the conditions that would allow the former court to block the enforcement of the judgment that had been declared enforceable. Such an interpretation would undermine the very principles on which that Regulation is based'.[53] This is an important clarification, because it underscores how Article 20 should be interpreted in light of the principles that underlie the Regulation. That is, it should generally be interpreted restrictively, since it is an exception to the system of competences provided for therein.[54]

This also applies to the second condition provided by the rule, which establishes the requirements for immediate enforcement of a provisional measure: namely, that it concerns persons or assets located within the Member State. This provision is fully consistent with the criterion of proximity: the court of the State where the minor is temporarily located,[55] since it is, at that time, the closest to the subject in need of protection, may intervene on a temporary basis, then leaving the court with jurisdiction over the substance of the matter to make all final decisions, using the primacy mechanism under Article 20(2).[56]

The choice to explicitly lay out the elements of connection with the territory of the Member State that would allow its courts to exercise interim jurisdiction can only be seen as a positive thing, since it makes it easier for national courts to apply the rule.[57] Its value is particularly evident in contrast with the unsatisfactory situation brought about by the 1968 Brussels Convention, in which the CJEU attempted to fill the gap left by the absence of any such provision. The outcome was the requirement, vague and difficult to apply, that there be a 'real connecting link' between the subject matter of the measures sought and the territorial jurisdiction of the Contracting State of the seised court.[58]

---

53 CJEU, case C-403/09 PPU, above n. 18, para. 47.

54 Ibid., para. 38.

55 CJEU, case C-523/07, above n. 14, para. 48: 'Those measures are applicable to children who have their habitual residence in one Member State but stay temporarily or intermittently in another Member State'.

56 On such a mechanism, see below, para. 4.

57 See e.g., *Krajský soud v Českých Budějovicích*, 14 January 2009, 5 Co 32/2009, EUFam's: CZS20090114; Corte di Appello di Catania, 17 March 2014, EUFam's: ITS20140317, both available on the EUFam's data-base <www.eufams.unimi.it> accessed 20.10.2018.

58 CJEU, case C-391/95, above n. 12, para. 40.

However, the more generic re-formulation of the requirements laid out in the Hague Conventions (which refer to the physical presence of the child or of his or her assets in the State), in order to adapt them to the broader scope of *ratione materiae* application of the Regulation, has caused some interpretive uncertainties.[59] The CJEU's observation in *Detiček*, that provisional measures impacting custody concern the minor as well as both parents,[60] engendered doubt as to whether the requirement that the 'persons' in relation to whom the measure is adopted must be physically present in the Member State and must always apply to all the subjects involved.[61] The answer appears to be yes when it comes to measures that are specifically intended to modify the arrangement for exercising parental responsibility that was previously established by the court with jurisdiction over the substance of the matter (as in the case referred to the CJEU for a preliminary ruling). However, it does not appear that the CJEU was intending to establish an analogous limitation for other types of measures, i.e. that, generally speaking, actions under Article 20 are blocked where even just one of the child's parents is not present in the Member State where judicial action is sought. Indeed, in the CJEU's reasoning, the need to ensure respect for the child's right 'to maintain on a regular basis a personal relationship and direct contact with both his or her parents', enshrined in Article 24(3) of the EU Charter,[62] is crucial, since 'respect for that right undeniably merges into the best interests of any child'.[63] Thus, it is clear that the requirement in question cannot be interpreted without taking into account the specific effects that the provisional measure will have on the particular scenario. On the contrary, it must necessarily be interpreted in light of these effects and may, therefore, vary on the basis of what the specific object of the requested measure is and the intended result of implementing it. However, in order to prevent uncertainties about interpretation from undermining the protection of children, the decision of the EU legislator to endorse the Commission's proposal to modify the rule, aligning its text with that of the Hague Conventions, is certainly appropriate,[64] despite the fact that, precisely because of such an alignment, the new provision will not apply to divorce, separation, or annulment of marriage disputes. This outcome is not particularly worrisome, given that coordinating with the other

59 Indeed, Article 20 applies to all disputes falling under the second chapter of the Regulation, including those in the areas of divorce, separation, and annulment of marriage.

60 CJEU, case C-403/09 PPU, above n. 18, paras. 50–52.

61 According to T. Kruger and L. Samyn, above n. 6, p. 149, 'This judgment seems to imply that provisional measures can only be granted if all persons involved are present on the territory of the court'.

62 [2016] OJ C202/389.

63 CJEU, case C-403/09 PPU, above n. 18, para. 54.

64 Article 12 of the proposal, above n. 6. The wording suggested by the Commission has been retained, with some drafting changes, in the Recast: see Art. 15.

EU Regulations specifically intended to regulate financial claims that may arise in the context of such cases leaves very little space for applying Article 20.[65]

Looking at the issue from a different angle, it bears noting that the CJEU's case law seems intended to deny that Article 20 entails a ground of jurisdiction.[66] This interpretation has consequences on two distinct levels. The first, obviously, concerns the exercise of jurisdiction: the adoption of provisional measures by a court other than the one with jurisdiction over the substance of the matter can only occur where the court's power is granted by an internal jurisdictional rule and, at the same time, where the requirements in Article 20 have been satisfied. Thus, the court is obliged to carry out a two-fold verification, which, however, we rarely see in practical application (probably not least of all due to the extreme brevity of the reasoning section of rulings adopting provisional measures), and which, perhaps, amounts to a superfluous burden on the courts. Indeed, it is difficult to see the usefulness of applying domestic jurisdictional rules in the context of a Regulation which, on the one hand, it is not interested in the criteria that such rules lay down and, on the other, focus the attention exclusively on the limits that rein in their application.

The denial of Article 20's ability to directly grant jurisdiction also has effects at another level: that of the territorial effectiveness of measures adopted by courts not having jurisdiction over the substance of the matter, which are excluded from the system of recognition and enforcement.[67] The CJEU reaches this conclusion on the basis of a systematic analysis, basing its reasoning on the Regulation's draft and explanatory documents,[68] and, *a contrario*, on the framework established by the 1996 Hague Convention.[69] It is plausible that the Court's chief purpose was that of avoiding the 'remedy shopping'[70] phenomenon, which emerged in the wake of the 1968 Brussels Convention, after judicial affirmation that provisional measures adopted by courts without jurisdiction over the substance of the matter do qualify for recognition and enforcement.[71]

---

65 See M. Pertegás Senders and C. Mariottini, above n. 9, p. 274 ff.

66 On precisely this matter, see Advocate General Sharpston, opinion delivered on 20.05.2010, CJEU, case C-256/09, *Purrucker I*, ECLI:EU:C:2010:296, para. 169: 'a court acting by virtue of Article 20 alone does not enjoy any jurisdiction conferred by the Regulation. It is merely "not prevented" from taking such urgent measures as are necessary and as are available under national law, in respect of persons or assets within its territorial jurisdiction'. This issue remains controversial, however; see Advocate General Kokott, opinion delivered on 29.01.2009, CJEU, case C-523/07, *A*, ECLI:EU:C:2009:39, para. 57.

67 CJEU, case C-256/09, above n. 10, para. 87.

68 Ibid., paras. 84–86.

69 Ibid., paras. 88–90.

70 Ibid., para. 91, which explicitly describes the need to avoid any risk of 'of circumvention of the rules of jurisdiction laid down by that Regulation and of forum shopping, which would be contrary to the objectives pursued by that regulation'.

71 See CJEU, case 143/78, *De Cavel v. De Cavel*, ECLI:EU:C:1979:83, para. 9; case 125/79, above n. 33. On the possibility of interpreting these judgments differently, see L. Collins,

Thus, the CJEU's interpretation further distinguished the regulation of interim protection under the Brussels IIa Regulation both from the aforementioned Hague Convention and from those other Regulations currently in force that borrowed from the model of the Brussels Convention, in order to ensure that legislative choices about how to further the best interests of the child in the context of assigning jurisdiction should not be undermined.[72] It remains in doubt, however, whether this goal has been fully reached. In fact, by simultaneously allowing the possibility of recognising measures adopted under Article 20 of the Regulation on the basis of other international instruments (chiefly the 1996 Hague Convention, once again), or on the basis of the applicable national rules of the requested member State, the CJEU has left the door open to potential opportunistic manoeuvring by the parties to a dispute.[73]

Leaving this murky area aside, the CJEU's case law on Article 20 of the Regulation has surely contributed significantly to outlining a system capable of guaranteeing adequate protection for children in the majority of disputes over parental responsibility. One notable exception, however, includes cases of international child abduction, an area where experience reveals that different solutions are needed. In particular, it has become clear that, where a child is at risk of physical or psychological harm, or of living in an otherwise intolerable situation following his or her return to the State of habitual residence, Article 11(4)'s obligation to order the child's return in any case, as long as there is evidence that adequate steps have been taken to ensure the child's protection, has been ignored in many cases. It is worth recalling that, within the European area of freedom, security and justice, even because of the freedom of movement that it allows, such an obligation is crucial in order to ensure the highest possible level of protection of children in cases of wrongful removal or retention, that is, in pursuing their best interests. Yet, it is likely that establishing a climate of mutual trust, which forms the basis of the reinforced duty to return with regard to the one provided for under the 1980 Hague Convention, is complicated by the practical difficulties that still hinder cooperation between the judiciaries of the

---

'Provisional and Protective Measures in International Litigation' (1992) *Recueil des Cours*, Vol. 234, 126 ff.

72 I.e. Regulations Brussels I, 650/2012, 2016/1103 and 2016/1104, above n. 47, and 4/2009, above n. 32.

73 CJEU, case C-256/09, above n. 10, para. 92, where it states that appeal may be made to these rules 'in a way that is compatible with the regulation'. For more on this, see P. Beaumont, L. Walker and J Holliday, 'Conflicts of EU Courts on Child Abduction: The Reality of Article 11(6)–(8) Brussels IIa Proceedings across the EU' (2016) *Journal of Private International Law*, 211–260, 219–221; U. P. Gruber, 'Die Anerkennung einstweiliger Maßnahmen in der EuEheVO' (2017) *IPRax* 5, 467–470. This opportunity was taken by Oberlandesgericht München, 22.01.2015, 12 UF 1821/14, EUFam's: DES20150122, available on the EUFam's data-base <www.eufams.unimi.it> accessed 20.10.2018.

different Member States, each of which, in turn, shows reluctance to delegate the protection of a child to another court.[74]

This problem is so serious that the Commission had proposed allowing the courts of the host State to intervene of their own accord, if only on a provisional basis, to institute the protective measures that, once recognised and enforced in the other Member State, can make the child's return safe. The intention was to bring about a system in which, as the Commission stressed, protective measures can 'travel with the child', preventing dangerous gaps in child protection.[75] It is worth noting that, in the Commission's proposal, the scope of the suggested modifications would not have been limited to cases of international abduction of children, but would have extended more generally to all protective measures adopted by courts not having jurisdiction over the substance of the dispute. That was because Article 12, which reproduces the text of the current Article 20, with some modifications, became a proper rule establishing jurisdiction.[76] This was intended to create the preconditions for decisions adopted on its basis to be recognised and enforced in other Member States. Indeed, the proposal expressly provides for this possibility at Article 48, limiting it to measures adopted in adversarial proceedings.

Thus conceived, the modifications to the Regulation would have exceeded the need for reform as it emerged from the evaluation of its operation and application. Furthermore, they were bucking the current trend in favour of a restrictive approach to the circulation of provisional and protective measures ordered by a court other than the one with jurisdiction over the substance of the matter, which has emerged with the recast Brussels I Regulation.[77] As the next section describes, this different option could have been justified in light of the fact that Brussels IIa contains a valid mechanism for circumventing the inconveniences that have dogged this possibility in the area of civil and commercial disputes. However, it was chiefly due to the need to balance the above-mentioned difficulties in enforcing abroad the measures granted by the judge dealing with the merits. These, in turn, were a direct result of the adoption, in the Commission's proposal, of the above-described strictes approach to the assessment of the child's opinion at the enforcement stage. Indeed, in such a scenario, the court of the Member State where the child is present would have

---

74 Convention on the Civil Aspects of International Child Abduction, The Hague, 25.10.1980 (hereinafter: 1980 Hague Convention). On the added value of the Brussels IIa regime on child abduction compared to the 1980 Hague Convention see L. Carpaneto, above n. 42, 934 ff. On the interdependent relationship between mutual trust among the judicial authorities of the Member States and the protection of the best interests of children, see K. Lenaerts, 'The Best Interests of the Child Always Come First: The Brussels II Bis Regulation and the European Court of Justice' (2013) *Jurisprudence* 4, 1302–1328, 1326.

75 See the proposal, above n. 6, pp. 10 and 14.

76 The provision was inserted into Chapter II, section 2, on parental responsibility.

77 See Article 2(a) of Regulation 1215/2012, above n. 40.

had a better chance to hear him or her, without impairing the speediness of the procedure and, thus, to adopt measures proving effective, even in the case of a child moving from a Member State to another.

Once it was decided to retain the grounds for the refusal of enforcement as they currently are, it comes without surprise that the legislator has substantially taken over the suggested modifications to Article 20 (relieving courts from the burden of the currently required two-fold verification in order to exercise jurisdiction), yet opting for a more prudent approach as to the circulation of provisional and protective measures granted by a court that is not competent on the merits. Consequently, under the Recast, the possibility to have such measures enforced in another Member State is limited to those ordered in accordance with its Article 27(5) in conjunction with its Article 15, i.e. to interim measures ancillary to return orders and intended to secure the protection of the child after his or her return in the circumstances referred to in point (b) of Article 13(1) of the 1980 Hague Convention.[78]

Albeit minimalist, this choice will probably prove sufficient in achieving the purpose of reinforcing the duty to return the child in abduction cases, and thus in pursuing the best interests of minors. Indeed, in this connection, it is submitted that, given the context in which a declaration of enforceability is no longer strictly necessary in order to proceed with the enforcement,[79] the solution outlined by the Recast may be more efficient, both in terms of economy of procedure and of the resulting protection of the child, than the so-called 'mirror orders', which cropped up in applications of the 1980 Hague Convention, particularly where the enforcement may only be opposed in exceptional cases, and cannot be used as a stalling tactic.[80]

4. COORDINATION BETWEEN MEASURES AND IMPACT ON THE NOTION OF 'PROVISIONAL AND PROTECTIVE MEASURES'

The two-fold track for instituting interim protection under Brussels IIa creates the need to coordinate among the different authorities which may, for different reasons, oversee the same case, so that no contradictions may even temporarily arise between their decisions until the proceedings on the substance of the case

---

78 See art. 2 par. 1 of the Recast.

79 Ibid., Article 34.

80 Namely the adoption in the State of habitual residence of measures that replicate the ones adopted or requested in the State where the child is present. On this practice, see HCC, Guide to Good Practice Child Abduction Convention: Part III – Preventive Measures, 2005, p. 20, where as an example it is mentioned the case *Gumbrell v. Jones* [2001] NZFLR 593, available on INCADAT < https://www.incadat.com/en> accessed 20.10.2018, at: [HC/E/NZ 446].

have been concluded. This is a common problem for other EU Regulations on jurisdiction as well and, before, for the Brussels Convention, wherein only the intervention of the CJEU has given the court with jurisdiction over the substance of the matter a central role even in the phase concerning protective measures.[81] This has led to the somewhat unsatisfactory outcome[82] that has necessitated, in the recasting of Regulation Brussels I, the interventions discussed above, which seek to limit the potential circulation of protective measures.[83]

At the regulatory level, this issue was addressed only in the Brussels IIa Regulation, which expressly provides at Article 20(2) that the provisional measures adopted under the first section of that Chapter will cease to apply when the court with jurisdiction over the substance of the matter has adopted the measures it deems appropriate.[84] It is important to stress that as the Brussels I Regulation was being recast, the idea of introducing a modification to bring about a similar result ran into opposition from the Member States.[85] This suggests that it was the specific characteristics of parental responsibility disputes – in which the protection of the child is pivotal, and in which it is broadly accepted that the protection of the child's interests takes priority over the need to resolve the opposing interests of the parties – which allowed for the creation of a unique way of regulating the relationships between the judicial authorities involved and between the various measures adopted.

Although the solution in Regulation No. 2201/2003 is unique in EU legislation, national judges have not run into particular difficulties in applying it. This suggests that the division of the roles between the court with jurisdiction

81 See the case law which aims to prevent protective measures from being used as a tool to circumvent the criteria to establish jurisdiction on the substance of the matter, in particular: CJEU, case C-391/95, above n. 12, para. 46; case C-99/96 *Mietz v Intership Yachting Sneek BV*, ECLI:EU:C:1999:202, paras. 47 and 55.

82 See, in particular, CJEU, case C-80/00 *Italian Leather spa v. WECO Polstermöbel GmbH & Co.*, ECLI:EU:C:2002:342, which recognises a judgment by the requested State denying the adoption of similar protective measures, under Article 24 of the 1968 Brussels Convention, as grounds for refusing to recognise a preventive measure adopted by the judge with jurisdiction over the substance of the matter.

83 See Article 2(a) of Regulation (EU) 1215/2012, above n. 40.

84 In the broader context of the instruments adopted as a part of judicial cooperation in civil matters, we may observe an attempt to coordinate those geared toward 'promoting the compatibility of the rules on civil procedure applicable in the Member States' provided for by Article 81(2)(f) TFEU. See, in particular, Article 16 of the Regulation (EU) 655/2014 of the European Parliament and of the Council of 15 May 2014 establishing a European Account Preservation Order procedure to facilitate cross-border debt recovery in civil and commercial matters [2014] OJ L189/59, where, however, the means of coordinating are radically different, since they are specifically intended to avoid excessive protection of creditors to the detriment of debtors.

85 See A. Dickinson, 'Provisional Measures in the "Brussels I" Review: Disturbing the Status Quo?', (2010) *Journal of Private International Law*, 519–564, 550 ff.; L. Sandrini, 'Coordination of Substantive and Interim Proceedings' in F. Pocar, I. Viarengo and F. Villata (eds.), *Recasting Brussels I*, Cedam, Padua, 2012, pp. 273–284, p. 275 ff., as well as the bibliographical references therein.

over the substance of the matter and the court with jurisdiction under Article 20, as clarified by the case law of the CJEU, does indeed respond to the peculiar needs of this area of law.[86] Of particular relevance here are a set of Italian decisions in which, on the one hand, courts seised with the substance of the matter intervened to replace measures adopted in other Member States under Article 20 and, on the other hand, courts seised under Article 20 instead rejected requested protective measures. In these latter cases the Italian courts held that, in light of the specific circumstances, adopting the measures would have amounted to undue interference with the exercise of jurisdiction by the judiciary of the State of the child's habitual residence.[87] One thing that has surely enabled the correct application of EU legislation in this area is that it was previously tested out in the broader context of international cooperation. Indeed, the very same regulatory solution appeared in the 1961 Hague Convention,[88] and was later replicated, with some modifications, in the 1996 Convention.[89] From a different point of view, it is clear that the subordinate relationship that this regulatory scheme establishes between the different judicial authorities cannot always be realised, due to the necessarily final and irreversible effect of some urgent provisional measures, which may take the form of judicial approval to proceed with medical treatments concerning the child, for example.[90]

Aside from specific scenarios like this one, however, Article 20(2) has the result of guaranteeing that protective measures adopted by courts without jurisdiction over the substance of the matter will, indeed, be provisional. Thus, it resolves the issue of how to categorise measures that fall under the rule, allowing for its avoidance. That is what until now this issue has not come up in the context of the Brussels IIa Regulation with the same urgency that it has had in other sectors. However, the new framework outlined by the proposal could have potentially given rise to interpretative uncertainties about it. Indeed, the practice applying the 1968 Brussels Convention demonstrates that such uncertainties are more likely to arise when a different Member State is called upon to enforce a measure. In this scenario, the limits on the exercise of provisional jurisdiction by a court not having jurisdiction over the substance of the matter – without prejudice to the prohibition of review of jurisdiction of the court of origin[91] and the prohibition

86 See, in particular, CJEU, case C-523/07, above n. 14.

87 See Corte di Appello di Catania, 3.06.2015, EUFam's: ITS20150603; Tribunale di Arezzo, 15.03.2011, EUFam's: ITF20110315; Tribunale di Cagliari, 12.12.2015, EUFam's: ITF20151212; Tribunale di Roma, 18.05.2017, EUFam's: ITF201702518, available on the EUFam's data-base <www.eufams.unimi.it> accessed 20.10.2018.

88 See Article 9 of the 1961 Hague Convention, above n. 49.

89 See Article 12(3) of the 1996 Hague Convention, above n. 49.

90 In this respect, see M. W. de Steiger, Rapport Explicatif (1961) Actes et documents de la Neuvième session (1960), tome IV, 'Protection des mineurs', p. 7.

91 Article 24 of Regulation Brussels IIa and Article 50 of the proposal, above n. 6. See CJEU, case C-455/15 PPU, *P v. Q*, ECLI:EU:C:2015:763, paras. 42–46, and the remarks by S. Corneloup, 'Actualité du règlement Bruxelles II bis', (2016) *Revue critique de droit international privé*, 479.

of review of the merits,[92] which prevent reviews concerning the existence of the urgency requirement – may well leave room for oversight concerning the nature of the measure.[93] Indeed, this is not excluded even where there is a reference to the national legal systems, which can be found both in Article 20(1) of the Brussels IIa Regulation and Article 24 of the Brussels Convention (and in the corresponding rules of the provisions which replaced it). In fact, even in this scenario, national regulations may only be applied in compliance with EU law.[94] Thus, it is perhaps for the very purpose of mitigating the interpretive problems that could derive from the aforementioned reference to national law, in a system that allows for the circulation of protective measures adopted by courts without jurisdiction over the substance of the matter, that the Commission proposed eliminating it from the text of the Regulation. This kind of intervention, in light of the case law of the CJEU concerning the interpretation of EU law, would have pointed toward the definition of an autonomous meaning.[95] However, since this is not even loosely sketched out by the Regulation, it would have required intervention by the CJEU in order to truly be defined. The shortcomings of this method, specifically when it comes to the regulation of provisional protective measures, have already come to light.[96] On the other hand, the Commission's

---

92 Article 26 of Regulation Brussels IIa and Article 52 of the proposal, above n. 6.

93 In the system envisioned by the Commission, this check could take place within proceedings to refuse enforcement under Article 40 ff. of the proposal.

94 This is one of the boundaries that the Court draws even in areas reserved for the competences of the Member States. An emblematic topic in this category, the object of which is an institution expressly recognised as belonging to domestic jurisdiction, is case law concerning citizenship: see, among many, CJEU, case C-360/90, *Mario Vicente Micheletti and others v. Delegación del Gobierno en Cantabria*, ECLI:EU:C:1992:295, para. 10, which states that, 'Under international law, it is for each Member State, *having due regard to Community law*, to lay down the conditions for the acquisition and loss of nationality' (emphasis added). In accordance with the same orientation, as to the 1968 Brussels Convention, CJEU, case C-261/90, *Mario Reichert, Hans-Heinz Reichert and Ingeborg Kockler v. Dresdner Bank AG.*, ECLI:EU:C:1992:149, para. 34, explained that, 'The expression "provisional, including protective, measures" within the meaning of Article 24 must therefore be understood as referring to measures which, in matters within the scope of the Convention, are intended to preserve a factual or legal situation so as to safeguard rights the recognition of which is sought elsewhere from the court having jurisdiction as to the substance of the matter', thus obliging the judge to carry out a two-fold qualification, in light of domestic law and the characteristics laid out by the CJEU.

95 Concerning this, the formula that has been consistently reiterated in the cases of the CJEU state: 'the need for uniform application of Community law and from the principle of equality that the terms of a provision of Community law which makes no express reference to the law of the Member States for the purpose of determining its meaning and scope must normally be given an autonomous and uniform interpretation throughout the European Community, having regard to the context of the provision and the objective pursued by the legislation in question' (case C-523/07, above n. 14, para. 34; see also case C-393/18 PPU, above n. 14, para. 46 and the case law cited therein).

96 Concerning the 1968 Brussels Convention, the CJEU, in addition to the general indication provided in case C-261/90, above n. 94, in which it held that the *actio pauliana* of French

refusal to engage in the development of an autonomous meaning is fully understandable in light of the profound differences between the legal systems of the Member States when it comes to protective measures, and, at the same time, the variety of situations that call for the adoption of such measures, and which result in an equally varied panoply of provisions.[97] Under the circumstances, it is likely that any attempt to define an autonomous meaning that could be, at once, sufficiently precise and all-inclusive, as well as capable of gaining the Council's approval, would likely be unrealistic.

Given this challenge, one may well wonder whether an autonomous meaning is really necessary or whether it could be useful anyway when it comes to regulation of parental responsibility, and whether its absence will have an impact, as it has had in the areas of civil and commercial law. It would appear that the answer is no, considering the chiefly anticipatory nature of provisional measures intended to protect children, which is decisive in this context. What distinguishes provisional rulings from rulings on the substance can be reduced to the urgent need for a ruling (a requirement provided for in the Regulation and applicable in any case, even where the characterisation must be made *ex lege fori*), to the provisional nature of the effects of the former, and to the usually summary assessment of the case. The potential weaknesses of this third characteristic do not undermine the system outlined by the Regulation. By the same token, the same may be said of the provisional character of protective measures, which, even if it was not *ab origine* a feature of the adopted measure, would in any case come about *ex post* through the mechanism of the primacy of the measures adopted by the court with jurisdiction over the substance of the matter, as already mentioned. It is equally clear that the duty of communication that, '[i]n so far as the protection of the best interests of the child so requires', falls on the court without jurisdiction over the substance, with regard to the measures it adopts, which the Recast includes in the text of the provision on interim

law does not derive from Article 24 of the Convention, has spoken numerous times on the notion of protective measures, with regard to specific measures provided for under the national legal systems (see CJEU, case C-99/96, above n. 81, para. 53 ff.; case C-80/00, above n. 82, paras. 39 and 46; case C-104/03, *St Paul Dairy Industries NV v. Unibel Exser BVBA*, ECLI:EU:C:2005:255, para. 25). These pronouncements case by case, tied to the queries submitted by the referring courts, have nevertheless not led to the complete definition of this concept.

97 It is not possible to give a complete overview of the different measures that fit into the controversies on parental responsibility, which, as mentioned previously (see above, para. 2 n. 32 and corresponding text), differ significantly from State to State. In addition to those already mentioned here, however, it is worth recalling those intended to prevent the child from crossing the border with only one parent, since these are often adopted *ante causam* with respect to custody proceedings, in order to counteract the phenomenon of international abduction. See, e.g. Ústavní soud, 3.03.2011, 2471/10, EUFam's: CZC20110303; Tribunale per i minorenni di Venezia, 30.11.2011, EUFam's: ITF20111130, available on the EUFam database <www.eufams.unimi.it> accessed 20.10.2018.

measures, not only will facilitates speedy enforcement of the measures, but also their rapid replacement with whatever measures the court with jurisdiction over the substance of the matter considers most appropriate.[98]

Thus the regulatory framework, which already provides tools intended to react against potential abuses of the special provision on provisional and protective measures, whatever characteristics these may have (even in the absence of an autonomous meaning), will see their effectiveness strengthened when the Recast will come into application. It should therefore be welcome the choice to reconsider the elimination of the reference to the national legal systems in the re-formulation of Article 20.[99] Indeed, its elimination would not only have failed to add value, but, on the contrary, by denying the court of origin a sure and known regulatory reference point without providing a new one, it could have engendered uncertainty in the course of the procedure for issuing provisional measures and, thus, have deleterious effects for the underlying goal of the provision: speedy intervention to provide interim protection.

5. CONCLUSIONS

The fact that the Member States of the EU share the goal of ensuring the best interests of the child in international disputes and, more specifically, that of guaranteeing speedy and effective protection of children's rights has permitted a well-articulated and functional regulatory scheme for provisional and protective measures to develop within the Brussels IIa Regulation. This, in itself, is an important outcome, considering that in all other sectors, including those that appear equally connected to the field of family law (i.e. spousal maintenance and property issues deriving from marriage or a registered partnership), the provision of interim measures has so far resisted every attempt to further judicial cooperation in civil matters in the EU.

The CJEU's intervention has been intended to capitalise on the features of the regulatory scheme established by the legislator, rather than to fill any gaps in it. This does not, however, undermine the importance of its contributions. Indeed, the CJEU has consistently underscored the central role of the principle of the superior interests of the child in interpreting EU laws on parental responsibility.

---

98 See Article 15, para. 2 and para. 3, for communications from the court competent on the merits to that having issued protective measures. See also Article 12, para. 1 line 2 of the proposal, above n. 6. The provision imposing a duty of communication codifies the position taken by the CJEU in case C-523/07, above n. 14, paras. 57-64. For more on this, see A. Dutta and A Schulz, 'First Cornerstones of the EU Rules on Cross-Border Child Cases: The Jurisprudence of the Court of Justice of the European Union on the Brussels IIa Regulation from C to Health Service Executive', (2014) *Journal of Private International Law*, 1–40, 37 ff.

99 See Article 15, para. 1 of the Recast.

At the same time, it has clearly identified the limits that govern appeals to the superior interests of the minor as an interpretative rule in the EU system. Teleological interpretation, according to the CJEU, may indeed lead to a broad interpretation of the rules, but may not contradict the letter of the provisions. It has, therefore, ruled out the possibility that the superior interests of the child may be invoked in a particular case in order to sidestep a general evaluation made by the legislator in the abstract concerning the interests *of children*. This is an important indication, and one that is all the more significant since it comes from a court that has not hesitated in other contexts, where necessary, to exercise creative jurisprudence. Therefore, it follows that it is the duty of the legislator to find regulatory solutions that are flexible enough to allow courts to give the proper weight to the specific features of each individual, particular case.

As mentioned above, the EU legislator has taken on this duty, and has proposed to modify the aspects of the regulatory scheme that the CJEU and the practice of national courts have identified as lacking, including with regard to the area just mentioned. The proposed modifications and those eventually adopted in the area of provisional protective measures discussed here lend themselves to a few observations. These derive, first, from the composite nature of the concept of the superior interests of the child. The protection of the child consists in guaranteeing a set of rights that must all necessarily be respected. In particular, the emphasis that the EU places on the child's right to be heard cannot obscure the fact that the same degree of importance must attach to the right to speedy and effective protection from whatever harm, physical or psychological, he or she may be exposed to. The Commission's proposal did not appear to have sufficiently balanced these two rights. Instead, it seems that, in its attempt to generally bolster the guarantees that protect the child's right to be heard, it neglected to consider that the specific goal of protective measures and their provisional nature may call for solutions different from those outlined for recognising and enforcing rulings on the substance of a matter. The recently adopted Recast, on the contrary, by retaining substantially unchanged the current grounds for refusal of enforcement of decisions in matters of parental responsibility and the related exceptions, is certainly more effective in reconciling the different exigencies.

Second, it seems that a careful consideration of the interests of the child in the re-formulation of the Regulation's rule on protective measures has led to a fruitful re-thinking of the role attributed to the definition of autonomous meanings in the area of judicial cooperation in civil matters. More precisely, it could lead to the emergence (or re-emergence) of the instrumental function they carry out in light of the objectives that the act or the specific rule pursue, and to abandonment of the tendency to consider uniformity of legal meanings and concepts as a value in itself. Then, the reference to the law of the Member States could be judged positively, and not as a failure to progress toward a space of freedom, safety, and justice, whenever it may facilitate the task of national courts, without jeopardising the overall coherence of the system, as seems to be the case with interim reliefs in the field of parental responsibility.

More generally, the self-restraint shown by the EU legislator in carrying on the recasting deserves appreciation. Among the modifications put forward by the Commission, only those likely to result in an actual enhancement in terms of protection of minors have been eventually picked up, while more far-reaching interventions have been rejected. That is, relating to provisional and protective measures, the current rules have been modified to the extent strictly necessary in light of the shortcomings that emerged in almost fourteen years of application. This minimalist approach in pursuing the aims of the recasting will hopefully contribute to mitigating the inevitable interpretative uncertainties and the consequent difficulties of application that any normative reform always brings about. Lastly, but no less important, quite the contrary in fact, in the always changing scenario of the EU judicial cooperation, which seems characterised by a sort of regulatory hyperactivity, it will contribute to acknowledging the importance of the stability of the normative framework as one of the crucial factors to ensuring the best interests of the child, both at the procedural and substantive levels.

INDEX

A
adoption 110, 221–222, *see also* kafala, *see also* cross-border adoption
adoptee's right to respect for family life 147
commercialisation of international adoption 204
cross-border recognition of adoptions 91, 176, 182, 261
ordre public exception 175–176, 261
European Convention on the Adoption of Children 210, 222
legal parent-child relationship 201
France 199, 201
margin of appreciation 184
mater semper certa est principle 201
France 201
Negrepontis-Giannisis v. Greece 218
non-discrimination 19
recognition of status *filii* 181, 185, 211
right to identity 143, 146
same-sex couples 76–77, 181
joint adoption 77–78
second-parent adoption 77–78, 180
Wagner v. Luxembourg 217–218
African Charter on the rights of women
forced marriages 120
American Convention on Human Rights
forced marriages 120
annulment of marriages 147–148
Brussels II bis Regulation 148
Area of Security, Justice and Freedom 246
Article 24 (CFREU) 9–10, 16–17, 47, 49, 64–65, 70, 94, 116, 143, 154, 162, 228, 235, 267
adoptions 213
Åkerberg Fransson case 65
best interests principle 9, 47, 49, 150
child abduction 237, 240
cross-border situations 10
family reunification 70
forced marriages 116
jurisdiction rules 275, 305
maintaining a relationship with both parents 9, 154, 236, 290, 298
non-compliance 230
relationship with Article 3 CRC 64
rights covered 9
right to be heard 9, 16–17, 237
right to personal relationship with parents 64
right to the protection and care 64
well-being of the child 9
asylum law 12
family members 69
asylum seekers *see* child asylum seekers and refugees
autonomous residence permits 117, 121, 133
asking for protection 135
pre-conditions 136
protection from forced marriages 134
autonomous rights 4, 33, 42

B
best interests as primary consideration 223, 265, 284
Article 3(1) CRC 58, 162, 211, 265
Article 8 ECHR 62, 227, 234
Article 24 CFREU 9, 12, 47, 64, 67, 150, 162, 211
asylum seekers 69
child abduction 227, 234
Dublin III Regulation 69
family reunification 67, 73
New York Convention 5, 6, 111
biological link between child and parents 61, 111, 181, 188, 190–191, 196, 198, 200–202, *see also* biological parents
Braun v. France 201
Foulon and Bouvet v. France 191, 200
Labassee v. France 188
Laborie v. France 190
Mennesson v. France 188, 198, 202
Paradiso and Campanelli v. Italy 194–197
Saenz and Saenz Cortes v. France 201
biological parents 61, 111
best interests as primary consideration 111
biological father
children born outside wedlock 61
refusing consent for adoption 181
surrogacy 192, 200–201
biological mother
surrogate, as 200, 202
legal parent-child relationship 198
border security
family reunification rights 56, 64
Brussels I Regulation 303
Brussels II bis Regulation 154, 164, 303
annulment of marriages 148
child abduction 226, 230–231
case law 237
criterion of proximity 274, 290

evolution 267
habitual residence 151–152, 230, 273
parental responsibility 97, 144, 150–151, 229
provisional and protective measures 289, 300, 303–304, 307
return of children provisions 153, 259
rights of access to a child 149
rights of asylum and immigration exclusion 272
rights of custody 154
Brussels II Regulation
Brussels II a 267
Brussels II ter Regulation
age of capacity 273
execution of decisions
abolition of exequatur 277, 282, 294
more efficient enforcement 278
Hague Parental Responsibility Convention, relationship with 271
improved protection
interpretative dimension 284
procedural dimension 284
substantial dimension 285
mediation 279–281
parental responsibility 270
rights of asylum and immigration 272
scope of application 273

C

Charter of Fundamental Rights of the EU (CFREU) 70, 94–95, 116, 154, 162, 174, 211, 213, 215, 226, 228, 275, 305
Article 6 TEU 142
Article 7 9, 23, 33, 55, 58, 85–86, 95, 143, 174, 228
legal protection of identity 22
proportionality test 36
protecting family unit 55, 58
rainbow families 86, 89, 92
Article 24 *see* Article 24 (CFREU)
best interests as primary consideration 9, 12, 47, 64, 67, 150, 162, 211
cross-border adoption 211
forced marriages 116
legal protection of identity 35
maintaining a relationship with both parents 9
non-discrimination 9
prohibition of exploitative child labour 9
rainbow families 85, 89
discrimination on the ground of sexual orientation 93–94
right to private and family life 90–92
receiving free compulsory education 9
respect for private and family life 9
right to be heard 9
well-being of the child 9
child abduction 240
'substantial' assessment of the child's situation 283
abduction of refugee children 257
Aguirre-Zarraga v. Pelz 230, 236, 280
Brussels II a Regulation 226
children's rights obligation 240
Detiček v. Sgueglia 236
Doris Povse v. Mauro Alpago 237
duty to return the child 302
Ferrari v. Romania 234
habitual residence 230
Hague Abduction Convention 225, 229
Maumousseau v. France 232
mediation proceedings 281
Neulinger v. Switzerland 167, 232
overriding mechanism 283
return remedy 231
best interests principle 231
second chance procedure 283
Severe v. Austria 234
X. v. Latvia 168, 233
child asylum seekers and refugees
child's right to humanitarian protection 45
duty to respect, protect and fulfil children's rights 44
non-refoulement principle 256
right of the child to be heard 16
vulnerability 40
special protection 40, 44
child labour
Article 32 CFREU 9
child marriages *see* forced marriages
child's cross-border placement 110, 221, 282, *see also* kafala
kafala 99, 100, 113
State's consent 282, 283
child's right to humanitarian protection 45
children born out of wedlock
Italy 14
non-discrimination 12
Brauer v. Germany 13
Keegan v. Ireland 13
Marckx v. Belgium 13
Mazurek v. France 13
Sahin v. Germany 14
children of same-sex couples *see* rainbow families
citizenship
criterion of proximity 274
freedom of movement 11, 68, 87
coercion *see* forced marriages
Committee on the Protection of the Rights of All Migrant Workers and Members of Their Families 7
Committee on the Rights of the Child 52, 58, 227
asylum procedures 17, 19, 50
family reunification 58
migrant children 7, 43
monitoring role 7
Common European Asylum and Immigration Policy
best interests principle 47

Common European Asylum System 49
common law systems 166
  Hague Abduction Convention 252
competent authority
  adoption 103
  kafala 99–100
conflict of laws
  avoiding situations harmful to human rights 159
  ECtHR 159, 221
  kafala 210
  private international law 144, 146, 157, 217
  recognition of foreign judgments 173, 214, 216, 220–221, 223, 271
  status filii 172, 178, 211, 217
connection *see* citizenship, *see* domicile, *see* habitual residence of the child, *see* nationality, *see* proximity
continuity of status *filii* 177
  best interests test 178–184
Convention on Consent to Marriage, Minimum Age for Marriage and Registration of Marriages 119
Convention on preventing and combating violence against women and domestic violence (Istanbul Convention)
  age of consent 120
  autonomous residence permits 133, 135
  family reunification 127, 136–137
  forced marriages 116, 120–121, 124, 130, 134, 136–137
  gender-based violence 123, 124
Convention on the elimination of all forms of discrimination against women (CEDAW)
  forced marriages 117, 119
Convention on the Rights of the Child (CRC) 3, 119, 162, 226, 239, 242
  best interests principle, function of 59
  best interests principle, importance of State 165
  commercial surrogacy 204
  definition of the child 58, 128
  family reunification 59
  forced marriages 119, 122
  Guidelines on Determining the Best Interests of the Child 53
  migrant children 58
    best interests of the child 43
    family reunification 58
    non-discrimination 43
    right to be heard 43
    right to life and development 43
  universal reach 7
Court of Justice of the European Union (CJEU) 4, 73, 81, 93, 128, 164
  child abduction 226
    Aguirre-Zarraga v. Pelz 236, 280
    children's rights obligations 240
    Detiček v. Sgueglia 236, 298
    Doris Povse v. Mauro Alpago 237
  Child and Family Agency case 169, 276
  Dynamic Medien case 11
  equality principle 153
  family reunification
    forced marriages 128
  Family Reunification Directive
    Chakroun case 65
    O., S., & L. case 66
  free movement of persons 14, 81
    Babanarakis case 14
    Coman case 81, 88
    maintaining relationships with other family members 14
    Zhu and Chen case 81
  interpretation of Brussels II bis Regulation 153–154
  rainbow families
    Coleman case 93
  recognition of status legally acquired abroad 28–30
  return of children
    J. McB case 153
  right to family life 8, 73
  transnational families 21
  uniform application 153
crimes against humanity 124
  forced marriages 124
cross-border adoption
  CFREU 211
  child-centred approach 222
  domestic regulation 209
  ECtHR 211
  EU law
    lack of harmonisation 209
  European Convention on the Adoption of Children 210
  Hague Adoption Convention 210
  legitimate expectation 219
  margin of appreciation 220
cross-border continuity of rights and status 146, 221
  conflict-of-law rules 221
  Harroudi v. France 221
cross-border legal recognition of adoption 91
cross-border legal recognition of rainbow families 83
cross-border legal recognition of surrogacy agreements 91
cross-border surrogacy 219
  ECtHR advisory opinion 218
  Foulon and Bouvet v. France 191–192
  Labassee v. France 188–190
  Laborie v. France 190–191
  Mennesson v. France 188–190
  ordre public exception 190
  removal of the child from the intending parents
    Paradiso and Campanelli v. Italy 177, 194–197, 219
  travel restrictions on children
    D. v. Belgium 192–194
cross-examination of children 17

D

dependency defined 34
descendants
  definition 78, 80, 104–105, 109
  family reunification 104–105
  kafala 105, 108–109
  minors 104
detention
  migrating children 6, 45
  prohibition of inhuman and degrading treatment 20
discrimination on grounds of gender 7, 118, 137, 258, *see also* forced marriages
discrimination on grounds of nationality 27–28
discrimination on grounds of race 118
discrimination on grounds of sexual orientation
  CFREU 93, 95
  ECHR 93
  EU law 93
  rainbow families 93
discrimination on grounds of sexual orientation 29, 83, 95, 181, 214, 263, *see also* same-sex couples, *see also* same-sex parenthood
domestic family law
  children born out of wedlock 12–14
  maintaining relationships with other family members 14–15
  prohibition of inhuman treatment 17–19
  recognition of family status 172
  right of the child to be heard 15–17
domestic violence 135, 251
  child abduction 169, 231, 248, 250, 257
  forced marriages 123
  non-refoulement principle 131
domestic violence 7, 137, 258, *see also* Convention on preventing and combating violence against women and domestic violence (Istanbul Convention), *see also* forced marriages
domicile 151, 166
Dublin II Regulation 49
Dublin III Regulation 12, 49, 68–70
  concerns
    lack of appeal remedies 69
    removal of asylum seekers 69
    separation of families 69
    use of discretionary provisions 69
  M.A. and Others v. UK 69
duty of cooperation 281
duty to collect and exchange information 281

E

entry and residence of a child placed in kafala care 99
  child entrusted to kafala care by competent authority in the child's State of habitual residence 99
  State in which the kafala was ordered 98
entry and residence of foreign nationals
  free movement of persons 100
  immigration policy 101
  kafala 108
Equality Framework Directive 2000/78
  discrimination on grounds of sexual orientation 93
equality principle 108, 153
EU accession to ECHR 57
EU legislator 290, 295, 298, 308–309
European Commission
  family reunification 66
  forced marriages 126, 128, 134
European Convention on Human Rights (ECHR) 4, 8, 61, 226
  child-centred approach 227
  conflict of laws 159
  kafala 111
  right to marry 129
  right to respect for private and family life (Article 8) 11, 61, 143, 215, 227
    Bronda v. Italy 14
    ECtHR interpretation 61
    Josef v. Belgium 19
    kafala 111
    kafali 105
    maintaining family relationships 14
    Manuello and Nevi v. Italy 14
    Nistor v. Romania 14
    rainbow families 92
European Convention on the Adoption of Children 210, 222
European Convention on the Exercise of Children's Rights (Strasbourg Convention) 16
European Court of Human Rights (ECtHR) 4, 72, 90–92, 94
  adoption
    Negrepontis-Giannisis case 147, 218
  balance between public interest and right to a family life 175
    cross-border adoption 221
  best interests principle
    public policy limitation 167
  child abduction 226
    children's rights obligations 240
    Doris Povse v. Mauro Alpago 238
    Ferrari v. Romania 234
    impacts of the Hague Abduction Convention 235
    Maumousseau v. France 232
    Neulinger v. Switzerland 232
    Severe v. Austria 234
    X. v. Latvia 233
  child-oriented interpretation 163
  children born out of wedlock 13–14
    Brauer v. Germany 13
    Keegan v. Ireland 13
    Marckx v. Belgium 13
    Mazurek v. France 13
    Sahin v. Germany 14

commercial surrogacy 205
cross-border adoption 211
forced marriages
Z.H. and R.H. v. Switzerland 128
Jeunesse case 11, 62
kafala 111–112
Chbihi Loudoudi and others v. Belgium 112
Harroudi v. France 111, 221
ordre public exception 167, 175, 216
Wagner case 167, 216
rainbow families
Gas and Dubois v. France 90, 92, 94
Labassee v. France 91
Marckx v. Belgium 90
Mennesson v. France 91
Wagner v. Luxembourg 91
residence 63
right to private and family life
El Ghatet v. Switzerland 72
Jeunesse case 62
Neulinger and Shuruk v. Switzerland 72
Nunez case 62
Rodrigues da Silva case 62
European Economic Area (EEA)
free movement of people 67
European Free Trade Association (EFTA)
free movement of people 67
European Parliament 82, 85, 121
forced marriages 121
freedom of movement 104
mediation proceedings 281
rainbow families
legal recognition 82, 84–85
European Parliament Coordinator on children's rights 281
exequatur
abolition 277–278, 282, 284, 294–295

F

family and child-related matters
civil rights 143
cultural, economic and social rights 143
family reunification 73, 81, 101–102, 133
age limit 126–127
age limits and forced marriage 126
asylum law 12, 67
best interests 63
Chavez-Vilchez case 71, 73
child as direct descendant of a Union citizen 80
children of same-sex parents
child is Union citizen, parents from third country 81
non-dependent child is a Union citizen 81
other situations 81
children's rights 78–82
Chakroun case 65
El Ghatet v. Switzerland 72
Neulinger and Shuruk v. Switzerland 72
O., S., & L. case 66
Coman case 81
denial causing violence against women 133
economic activities of family 65
EU law 101–105
Citizens' Rights Directive 104
family reunification directive 102–104
income requirement 66
Italy 14
Jeunesse case 11, 62
MA and others case 12
Marjan Noorzia v. Bundesministerin für Inneres 127
nationality of person applying for reunification 101
third-country nationals residing in a Member State 101
Union citizens 101
protection family unity
right not to be separated from parents 32
Ruiz Zambrano case 11, 70
sponsors of reunification 126
third-country nationals 104
Zhu and Chen case 81
Family Reunification Directive (2003/86) 10, 65, 67–68, 99, 102, 116, 125, 133
forced marriages 116, 125, 133, 137
interpretation 66
female genital mutilation 4, 17–18, 133
non-refoulement principle 17
risk of refoulement 7
forced marriages 4, 115
age of sponsor's spouse 126
autonomous residence permits 134
child abduction 258
crimes against humanity 124
cultural/religious perspective 118, 124, 129
margin of appreciation 129
definition of a child 117
domestic violence 123
family reunification law 125
health consequences 122
Istanbul Convention 136
Marjan Noorzia v. Bundesministerin für Inneres 127, 133
prohibition in international law
Convention on Consent to Marriage, Minimum Age for Marriage and Registration of Marriages 119
Convention on the elimination of all forms of discrimination against women 119
Convention on the Rights of the Child 119, 121
prohibition in regional law
American Convention on human rights 120
Council of Europe 120
European Parliament 121
Istanbul Convention 121
Maputo Protocol to the African Charter on the rights of women 120

protection in the destination country 137
reasons 118
right to education 123
risk of refoulement 7
statistics 117
Z.H. and R.H. v. Switzerland 116, 132
forum law 27, 146, 152, 172, 273
family status restrictions 173
ordre public exception 172
recognition of family status 172
status *filii* 177
forum shopping 263, 277
fraude à la loi 178
Foulon and Bouvet v. France 191–192
Free Movement Directive (2004/38) 33, 67
adopted children 104
family reunification 104
family reunification rights 79, 99
genuine residence 33
kafala 105
protection of family unity 33
free movement of persons 35, 78, 86, 95
family reunification 67
non-recognition of a child's name 26–28, 35
rainbow families 87–88, 95

G
gender-based discrimination 7, 128, 137, 258
see also forced marriages
gender-based violence against women 135, 169, 231, 257, *see also* domestic violence
forced marriages 124
genetic parents *see* biological parents
grandparents
children maintaining a relationship with 13–15, 104
Grunkin Paul principle 29, 37, 87
guardianship 99, 107, 110, 145, 147, 196, 221, *see also* kafala

H
habitual residence of the child 160, 166, 274–275, 290, 304
Brussels II bis Regulation 151, 230, 239, 273
Brussels II ter Regulation 275
child abduction 230
connection criteria 161, 166
Hague Abduction Convention 255, 259
kafala 99, 100
Hague Convention on Jurisdiction, Applicable Law, Recognition, Enforcement and Cooperation in Respect of Parental Responsibility and Measures for the Protection of Children (1996 Hague Convention) 97, 110, 145
provision of care by kafala 99
Hague Convention on Protection of Children and Co-operation in Respect of Intercountry Adoption (Hague Adoption Convention) 210–211
adoption by same-sex couples 214
ambiguity of term 'family' 214
interpretation of the concept of family 214
origins 212
procedural safeguards 212
purpose 212
safeguarding of national public concerns 214
Hague Convention on the Civil Aspects of International Child Abduction 1980 (Hague Abduction Convention) 167, 222, 225, 229, 239–240
Article 20 246
ambiguous relationship with other rules 247
Article 13, relationship with 248
best interests of the child 254
children with asylum and refugee status 256
custody proceedings 255
defining scope of application 246
discriminatory treatment 253
failure of domestic judicial system 252
forced marriages 258
grave risk' exception 250
grounds for triggering 252
habitual residence 255
subjective scope of application 247
ultimate safeguard clause 249
Article 20 in EU cases
mutual trust principle 259
public policy exception 261
fundamental rights violated by returning the child 260
refusal to return an abducted child 244–246
public policy 244
scope of application 245–246
serious risk of harm to the child on return 230
Hague Protocol of 23 November 2007 on the law applicable to maintenance obligations 152
harmonisation within the EU 155
guardianship 147
judicial cooperation in civil matters 144
legal security 147
right to identity 147

I
'interim' jurisdiction
identity *see* right to identity
inheritance rights 13, 28, 84, 173, 199
Inter-American Court of Human Rights
best interests of the child 164
urgency requirement 296
interim protection *see* provisional and protective measures
interim relief
Brussels II bis Regulation 289
Brussels II ter Regulation 290
International Convention on the Protection of the Rights of All Migrant Workers and Members of Their Families 60

International Covenant on Civil and Political Rights (ICCPR) 4–5, 215
internationalisation of relationships 160
Islamic law *see* kafala

J
judicial cooperation
- child abduction 161
- civil matters 144, 278, 307–309
- criminal matters 131

judicial discretion 31, 154
jurisdiction
- Brussels II bis Regulation 275
- Brussels II ter Regulation 275
  - parental responsibility 276
  - transfer to a more appropriate forum 276
- citizenship 274
- proximity 274

K
kafala 98, 221
- 1996 Hague Convention 99, 110
- Citizens' Rights Directive 105
- consensual kafala 109
- Family Reunification Directive 110
- *Harroudi v. France* 221
- Italy 106
  - best interests of the child 108
  - conformity with the Constitution 108
  - Court of Cassation interpretation 107
  - third-country national as sponsor 106
- kafala ordered by a judge 109
- state practice 105–110

L
legal aid 16
legal protection of identity
- Article 7 CFREU 22
- Article 8 ECHR 22
- Article 51 CFREU 25, 37
- child welfare 23
- right to private and family 22
- scope of EU law 24–25
- Treaty law 25

legal representation to children 16

M
maintaining family relationships 236
- with both parents 9, 154, 236, 290, 298
- with grandparents 13–15, 104
- with other family members 14–15

margin of appreciation
- adoption 184, 220
- family reunification 65
- *ordre public* exception 175–176
- recognition of status legally acquired abroad 31
- removal of children 51

mater semper certa est principle 201
mediation procedures
- child's right to be heard 279

Mediator for International Parental Child Abduction *see* European Parliament Coordinator on children's rights
medical treatment 233, 304
- parental consent 83, 146
- surrogate mothers 183

medically assisted insemination
- same-sex couples 76–78
- single persons 77–78

migrant children 4, 44
- definition 39
- detention 6, 45
- duty to respect, protect and fulfil children's rights 44
- Italy 51
- minorities or indigenous communities 44
- risk of refoulement 7
- separation of families 56

migration law 11
monitoring
- Committee on the Rights of the Child 7
- Hague Abduction Convention 251

N
nationality
- connection criteria 160, 166
- discrimination on grounds of nationality 27–28

New York Convention 5
- cross-border adoption 212, 215
- kafala 111

non-discrimination 8, 162
- Article 21 CFREU 9
- children born out of wedlock 12, 19
  - *Brauer v. Germany* 13
  - *Keegan v. Ireland* 13
  - *Marckx v. Belgium* 13
  - *Mazurek v. France* 13
- migrant children 43
- recognition of a child's name 27
- right to identity 25

non-refoulement principle 60, 131, 256
- prohibition of inhuman and degrading treatment 17, 131

nuclear families 76, 84, 92, 95
- family reunification rights 94

O
Optional Protocol on the Sale of Children, Child Prostitution and Child Pornography 204, 208
ordre public exception 161, 172
- *Labassee* case 177
- margin of appreciation 176
- *Mennesson* case 175
- *Negrepontis-Giannisis* case 175, 218
- *Paradiso and Campanelli* case 177, 194, 219
- recognition and enforcement of judgments 175
- *Wagner* case 176, 216

P
party autonomy 160, 267
  choice of court 275
  habitual residence of the child 275, 284
Préjudicielle d'Urgence (PPU) 268, 285, 296, 305
primacy principle 101
  CRC 45, 185, 235
  EU legislator 291
principle of inalienability of civil status (France) 189
private international law 212
  adoption
    balancing human rights 220
    Hague Adoption Convention 212
  family and child-related matters 155
  human rights-oriented interpretation 152–155
  human rights, relationship with
    conflict of laws 159
  impact of human rights 148–152
    choice of connecting factors 150–152
    openness towards foreign judgments and law 148–149
    protection of human rights in particular circumstances 151–152
    rules primarily reflecting a concern for rights 150–151
  protection of human rights 142–143
    Convention on the rights of persons with disabilities 142
    Convention on the rights of the child 142
    cross-border situations 144
    Treaty on European Union 142
    Treaty on the Functioning of the EU 142
prohibition of exploitative child labour 9
prohibition of inhuman or degrading treatment 6
  detention cases 20
  non-refoulement principle 17, 19
prohibition of review of jurisdiction 304
prohibition of review of the merits 305
promotion of the individual in family relationships 160
proportionality test
  necessity test 180
  recognition of status legally acquired abroad
    freedom of movement 31
    inconvenience 32
  suitability test 180
protecting family unity
  Article 7 CFREU 55
  Article 8 ECHR 55
  proportionality 35
  removal of a child's family member 33–35
  right to family reunification 32–33
protection from discrimination *see* non-discrimination
provisional and protective measures 288
  'interim' jurisdiction 295–302
  interim relief 289–295
proximity
  connection criteria 166, 274, 290–291, 297
public policy exception *see ordre public* exception

R
rainbow families 76
  definition 75
  legal recognition 76–78, 85
  right to free movement 85
rainbow families 29, 83, 95, 181, 214, 263, *see also* same-sex couples, *see also* same-sex parenthood
ratione materiae 271, 298
ratione personae 273
rebus sic stantibus principle 278
recognition and enforcement of judgments 97, 144, 147, 154–155, 164, 237, 259, 274, 290, 307, *see also* Brussels II bis Regulation
  ordre public exception 175
recognition and enforcement of privileged decisions 278
recognition of a child's name 37, 143, 175, *see also* right to identity
  free movement of persons 26–28
  non-discrimination 27
recognition of foreign family status 171
recognition of foreign judgments 146–147
  conflict of laws 173
  right to marry and found a family 147
recognition of same-sex couples' parental status 78, 84, 95
  CFREU 91
  ECHR 91
recognition of status *filii*
  adoption 181, 211
    Hussin v. Belgium 216
  conflicts of law
    foreign 173
    right to identity 175
  continuity of status *filii* 177
  domestic law 172
  international law 171
  margin of appreciation 179
  ordre public exception
    European Court of Human Rights 174–178
    margin of appreciation 174–178
  surrogacy 181
recognition of status legally acquired abroad
  benefit rights 28
  citizenship rights 29
  Coman case 30
  freedom of movement 29
    margin of appreciation 31
    proportionality test 31
  Grunkin Paul case 29, 37
  inheritance rights 28
  recognition of parental links 29
  restrictions 30–32
  right to identity 28

recognition of the parent-child relationship 218
  cross-border surrogacy
    ECtHR approach 207
    Foulon and Bouvet v. France 198
    Mennesson v. France 198
    Saenz and Saenz Cortes v. France 201
  legitimate expectation 219
refugees *see* child asylum seekers and refugees
registration of identity 22
removal of children 50, 130
  Dublin Regulation 50–51
margin of appreciation 51
removal of family members 33–35
residency 63, 100, 151, 166, 239, 259, 275, 290, 304, *see also* habitual residence of the child
right to identity 33
  acquisition of citizenship 22
  adoption 143
  CJEU case law 36
  legal protection 22
    right to private and family life 22
  margin of appreciation 175
  Mennesson case 175
  Negrepontis-Giannisis case 175
  non-recognition of a child's name 26–28, 143
  O. B. & S. case 36
  recognition/transcription of status 25
  recognition of a child's name 26–28
  recognition of status legally acquired abroad 28–30
  removal of relatives from third countries 26
  right not to be separated from parents 32–33
    removal of a child's family member 33
  right to family reunification 25
  right to identity 22
  Ruiz Zambrano case 36–37
  Sayn-Wittgenstein case 36
  Treaty law 35
right of residence 81, 104
  derived from child's EU citizenship 72
  habitual residence 68
  third-country nationals 33, 68, 71
right to be heard 5, 9, 16–17, 162, 279
  Article 12 CRC 16
  Article 24 CFREU 9, 16
  Italy 17
  judgments regarding parental responsibility 5
  mediation 279
right to education 9, 44, 122, 143, 145
  Article 14 CFREU 9
  forced marriages 123, 135
right to life 43, 162, 227
right to marry 147–148
  recognition of foreign judgments 148
right to private and family life 8
  Article 7 CFREU 9, 95
    legal protection of identity 22
    rainbow families 92
  Article 8 ECHR 11, 23
    legal protection of identity 23
    rainbow families 90, 92
  Jeunesse case 11, 18, 62
    exceptional circumstances test 18
  maintaining relationships with other family members 14
  migration 57
  non-recognition of a foreign status *filii* 174
  rainbow families 90–92
  right to family reunification 57
  Ruiz Zambrano case 11
right to respect for physical integrity 4

S

same-sex couples 76, 214
  adoption 181, 214
  co-parents, as 78
  cross-border legal recognition of same-sex marriages 83
  joint adoption 77–78
  medically assisted insemination 77
  non-recognition of parental rights 83
  parental rights 77
  surrogacy 181, 263
same-sex couples 29, 95, *see also* same-sex parenthood
same-sex parenthood 29, 76, 95
  lack of EU competence 77
stateless children 44, 70
  duty to respect, protect and fulfil children's rights 44
status filiation is 29, 161, 209, 211, 263
subsidiarity principle 101
substantial and procedural value of the best interests principle 168
surrogacy 77, 177, 194, 219, *see also* cross-border surrogacy
  biological parentage 202
  commercial and altruistic surrogacy distinguished 203–207
  non-discrimination 19
  recognition of status *filii* 181
  regulation 206
  regulation of commercial surrogacy
    Optional Protocol on the Sale of Children, Child Prostitution and Child Pornography 204
  same-sex couples 184, 263

T

third country nationals (TCNs)
  child's primary caregiver, as 34, 71
  dependency of child 34–35
  right to family reunification 32
    Chavez-Vilchez case 71, 73
    Dereci case 34
    removal of a child's family member 33–35
    Ruiz Zambrano case 34

trafficking 194
  duty to respect, protect and fulfil children's rights 44, 212, 222
transfer of children *see* removal of children
travel restrictions on children
  cross-border surrogacy 192–194
Treaty on European Union (TEU) 9, 142
  Article 6 56, 89, 142–143
  best interests principle 47, 56
  CFREU 64, 89
  Lisbon Treaty 89
Treaty on the Functioning of the European Union (TFEU) 85, 142
  best interests of the child 56–65, 267
  free movement of persons 33, 67, 71, 78, 85, 101
    rainbow families 87
  judicial cooperation in civil matters 144
  legal protection of identity 25, 35
  non-discrimination principle 27
  right of residence for TCNs 33–34, 70
  free movement of persons
    rainbow families 87

U

uniform application of EU law 153, 155, 260, 263, *see also* harmonisation within the EU
United Nations General Assembly (UNGA) 4, 122
United Nations Human Rights Council (UNHRC) 205
  commercial surrogacy 205
  forced marriages 122
Universal Declaration on Human Rights (UDHR) 4, 215
urgency requirement 268, 285, 296, 305

V

victims of trafficking *see* trafficking
violence against women 124, 133, 135, 169, 231, 257, *see also* domestic violence, *see also* gender-based violence against women
  denial of family reunification 133
  forced marriages 128

ABOUT THE EDITORS

Dr Elisabetta Bergamini is Associate Professor of International Law at the University of Udine since 2013. After obtaining her PhD in EU Law at the University of Bologna, she became Researcher of International Law at the University of Udine, where she coordinated, from 2014 to 2017, a Jean Monnet Module on European Family Law. She teaches, researches and writes on International Law, EU Law and Private International Law, with particular emphasis on Family Law, and has been involved in national and international projects on the subject.

Dr Chiara Ragni is Associate Professor of International Law at the University of Milan since 2015. After obtaining her PhD in EU and International Law, she became, in 2005, Researcher in International Law at the University of Milan, where, from 2013 to 2016, she coordinated a Jean Monnet Module on European Family Law and Human Rights. Throughout her career, she has been frequently involved in national and international research projects, conferences and lectures on International and European Family Law, a field on which she has always focused her research activities, having authored a number of journal articles and book chapters examining different aspects of this legal area.

www.ingramcontent.com/pod-product-compliance
Ingram Content Group UK Ltd.
Pitfield, Milton Keynes, MK11 3LW, UK
UKHW051847100926
8556IPUK00005B/492